Painting Birds

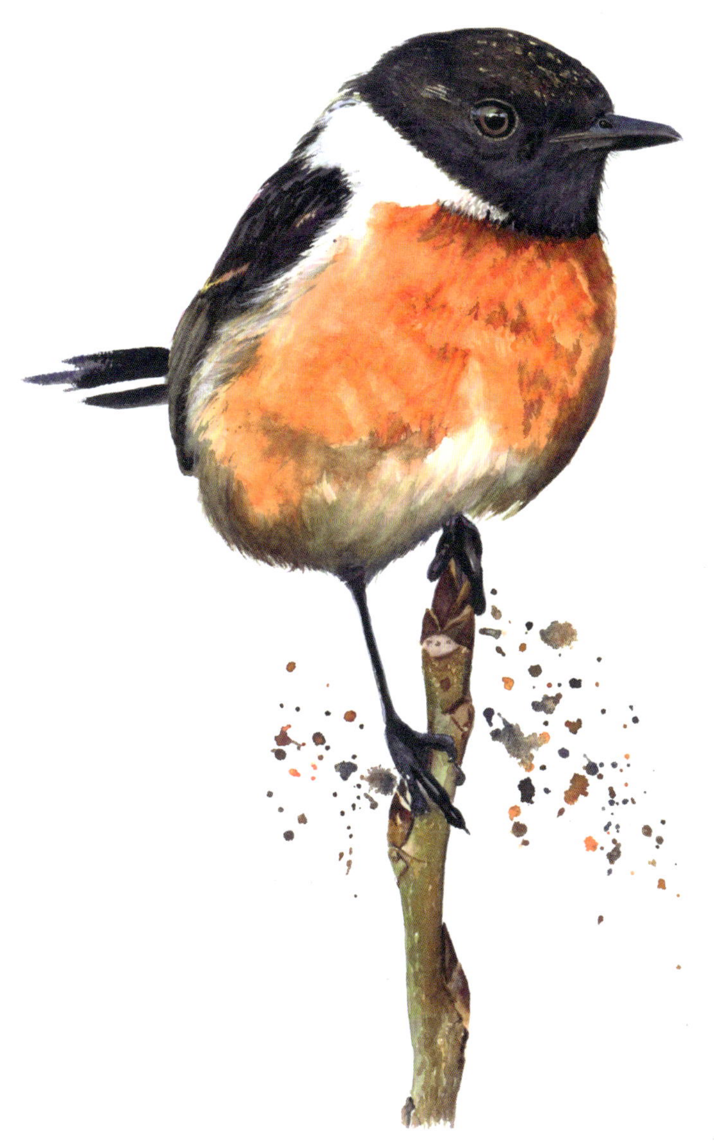

HERBERT PRESS
Bloomsbury Publishing Plc
50 Bedford Square, London, WC1B 3DP, UK
29 Earlsfort Terrace, Dublin 2, Ireland

BLOOMSBURY, HERBERT PRESS and the Herbert Press logo are trademarks of Bloomsbury Publishing Plc

First published in Great Britain in 2024

A catalogue record for this book is available from the British Library
Library of Congress Cataloguing-in-Publication data has been applied for

ISBN: 978-1-7899-4133-3; ePub: 978-1-7899-4132-6

2

Designed and typeset by Austin Taylor

Printed and bound in Turkey by Elma Basim Printing Solutions Limited

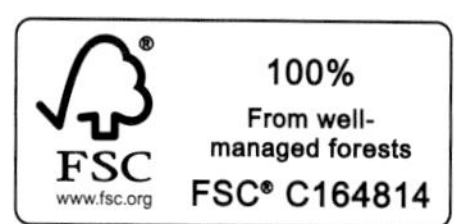

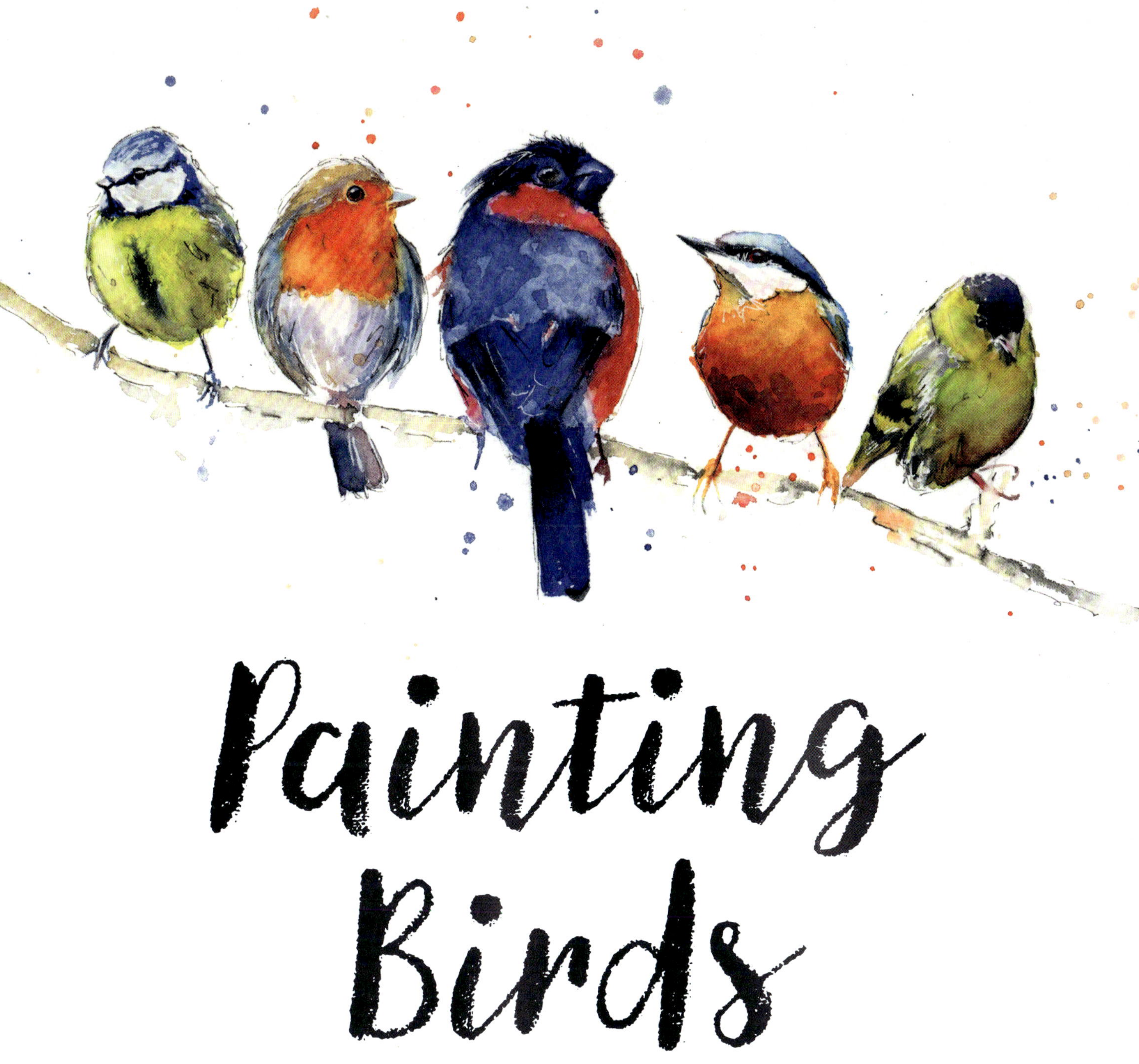

Painting Birds

Expressive Watercolour Techniques

Sarah Stokes

HERBERT PRESS
LONDON • OXFORD • NEW YORK • NEW DELHI • SYDNEY

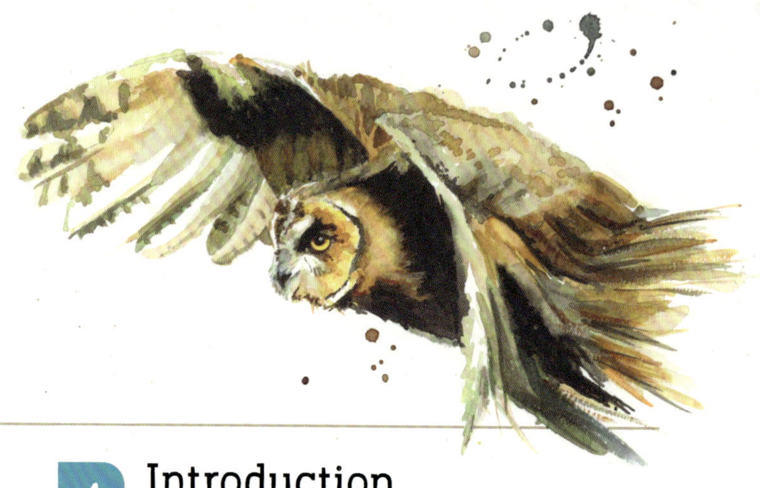

Contents

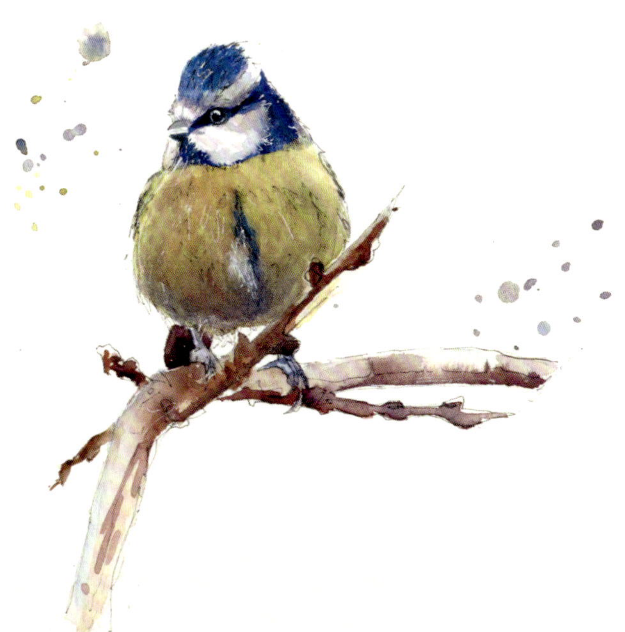

PART TWO:

Advanced Techniques 99

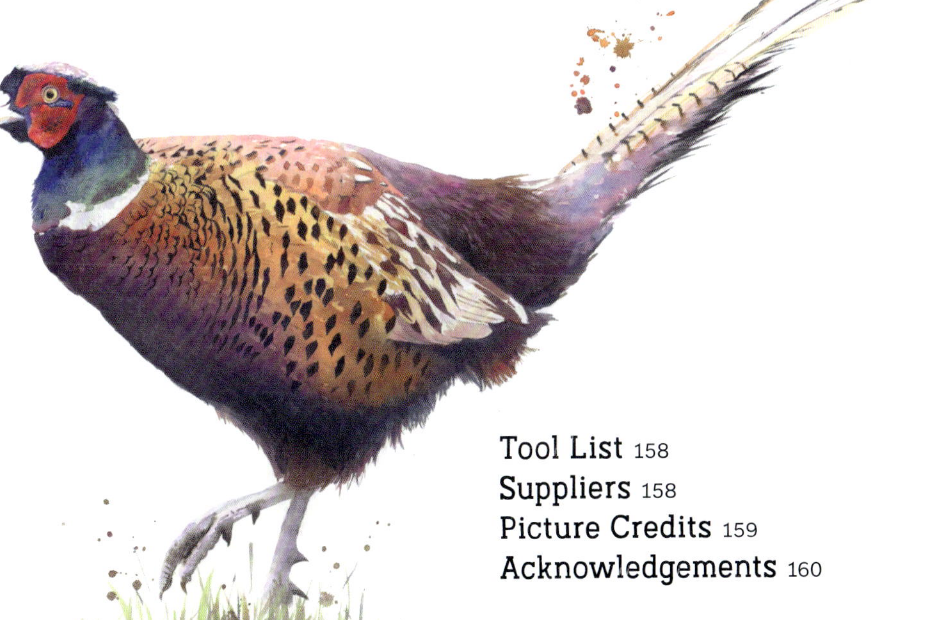

ODE TO SPRING

Angela Miriam Stokes, 2022

The Spring has arrived and once again, the migrating birds have returned from far off lands as winter quietly slips away.

Their singing fills the air and lifts our spirits as we marvel at the strength and beauty of these small, delicate creatures who have travelled so many miles with their songs.

In this busy world they arrive, whether it be to the countryside or to the bustling city streets, so let us find time to listen to their song and rejoice in the joy it brings.

In memory of Miriam

DEDICATION

This book is dedicated to my wonderful husband, Simon, for his unwavering support and patience while I wrote this book; to my Mum and Dad for opening my eyes to the beauty and fragility of the animal kingdom; and to my brother Russ and his beautiful little family for always encouraging me to chase my dream. I love you.

→ (*Opposite*) 'The Gardener's Companions', 2020, watercolour.

↓ 'Ode to Spring', 2023, watercolour.

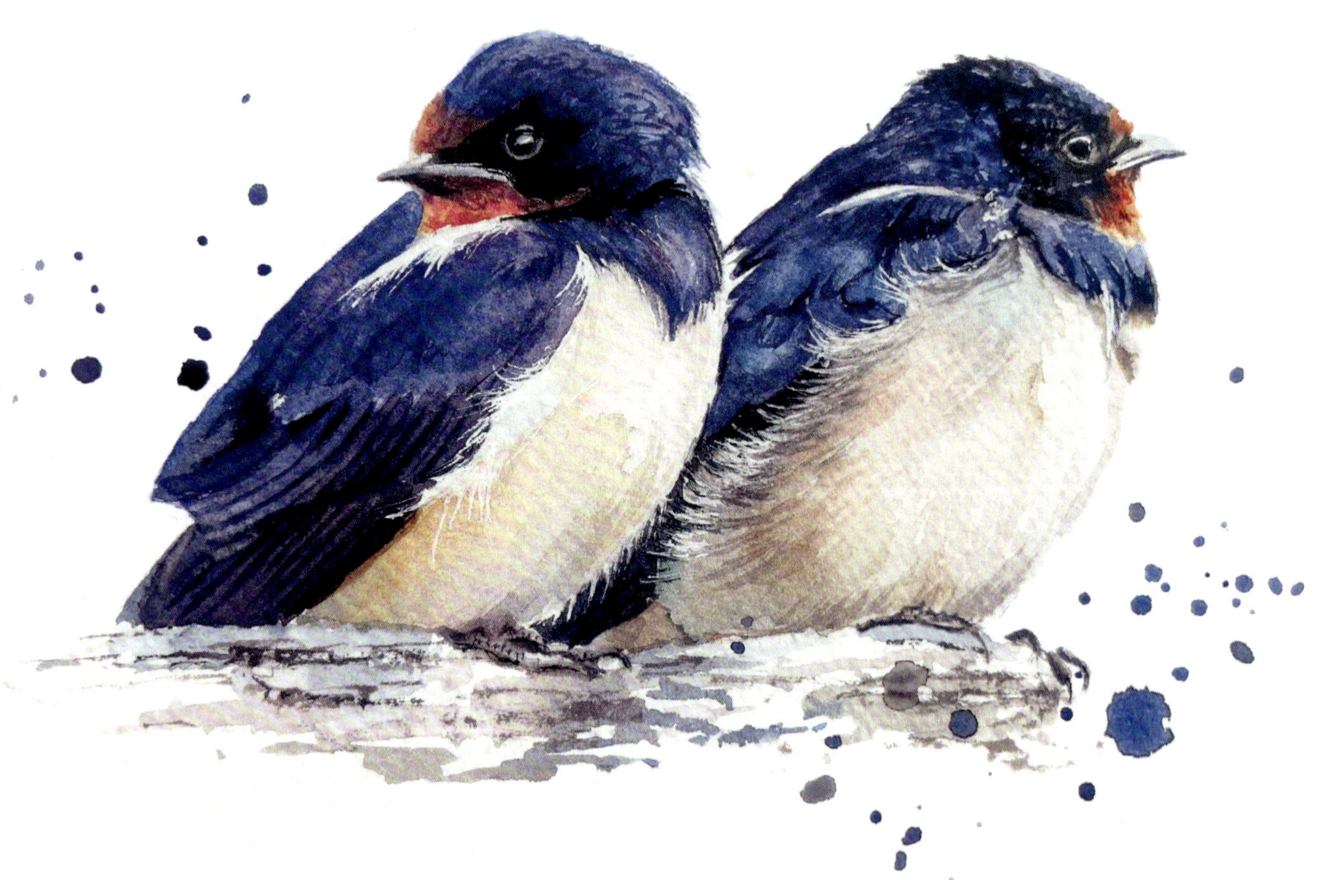

Introduction

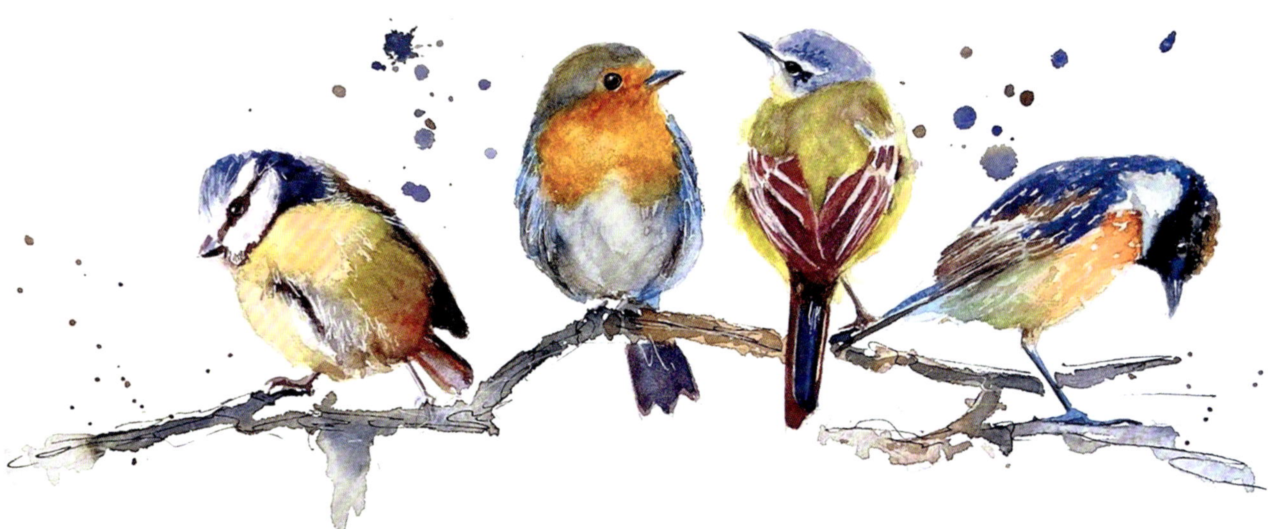

Why birds?

Why have I chosen birds to be the main subject for my first book? Perhaps most importantly, birds bring us joy, hope and wonder; whether it is the sight of a little robin watching over us as we garden or the hypnotic sound of swans flying overhead. The chirps, trills, caws and hoots of bird calls are some of the most uplifting sounds I experience when walking my dog locally. That wall of sound coming from deep in the woods is both exhilarating and humbling; it reminds me that although I can't see the birds, they are there, deep among the trees, going about their daily business.

Birds are wonderful subjects to paint as they are generally accessible to most of us. Even if you live in a city, birds can be attracted to balcony spaces with feeders, and they abound in local parks and green spaces.

Birds also present us with an amazing array of colours, textures and characteristics, from the iridescent plumage of a hummingbird to the tuxedo-like appearance of a puffin. This will give you the chance to discover the versatility of watercolour, which in turn will put you in good stead to paint any animal of your choice, not just of the avian variety.

Finally, painting birds gives us the perfect chance to explore composition and texture by creating an array of environments incorporating skies, water, woodlands and foliage. What better way to start our journey into expressive, dynamic watercolour?

What do we mean by expressive, dynamic watercolour?

Terms such as 'expressive' and 'dynamic' are used to describe one of the most popular styles that many watercolour artists aspire to, but the apparent effortlessness of the look belies the fact that it is one of the most difficult techniques to master. It is also open to interpretation.

Quite often, a painting may appear 'expressive' or 'loose' in style, but closer examination reveals that it is very tightly rendered in certain sections. Many of the larger shapes, tones and even colours may also have been interpreted with much accuracy. However, the application of lighter, more playful notes, such as splashes, painterly brushstrokes, abstract backgrounds and so on, can give the illusion of 'looseness'. So, it can sometimes be a case of smoke and mirrors!

The trick is to achieve an acceptable balance between expressive and more restrained brushwork that brings satisfaction primarily to the creator and hopefully to the viewer, and that in itself is very subjective. It is a struggle that many artists experience, both improvers and professionals alike; it is a constant journey of discovery, wonder and learning, with a fair smattering of frustration.

This approach to painting is diverse in range

and open to interpretation because an artist's painting style is (or should be) as individual as their handwriting. Therefore, it can describe anything from a painting that borders on the abstract to one that is far more representational in nature. My gallery pieces tend to fall into the latter category, but my playful pieces and studies are far looser in approach. My priority is to make sure that, in either case, there is a marriage of both subject and medium enabling each to shine to maximum effect.

Being 'expressive' is as much about your mindset as it is about specific techniques. It involves adopting a fresh approach to painting: the willingness to experiment and play without the fear of 'making mistakes', without worrying about wasting time and paper. It is only through letting go and allowing your mind and hand to explore the medium that you can find your voice; your signature style.

In practical terms, a loose style of painting involves a more reductionist approach to the creative process. It means acquiring the skill set and discipline to see and paint the larger shapes while just hinting at the finer details, allowing the viewer to fill in the gaps. Many of us struggle with this concept. Although we love the idea, we can be tempted to paint excessive detail and then we are in danger of creating flat, lifeless or overly busy pieces. The tendency to include too much detail, with minimal thought to the larger shapes, seems to be one of the biggest hurdles to overcome and this book sets out some useful exercises to help artists in this quest.

Learning the basic rules of composition can help you to create eye-catching artwork. You may have painted a beautifully rendered bird piece in the past, only for it to have been spoilt by some misdirected splashes, a lacklustre background or a busy foreground. It is important to remember the conversation we are having with the viewer. How do we draw them onto our piece, to effectively guide their eyes around and evoke emotion?

In this book, I will set aside some of the myths and

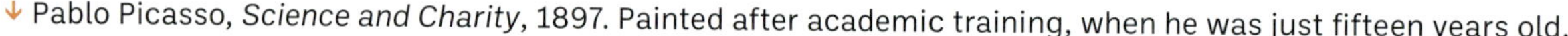

↓ Pablo Picasso, *Science and Charity*, 1897. Painted after academic training, when he was just fifteen years old.

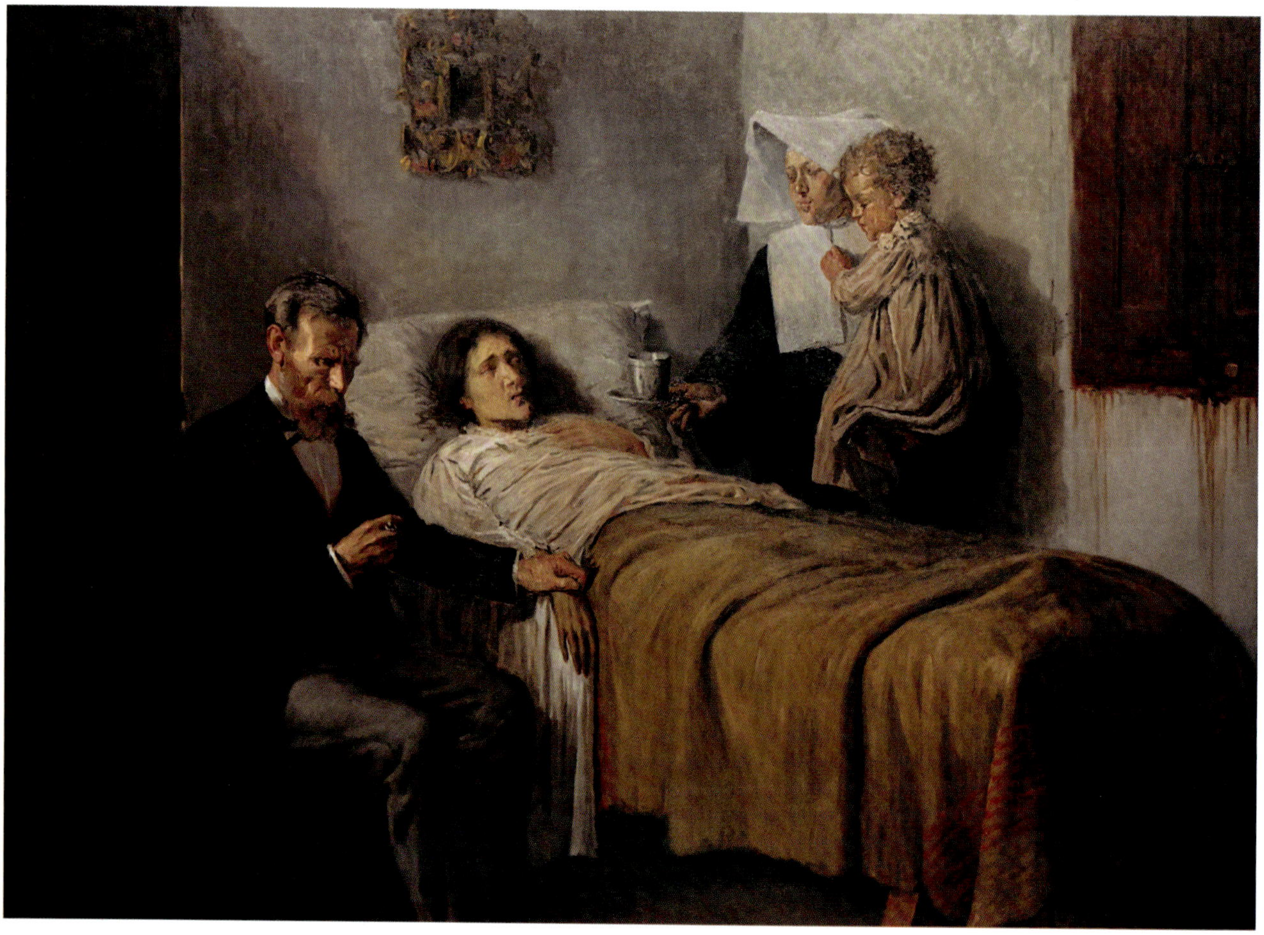

→ Pablo Picasso, *Les Demoiselles d'Avignon*, 1907. Painted just ten years after *Science and Charity*, and in his more distinctive and unique style. What a difference in approach!

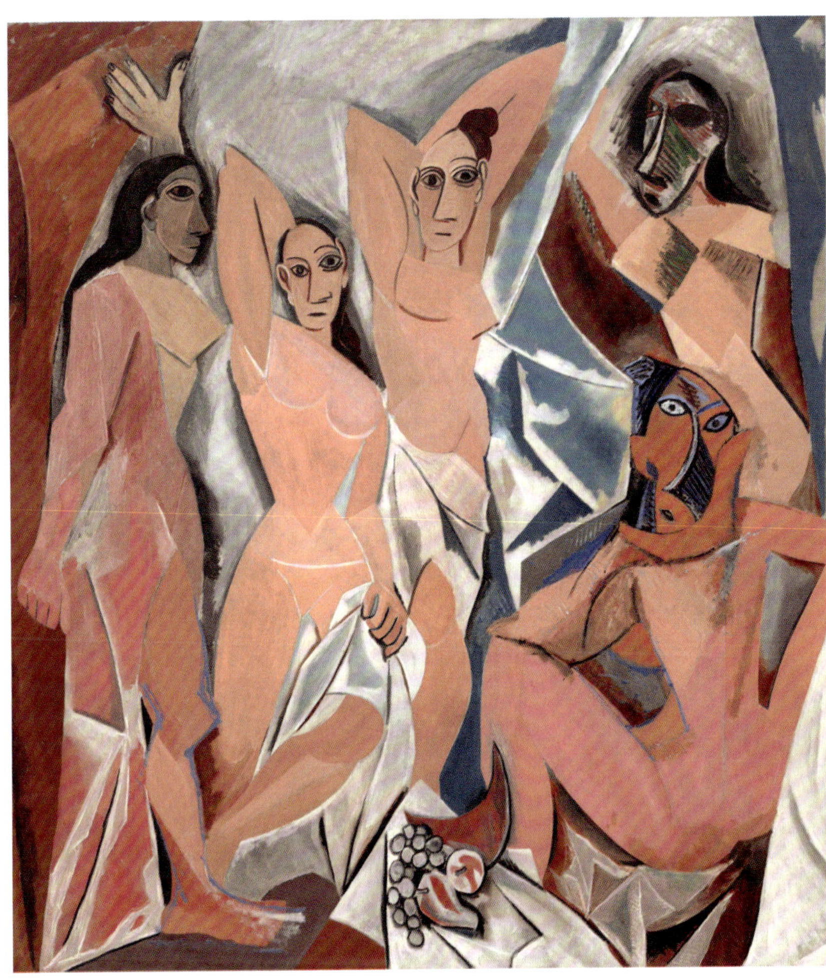

teach you practical techniques for starting your journey into expressive watercolour painting. Eventually, with practice, you will find a happy compromise between loose and more realistic marks to create a unique, recognisable style.

Watercolour provides us with the ideal medium for expressive techniques with its translucent, colourful and playful qualities. The painting process is a two-way conversation. It is about how we interact with the medium; allowing watercolour to do its thing and then reacting to what we see on the page as we drop, splash, blend and lift the paint. Sometimes we have to do the hardest thing of all... wait!

One word of caution in this discussion of looser styles: 'expressive' doesn't mean sloppy or careless artwork; although it is fun, it is also considered, skilled and sometimes even slow paced. The trick is to give the piece a sense of energy and excitement, even though in reality many of the marks will have been made with thoughtfulness.

Like anything worth creating, repetition and practice will make for more successful pieces. There is no quick fix. This might sound obvious, but so often I see students getting frustrated if something isn't falling into place straight away, be it colour mixing, drawing, layering or some other learnt skill. Established artists have a knack of making something look easy, but their adeptness comes after many hours of painting. So please don't be hard on yourself if something doesn't 'click' straight away. It was only after I had been painting for many years that some of the original self-help books that I had bought actually made sense, particularly when it pertained to subjects such as timing, consistency, edges and mark making.

The structure of the book

This book contains a sequence of exercises and projects that are designed to take you through the fundamental building blocks of creating successful artworks through to more advanced watercolour techniques.

Although each chapter can be taken in isolation, if you are a beginner to painting, I recommend that you approach the book logically, taking it a chapter at a time. If you are a more experienced artist, you may prefer to dip and dive in and out of projects, and to this end I have repeated certain messages throughout the book that I feel are important to the process.

Part One deals with some of the basic and essential aspects of drawing and painting. You may be surprised to discover that we don't even pick up a paintbrush until Chapter 2. Learning the 'rules' is key

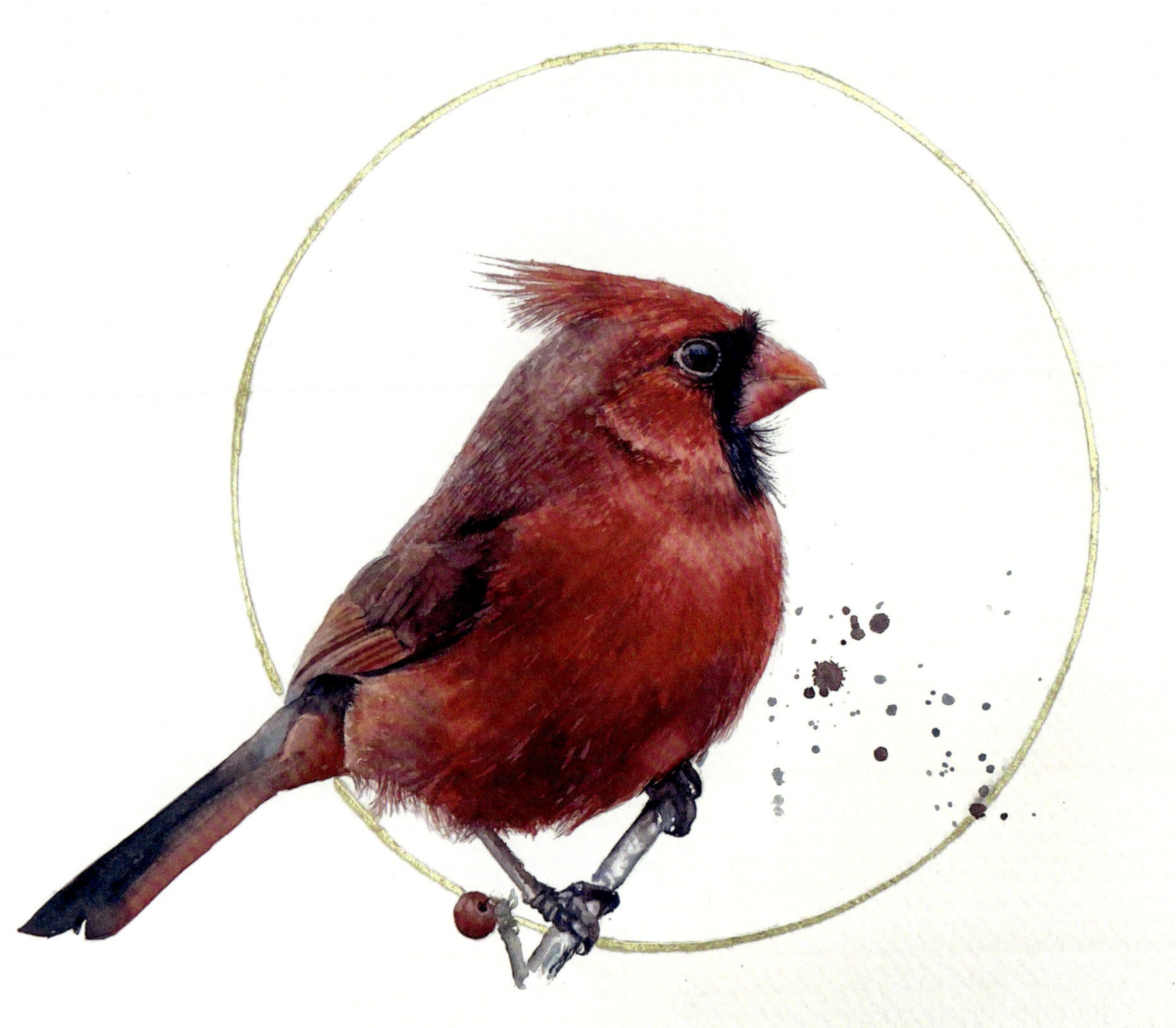

to painting expressively, so we can make informed choices about which ones we want to break! As Picasso said, 'Learn the rules like a pro, so you can break them like an artist.'

Part Two covers more advanced techniques such as developing your style through mark making, incorporating background washes and foreground details, and experimenting with mixed media.

To create a convincing bird portrait in whatever style you choose, it is very important to have a working knowledge of shape, tone, composition, colour and edges. It is with shape and tone where our journey will begin.

↑ 'Male cardinal', 2021, watercolour and gold leaf.

WHAT TOOLS WILL I NEED?

You will need a mixture of drawing and painting tools for the projects in this book. Each exercise lists the tools that I have used, and there is a tool list on page 158. Don't worry if you haven't got exactly the same equipment and materials to hand, as many can be substituted for similar items.

It's important to develop your own style and colour palette over time; carbon copies of these exercises would be dull! In general, particularly when it comes to the painting section, it is advisable to get the best quality paint and paper that you can, so that you enjoy the process. There is nothing worse than battling with poor tools and materials.

PART ONE

The Fundamentals

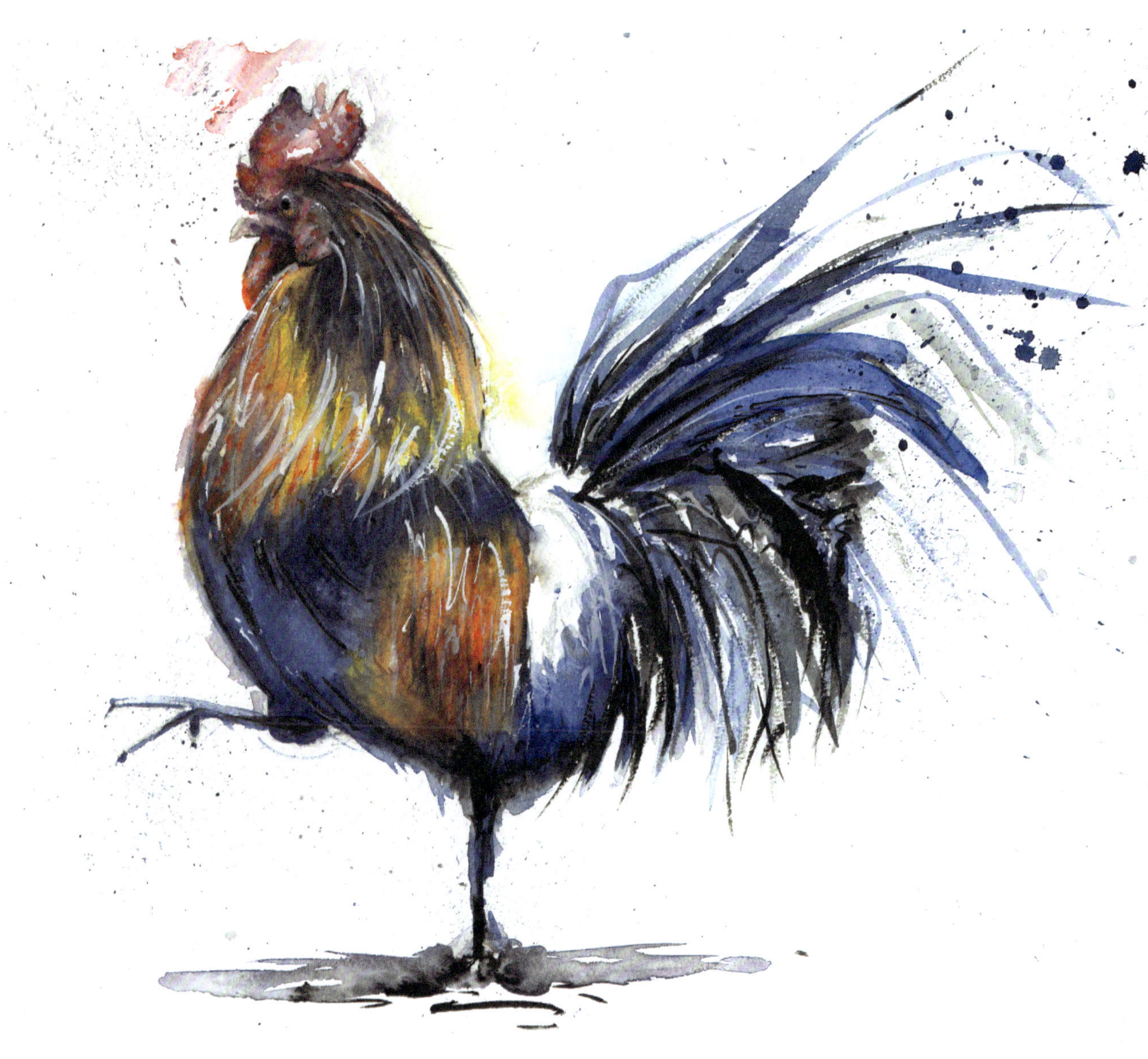

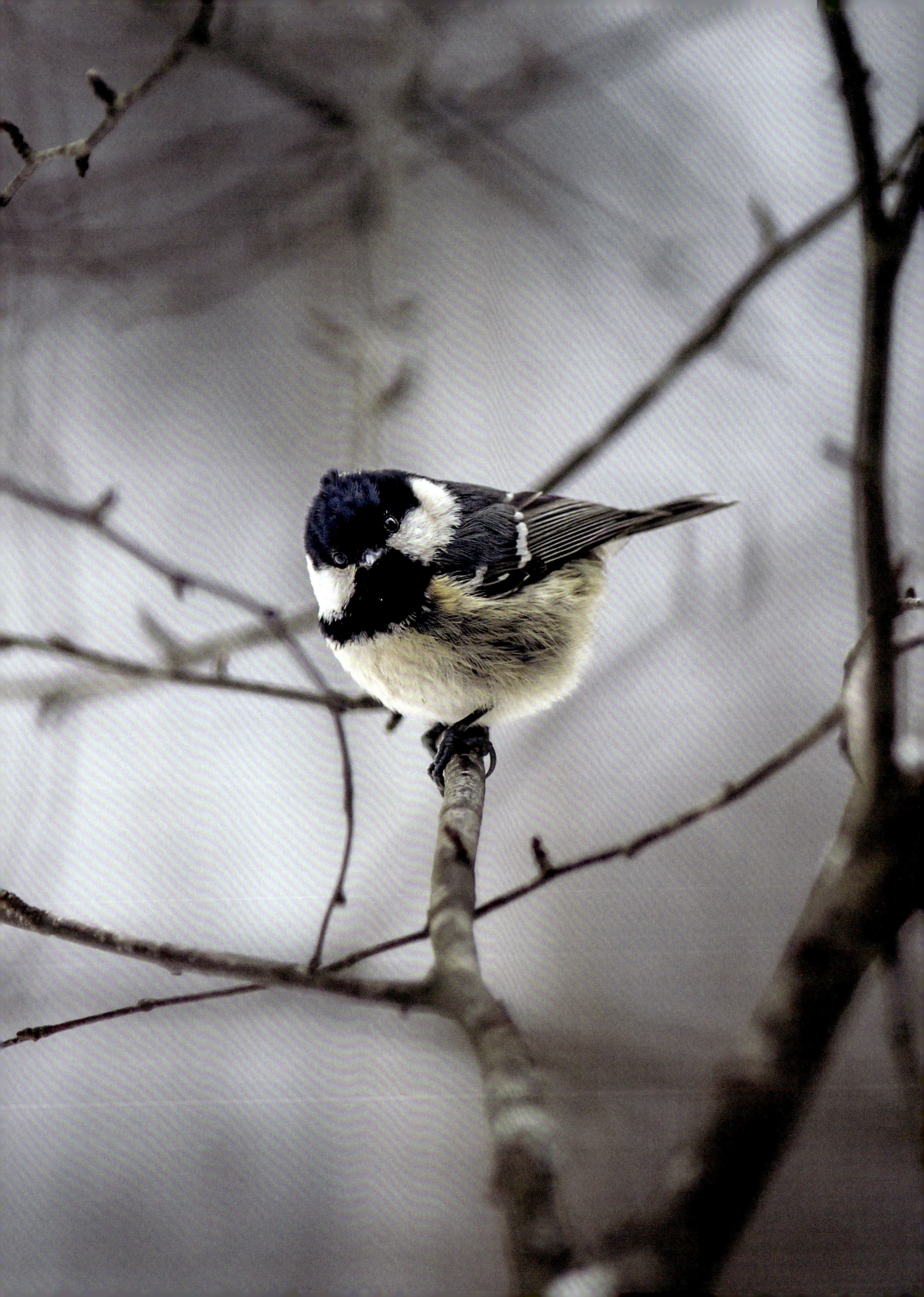

CHAPTER

1

The Importance of Shape and Tone

Before we get involved with the complexities of watercolour paint, I have found that all my students benefit from gaining a sound understanding of shape and tone.

Why are shapes so important?

This might sound a strange question, but as soon as we start to see things as shapes, as opposed to specific parts of a bird, it becomes much easier to build up a painting effectively into a dynamic and interesting piece.

Whatever medium you're working in, lay down your larger shapes first, before adding the smaller details. I tend to stick to an 80/20 rule; the majority of my time will go into depicting larger forms with only a small percentage of my effort being used to create the smaller elements of the piece.

This rule also applies to the visual aspect of the piece, in that the larger shapes should dominate most of the viewer's attention, with the detailed sections taking up smaller interest. If you bear this in mind, you will create a far more interesting piece in which the viewer gets to fill in the gaps. It will also make for a far more rewarding painting experience, avoiding the pitfalls of getting bogged down in minutiae.

Looking at the peacock, it's amazing how little information a viewer needs to determine the nature of the subject. Even when we have stripped this bird of its iridescent colours and tiny feathery details, the basic shapes still inform us that this is a peacock's head. Note that the 'feathers' that worry so many students are in this case represented by simple, wayward lines of white angular shapes.

In its most basic sense, I always look at painting as placing correctly judged blocks of shape (of the correct colour and tone) on the paper; large first and smaller later. Clearly there's far more to painting a successful piece than this, but I find that this mindset helps me overcome

← Just look at the multitude of colours and textures in the body of this bird.

any anxiety I might feel about tackling a certain aspect of the work.

Seeing the larger shapes first takes a bit of getting used to. It's easy to become overwhelmed by the myriad details in front of us, especially if we are new to painting that particular subject. The amount of colour and detail can be perplexing, not to mention the existence of other more abstract concepts such as luminosity, shininess and fluffiness. In essence, a shape's boundary can often be defined by a simple line, a change of colour, tone or edge, or quite often by a mixture of any of these components. One of the best ways of seeing shape is by squinting your eyes. This tends to knock out all of the tiny colour details and differences in tone, allowing you to see the bigger forms.

I must confess that when I started landscape painting a while back, I felt a similar level of perplexity when confronted with a busy scene, but regardless of the subject matter, the same rules apply: namely identify and paint your larger shapes first, moving on to the smaller details in the final stages. This approach will quite often result in an 'ugly duckling' phase of a painting when everything looks flat, but it'll be those subsequent layers of darker and more saturated shapes that will pull the piece together.

We will be looking at colour extensively in Chapter 4, but now's a good time to look at tone.

What is tone?

The peacock image (p.13) is simply a collection of black and white shapes, but tone is needed to give everything a sense of being three-dimensional.

Tone, or tonal value, is the lightness or darkness of a colour. It's how near a colour is to black and to white; it's what we depict when we add 'shading' to a piece, and it's essential to give the subject a sense of form, space and depth.

Tone is such an important factor in determining the success of the eventual painting that consideration of tone even informs my decision as to which photograph I use as a reference. I will always use a reference photograph with a variety of contrasting tones, as this will help prevent my painting from looking flat and lifeless.

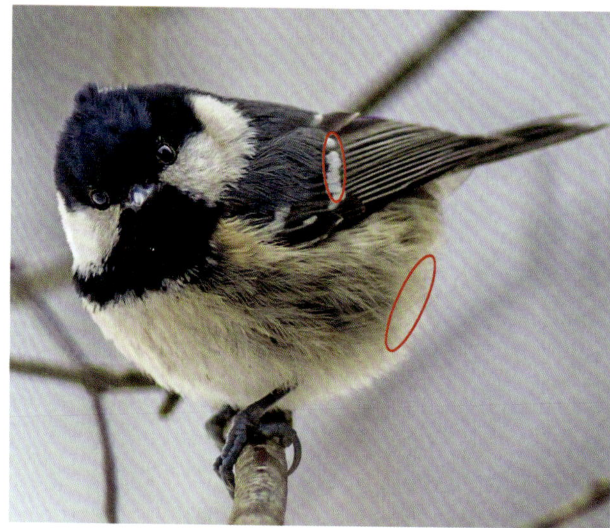

↑ A cursory glance leads us to believe that lighter wing markings are white and the edge of the body is beige; however their tones are very similar, as seen opposite.

SEEING TONE

Tone can be pretty difficult to work out in colour photographs because individual colours have different qualities, such as saturation and intensity, which can be difficult to gauge. We can also perceive them as being brighter, duller, lighter or darker according to the colours that they sit next to; a phenomenon known as simultaneous contrast.

Furthermore, the left-hand side of our brain, which amongst other things controls our language centre, quite unhelpfully fools us into believing things that simply aren't true. For instance, when painting the sclera of the human eye (the so-called 'white' of the eyeball), we tend to think of it as being white. However, the eyeball is a sphere and partly in shadow so, in order to paint a realistic eye, we need to accurately depict the various colours and shades on the surface of the sclera. As a rough rule of thumb, younger people will have a bluish sclera while older people have a reddish sclera. If we were to leave it entirely white, then the painted eye would look flat and quite unnatural.

In addition, a colour photograph can be overwhelming in terms of the level of information that it throws at us, as can be seen in the full-colour photo of a coal tit above.

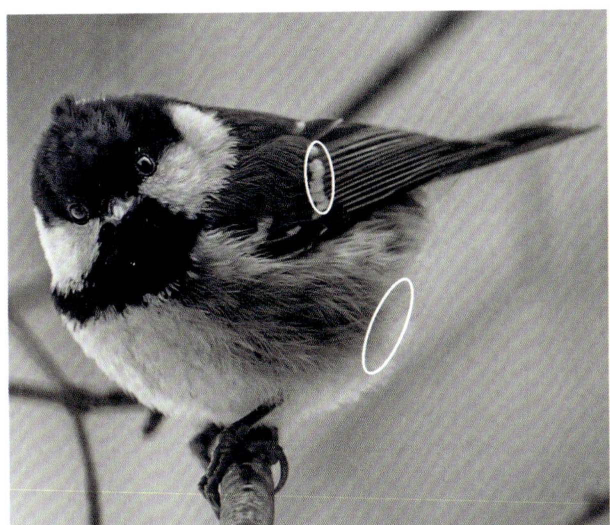

↑ As this desaturated photograph shows, the two areas are of a very similar tone. In fact, the 'white' markings are made up of pale, neutral, cool blue-greys – not white at all.

THE CHALLENGE OF ASSESSING TONE

When starting out in drawing, tones can be really difficult to gauge, even in monochromatic format. Our perception of how bright something is changes depending on the tones that surround it.

There are grey scale finders (both printed and digital versions) on the market that can help you work out values, but with practice it will become second nature. I often liken it to walking into a darkened room; eventually your eyes adjust and you will see the various values and their relationship to each other.

As a general rule of thumb, students don't apply dark enough tones, so much of their drawings

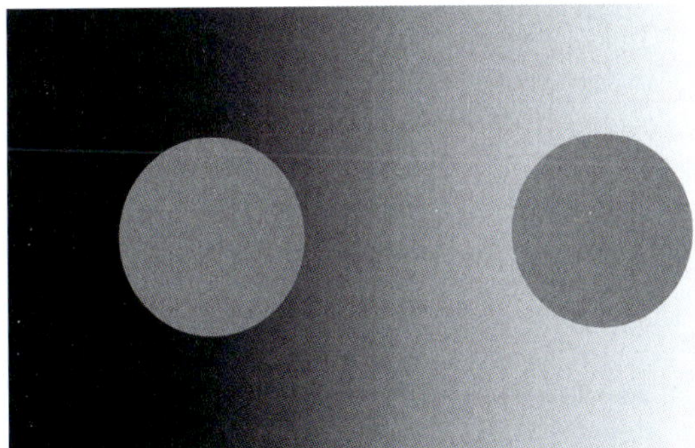

↑ This shows the same grey circle surrounded by both black and white. Notice how the grey circle looks much darker against a lighter background.

become a mid-grey, with little relief. Make the most of those darks and lights! They will give your drawing some punch. When looking at a photograph it can often be difficult to see the tones, so try squinting your eyes to reveal the bigger shapes.

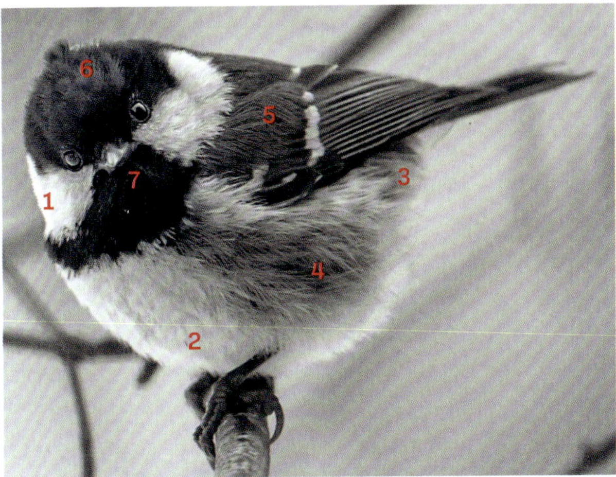

↑ The numbering gives you an idea of the variety of tones in this photograph, with 1 being the lightest and 7 being the darkest. There are even more tones than this, but I've marked off the main ones that will help us draw this piece.

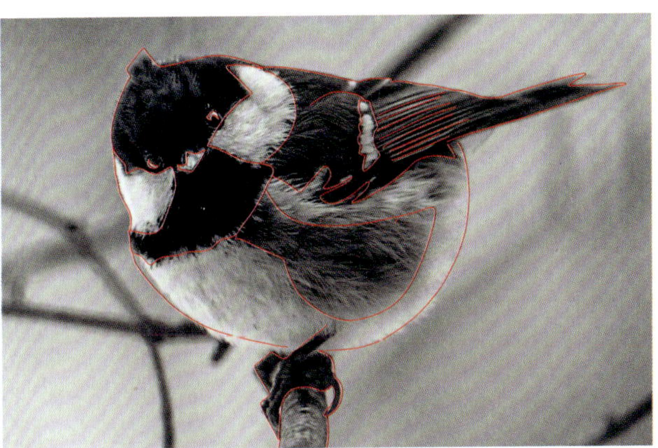

↑ Here you can see where I've outlined the major shapes. How much detail you put into these shapes and how expressively you make those marks will be your choice. Having the basic proportions and tones in the right place is an excellent starting point.

When it comes to drawing or painting, try not to think about the 'feathery' nature of a bird or, for instance, the 'shininess' of an eye. Instead think about shapes (big to small, obvious to more obscure), tones (dark to light) and edges (hard to soft). This will really help you draw and paint what you see without getting overwhelmed with the detail of the subject. If you get the shapes and tones right, you will automatically be able to portray these attributes.

PROJECT 1

Exploring tone – drawing a coal tit in charcoal

Depicting tone is easier to do when working in one colour and with a medium that stays put, such as charcoal. Unlike its watercolour counterpart, charcoal doesn't move around the paper, throwing in unexpected surprises when you least want them. It's a lovely steady medium to ease yourself into the process.

The main point of this project is for you to see and draw the shapes, allocating the correct shade. By doing this correctly, you'll produce a coal tit drawing without worrying about drawing a single feather.

If you apply the right tonal values in the correct places, the feathers, beak and other features will draw themselves! I apply this thought process to my paintings, whether in monochrome or colour.

As with all of my projects, I will list the materials that I have used to achieve a particular piece; however, please use whatever you have to hand. These are only recommended tools and you may have found others that suit your style better.

↓ Tools and materials needed for the charcoal coal tit.

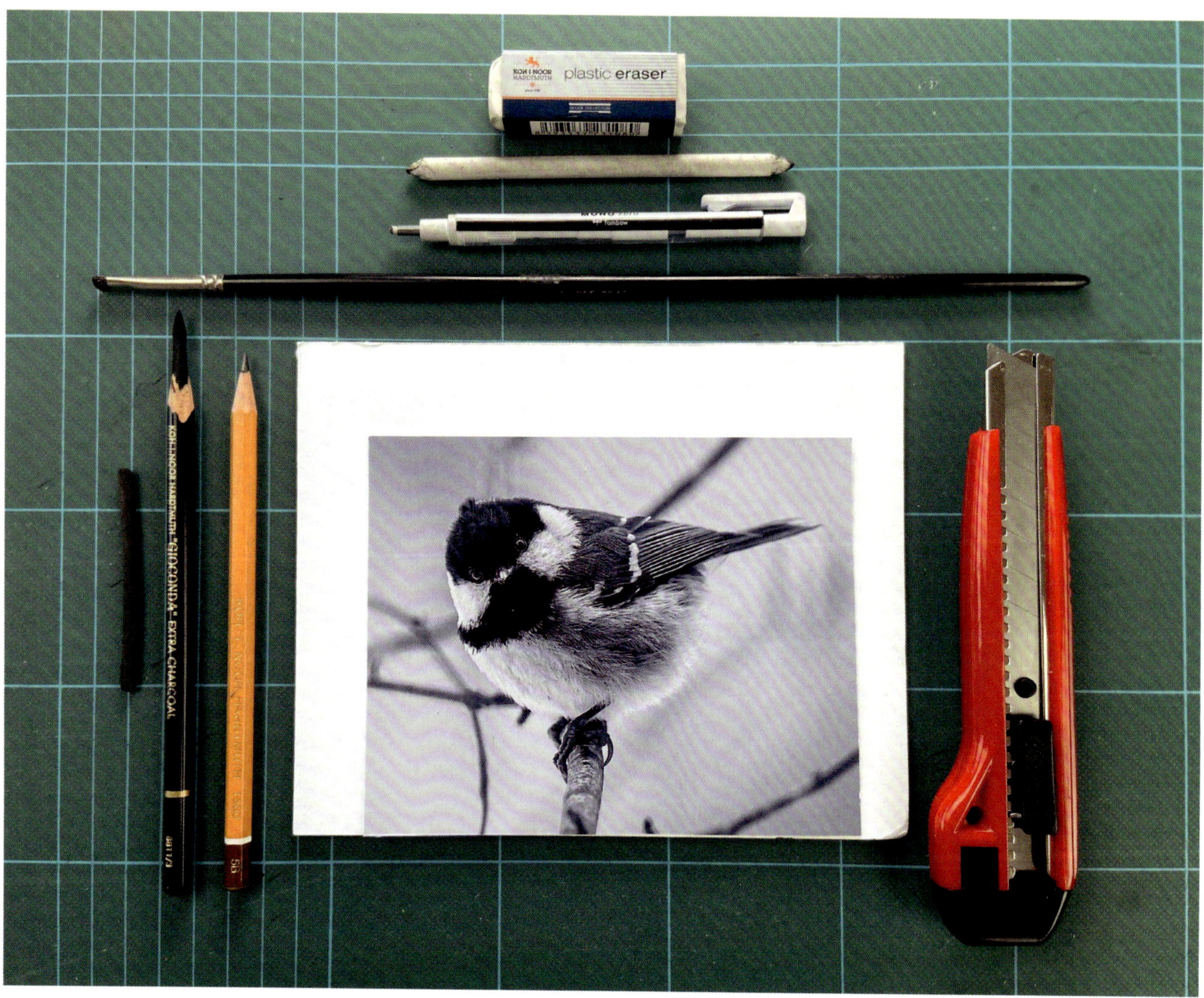

You will need

- Photographic reference of a coal tit
- 220 gsm (or heavier) smooth drawing paper or line and wash board
- Dark charcoal pencil and a slim stick of vine or willow charcoal
- Stationery: soft 5B pencil, plastic and mono erasers, spray fixative, blending stump, stiff-bristled brush
- Wax-free transfer or tracing paper (optional)
- Cutting mat, ruler and craft knife (optional)

FAMILIARISE YOURSELF WITH THE TOOLS

I used a charcoal pencil made by Koh-I-Noor, but Derwent also produce a good-quality dark pencil. It is crucial to sharpen your charcoal pencil to a long point so you can apply accurate marks where needed. I use a craft knife to sharpen mine to avoid charcoal breakage; I then fine-tune the point with a sandpaper block. The slim stick of vine or willow charcoal will help you to achieve beautifully subtle light and mid tones that can be easily blended and lifted to suit.

If you haven't used charcoal tools before, take a few moments to play with them on a blank sheet of standard copier paper. Use the charcoal pencil and stick to make a variety of marks of different levels of darkness and widths. Explore the characteristics of the tools by using them on their sides as well as by their tips. Create hard and barely-there lines. Drag, pull and swirl the tools across the page to see the effects that you can create. Rub parts of the marks with a variety of objects such as your fingers, tissues and brushes to see how they soften, blur, blend and in some cases almost disappear. I use an old brush to blend my charcoals, which has the correct amount of stiffness and works well on the Daler-Rowney line and wash board that I use. I prefer to use line and wash board as it doesn't crease and can take a hammering from the blending tools I use. However, if you prefer using paper, I recommend Strathmore 300 Series Bristol, smooth.

One of my favourite sets of tools are the erasers. I use erasers to create lighter shapes and textures within a charcoal piece and we will be using them in this project to regain lighter tones and create texture. The mono eraser is an invaluable little tool that helps me pull back the white of the paper to create delicate lighter marks. I also use a selection of standard plastic erasers, many of which have been carved into points and flat angles to achieve certain effects, to recover large areas of light or to sweep through sections of a drawing to create interesting marks, suggesting feathers, among other things. Note how the erasers lift the lighter willow and vine marks away more easily than the darker compressed charcoal ones.

Spray fixative, as the name suggests, fixes your work and ensures that the charcoal doesn't smudge. I use the Professional Fixative Spray from Winsor & Newton. For the purposes of this project you may decide not to fix at all, or to use hairspray to fix – be careful as hairsprays can turn the paper or board yellow over time.

I prefer to work from a physical photograph printed onto glossy paper of the same size as my final piece. However, you may prefer to work from the image in the book or from the image on a computer or tablet screen. I use the cutting mat and craft knife to cut larger boards of card down to size and to score a grid into my reference photo.

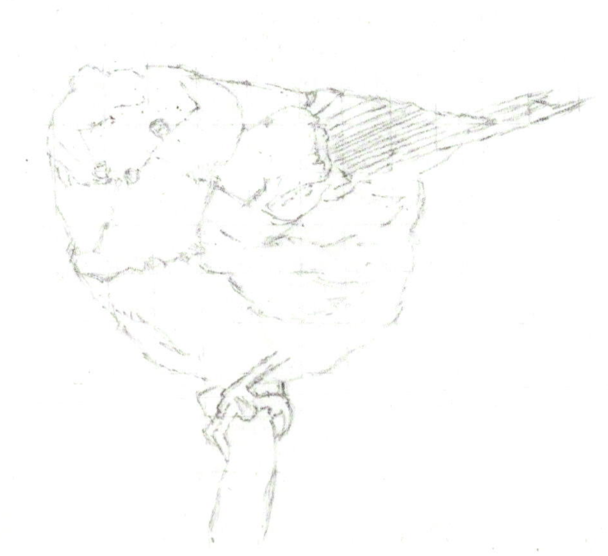

← My sketch, which indicates the outer perimeter, key features and major changes of tone in the original reference photograph.

CREATE A LINE DRAWING

1 You will need to create a line drawing, which should incorporate the outer edge as well as the larger tonal shapes inside the subject. As this is the scaffolding to our piece, it's important to draw this with accuracy.

I used the gridding method of drawing, by which I grid both my reference photograph and my card and draw each section of the bird box by box, but feel free to copy the reference with whatever method suits you, whether it be freehand, traced, gridded or using another technique. If gridding up or freehand drawing methods don't appeal to you, you could, as many of my students do, use a wax-free transfer paper such as Tracedown by Frisk.

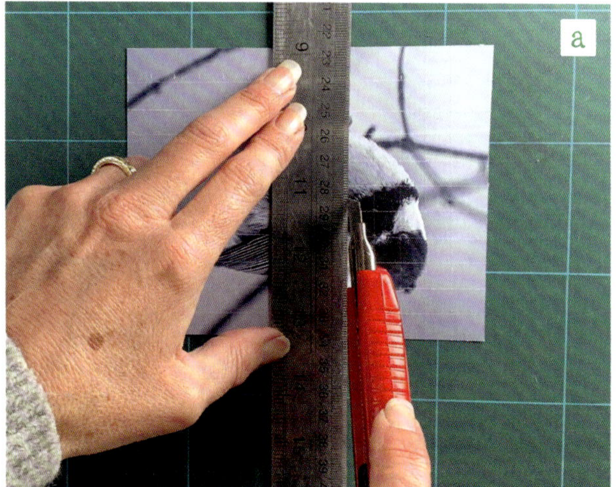

↑ Grids can be overlaid digitally (prior to printing) or manually (after printing) using a craft knife and metal ruler on a cutting mat to score the surface.

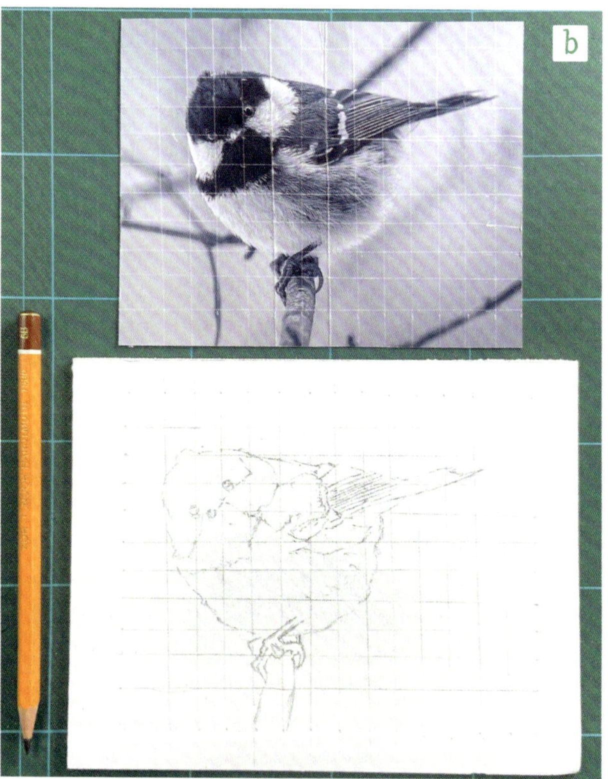

↑ By breaking the image down into smaller squares, it is much easier to draw the bird. Tackle one small square at a time to accurately draw the full picture.

BLOCK IN THE MAJOR TONES AND SHAPES

2 Use a very sharp, dark charcoal pencil to gently and precisely lay down darker tones. The eyes need to be precise – if you are creating a small drawing, this can be fiddly. I found it useful to zoom in on the eye to ensure that my shapes and values were accurate. This is the only section of the drawing that requires such accuracy, but it's important to get it right. Look at the angles and tones in the reflected lights, as getting these right will help to give character and expression to the bird.

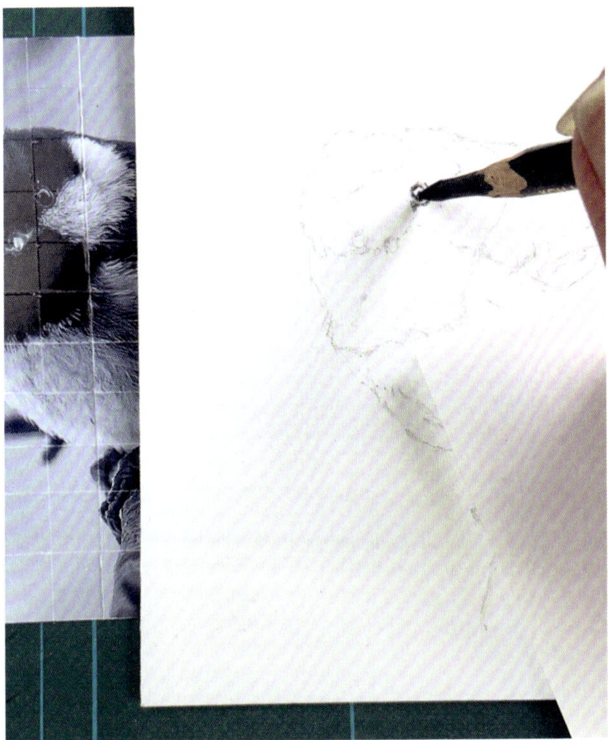

↑ A sharpened charcoal pencil will make fiddly tasks much easier.

Top tip

The charcoal process can be quite messy. I often place a sheet of copier paper underneath my drawing hand so I don't accidentally smudge the wrong area.

3 Work around the bird, applying different pressures to the pencil to achieve lighter and darker tones. The white of your surface material and a soft willow stick will create your lighter and mid tones, so be sure to leave these clear of charcoal for now.

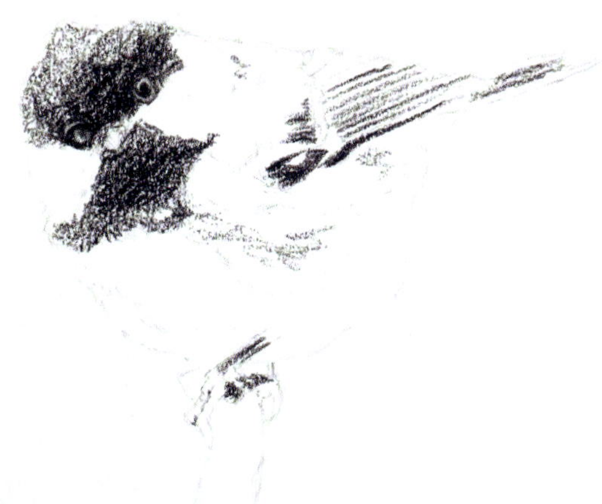

↑ These darker tones have all been achieved with the charcoal pencil applied both firmly and gently to achieve different values.

4 Use your willow or vine stick to apply charcoal to the mid-tone areas. At a later stage we will be blending these out and the residue will constitute our lighter tones, so go steady at this stage.

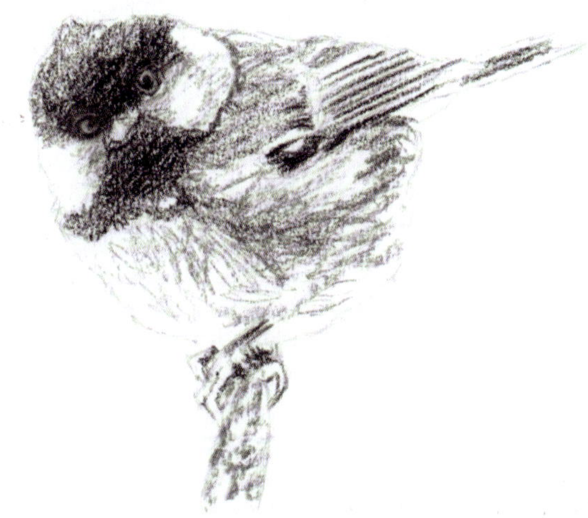

↑ Both the charcoal pencil and willow stick have been used at different pressures to start the process of laying down value and shapes.

BLEND THE SHAPES TOGETHER AND START ADDING DETAIL

5 Use the variety of tools that you have to hand to push, pull and blend the values together. Keep your eye on the photographic reference to ensure accuracy so that you don't inadvertently go too dark in any one area. I love this part of the process because the piece comes together very quickly at this point.

I blended the various sections using my fingers, a blending stump and an old oil brush to further define and refine my main values. I choose very smooth paper as my style is to remove evidence of the paper below by rubbing the charcoals into it. However, many charcoal artists will use a paper with a 'tooth' in it, to enable the textural marks of the charcoal tools to show. This is a matter of style, so go with whatever feels right to you!

→ Blending stumps are available in a variety of sizes. I use a medium one to blend and drag charcoal over the page. It is rarely cleaned as I use the excess charcoal residue to create soft marks in other sections of the drawing, such as the feet.

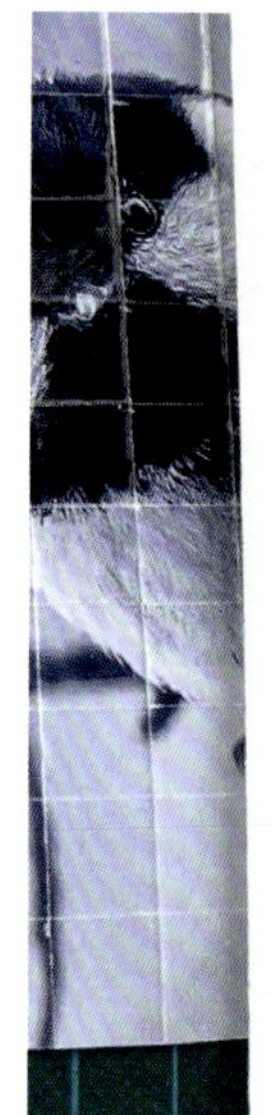

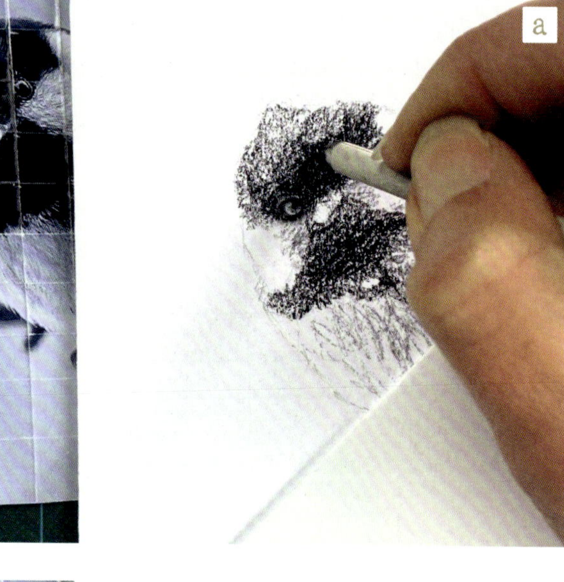

a

→ My favourite old oil brush for blending has a stiffness that is very effective at blending the charcoal together and removing the light pops of card that show through.

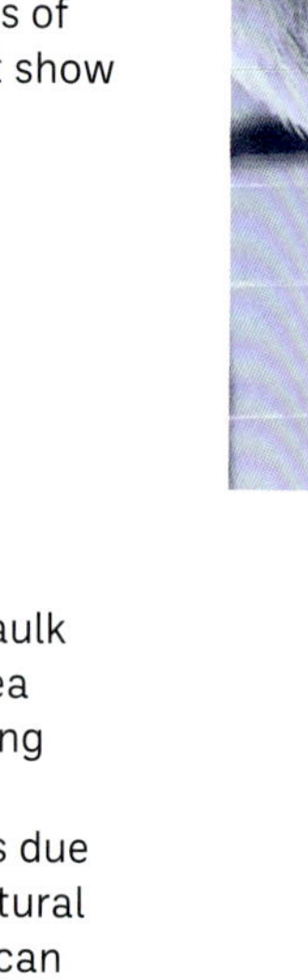

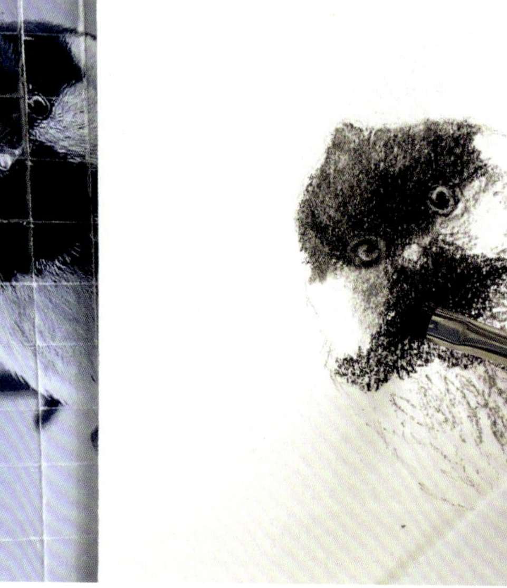

b

→ Some artists baulk at the idea of touching surface materials due to the natural oils that can be passed on to them, but I find it an invaluable, intuitive and fun method of blending.

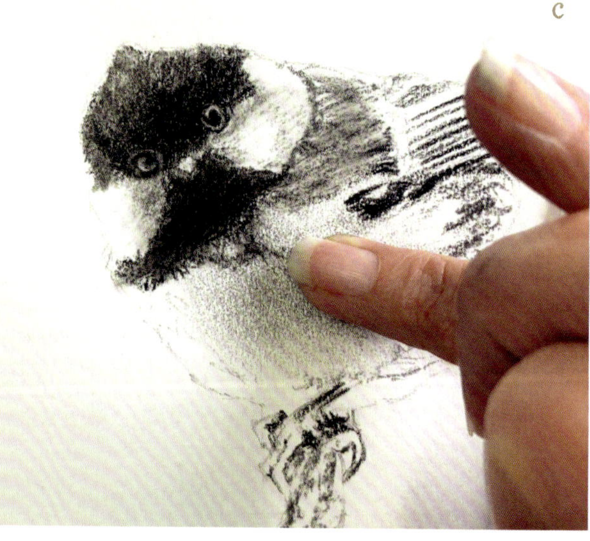

c

6 As you blend the tones together, you will invariably lose some of the darks. You'll need to add more darks as you work through the process.

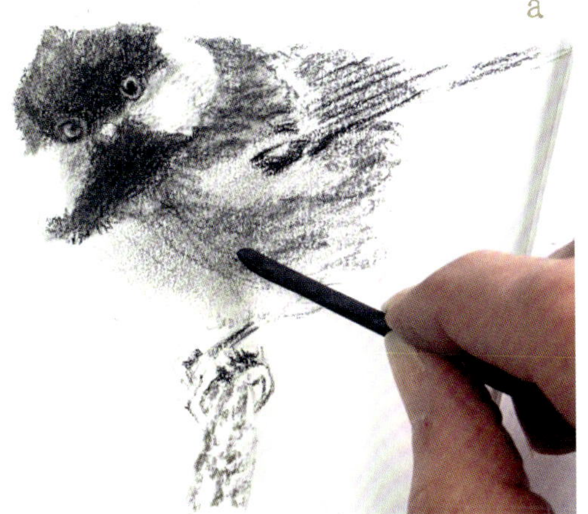

↑ Reapplying tone using a willow stick.

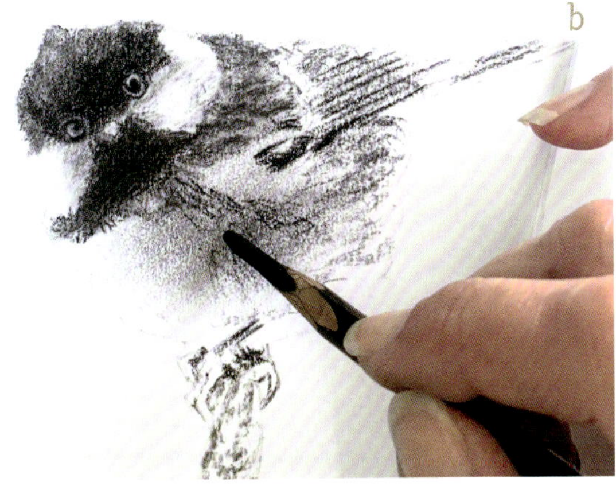

↑ Adding more tone using a charcoal pencil.

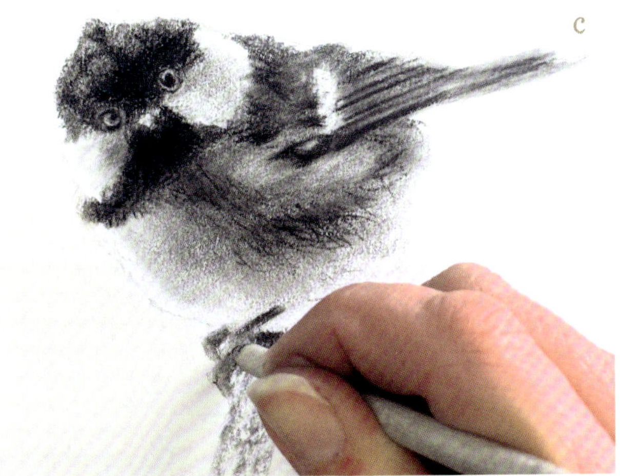

↑ Using the excess charcoal on a blending stump to help describe the feet.

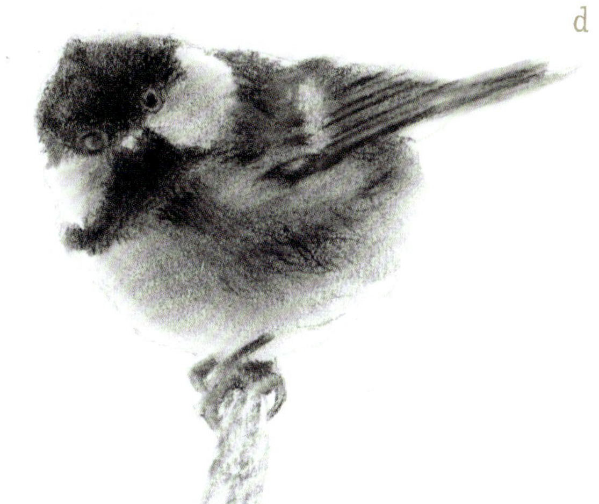

↑ At this stage, most of the values are completed but the drawing needs a little more work for accuracy and finishing touches.

FINE-TUNE FOR TEXTURE AND DETAIL

This is my favourite part of the process, where I get to add the finishing touches. Generally speaking, this is where I will make sure that my darks are dark enough, that I've re-established any lights and that I've added sufficient loose marks.

7 Fine-tune the areas by lifting out lighter parts using your erasers. Run the mono eraser over the piece where more delicate, lighter values are required.

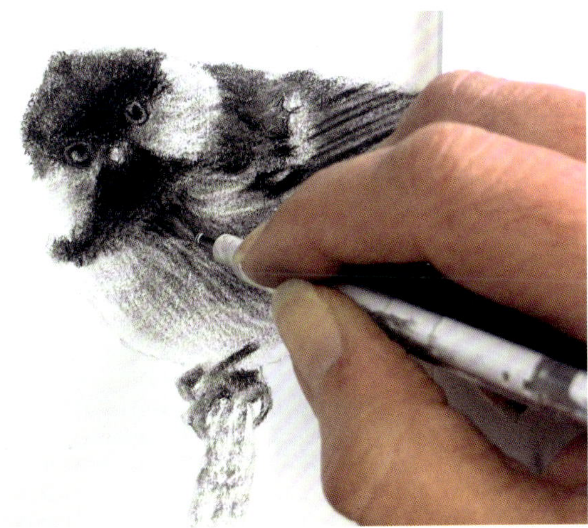

↑ Using a mono eraser to regain the light and add texture.

8 Re-establish darker areas, as and when needed, with the dark charcoal pencil and willow stick. Go back and forth with both erasers and charcoal to create interesting marks and effects.

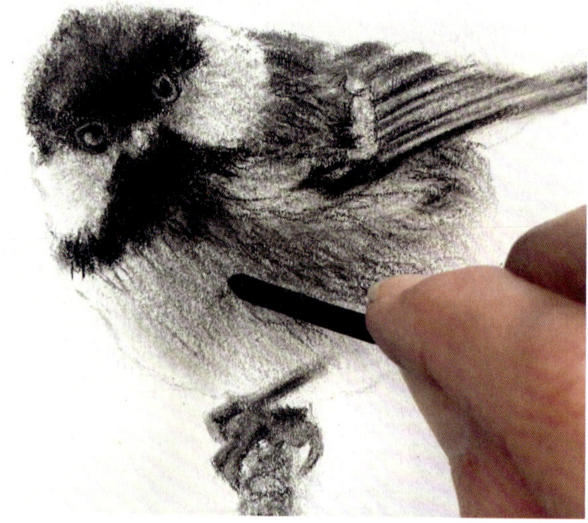

↑ Introducing more texture by adding delicate marks with the willow stick.

9 How much detail you put in at this stage is again an artistic choice; you may decide to leave the drawing with minimal detail. Once you are happy with your piece and have no further amendments to make, clean the surface thoroughly of any unwanted marks with a clean eraser and then fix the charcoal with a suitable spray fixative, following the guidance on the container.

Top tip

You need to get the dark tones dark enough for the light tones to pop.

↓ This is the finished piece. There aren't many differences from the previous stage, but just enough to call it complete.

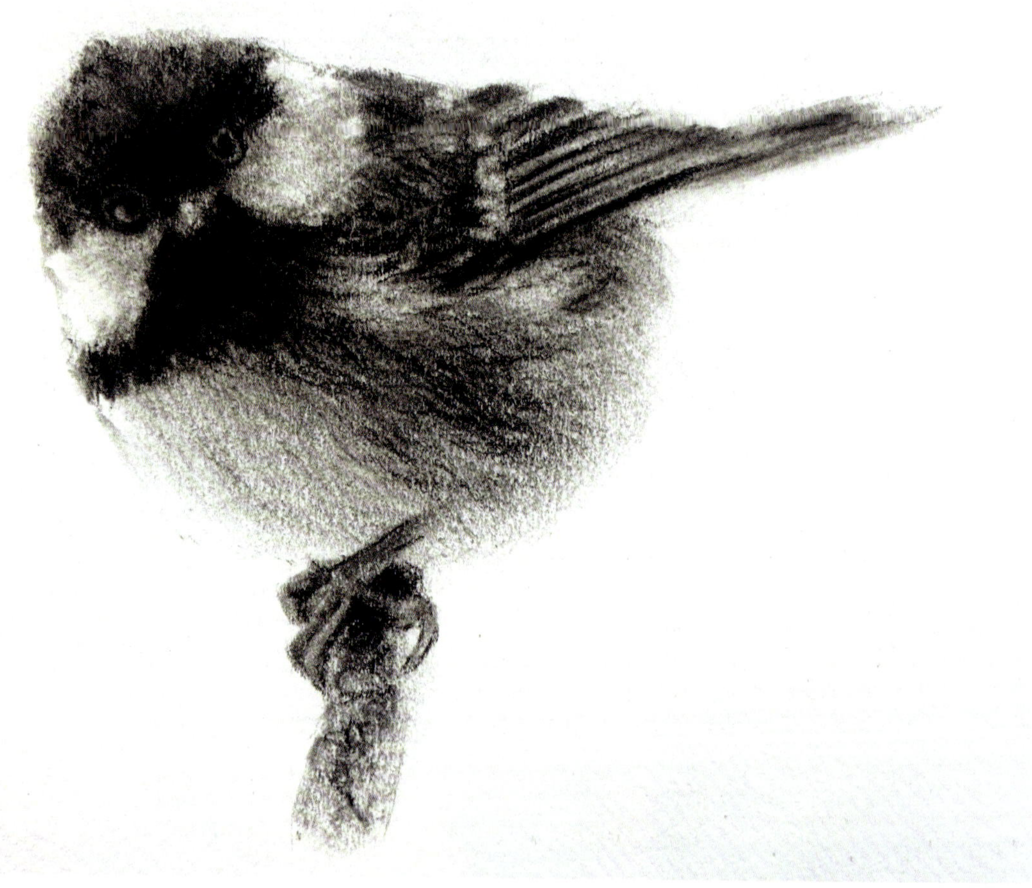

Further examples of tonal drawings

In these four pieces I used the same methods as described earlier; however, I drew them on toned paper. I wanted brighter whites than just leaving the toned paper to show through, so I added white towards the end of the process using a mixture of white charcoal pencil and white pastel. The branches have been kept deliberately loose in style, as have the outer feathers of the birds, but all the larger tone values are in the right places to give everything shape and form. I used willow charcoal for some of the lighter grey tones.

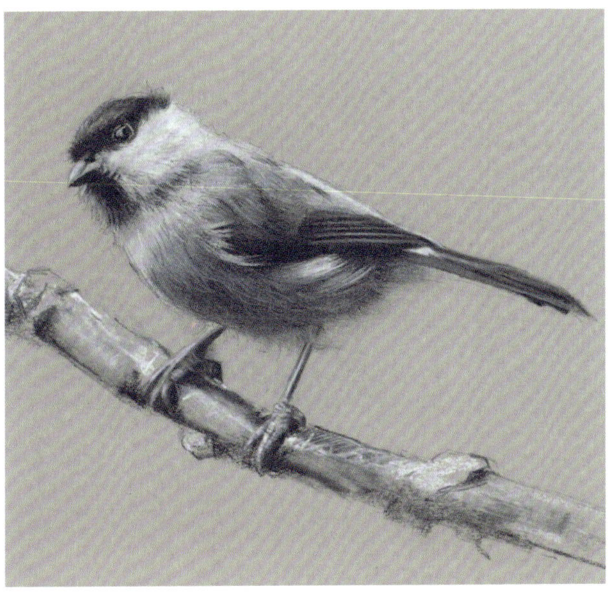

↑ 'Coal Tit', 2021, charcoal and pastel on toned paper.

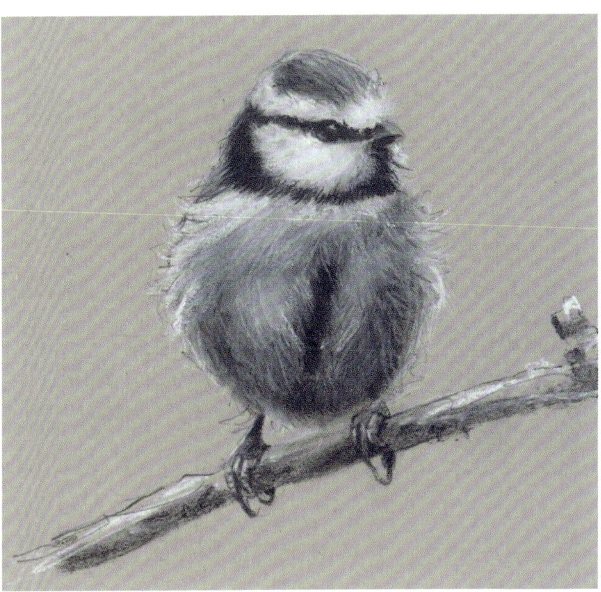

↑ 'Blue Tit', 2021, charcoal and pastel on toned paper.

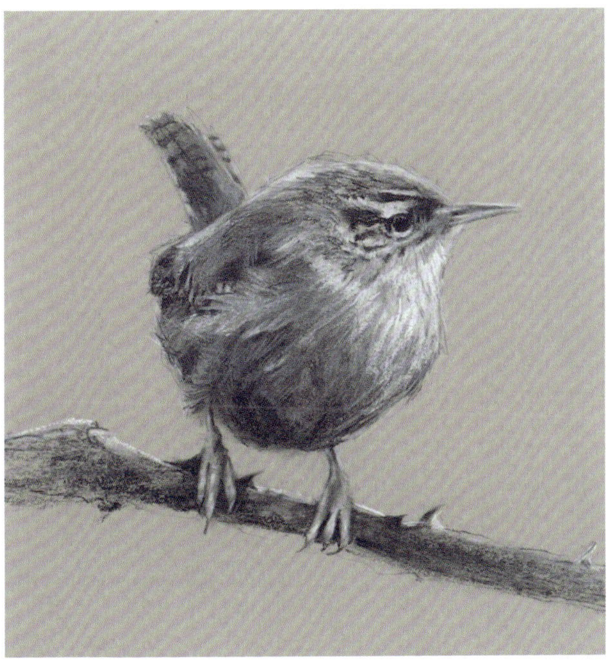

↑ 'Jenny Wren', 2021, charcoal and pastel on toned paper.

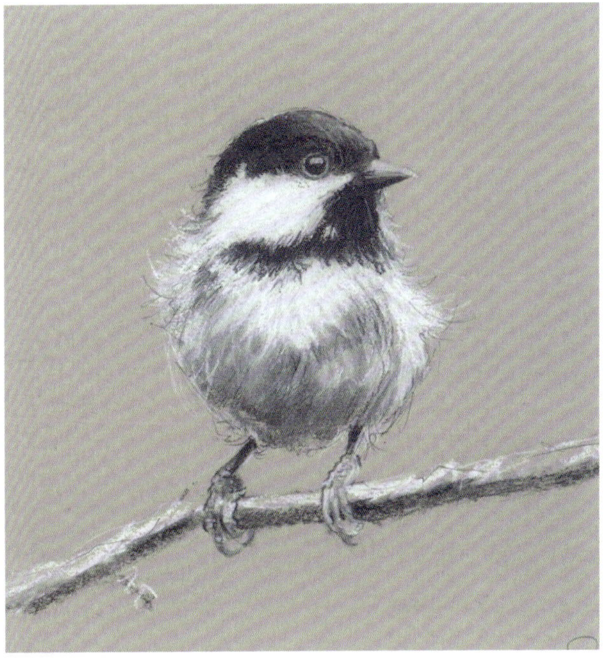

↑ 'Coal Tit', 2021, charcoal and pastel on toned paper.

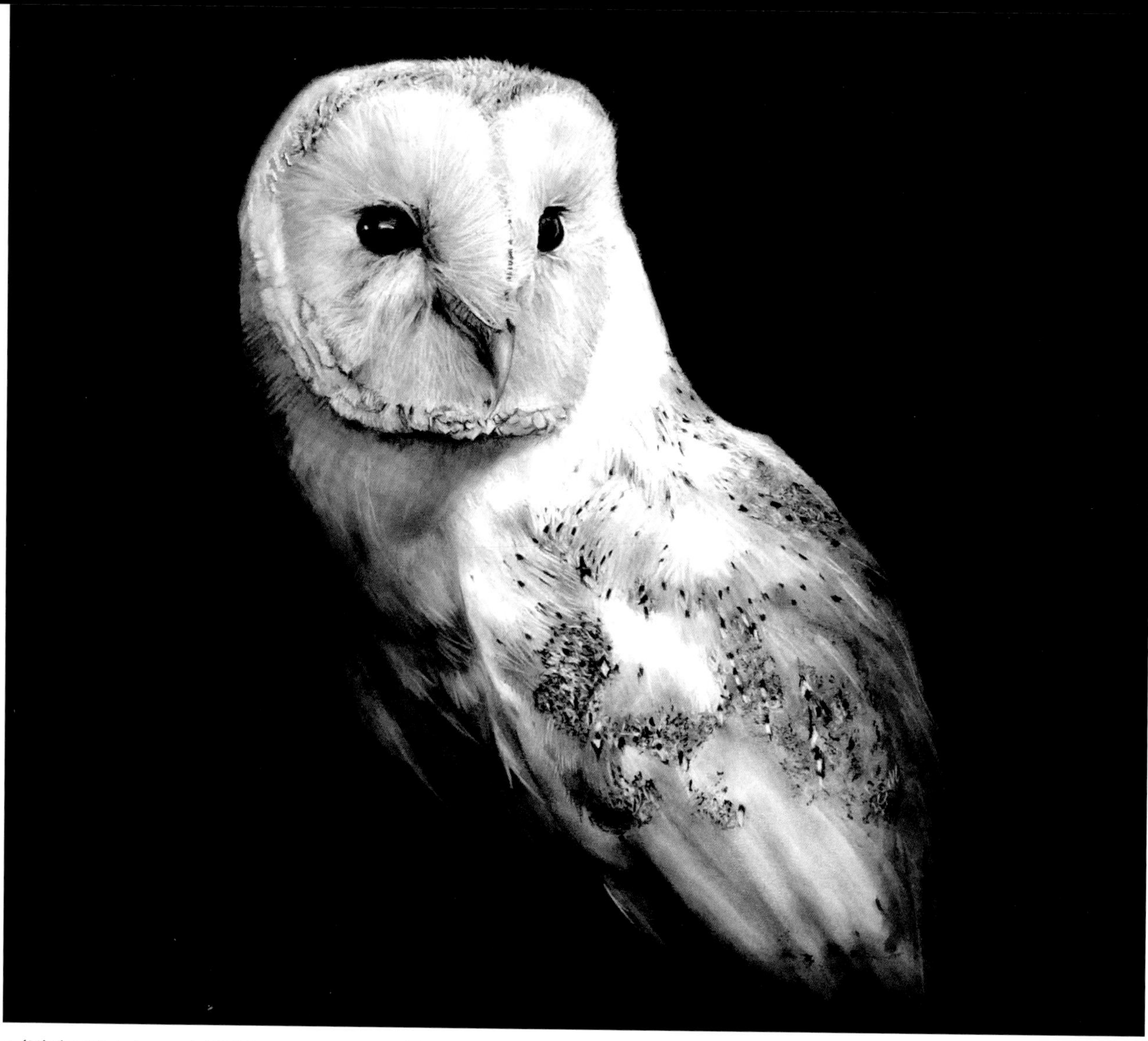

↑ 'Night Watchman', 2020, charcoal on board.

↓ 'Dominion', 2020, charcoal on board.

↓ 'Parrot', 2023, charcoal on paper.

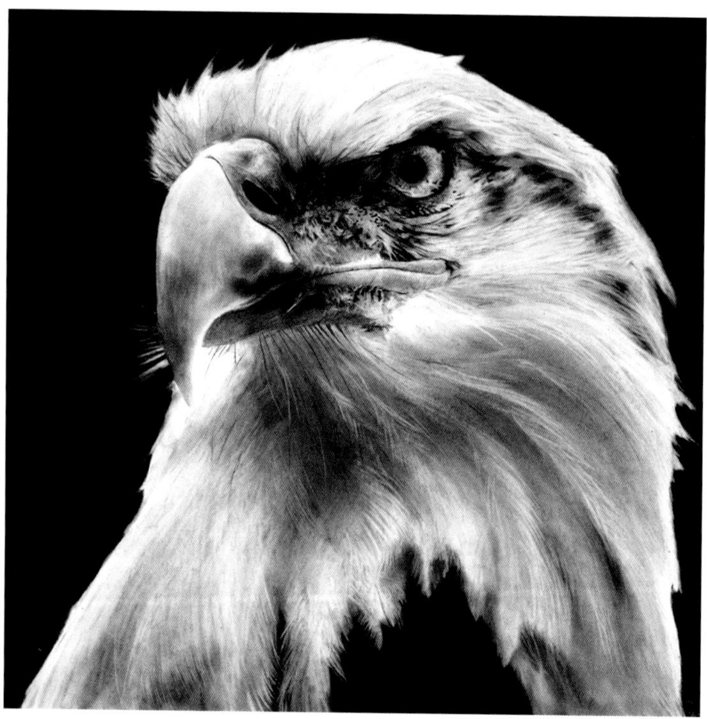

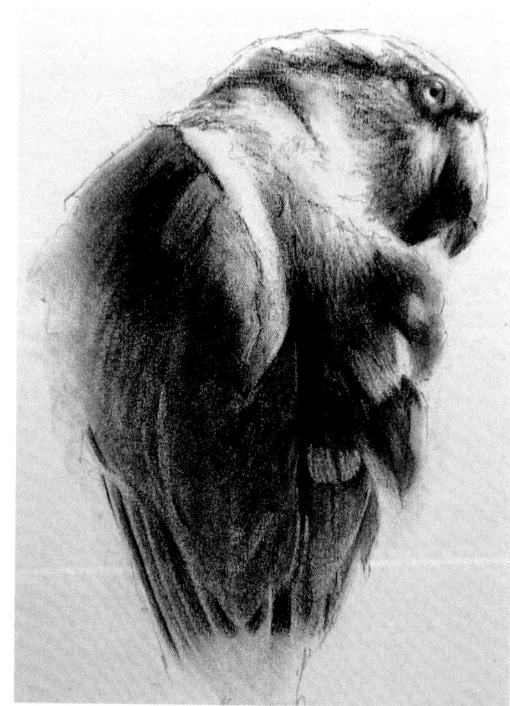

An observation about chroma and tone

I create a lot of charcoal art, and during the preparatory stages I always desaturate the photo first as it normally makes the dark, light and mid-tone shapes easier to see. It also informs me whether the image will make for a good charcoal piece. However, sometimes a colour's chroma (also known as its saturation or intensity) can really throw a curveball when you desaturate an image.

A good example of this can be seen in this beautiful photograph of a robin. The brightness of the orange breast leads us to believe that the tone would be similar to the surrounding greys, perhaps just a little lighter. However, the orange area, when desaturated, is much lighter than first expected. The brightness and chroma of a colour can really throw our way of thinking about colour and tone.

→ Colour robin.

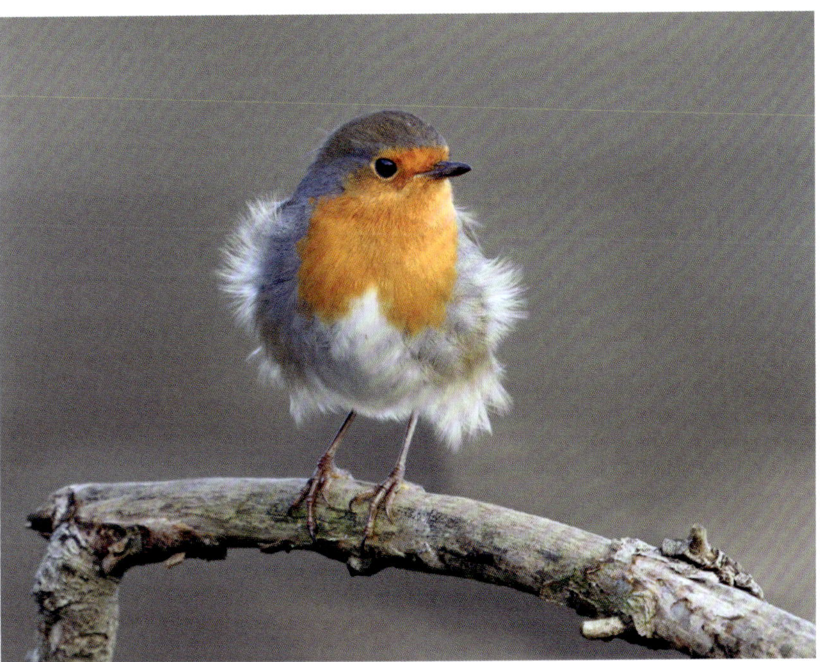

→ Monochrome robin.

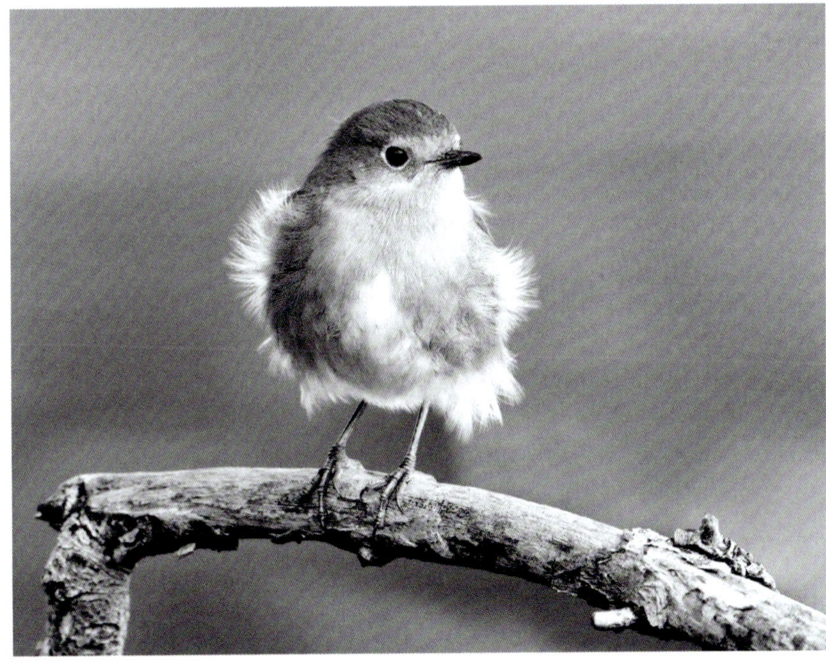

The whole issue of colour theory is fascinating and I would recommend James Gurney's book, *Color and Light: A Guide for the Realist Painter*, for those of you who want to delve deeper into the subject.

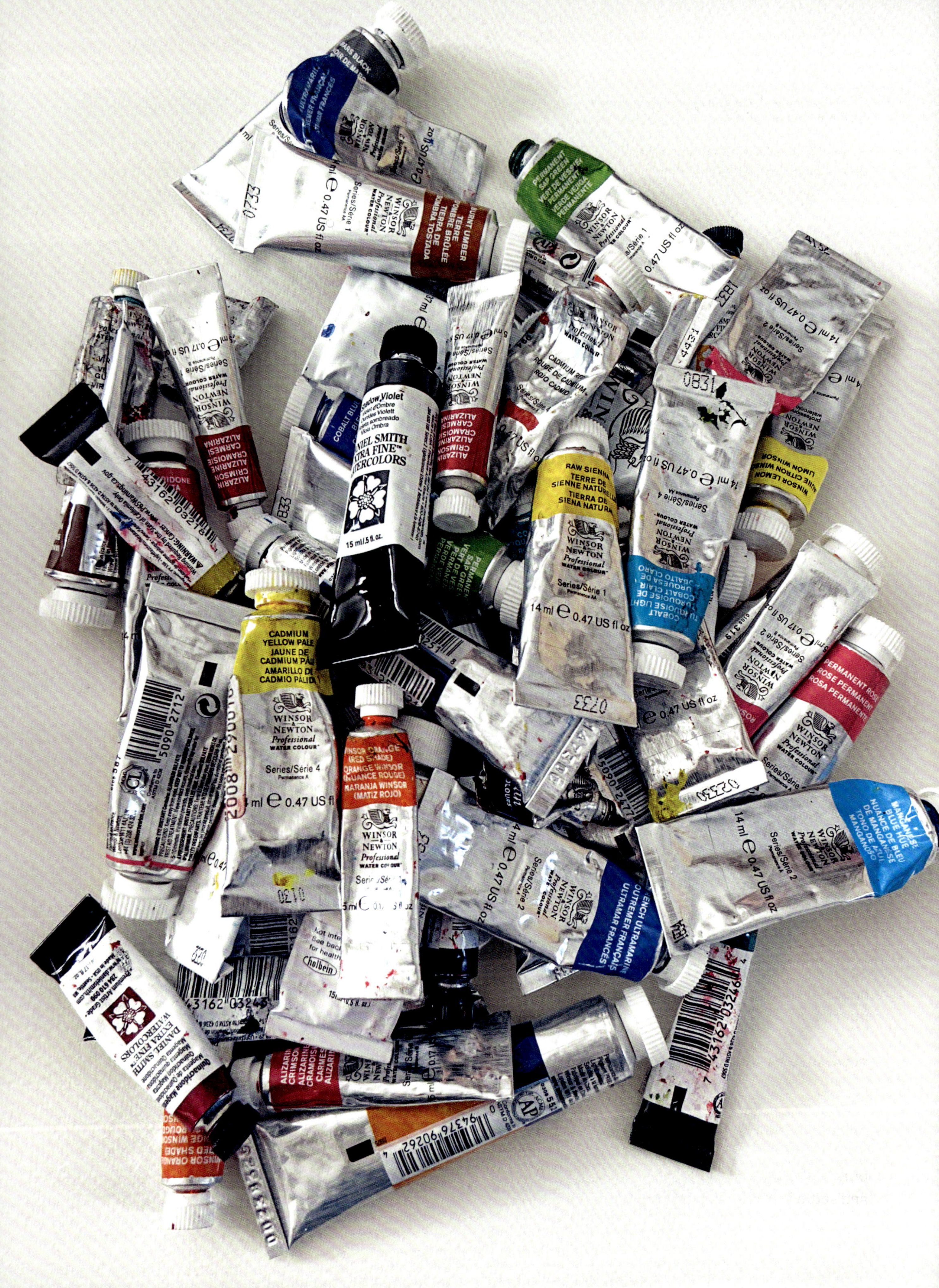
CADMIUM YELLOW PALE
JAUNE DE CADMIUM PÂLE
AMARILLO DE CADMIO PÁLIDO
WINSOR & NEWTON
Professional
WATER COLOUR
Series/Série 4
RAW SIENNA
TERRE DE SIENNE NATURELLE
TIERRA DE SIENA NATURAL
WINSOR & NEWTON
Professional
WATER COLOUR
Series/Série 1
14 ml ℮ 0.47 US fl oz
WINSOR ORANGE (RED SHADE)
ORANGE WINSOR (NUANCE ROUGE)
NARANJA WINSOR (MATIZ ROJO)
WINSOR & NEWTON
Professional
WATER COLOUR
15 ml/.5 fl. oz.
0733

CHAPTER

2

Exploring Watercolour Paint

With watercolour paint you get the best of both worlds. It can be tightly controlled to render particular details of interest, or it can be used expressively, helped along with a multitude of other substances such as salt, cling film, bleach, granulating fluid, inks, acrylics, gouache and, of course, water itself!

PROJECT 2

Discovering how watercolour works through experimentation and play

In this project, you are going to explore these two sides of watercolour through five exercises that will enable you to paint a great egret with a beautifully loose background in the next chapter.

MY REGULAR TOOLS

I only use a handful of items to paint with, but I've added some optional extras to the list below that you might want to experiment with. If you've got some unusual brushes or tools that you've never had chance to use, this is a great time to see what marks they will make.

Watercolour paper

I use two types of paper, both cold press. Cold press paper has a slightly bumpy texture, which means you can make a range of marks, from solid lines to broken ones. It also allows the paint to pool, merge and settle in exciting and unexpected ways as it gathers and dries in the dips of the paper's surface. I use a mixture of expressive and detailed brushwork, so this type of paper is best suited for my style of painting.

You may have other papers to hand, such as rough or hot press. Rough press is more heavily textured than cold press, and is great for glazing, dry brush techniques and loose painterly strokes, but it can be a little more problematic when it comes to depicting fine detail. Hot press paper is much smoother than both cold and rough press, and as such, you will find it more difficult to achieve some of the more expressive techniques mentioned in this book.

For my gallery pieces, I use Saunders Waterford 100% cotton, 638 gsm, cold press, high white paper by St Cuthberts Mill. This is especially useful for larger pieces as it doesn't buckle when using large quantities of water. It is also thick enough to take a lot of scrubbing and withstand any potential damage that I do to it when vigorously lifting dried paint with a brush. The paints pool on it beautifully and you can build up gloriously rich colours with layering.

↑ An assortment of paper: Daler-Rowney (top), Saunders Waterford (middle), Seawhite of Brighton (bottom).

For smaller exercise pieces, as in this chapter, I use a lighter weight (350 gsm), cold press paper by Seawhite of Brighton. It is fairly robust, doesn't buckle easily and colours are easy to lift. It's also significantly cheaper than the thicker paper, so is ideal for experimenting.

If you are using lighter weight paper, you may find it has a tendency to cockle, especially if you are applying large washes to recreate a sky, for instance. If this is the case, you may wish to stretch the paper first. You can do this by soaking it thoroughly first and then attaching it to a rigid board using gummed tape. Once it has dried flat and taut, it is ready to use.

Top tip

You can purchase samples of papers from several manufacturers.

Brushes

Round brushes (synthetic)

I use sizes 6 and 12 generally, but anything similar will suffice. Round brushes are versatile because you can use both the tip and the body of the brush to create anything from tiny details to large sweeps of paint. I prefer synthetic over animal hair brushes as I feel I have more control with them and I like the resistance they have.

Rigger brushes (synthetic, slim)

I use a size 2 brush, but a size 0 or 1 would also be suitable. These are great for making long wispy shapes.

Detailer brushes (synthetic)

I use a small oval brush, but a size 00 or 1 round brush is also ideal for adding the smallest of details, such as around beaks and eyes.

Flat brushes (1 inch)

I use these to create large washes for skies, rivers and seas.

Size 12, round, synthetic, Escoda Prado.

Size 6, round, synthetic, Escoda Prado.

Rigger, size 2, synthetic, Major.

Small oval brush, size 4, synthetic, Escoda Prado.

Flat wash, 1 inch, synthetic, Winsor & Newton.

Scrubbing/lifting brush, synthetic, Escoda Perla.

Lifting brushes

Sometimes I need to lift paint. For damp paint, I use one of my regular brushes, but I use an old nylon watercolour brush for lifting dried paint. Generally speaking, I don't lift with any exact precision so the bluntness of this brush serves me well. However, some artists need to lift with precision, for example to reveal slim passages of light in the wings, in which case small flat brushes can be useful.

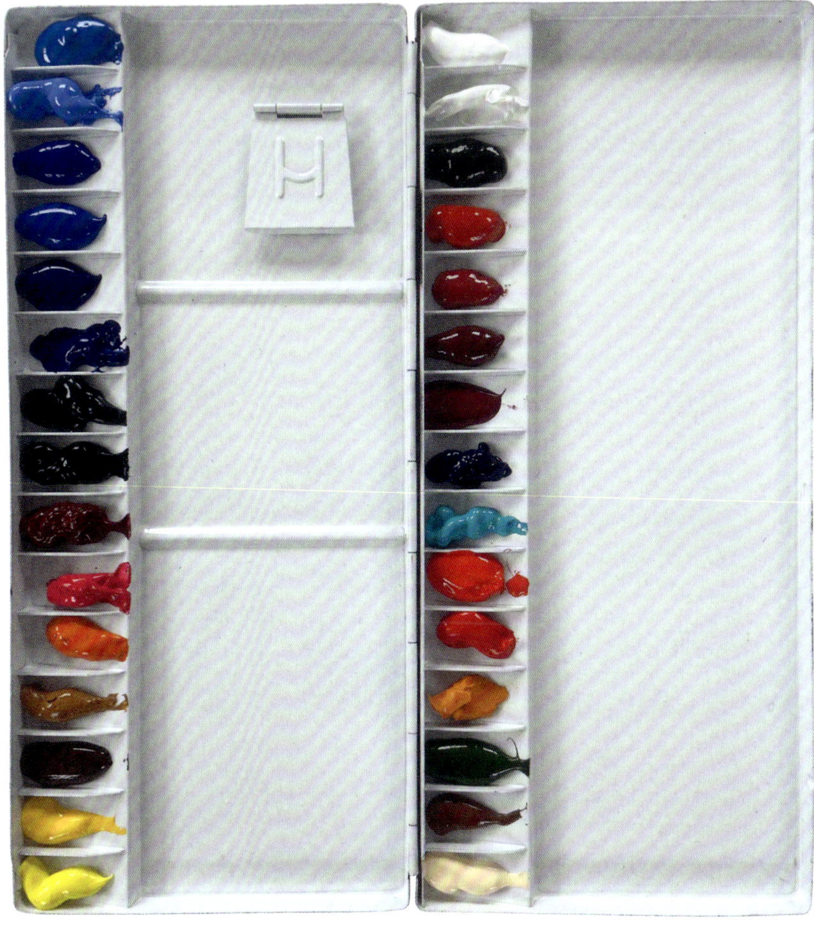

↑ It is important to familiarise yourself with the layout of your palette as you will need to work quickly and intuitively with watercolour. It needs to become as second nature as finding the accelerator and brake pedals!

Palette

For much of this book you will only be using four to six colours at a time, so something as simple as a white china plate will suffice. When I paint using a larger range of colours, I use a tin palette. This allows me to decant my favourite tube paints into the side slots. The paints harden over time but can be reactivated by misting them with water from an atomiser.

I prefer tin over plastic palettes as I like the way that the water pools in large amounts on the surface when mixing colours. On some of the cheaper plastic palettes, the pools of water have a tendency to bead and separate off.

If you are filling up a palette with your own choice of paints, it's important to place them in a clear and logical order. I put my favourite colours on one side of the palette, with lesser-used ones relegated to the furthest side. I lay the cooler colours in a row (blues, greens and black) followed by the warmer ones (pinks, reds, oranges and yellows).

Paints

Four paints are the basis of much of the painting in this book: Manganese Blue Hue, Quinacridone Magenta, Winsor Lemon and Mars Black (a CMYK palette). I use both tube and pan paints (rectangular 'cakes') by Winsor & Newton. I don't prefer one over the other as my tube paints also harden into blocks after they've been left in the well of a palette for a day or so.

In terms of whether you buy student-grade or professional-grade paint, it really is a matter of choice. I tend to buy a mixture of both. There are some colours that I love that only come in the professional ranges. I have found that the paint from the professional range is much denser in colour, so a little goes a long way.

In the following exercises I'd encourage you to experiment with any of the paints you have to hand to see what effects they create. They will vary in terms of transparency, chroma and granulation; playing with them is the best way to familiarise yourself with their qualities.

Masking fluid

Masking fluid allows you to protect sections of the paper from the paint, enabling you to work freely on your layers, leaving sections of the white paper reserved. It can be applied in a range of ways: splashed, flicked and painted, to name but a few.

Paper towels

Paper towels are useful for lifting paint and regulating paint on the brush.

Water

I often have two jars of water on my table: one with clean water and the other for swilling out dirty brushes. This saves a lot of time changing water and prevents me from getting muddy colours on those initial washes.

Optional extras

This is the time to root around your cupboards, drawers, outhouse, garage and green spaces to see what treasures you can come up with to help you create some wonderful marks. Think of all of those things that you bought on a whim from a craft shop or got handed down from a well-meaning relative and never knew what to do with! Here are some suggested ideas to get you started:

Credit card, nib pen, cocktail stick, twigs

To apply, lift and drag paint, and score paper.

Palette knife

The flat and the tip of an oil palette knife can be used to drag paint across the page, excellent for creating trees, branches, twigs and the suggestion of grasses.

Feather

I use a pigeon feather to create lost and found lines with the 'nib' to suggest branches and foliage. I also use the feathery end to make a range of marks to denote, for instance, distant trees.

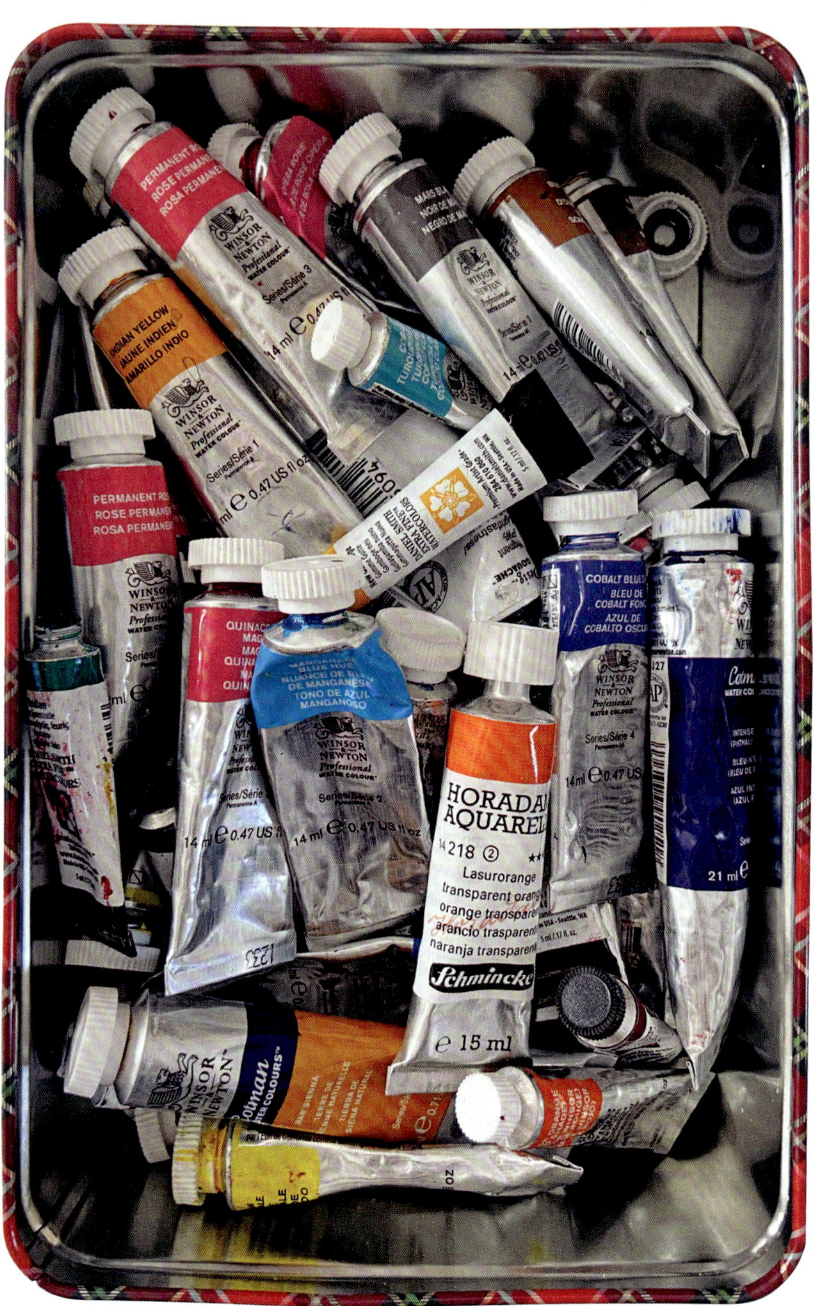

← Collection of my paints.

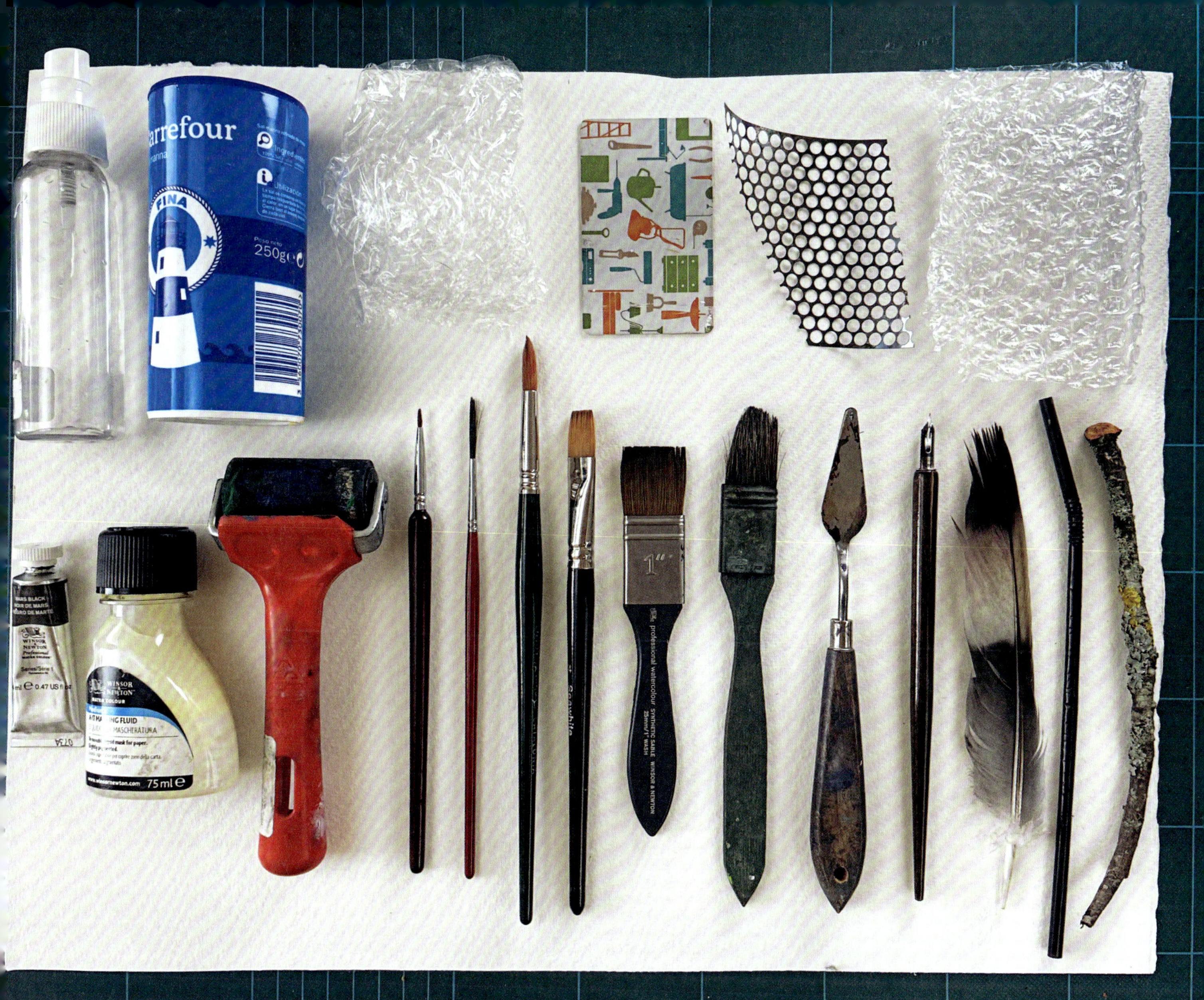

↑ Foraged, found and gifted items put to good use.

Atomiser

For spraying a fine mist of water. I use one that I bought from my local pharmacy.

Table salt

Normal or rock salt to create textures on branches and other environmental elements.

Cling film and bubble wrap

These create interesting effects that can be useful when depicting rocks or a tangle of undergrowth.

Bendy straw

These are great for blowing paint around the page. They create twiglike effects coming off trees or can suggest movement in a bird as can be seen in 'Eric in Flight' (p.59).

EXERCISE 1: PRACTISE LAYERING AND LIFTING TECHNIQUES

One of the basic principles of using watercolour is the practice of adding layers of watercolour pigment on top of each other to achieve a range of colour, tones, shapes and edges. Equally important is the ability to lift watercolour. This exercise covers the basics of these two essential principles as an invaluable way of getting to know how your paint and paper will work together when creating your final pieces.

Watercolour paint has a reputation for being difficult to remove and while this is true of some colours due to the staining qualities of individual pigments, most can be lifted off to good effect. Admittedly, you will never recover a bright white sheet, but you can often lift an overworked section in order to recover light areas in readiness for subsequent layers.

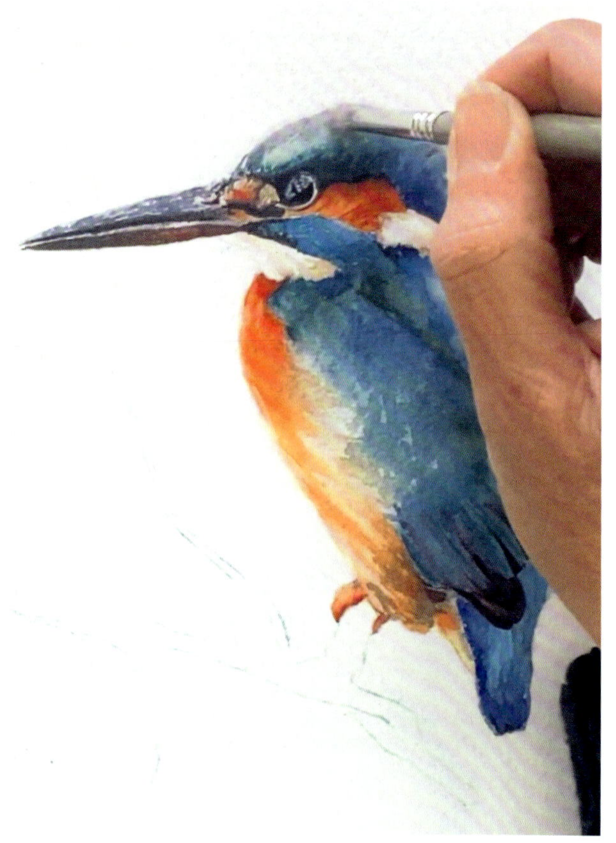

← An example of lifting paint. Here an area of paint is being gently lifted from a kingfisher's head.

1 Draw a line of boxes onto the watercolour paper.

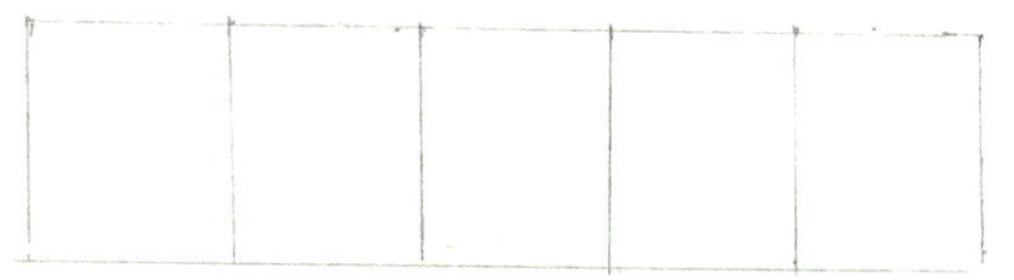

↑ Boxes drawn on paper using a pencil and ruler.

2 Mix up some black paint with water to make a light grey wash and add a layer of this to the paper using your size 12 brush.

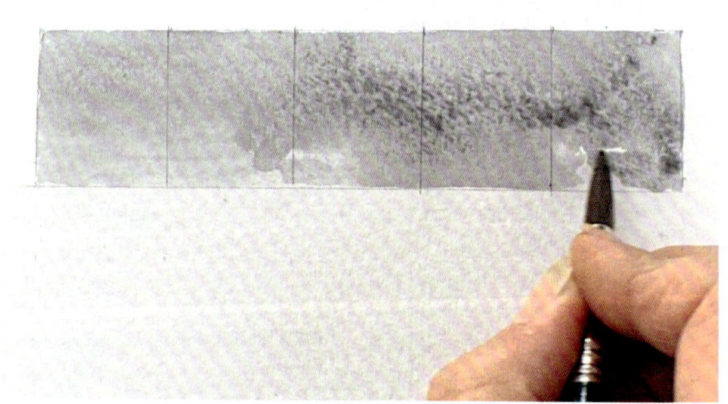

↑ Completing the first layer with a thin wash of black paint.

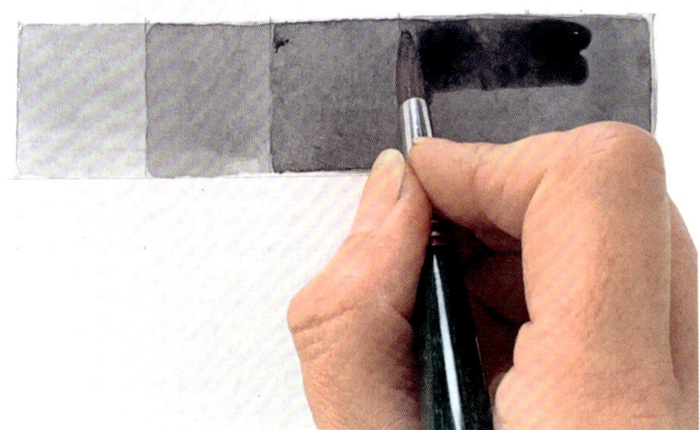

↑ Applying the fourth layer to the fourth and fifth box using the same consistency of paint.

3 Once this layer has dried, add another layer along all of the adjoining boxes, making sure to leave the first box clear of additional paint. Once dry, continue the process until you have reached the end box.

Five layers of pale wash have increased the tone quite considerably by the time you get to the final layer. In reality, I increase the amount of pigment on the brush for my second and third layers, which means that I don't need to apply five layers of paint when painting a piece. However, those lighter layers are essential to give the final piece a sense of light, and for that reason I always ensure that parts of layers remain untouched by subsequent brush marks.

↑ See how dark you can make the final box, simply by layering up light washes.

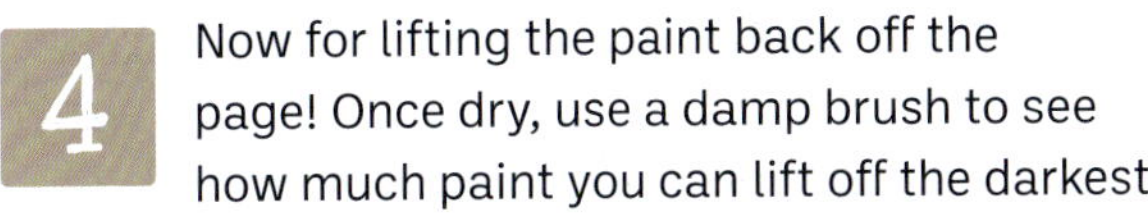

4 Now for lifting the paint back off the page! Once dry, use a damp brush to see how much paint you can lift off the darkest box. You may need to agitate the paint a little by rubbing the damp brush back and forth gently to reactivate the paint. Be wary of damaging the surface of the paper. Remove the unwanted paint by rolling your paper towel into a point to dab up the moisture. Experiment with different brushes to see which ones lift paint effectively and the shapes that they make. The success of how much paint you remove will vary according to the brand and pigment of paint, type of paper and the brush that you are using.

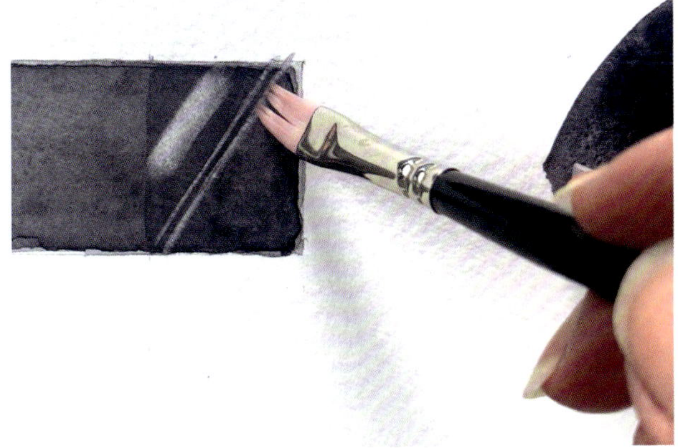

↑ Here I used my small round lifting brush then a small flat brush to lift paint off the page. This can be an essential way of regaining light, although you will never be able to get the paper back to its original brightness. We will use this technique in Chapter 11 to regain the light on an eagle's feathers.

Top tip

You will find that some colours are easier to lift than others, due to their staining qualities. A product called Lifting Preparation can be applied to your paper prior to painting, which will help if you find it difficult to lift pigments from your paper.

EXERCISE 2: EXPLORE PAINT AND WATER RATIOS AND THEIR EFFECT ON DAMP PAPER

One of the most important things to consider when using watercolour paint is the wetness of your paper and your brush. I paint on dry, wet and damp paper to achieve a variety of effects. The amount of moisture in the paper will affect how the paint reacts once it hits the surface. Similarly, the amount of pigment and water on your brush will determine the spread, shape, colour, tone and edge of the marks laid down. The following exercises are designed to explain what happens when you add paint of differing consistencies onto a damp layer of painted paper.

1 On a sheet of paper, add two swatches of paint. Make sure your paper is dry when you do this. Let the pigment settle for a few seconds.

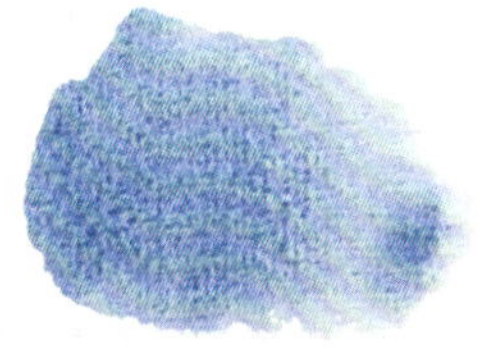

↑ Two swatches of paint applied to the paper.

2 While it is semi-damp, drop a splash of pure water onto one of your swatches. Watch how the paint reacts. As the fresh water hits the damp paint, blooms will occur as the water pushes the settling pigment away. You can even spray a fine mist of water using an atomiser to discover random and beautiful patterns that emerge.

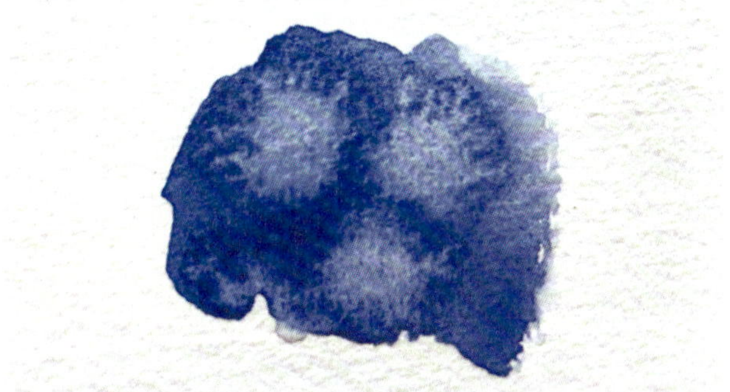

↑ Blooms appearing as the pigment dissipates.

Why is this technique useful?

This effect may be something that you'll either want to avoid or embrace. I often use drops of water on damp paint to dissipate pigment if an area needs breaking up. It is important to remember that dry paper will create hard edges, damp paper will create soft edges and wet paper will cause soft, lost edges. We will want to incorporate all of these types of edges into our work.

The image below was taken when I was painting a barn owl, a subject we will cover in Chapter 8. During the process, a large area of wing appeared flat and lifeless. I applied a drop of water to the damp paint and this helped to lighten the area softly. I was then able to gently coax the paint away from the darker area to recover an area of light. The cauliflower shape still remained, but I just embraced it as part of the final image.

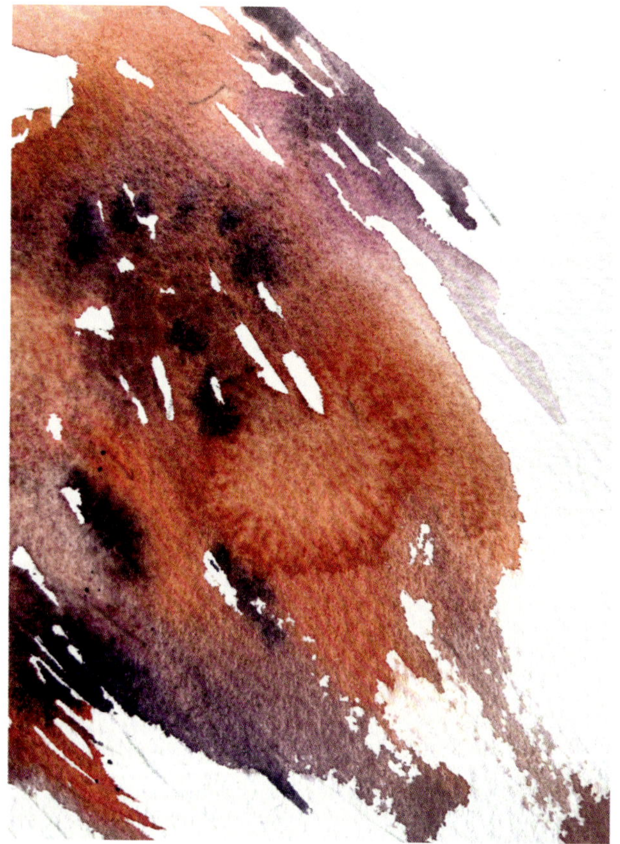

↑ Adding a drop of water to an owl's wing to regain the light on an overworked piece.

3 Load creamier paint onto your brush, so that the paint on your brush is thicker and darker than the paint on your swatch. Add a drop of this thicker mix of paint onto the damp swatch. Allow the paint to spread of its own accord.

This time a bloom won't happen, and, as long as your swatch is damp enough, the newly applied paint will softly spread into the lighter shade below. Look at how the darker paint moves into the lighter areas, creating soft edges as it dries.

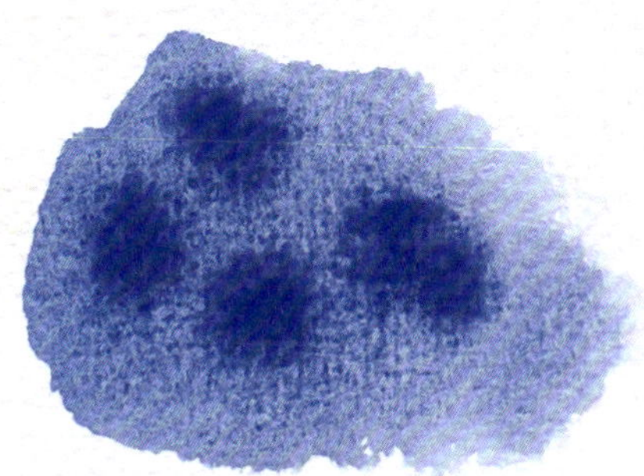

↑ Timing and pigment control are essential skills to master, and this particular technique features heavily in my work.

This technique is commonly known as 'wet-into-wet' – a particularly unhelpful phrase, as it is really creamy paint onto damp paper! When you carry out this experiment, if the darker, thicker drop of paint doesn't move much this is normally an indication that your paper was too dry when you dropped it onto the wash below.

Why is this technique useful?

Much of my painting process involves this technique and is applied predominantly with the first wash. It creates beautiful soft edges that are crucial when it comes to my particular style of painting.

This next photograph shows a section of a swan painting that we will be covering in Chapter 10. It shows how creamy greys and magenta/black mixes have been dropped into a still-damp pale blue wash to create soft edges. These effects are most apparent in the middle of the image. At the bottom right, however, you can see where the purple-coloured water is pooling. This very wet paint was hastily sucked up and removed with a screwed-up section of kitchen towel to avoid a bloom or back run appearing in the surrounding section.

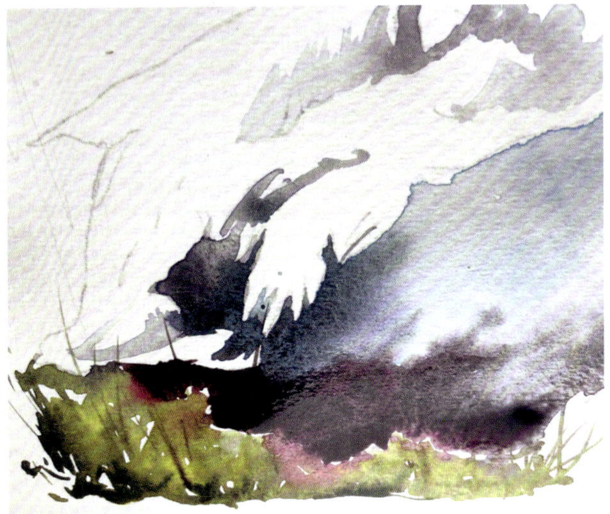

↑ Thicker paints dropped onto underlying light colours at just the right moment will create soft edges without disturbing the colours beneath.

As you can see, watercolour certainly keeps you on your toes! It is impossible to predict everything that will happen on the page. Therefore, much of the process is about understanding what is happening on the paper and reacting to it accordingly to achieve the outcomes you desire.

Timing, moisture and pigment control are some of the key features to creating a successful watercolour piece. They represent some of the trickiest elements for new artists to understand, as there are a number of variables that affect how the paint reacts on paper. Principally it can be down to the moisture on the paper, the mixture of water and paint on your brush and the temperature of your work space. The type of materials you use can also affect the outcomes. Once you've practised these techniques a number of times, timing and moisture control will become second nature.

Top tip

Check the dampness of your paper by bobbing your head up and down to gauge its shininess. If it is still glistening, it is most likely too wet; there should just be a fine subtle sheen.

EXERCISE 3: EXPERIMENT WITH SALT, CLING FILM AND BUBBLE WRAP

Now you can discover how to create interesting effects with household products. These items can create an array of textures that are particularly useful when it comes to depicting environmental elements such as rocks, branches, foliage and, of course, birds. Your imagination is your only limit, so go for it!

Using salt

1 To demonstrate this technique, I'll be using an Australian pink robin. Paint the first wash of light paint onto dry paper, then add thicker, darker paint, where needed, while the paint is still damp. Wait for some of the sheen to disappear.

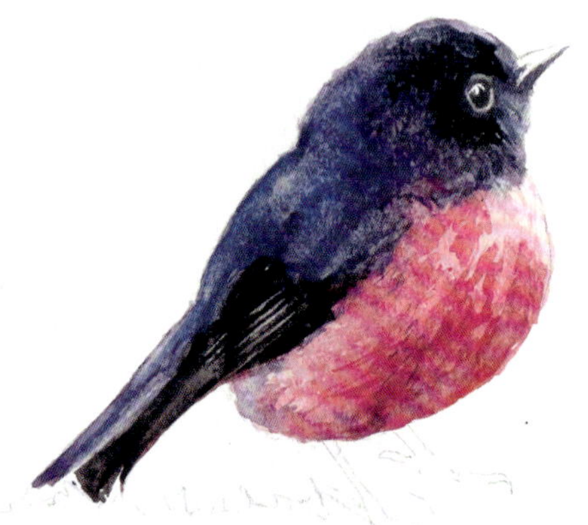

↑ The first layer drying. I used layering to get all of the pinks on the robin's chest.

2 While the paint is still damp, sprinkle salt over a section of the painting. In this case I added it to the top of the head and back area as that was where I most wanted texture introduced.

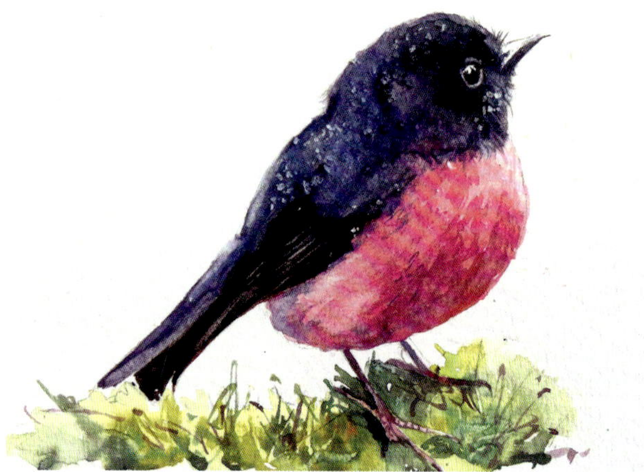

↑ A small sprinkle of salt added to the back and head of the robin, while the paint is still damp.

3 Wait for the salt to dry thoroughly before rubbing it away with your fingers. Small parts of the underlayer will peep through.

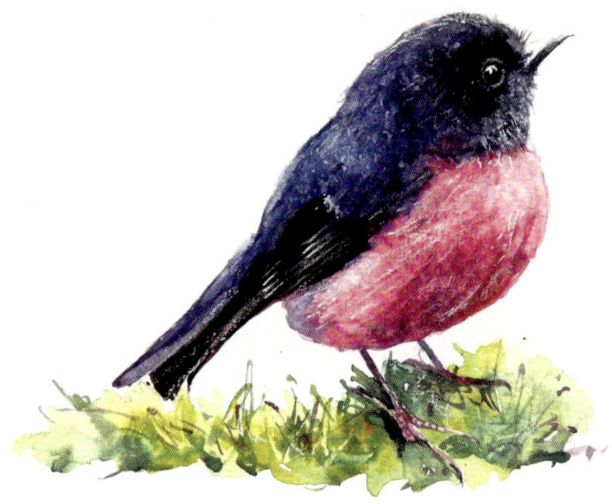

↑ The salt has removed a small amount of the paint, lightening the back and head and creating an interesting feathery texture.

4 A close-up of the head shows the variety of marks created by the salt. The effect will differ according to the moisture on the paper, paint density and the type of salt you use.

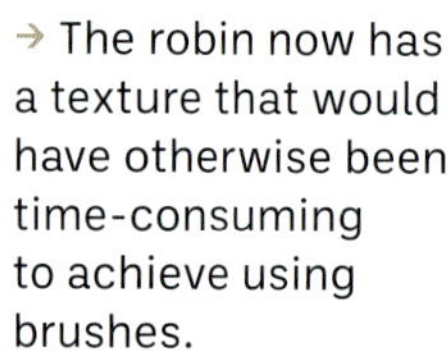

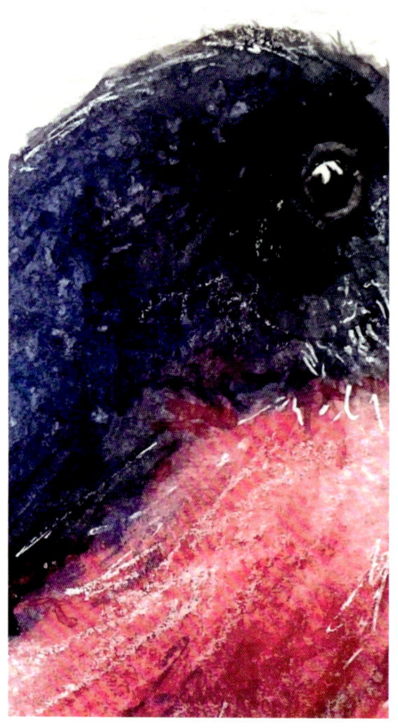

→ The robin now has a texture that would have otherwise been time-consuming to achieve using brushes.

Using cling film and bubble wrap

Cling film and bubble wrap can also create interesting effects.

1. Form some organic shapes, such as boulders or stones, using two or three colours and creating darker and lighter tones.

2. Press crumpled-up cling film or bubble wrap directly onto the surface of the wet paint. Allow the paint to dry thoroughly.

3. Lift off the cling film or bubble wrap when the paint is dry to reveal an exciting array of shapes and tones.

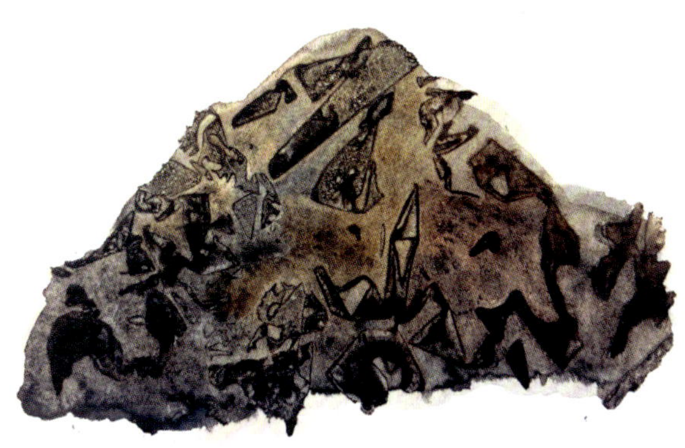

↑ Cling film has been used on this occasion to 'paint' a craggy rock. Imagine what this could represent in cooler hues... a mountain, perhaps?

EXERCISE 4: TIPS AND TRICKS WITH DIFFERENT TOOLS

Feathers

Feathers are a lot of fun to work with as they create a whole array of unpredictable marks. I used a found pigeon feather in the following examples. Be creative and expressive in your mark making and make sure you use both the quill and the feather.

1. Dip the feather into a watery black mix and move it in different directions. The ends of the feather have a tendency to bunch up, so you may need to spread them out a little to get some interesting lines.

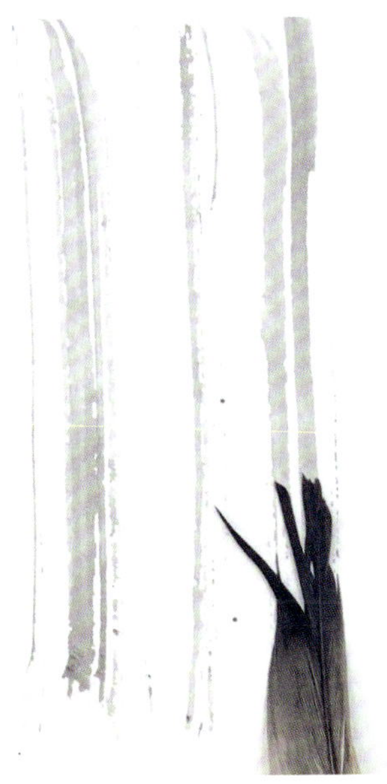

↑ In this case, I'm pulling the feather down from the top of the page to the bottom.

2. The sharpened quill creates a beautiful range of shapes. Scribble, splatter and make marks with abandon to replicate the unwieldy, tangled nature of vegetation.

↑ I quickly sharpened the quill with a craft knife and dipped it into runny black watercolour.

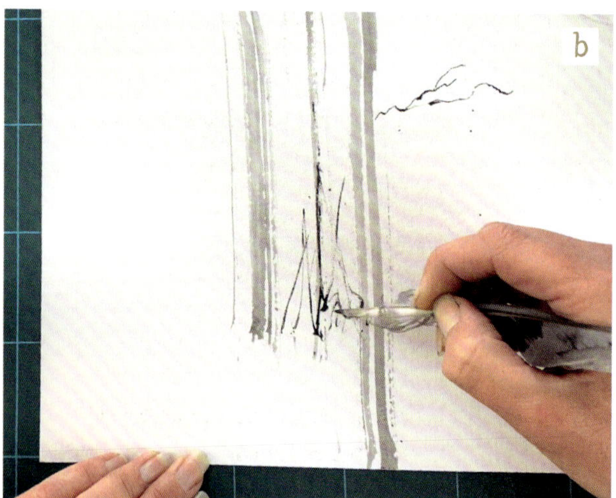

↑ Using different pressures, I twisted and turned the point of the quill as it moved across the page.

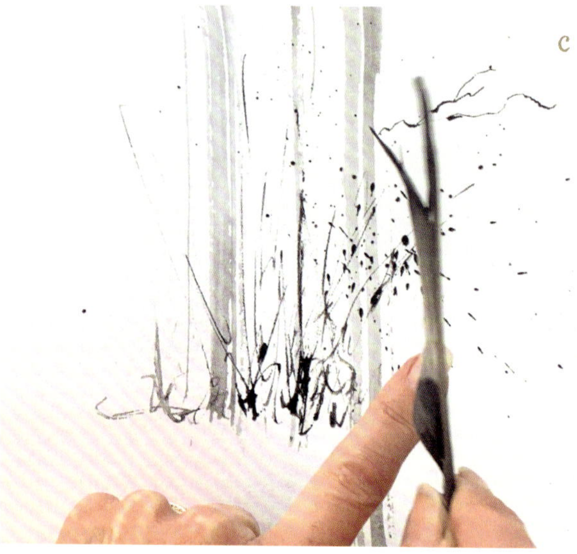

↑ Even loose splatters can be created by tapping the paint-laden feather on the back of a finger.

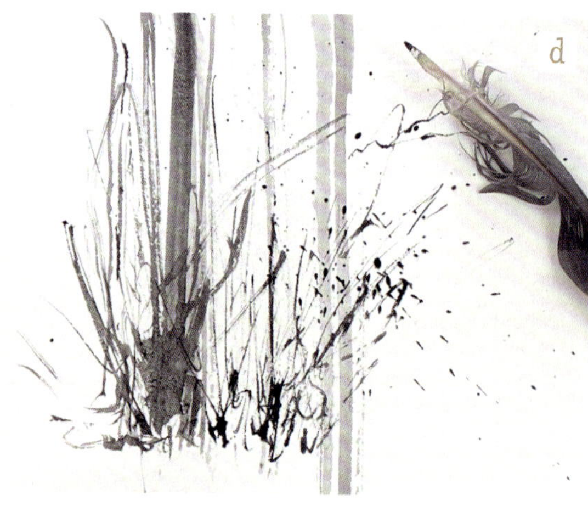

↑ Such a range of energetic marks can be made with the feather.

Palette knife

A palette knife is not a tool normally associated with watercolour but you can create the most wonderful range of marks with them.

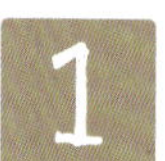

1 Run the tube of paint along one-half of the palette knife's underside to thickly coat it.

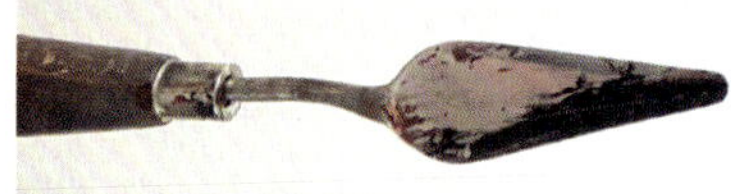

→ The coated palette knife.

2 Scrape the knife to one side as if you were cleaning it.

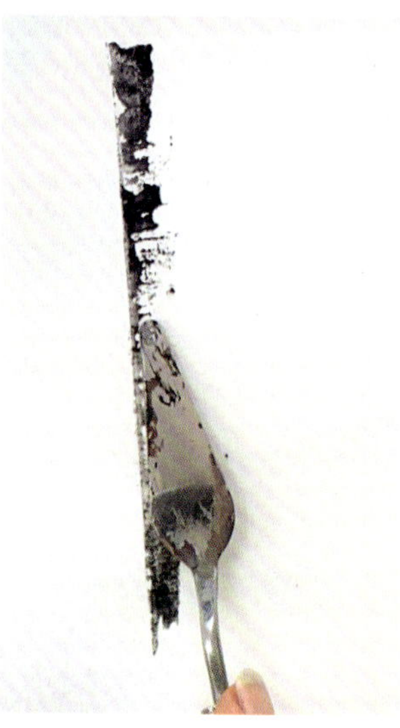

→ Scraping the coated palette knife creates some lovely broken markings.

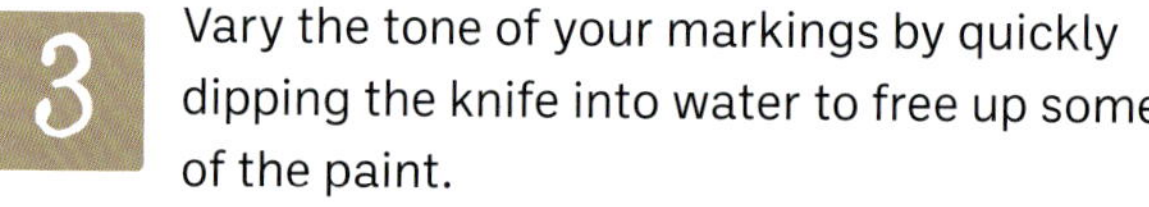

3 Vary the tone of your markings by quickly dipping the knife into water to free up some of the paint.

4 Use the tip of the knife and be creative and dynamic in your movements to create branches and twigs.

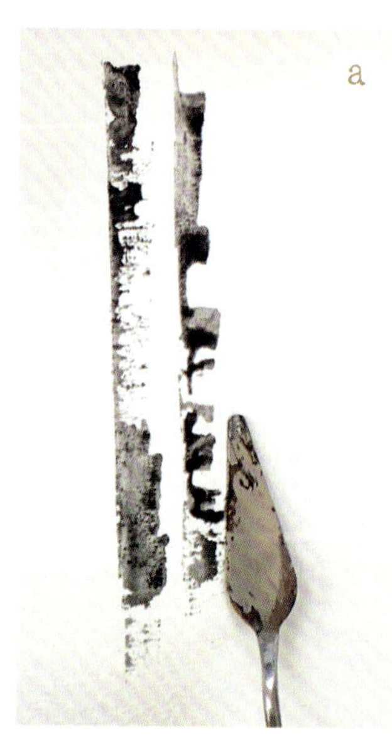

→ Using water will ensure that you have lighter, looser markings as well as darker, more textured ones.

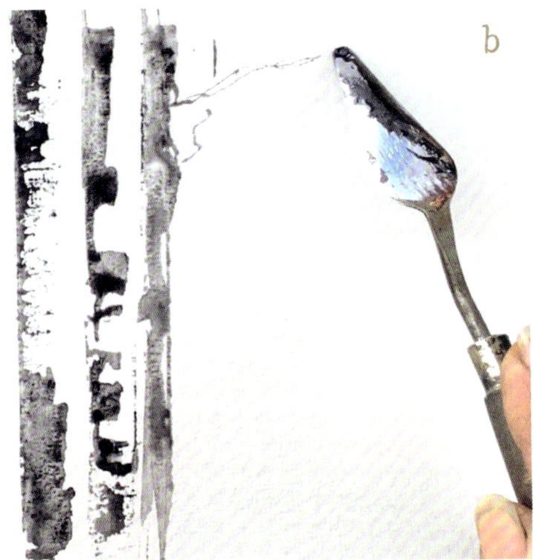

↑ Tiny branches and twigs can be created with the tip of the knife.

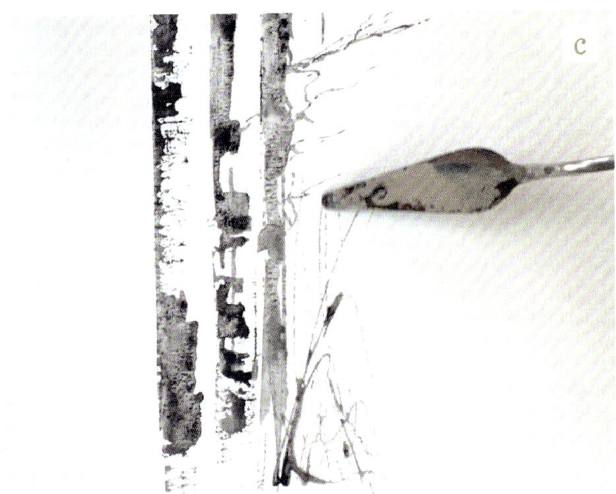

↑ Sweep upwards, sideways and crossways with speed and momentum.

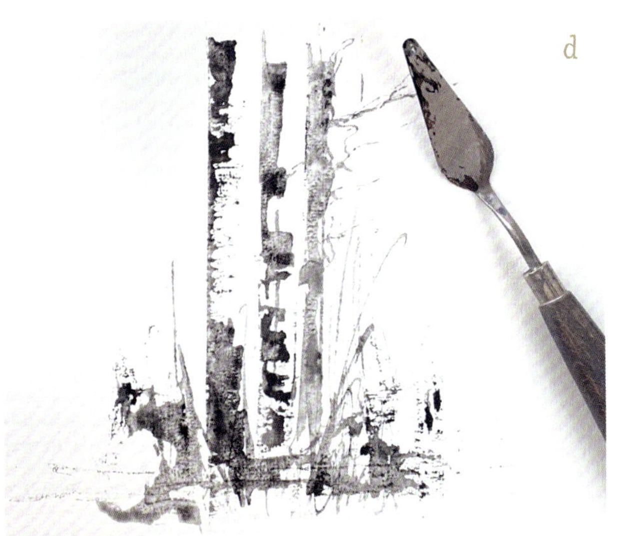

↑ A quick tree study, finished in a matter of minutes.

Masking fluid and palette knife

Using a palette knife to apply masking fluid can create some exciting results that are impossible to second guess. We will be using this technique in the next chapter to suggest foliage.

1 Decant some masking fluid into its lid and dip your knife into it. Apply the fluid in a range of ways – you can even splash it on. If it is too thick, you can thin it down with water to make it more malleable. Once you're happy with the marks that you've made, allow them to dry thoroughly. Depending on how thickly you've applied the fluid, this may take a few moments.

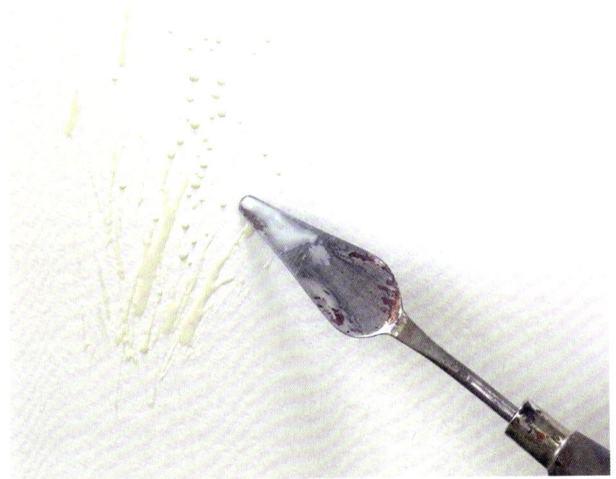

↑ Apply the masking fluid with the palette knife, just as you did with the paint.

2 Once dry, add a range of paints to it, using different thicknesses of pigment as you did when creating the rocks.

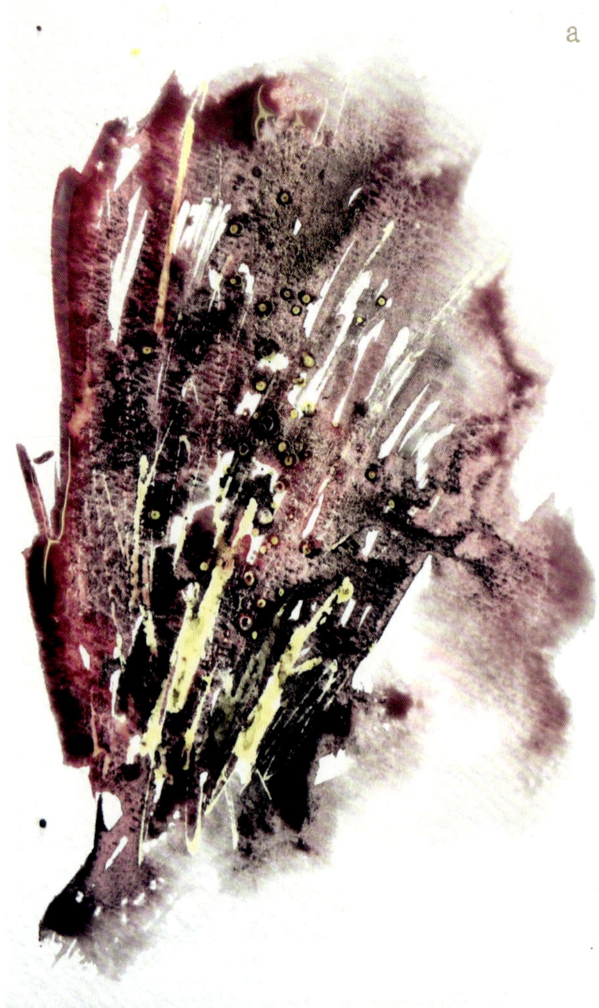

↑ Using a mixture of colours and consistencies to add interest to the finished section. Here, some of the masking fluid has been removed, revealing the untouched white paper below.

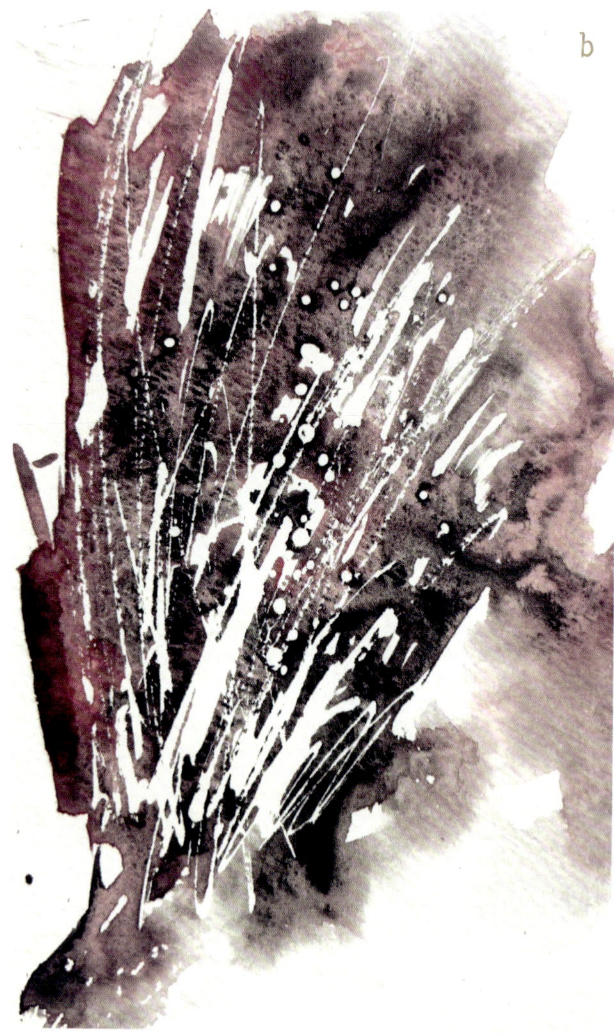

↑ The brightness and harshness of the lines make this a striking section if used in a finished piece. Some of the brighter marks will normally be knocked back so that they sit more comfortably in the composition.

3 Once the paint has dried thoroughly, remove the masking fluid. This can be done either by gently rubbing it away with a clean eraser or using your fingers. This will leave a bunch of sharp-edged bright marks on the paper. It's unlikely that you would want to keep them all as they can be a distraction from the main focal point. I often knock back some of them by adding colour and softening edges as and where needed.

EXERCISE 5: DISCOVER THE VERSATILITY OF YOUR BRUSHES

The first four techniques are a lot of fun, especially for incorporating background elements, but when it comes to painting birds your brushes will do the heavy lifting.

If you are unfamiliar with your brushes, test drive them on a blank sheet of watercolour paper to find out some of the marks they can make. Alternate the angle of your hand, the pressure applied and the consistency of your paint to achieve different marks.

Brushstroke examples using a size 12 round brush

Using my round size 12 brush as an example, below are some movements and marks that you might find useful to start with. Most of my work includes a mix of both expressive and controlled brushwork.

Thick and thin strokes

→ Altering the pressure of the brush will produce thick and thin strokes.

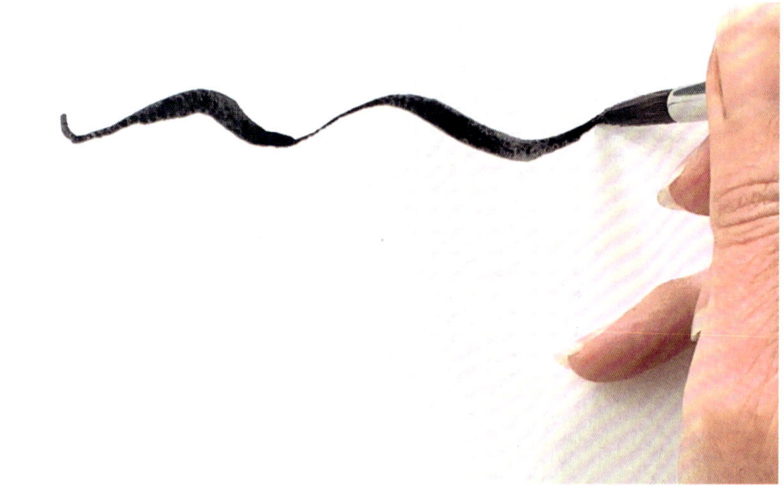

Dry brush effect

→ The brush can be swept on its side to spread paint or water on the page. As it runs out of paint, parts of the paper show through. This is called the dry brush effect and is best achieved on textured and rough paper. It can take a while to perfect and is achieved more easily if you paint with the flat of your brush, as opposed to the point.

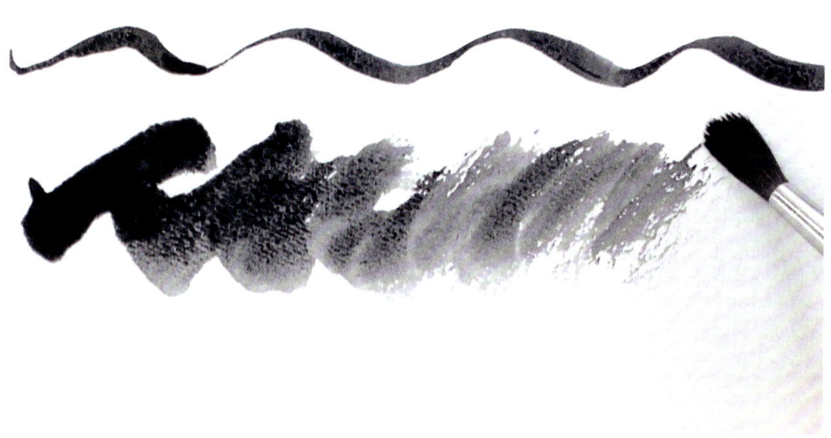

Calligraphic marks

→ The fine points allow calligraphic marks. Practise these... they will be as unique as your signature and will help you to develop your style. Try and build up a rhythm and style that is natural, almost like when we doodle with a pencil.

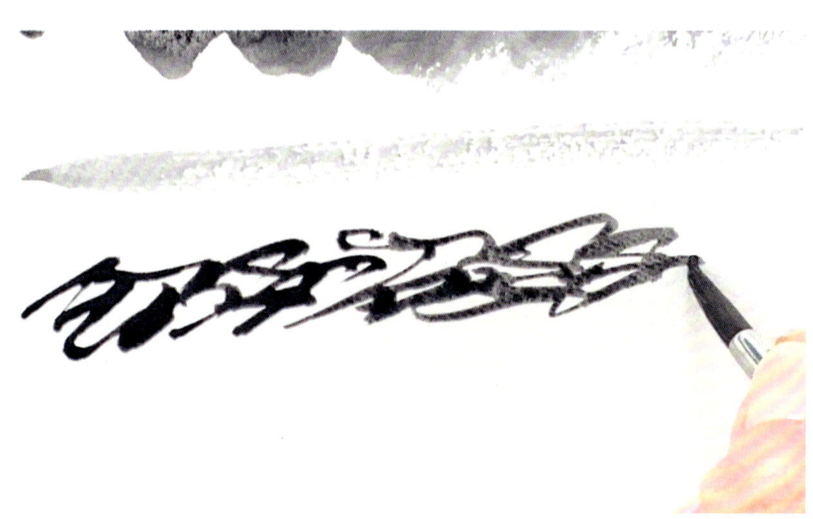

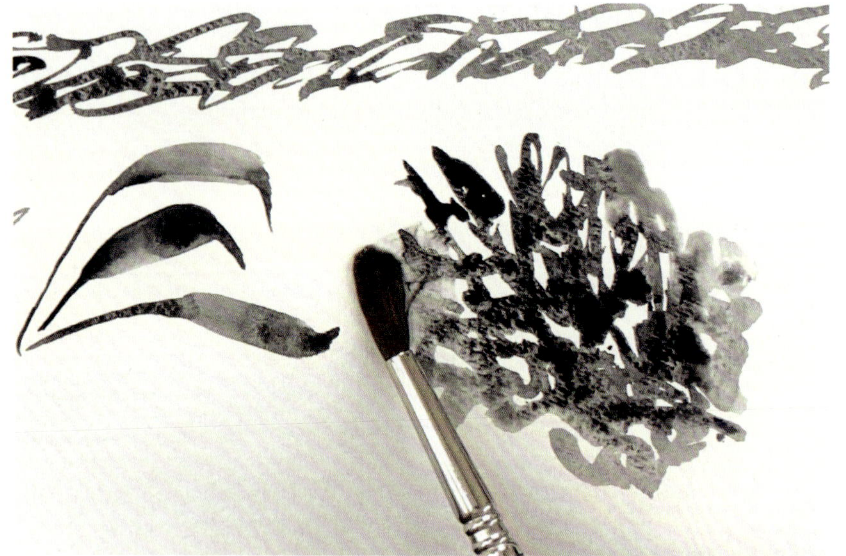

Side sweeps

← I often side sweep the belly of the brush during the painting process to spread paint out or soften edges with the addition of water.

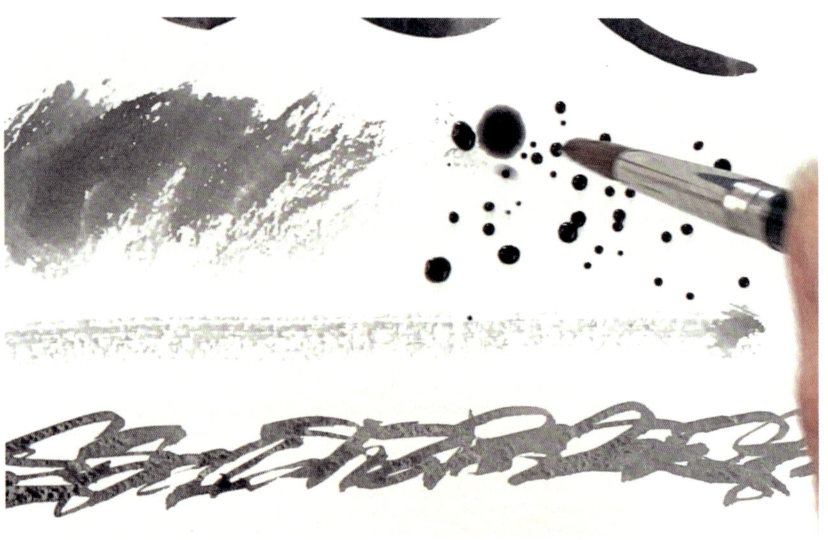

Splashes

← Splashes of different sizes can be created by tapping a loaded brush onto the back of an outstretched finger. Alternatively, forceful drops of the hand with a loaded brush can create larger splashes. The more watery the consistency, the bigger the splash.

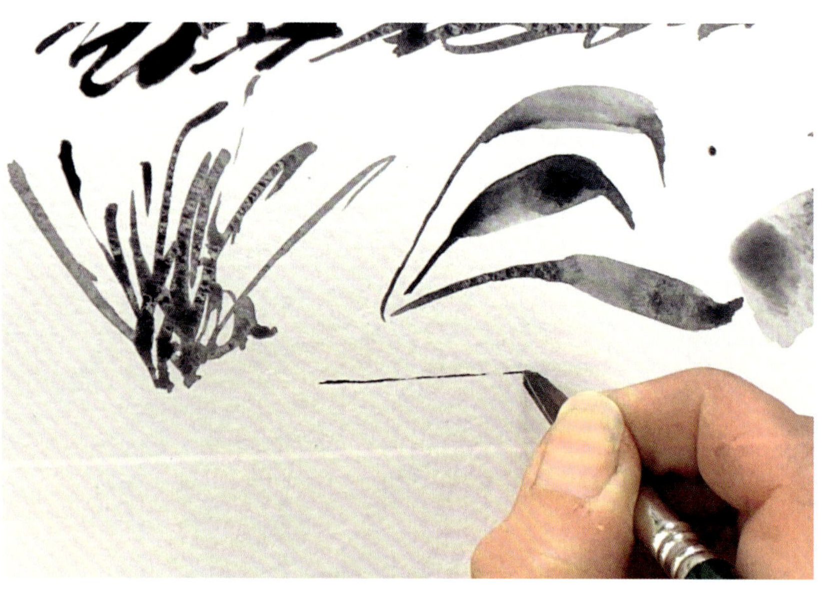

Fine lines

← Practise fine lines with the tip of the brush. They don't have to be perfect; in fact, broken lines often look more effective than clean, crisp, sharp ones.

MY FAVOURITE BRUSHES

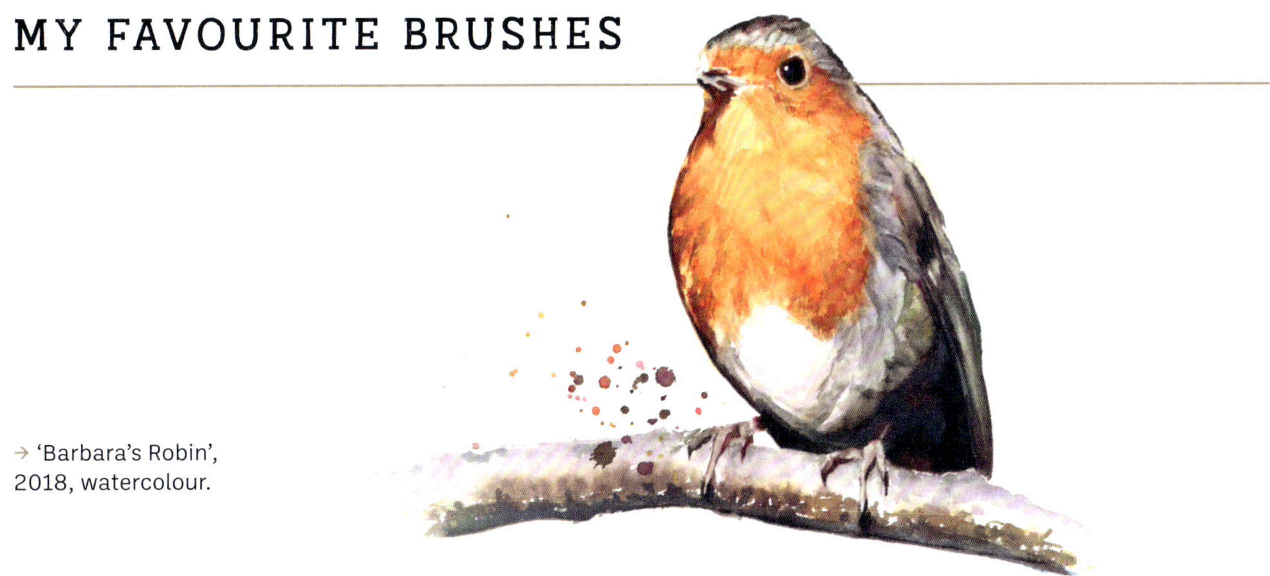

→ 'Barbara's Robin', 2018, watercolour.

Round size 12 synthetic brush

When you first start out in painting, this size brush can feel quite large and intimidating; however, its fine point means that you can still create precise details without the need to pick up an alternative brush. This can be invaluable if you're trying to maintain consistency of colour in a single stroke of various dimensions. I use this brush for the majority of my paintings to lay and spread washes using the flat of the brush, as well as to apply detail using the point.

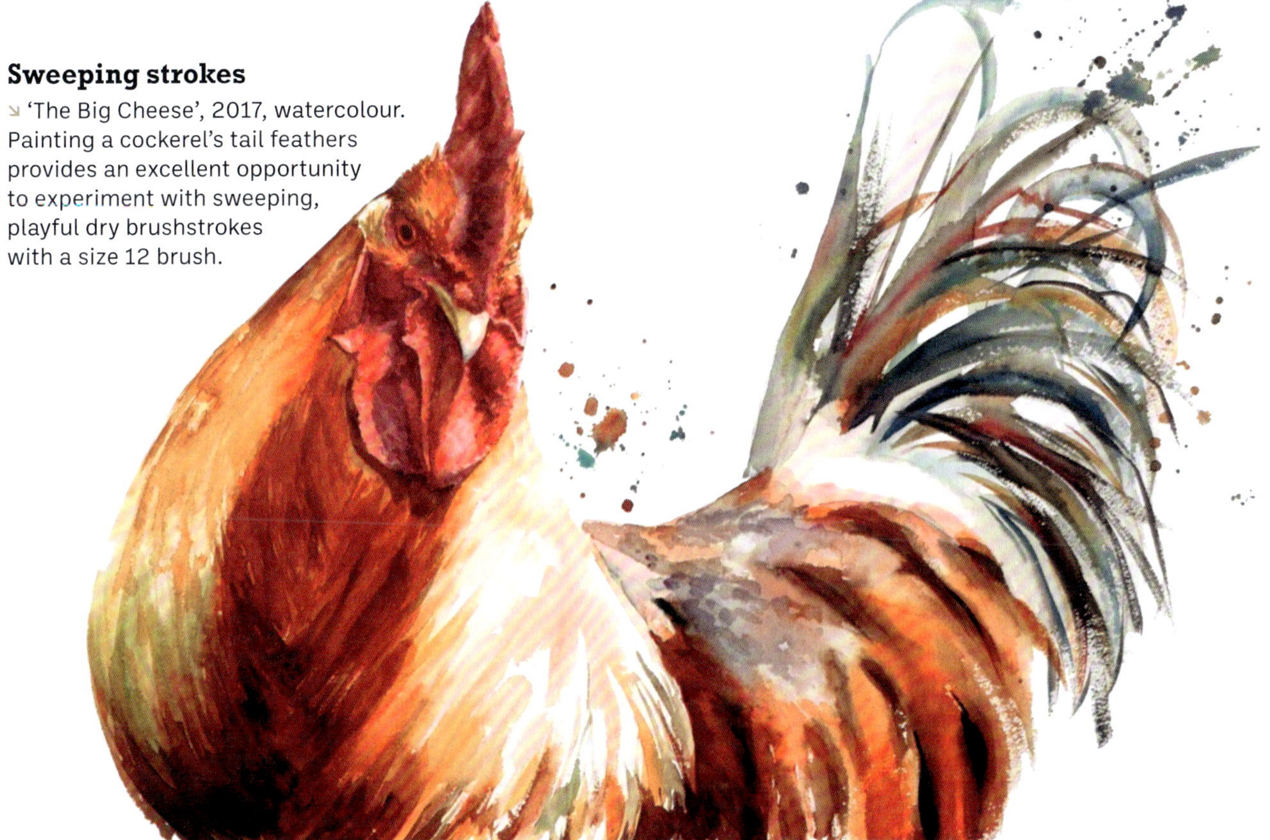

Sweeping strokes

↘ 'The Big Cheese', 2017, watercolour. Painting a cockerel's tail feathers provides an excellent opportunity to experiment with sweeping, playful dry brushstrokes with a size 12 brush.

Splashes

↓ The size 12 or even larger brushes are great for dropping on cold, confident splashes. Even better when one drops on top of the other to create even more glorious colour.

'Kingfisher', 2019, watercolour.

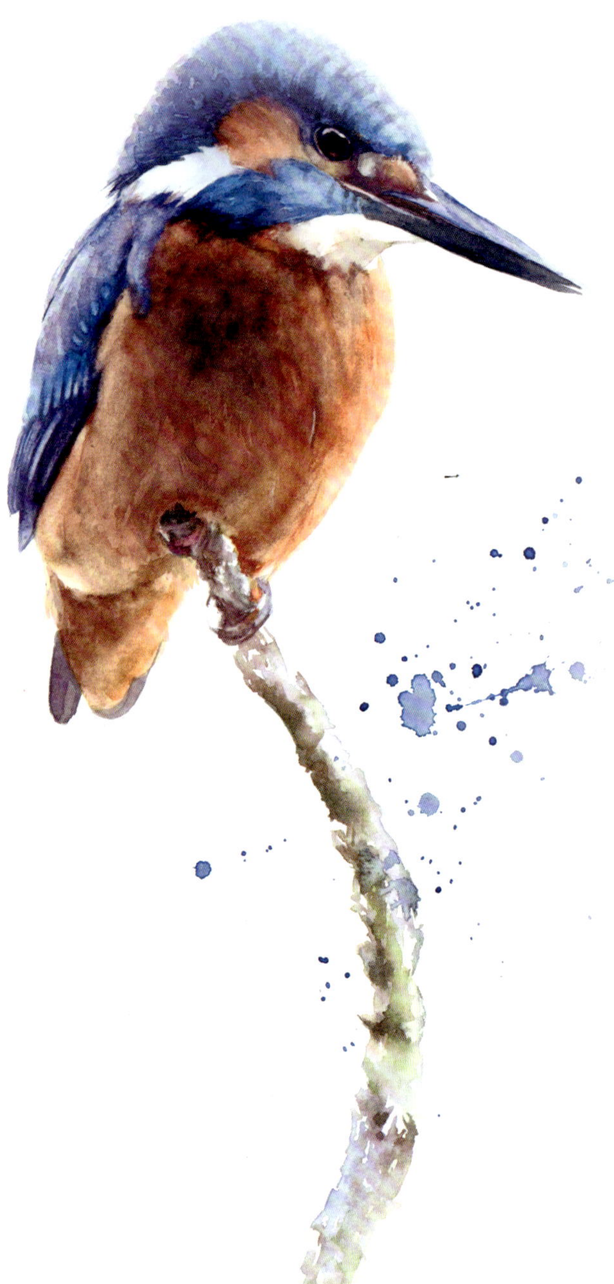

Colour washes

→ One of the essential uses of the size 12 brush is to lay down the initial wash of very diluted paint followed by dabs of thicker paint into the drying wash.

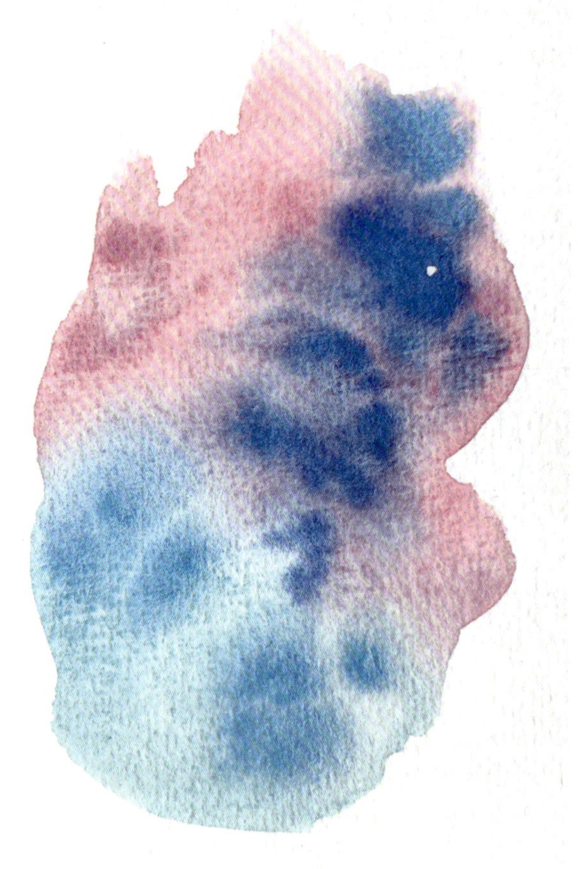

Round size 6 synthetic brush

This is just a smaller version of the size 12 brush. It can be used to create similar effects but on smaller sections of the painting.

↓ The size 6 is great for creating the first wash of a kingfisher's head, for example.

Precision brush

Even though this is a book about expressive techniques, I always incorporate precise details in my work, especially around the facial area. A small detailer brush is ideal for this. I prefer brushes that have very little give in the tip, so I have maximum control over it. I'm currently using a small oval brush, but most small brushes with a sharp small point would be suitable.

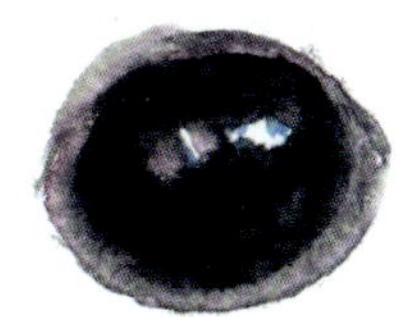

← Eyes, beaks, feet and some wing details are created more easily using a tiny brush.

Rigger brush

A rigger brush is an invaluable tool for creating the finest of lines. It takes a little practice to get the most out of it.

A rigger can create short and long, solid and broken fine lines in all directions. A steady hand is needed for using it, so I find it helpful to lean my painting arm on the table and to relax into the stroke. These strokes are great for recreating scruffy feathers that sometimes appear around the top of the legs or around the circumference of some birds.

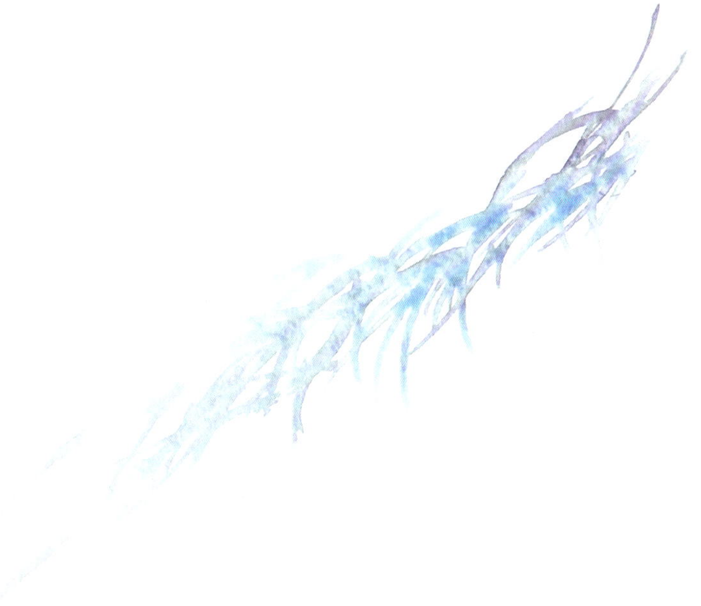

→ Even when using a rigger, I vary the direction and colour of the strokes to add interest.

1 inch flat brush

A 1 inch flat brush is perfect for creating supporting elements such as skies, water and trees. We will be using this brush to suggest trees in the next chapter and to create the sky and sea for a swan in Chapter 10.

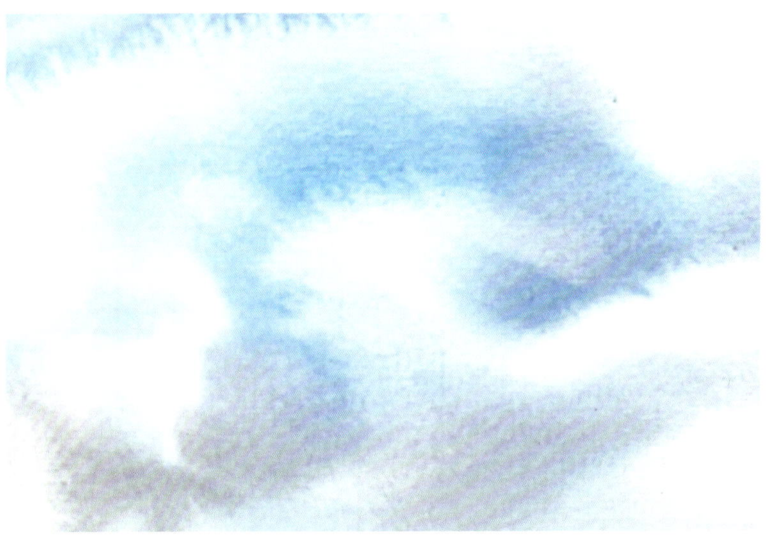

→ These brushstrokes were applied onto damp paper, with gaps left between them to allow the white paper to peep through as clouds. The residual moisture on the paper enables you to create beautiful soft edges.

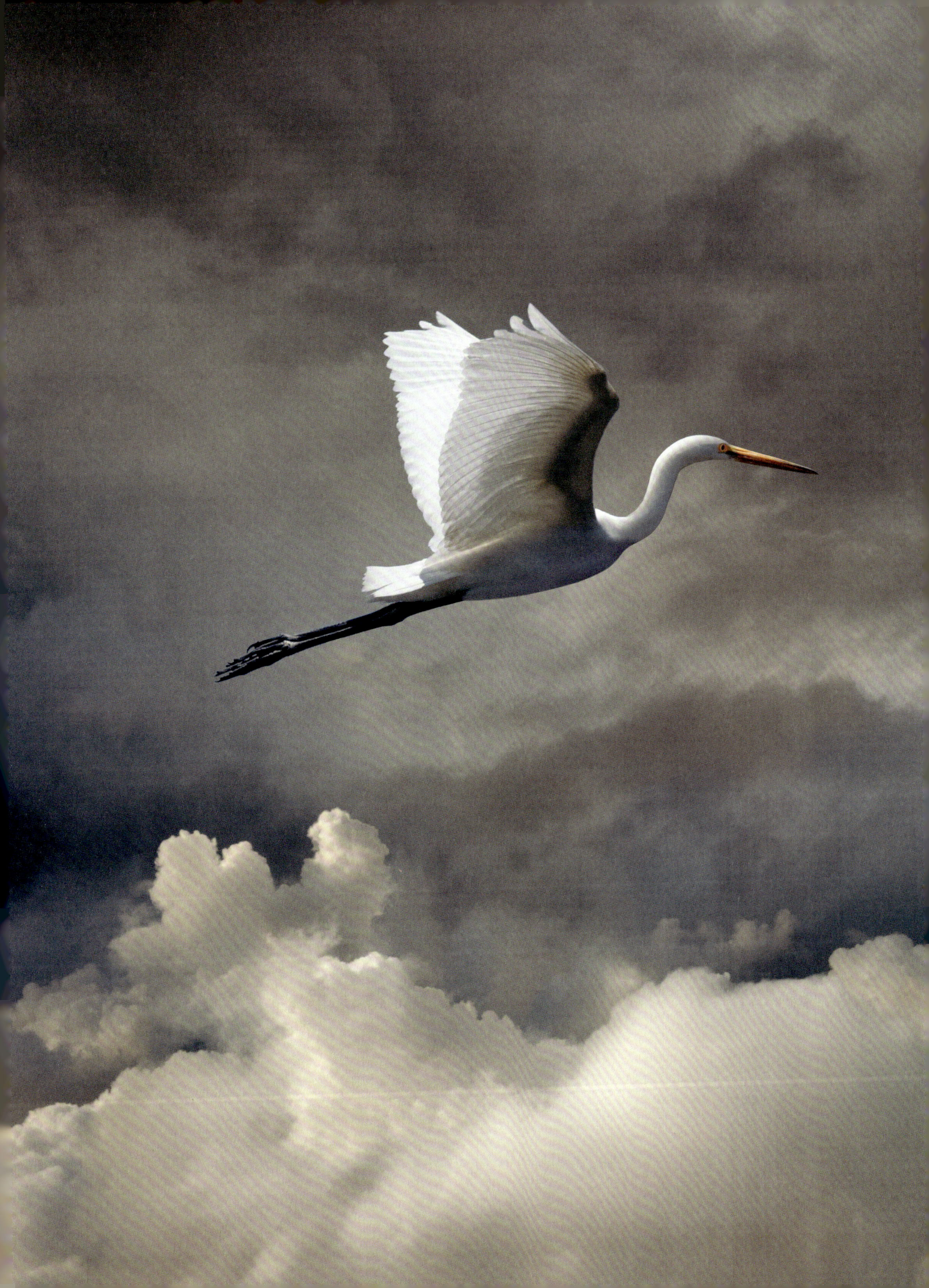

CHAPTER

3

Introduction to Composition, Layering and Expressive Mark Making

Sometimes students don't give enough thought to composition in the early stages of their painting process. Backgrounds, splashes and subject positioning are often afterthoughts. However, with planning, all of these compositional tools can be used to guide the viewer around a piece. In fact, they are so powerful that they can often make or break a piece of art.

PROJECT 3

Mixing expressive and controlled techniques – painting an egret in flight

You will need

- Photographic reference of a great egret in flight
- Paper: 300, 350 or 640 gsm, cold press, textured paper
- Brushes: synthetic round size 6 brush, 1 inch flat brush, size 0, 1 or 2 rigger brush and a detailer brush
- Paint: black tube or pan watercolour paint (p.158)
- Stationery: F or H grade hard pencil, ruler, eraser, plain paper
- Masking fluid and a small brush
- Salt, cling film, feather (optional)
- Wax-free transfer or tracing paper and low-tack washi tape (optional)
- Palette, water container, paper towel, washing-up liquid

Top tip

Lighter weight paper tends to buckle with the use of a lot of water, particularly if you haven't stretched it first. Either stretch the paper (see Chapter 2) or use thicker paper such as Saunders Waterford 638 gsm by St Cuthberts Mill.

WORK OUT COMPOSITION BY CREATING A THUMBNAIL SKETCH

If I am creating a more complex piece involving background or foreground elements, I find it helpful to carry out a thumbnail sketch on cheap copier paper prior to painting to see if a basic design is going to work. There are a multitude of compositional tools, but I will be using the following four when creating this piece.

These are just a few pointers to help you with your initial sketches and I hope they may help resolve a few issues that you might have had with previous paintings that just feel a little 'off'. Please don't get too hung up on them. Remember that rules are made to be broken and sometimes paintings just work without necessarily fitting into any of these categories!

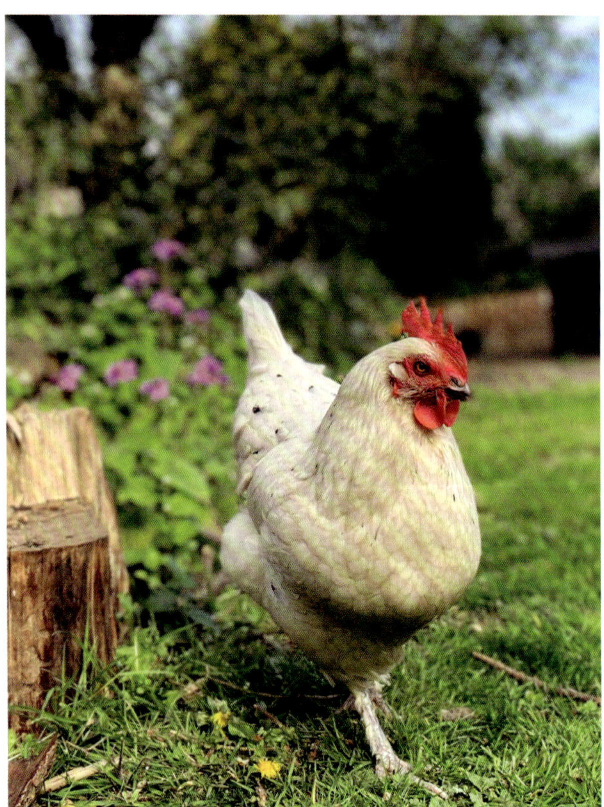

↑ See how the out-of-focus blurred background leads the viewer's eye to the chicken, which contains far more detail.

→ A visualisation of the rule of thirds.

1. Atmospheric perspective

Atmospheric perspective refers to the effect the atmosphere has on the appearance of objects when you look at them from a distance. You see objects further back into the distance less clearly and their colour changes in value, saturation and hue.

In this case, I'm painting in just one colour so I don't have to worry so much about colour and hue, but I will make sure that some of the backdrop is blurry to suggest trees and foliage in the distance. That way, the backdrop won't compete for attention with the egret.

In the past you may have produced a piece of work in which everything is too busy and the viewer's eye has nowhere to settle. This could well be an issue with atmospheric perspective. This technique can also be applied to photography – as can be seen in this photograph of one of our rescue hens.

2. The rule of thirds

The rule of thirds is a compositional guideline that breaks an image down into thirds (both horizontally and vertically) so you have nine pieces and four gridlines. According to the rule, by positioning key elements at the intersection of one or some of the gridlines, you'll end up with better compositions.

I have tilted the great egret upwards to ensure that the left wing and tail feathers are in the vicinity of the intersections. In addition, I've designed a thumbnail in which most of the activity is in two-thirds of the piece, leaving just a minimal amount of detail in the right-hand third.

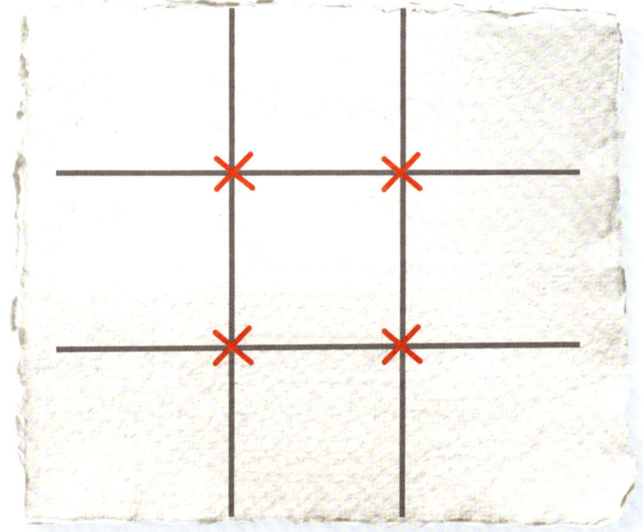

3. The rule of space

This rule suggests that you should place any negative space in your photo in the direction that your subject is facing as this creates a pathway for the eyes to follow. It also helps to enhance movement and create a directional flow in the image.

I have ensured that the great egret is flying from left to right, thus allowing it to fly into the negative space. If the reference photo had shown otherwise, I would have flipped the image using an illustration app, such as Procreate for iPad, to help me draw it flying in the chosen direction.

4. Counterchange

Parts of the egret are white, so I want the backdrop to help me describe this white. I don't want an overly oppressive backdrop, so I need to work out where to place the lighter and darker sides of my background. I'm using a compositional tool based on the principle of counterchange. This is when darker tones are laid against lighter ones and lighter tones are laid against darker ones. It can really help your piece to pop.

In my thumbnail sketch of the egret, the highlights of the white wings are laid over dark black marks; conversely, the dark beak and feet are laid over a lighter background. There are lovely slithers of light on top of the egret's legs that will also benefit from a dark backdrop. The viewer's eye will always be drawn to these areas of stronger tonal contrast. For the same reason, I will design a scene that is not too 'busy', to ensure that the viewer isn't distracted from the main subject, the egret.

An additional point to remember

Remember that the negative spaces, such as the faded area to the right of the image and the lights between the trees, are just as impactful as the positive, darker parts of the image that have been painted. Just because we can't name these spaces doesn't make them any less important.

MY THUMBNAIL SKETCHES IN PENCIL AND PAINT

Here are my thumbnail sketches, incorporating all four of the compositional rules. These give me a good idea of the techniques and effects I want to achieve in the final painting, including where I would like to create my looser, more expressive brushwork.

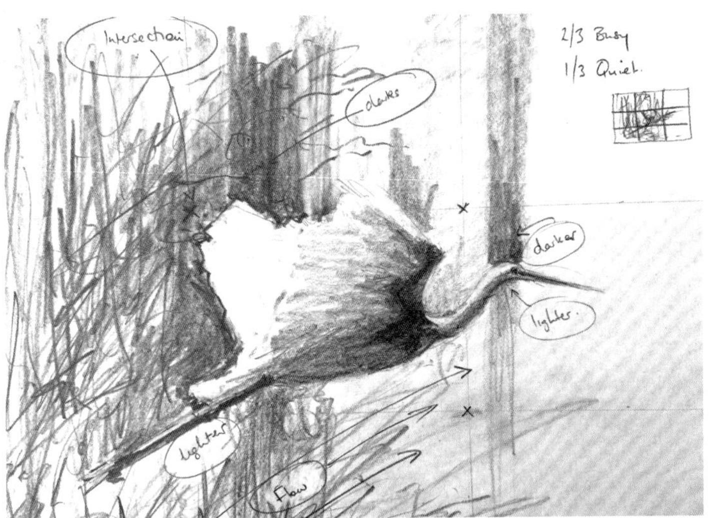

↑ A thumbnail drawing doesn't have to be anything fancy or well-rendered. It is just a quick sketch to work out whether your composition is going to work and it certainly doesn't stop you painting intuitively. It merely acts as a guide to the rough placement of tone and shape.

↓ This is a quick thumbnail painting in which the tones are put down with speed, not accuracy. It's another way of checking whether a composition will work. Painting your thumbnail sketch also has the benefit of acting as a warm-up exercise, enabling you to trial brushstrokes and effects without fear of 'ruining' a considered piece.

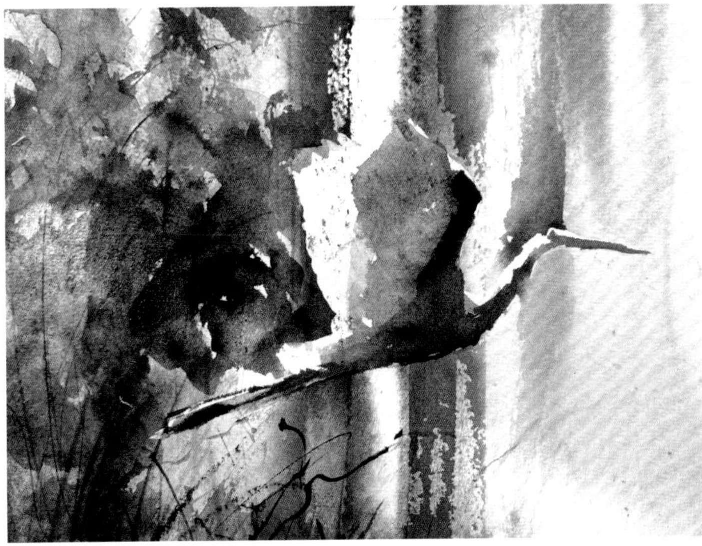

PRACTISE PAINTING THE EGRET USING THE LAYERING TECHNIQUE

Now to begin the drawing process. I created my line drawing in the same way as I did with the coal tit in Chapter 1.

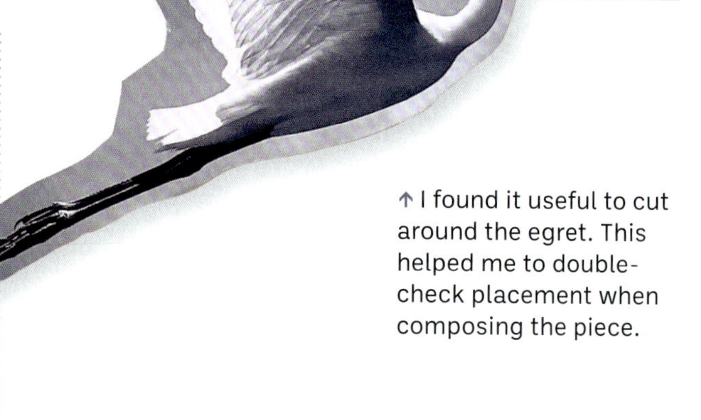

↑ I found it useful to cut around the egret. This helped me to double-check placement when composing the piece.

1 Outline the bird and main shapes. You may decide to trace your reference photo, grid it, or draw it freehand. I don't consider any of the techniques to be 'cheating'; use whichever you feel most comfortable in doing.

When creating the egret, look for the main shapes and tones, as you did with the coal tit. Try not to be distracted by the detail of the feet or the lines in the outstretched wings; these details can be suggested at a later stage.

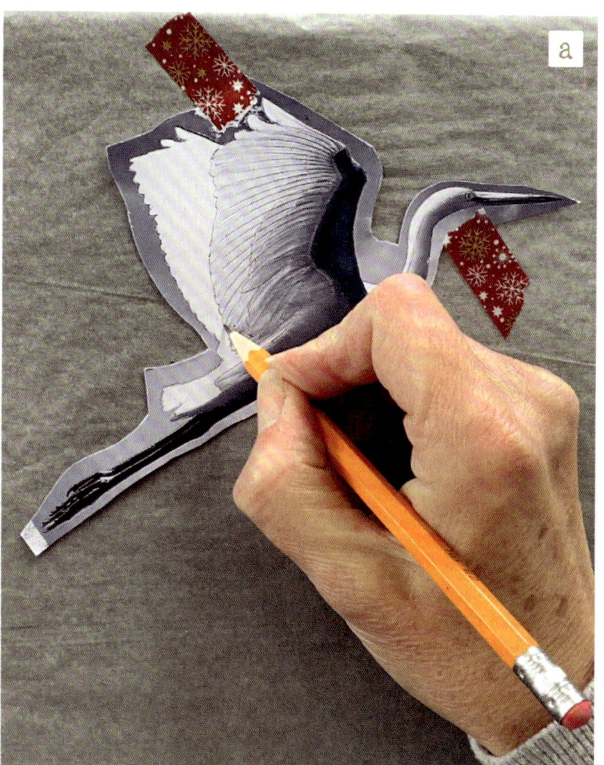

↑ Attach the carbon paper to the watercolour paper using low-tack washi tape. I used Tracedown by Frisk. Use a hard pencil, such as an F or H grade, to draw over the lines that you'd like to transfer.

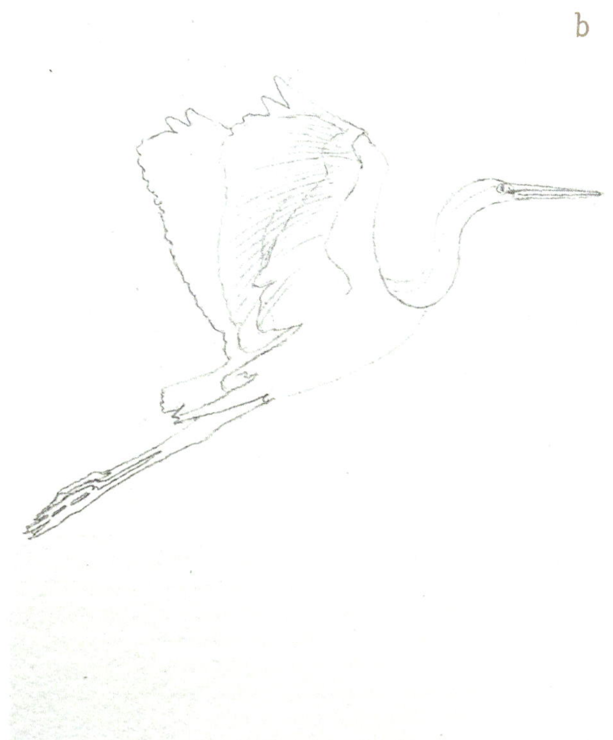

↑ Some of the lines might need enhancing by going back over them with a pencil. Others may need gently erasing, particularly if they feature in lighter areas of the piece, as you might not be able to remove them after water has been applied to the paper. I find that graphite cannot be erased from the heavyweight paper that I use, once the first wash has been laid down.

2 Starting on dry paper, gradually layer up the paint. I used my size 6 and detailer brushes for this piece as it's fairly small.

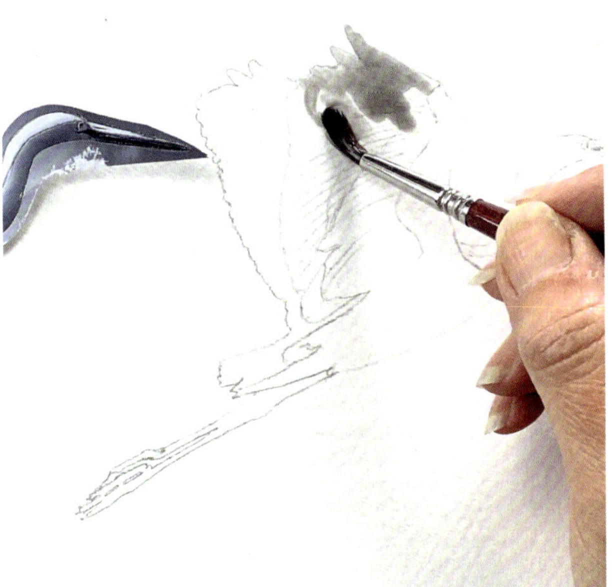

↑ Start by mixing up a very light wash of black, so that it is no darker than dirty water. Apply this wash to your lightest area. Remember that the left wing will be indicated by the white of the paper.

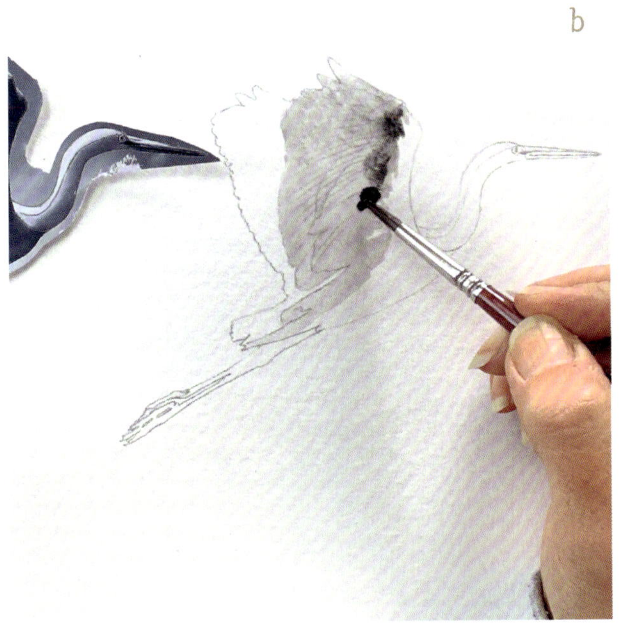

↑ Drop in thicker paint as the first layer is drying. If the paper is damp and your paint is thick enough, you should be able to create lovely soft edges as it spreads across the damp underlayer.

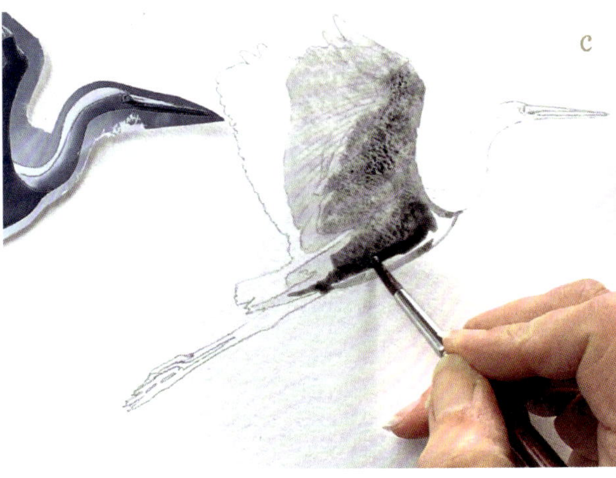

↑ Start working on the darker layers. There is no need to apply a really light wash here; it's quicker to go in with a darker mix in the first instance.

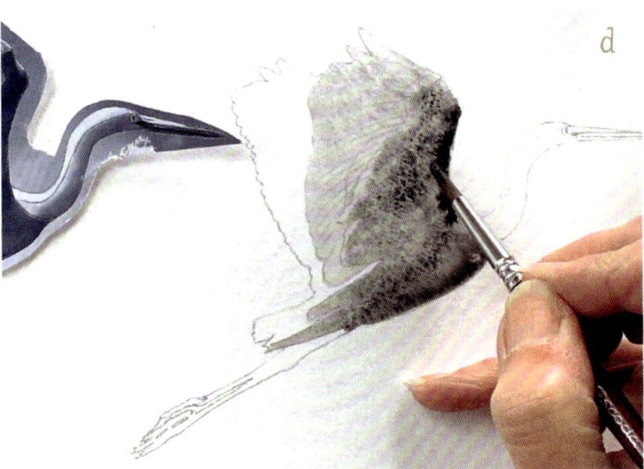

↑ The paint will appear lighter as it dries, so you will need to add pigment to get the depth of tone that you're after.

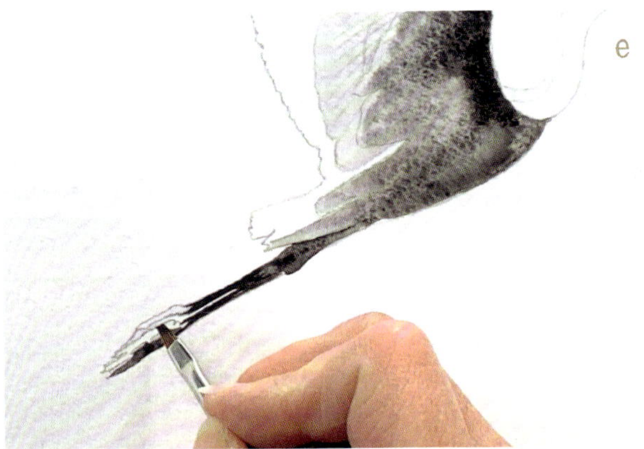

↑ For the feet, use a small detailer brush and much thicker paint from the outset. You will most likely need to do two layers here to get that really dark black. The edges need to be sharp and precise. Leave slithers of white paper popping through this area to indicate shards of light.

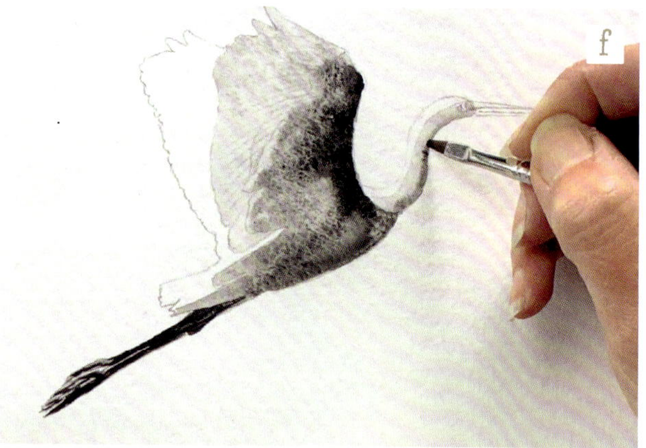

↑ With the body dry, this is a good opportunity to lay a pale wash on the neck. Drop in slightly darker paint at the edge and allow it to blend into the damp underlayer to achieve a lovely soft blend.

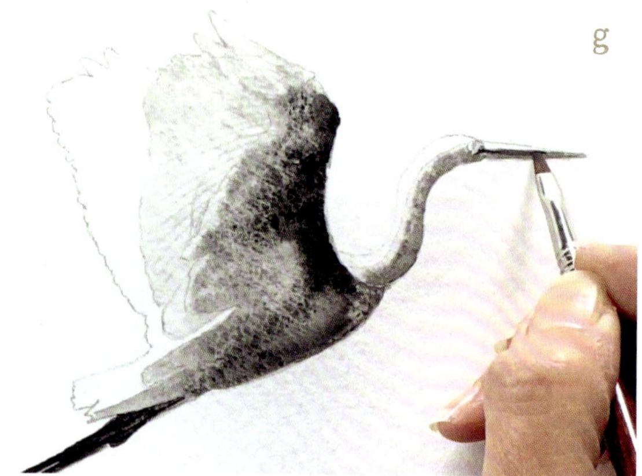

↑ The beak can be completed with a precision brush in just two layers of mid and dark black.

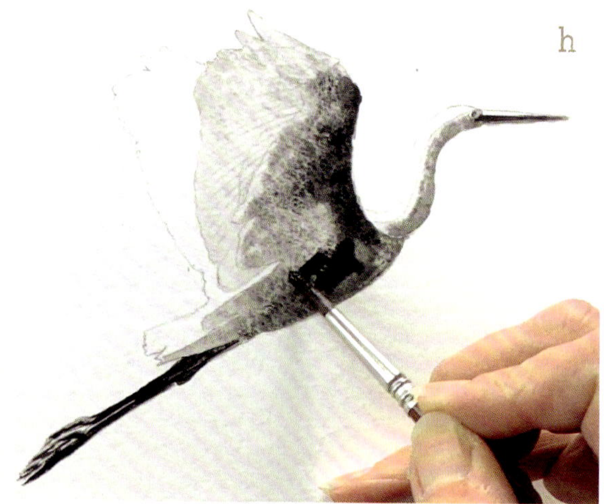

↑ I normally allow my painting to dry before adding a second layer. I tend to work on dry paper at this stage for maximum control. Some of the areas need darkening so I am dropping on darker paint and then spreading it over the required areas, sometimes loosening it with water.

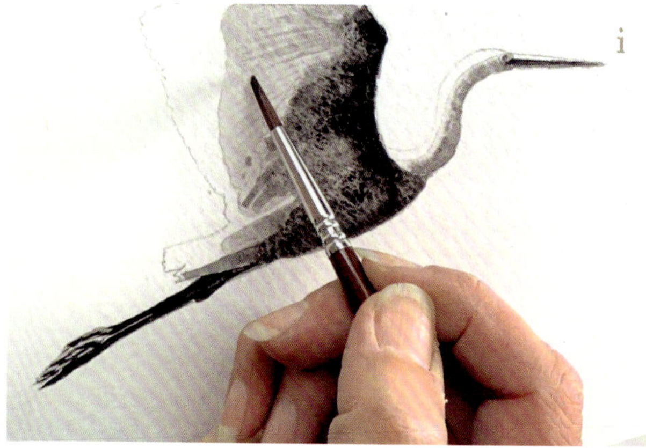

↑ Here, I am dragging out a little of the excess paint from the wings to suggest the individual feathers. Try not to paint these in a precise manner and only indicate a few.

3 When you think that you've replicated the major shapes and tones, it really is a question of style as to how much more detail you add. I have left mine at this stage. A good way of checking the shapes and tones is to take a photograph of the reference image and the painting side by side (see below), using your smartphone, then desaturate the image using your phone's photo software. This shows you clearly whether your tones and shapes are in the right places and if you need to lift, darken or soften anything.

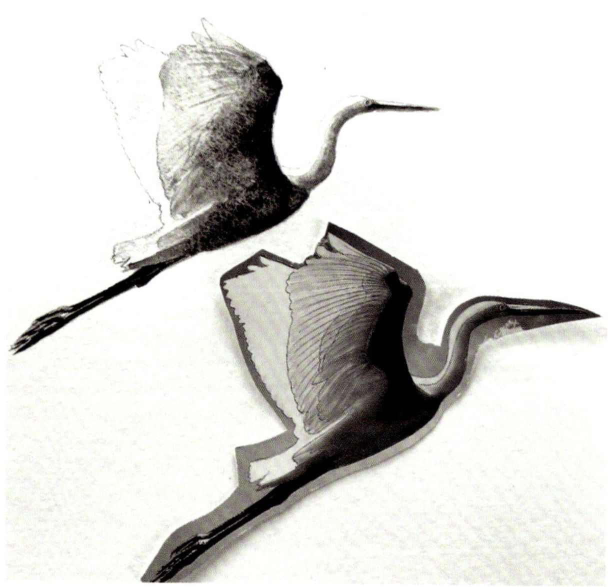

↑ The desaturated image shows clearly whether the painting and the photograph have the same tonal values. In this case, the painted neck is a little lighter than its photographic counterpart.

4 Why not use this practice piece to drop a wash in the background? It will help enhance the shape of the far wing. Have fun with the process, paint intuitively and try not to overthink it.

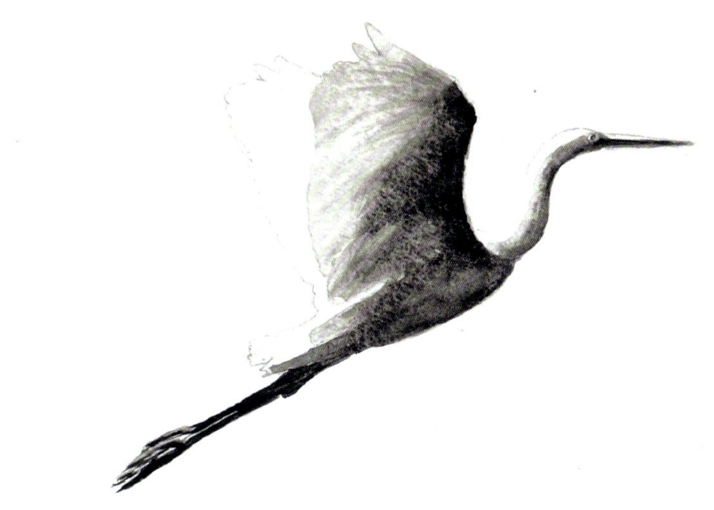

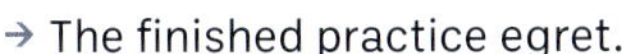

→ The finished practice egret.

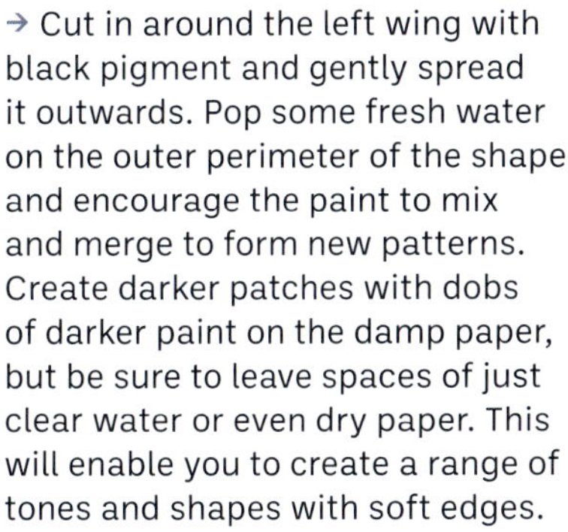

→ Cut in around the left wing with black pigment and gently spread it outwards. Pop some fresh water on the outer perimeter of the shape and encourage the paint to mix and merge to form new patterns. Create darker patches with dobs of darker paint on the damp paper, but be sure to leave spaces of just clear water or even dry paper. This will enable you to create a range of tones and shapes with soft edges.

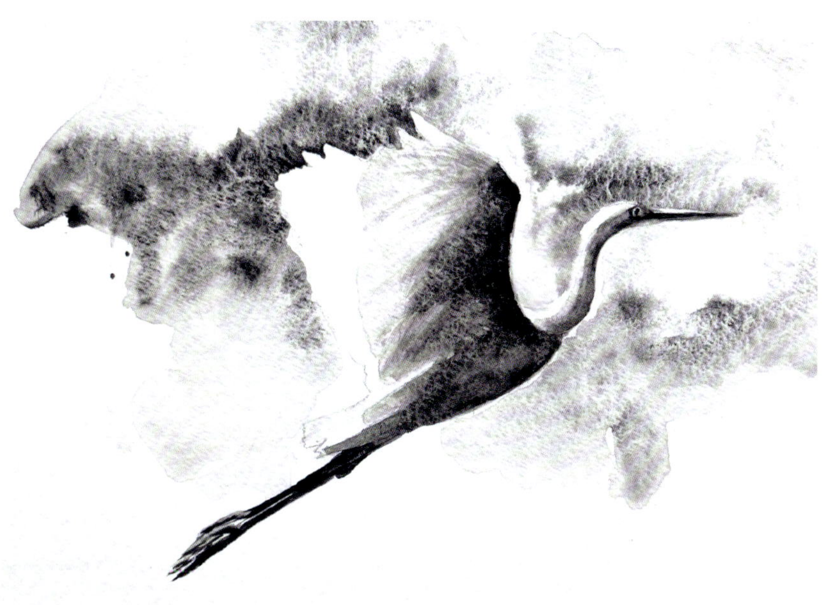

DRAW OUT THE MAIN PIECE, MASKING OFF AND INDICATING KEY AREAS

5 Now that you've practised painting the egret, use a fresh piece of watercolour paper and draw it out again. Using masking fluid, mask out your egret and add expressive marks, as shown in the previous chapter. Masking fluid will allow you free rein with the backdrop without worrying about maintaining the white of the egret.

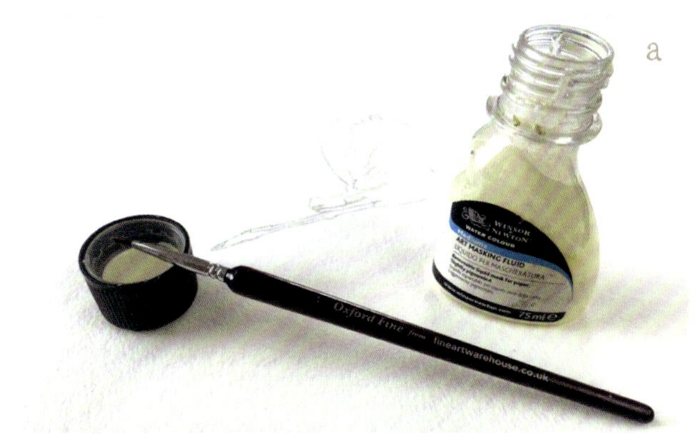

→ I find it easier to dip into masking fluid that has been decanted into the lid.

Top tip

When using a brush to apply masking fluid, coat the fibres in washing-up liquid first to ensure that your brush does not get damaged.

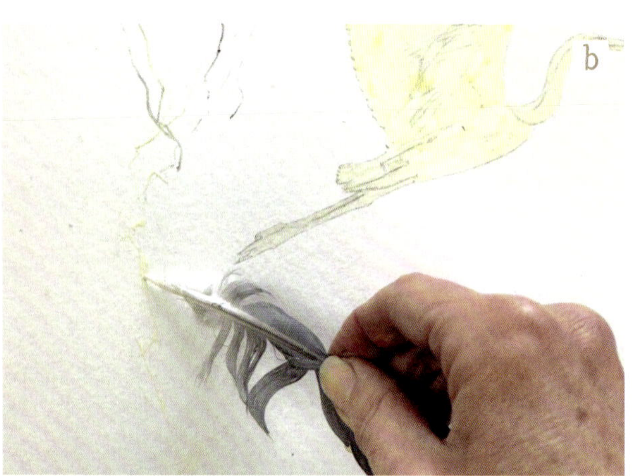

↑ Try applying masking fluid with a feather to create the tangled nature of vegetation. Add these marks intuitively and playfully. If you end up applying too many marks, they can be painted over at a later stage.

6 Scribble in some rough pencil marks to guide your colour placement.

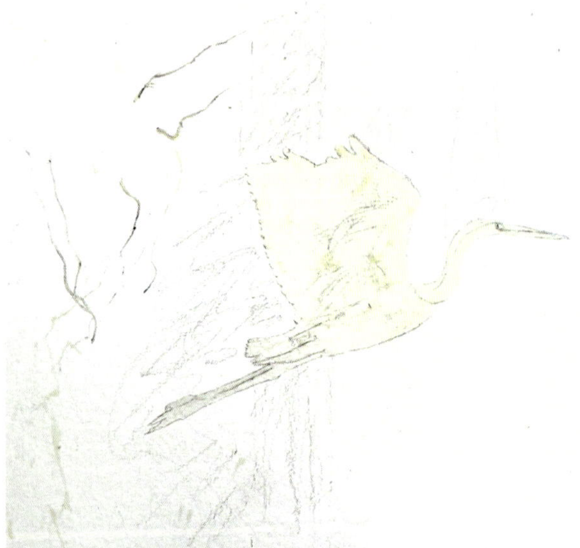

↑ While painting with speed, it is easy to overlook the original composition. These rough pencil marks remind me where I need to place my key tones.

APPLY PAINT TO CREATE THE BACKGROUND WASH

Here you will get to use some of the techniques learnt in Chapter 2 to apply a background wash to create an interesting backdrop. Keep your hand movements varied and have fun dragging, rolling and flicking with your paint tools. Employ your favourite methods, whether it be the application of salt, cling film or paint and water. This particular stage of the painting is fast paced, spontaneous and exhilarating, but be sure to pause every now and then to evaluate and assess tone and shape. Are any areas too dark or too bland? Is the paper getting overworked?

7 Use your 1 inch flat brush to cover the whole page in water and then proceed to create a series of brushstrokes and marks using a feather (both ends) and a range of brushes. Vary the quantities of pigment/water and work at different points of the drying process. This will give you a range of shapes and textures; some blurry and some sharp edged, some solid and some broken, some thick and some thin. Work with speed and energy, using your thumbnail sketch to remind you where to lay pigment and where to avoid paint. Take comfort in the fact that the egret is masked and use the techniques you experimented with in Chapter 2.

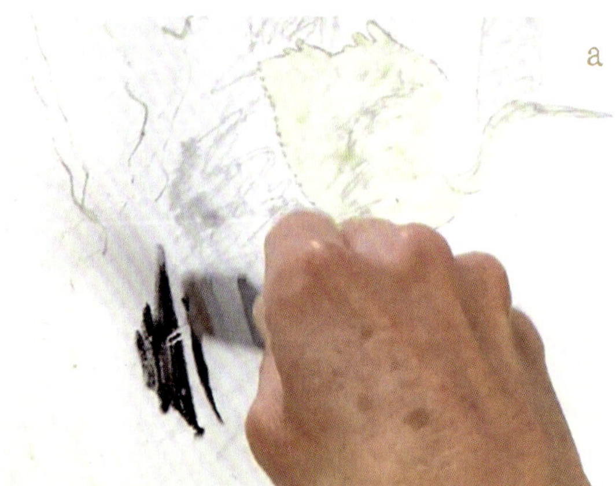

↑ Once the water has been applied to the paper, I add black paint using a flat brush vertically, using the tip to create slices. The paint is creamy in consistency because I have to allow for the wet of the paper lightening it. I ensure that pockets of light are maintained between some strokes to create a range of tones as the paper dries. I then continue to use the brush in a haphazard fashion by applying horizontal marks.

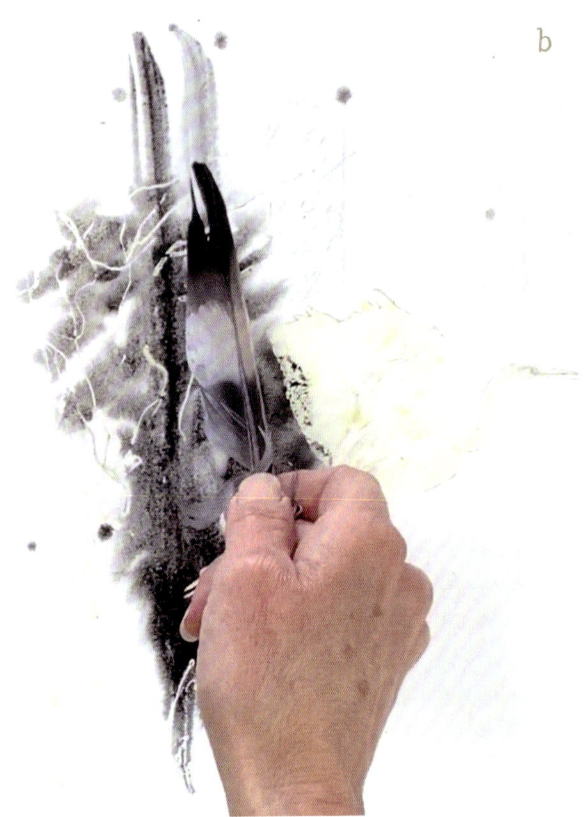

↑ Dragging a feather down the page can create some beautiful lines.

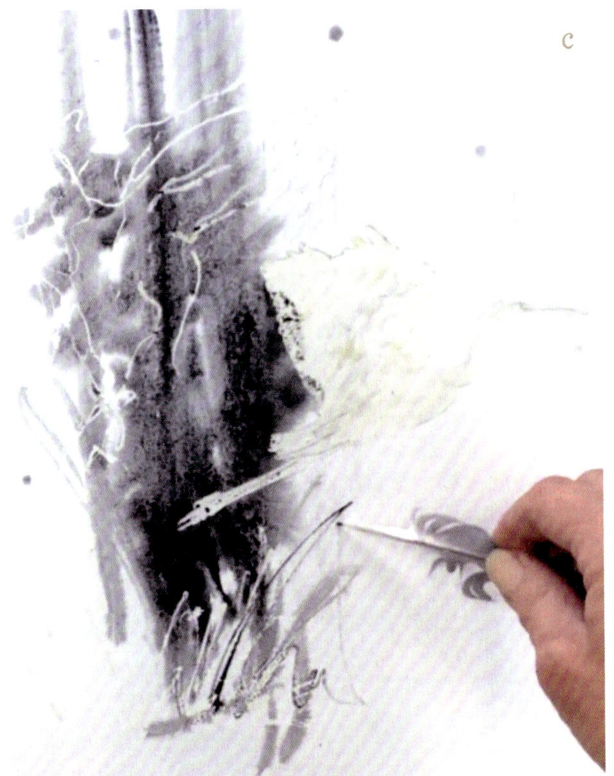

↑ The feather's quill is useful for sharper, thinner marks.

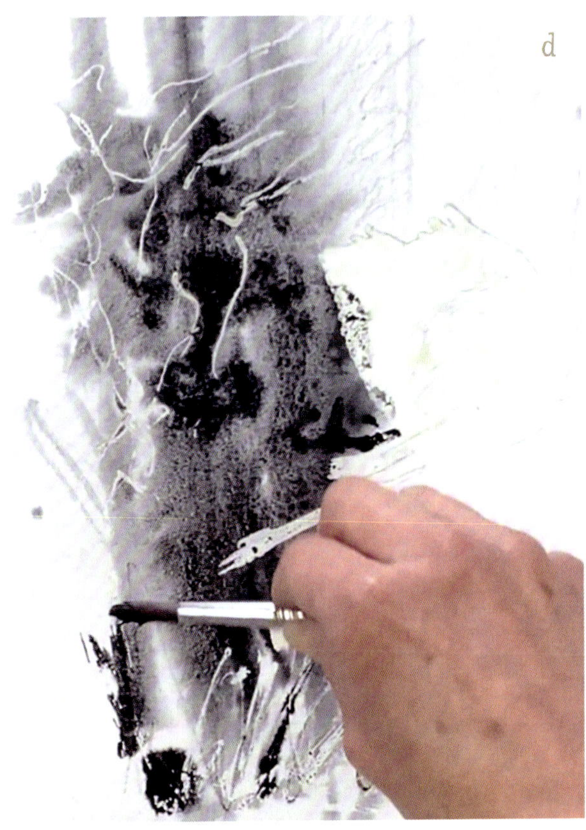

↑ Every brush gets used in a variety of ways. Here I am applying dark paint vertically using the flat of the brush and a scribbling movement.

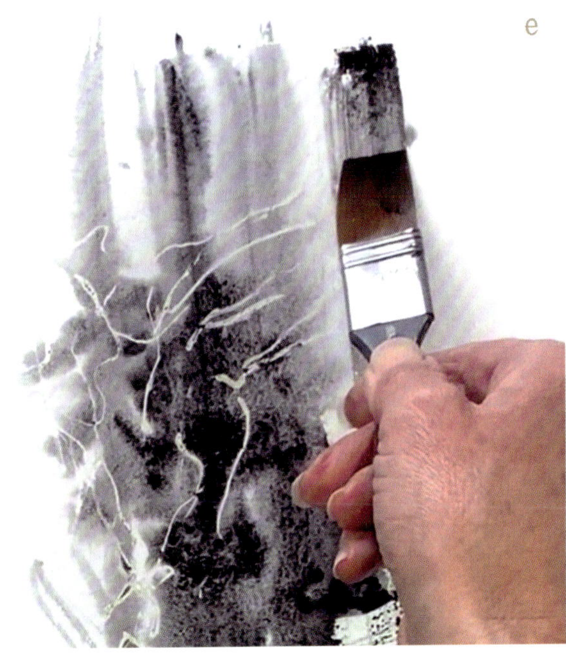

↑ The flat brush is great for suggesting distant trees. If you lay your brush down close to the paper, you are likely to create 'dry brush' marks resulting in a line that is broken up. This can be a lovely effect and more 'painterly' than bold sharp lines.

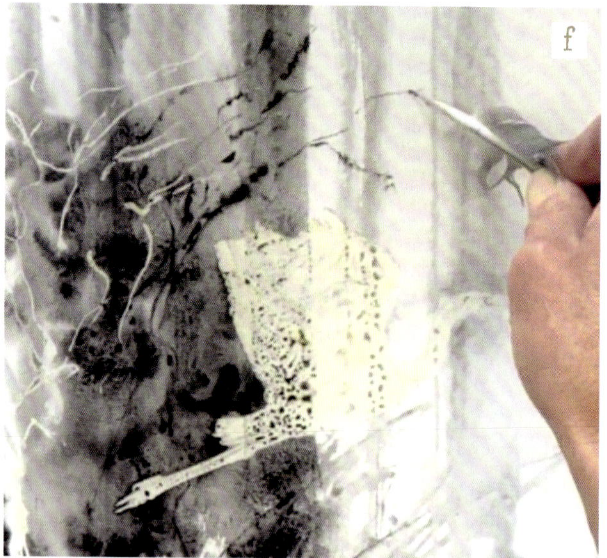

↑ The quill of the feather is an excellent tool for creating lost and found squiggly lines that suggest branches or twigs. The feathery end can also be used by dragging across the page to create movement.

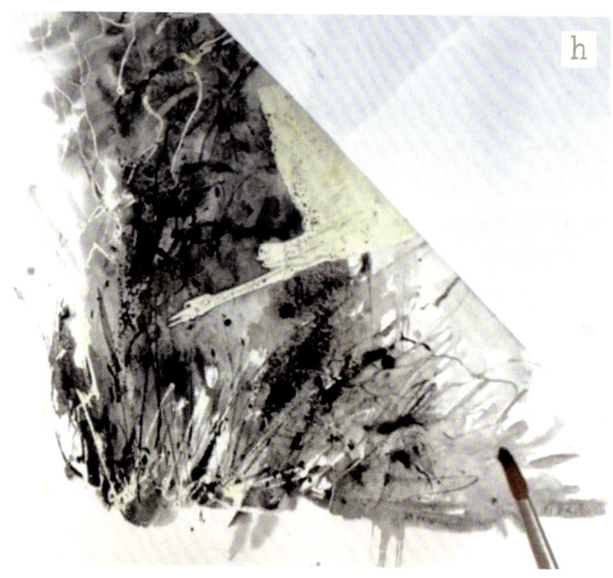

↑ Make sure you cover any exposed areas with paper before you get splashing.

Top tip

Tissue is a vital tool and here it was used to regain the light under the feet. The paint was still wet, so I rolled the tissue into a small ball and gently dabbed it off.

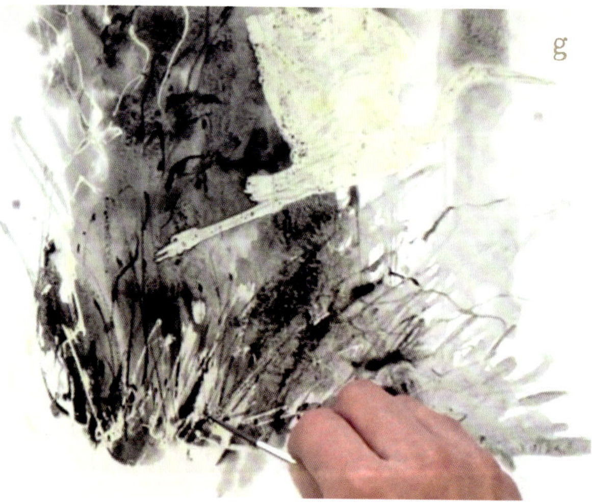

↑ The rigger can be dipped into very dark paint to create some striking calligraphic marks, suggesting vegetation.

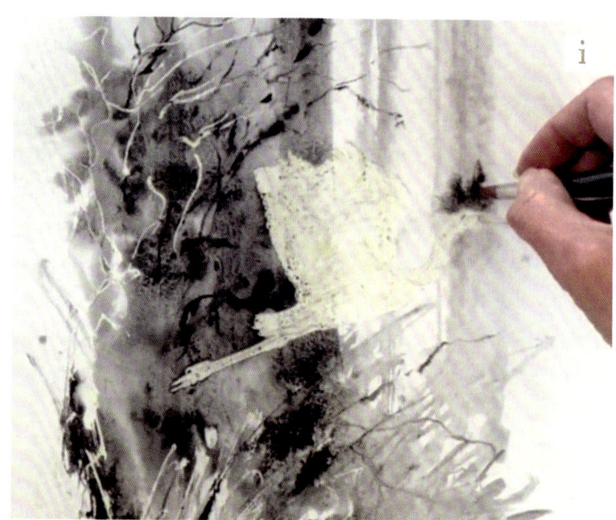

↑ Referring to my thumbnail sketch reminded me to add darks above the head of the egret to accentuate the white of its crown.

ENOUGH IS ENOUGH!

8 There comes a stage when you have to reluctantly pull yourself away from the work to allow this layer to dry. An exact time cannot be prescribed; it comes with experience. If you continue to 'play' on the same piece of paper without allowing any drying time, you are in danger of overworking the page and losing the beautiful array of tones and marks that you have created spontaneously.

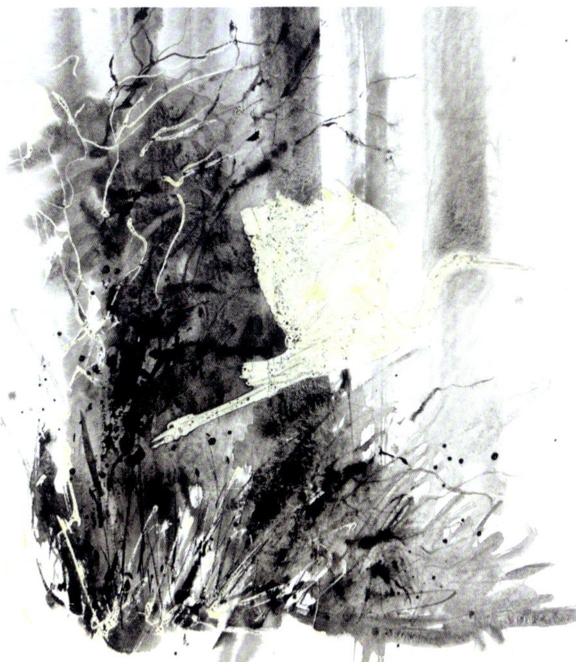

↑ This part of the process is exciting to create. My work table was a complete mess of tools, paint and other equipment when I completed this section, but it was so much fun!

9 Once the background wash has dried, carefully remove the masking fluid from the egret by rubbing gently with a clean eraser or finger, starting from the outer edge (see p.40).

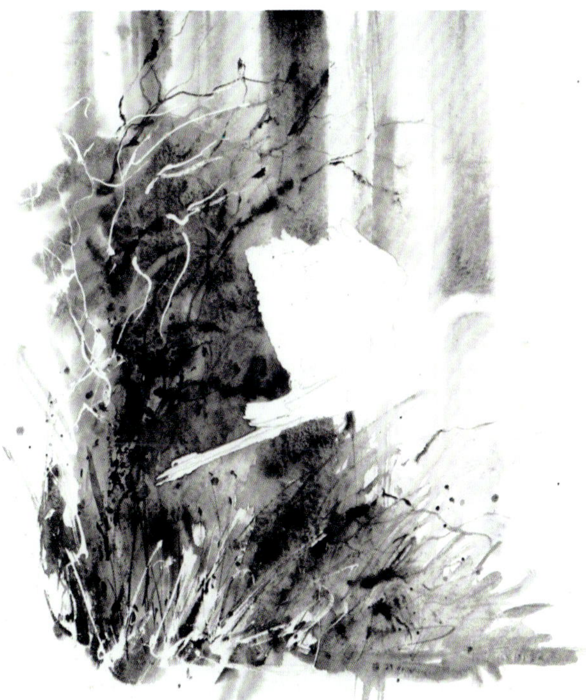

↑ The masking fluid has left the egret clean and ready to paint.

PAINT THE EGRET, ADD FINISHING TOUCHES AND ASSESS THE COMPOSITION

10 Now it's time to paint the egret using the methods outlined in the previous pages. Give yourself time to slow down the process so you achieve accuracy and precision. That doesn't mean that you have to paint every feather; it just means that your major shapes, tones and edges need to reflect what you observe in the photograph.

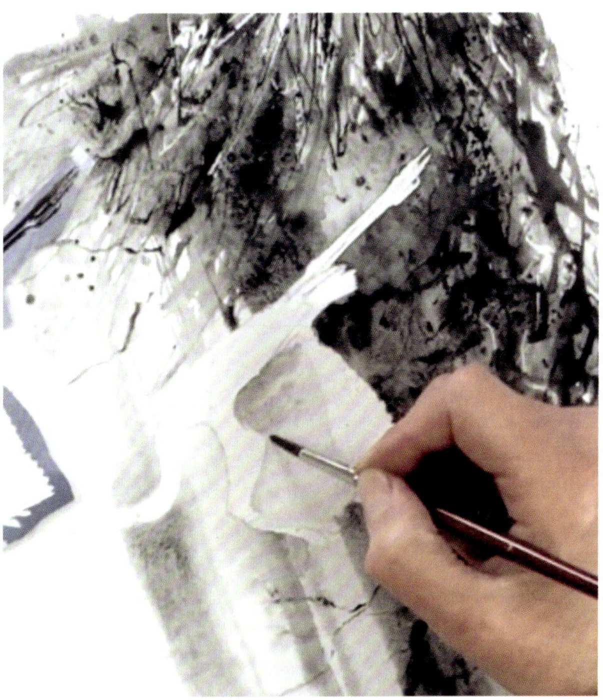

↑ Paint in a way that's comfortable to you, even if that means rotating the painting and the reference image upside down.

11 Once you have competed the egret, add any finishing touches to the surrounding areas. This might mean knocking back some of the stark white areas left by the masking fluid. You can do this easily by adding touches of paint or softening the hard edges by gently rubbing a damp brush over them. With my painting, I added a few darker branches, twigs and foliage and reduced the brightness of some of the areas where bare paper was exposed.

12 It can sometimes be difficult to know when to finish a piece and to decide on the final composition and crop. For instance, you may have applied brushstrokes or marks that you really love and would like to keep in the final piece.

I find the following methods really helpful when deciding this. Firstly, take a picture of the finished piece and view it on your phone or, alternatively, use a reducing lens. These tools enable you to critique your work in terms of assessing balance and gaining a good sense of composition.

Secondly, cut up an old mount into two sections and place the L shapes at differing points around the piece. Does the format actually look better as a square as opposed to a rectangular format? Or could a little bit of paint here or there resolve an issue?

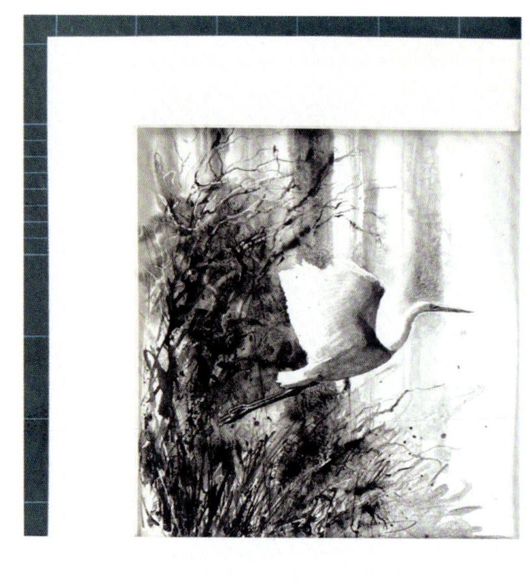

↑ Slide the sections around until you are happy with the format. With this option, it reveals some marks that I inadvertently made on the left-hand side. I love these marks, but are they too distracting or do they help lead the viewer to other aspects of the painting?

← The finished piece, demonstrating a mixture of expressive and more controlled techniques using just one colour. The left-hand edge has been removed so that the focus is on the giant egret.

Top tip

Don't underestimate the angle and movement of your paper when painting a piece. I created much of this work with my paper flat and in one position. However, you can achieve a whole host of exciting and dynamic effects by moving the paper when applying paint and water.

A summary of my process when painting a bird

My painting process evolved organically, no doubt by watching tutorials and reading books, until I eventually found a flow and rhythm that I understood, and that came naturally to me, and then I created a consistent style that I felt comfortable with. In the same way, you will pick up your own methodology. If I had to summarise it, these would be the steps, whether I was painting in one colour or a number of colours:

1 Apply a loose wash of colour over a small enough section that won't dry too quickly, making sure that any white areas are left dry.
2 When damp, apply a thicker wash, leaving spaces between the newly applied paint to allow for expansion and colour merges. Lift any unwanted dark patches with a thirsty brush.
3 Allow this first layer to dry.
4 Paint in some of your darker, more precise parts, such as eyes and beaks, onto dry paper, to bring the subject to life and to help you gauge the myriad mid tones later in the process.
5 Complete painting your mid tones on dry paper. Incorporate smaller details by adding creamy paint, sometimes diluting and dragging it on the paper to create soft edges. Continue this process until full tonal depth is achieved.
6 Assess values on a regular basis and lift any areas – small or large – that are overworked.
7 Once all the main values, shapes and colours are in the right place, spend a few minutes adding any tiny details using a smaller brush on dry paper.

GENERAL NOTES ABOUT STYLE AND METHOD

Although this book is about expressive techniques, my particular style of painting encompasses both loose and more representational brushwork. Here, I painted the egret in a much tighter, more representational style. This is just personal choice and is certainly not meant to be a prescriptive rule. You will have your own style and method, unique to just you, and this is to be embraced and encouraged.

In terms of methodology, when painting in watercolour, generally speaking the lightest tones are established by keeping the paper free of paint. Many watercolour artists, myself included, paint lighter tones first and then move into mid and dark tones respectively.

There are a couple of exceptions to my method. I will often add a section of dark tone early on in the process; in this case on the beak. This helps me to gauge the light and mid tones more accurately. Also, I may add lighter tones at the very end of the process using gouache, acrylic or white gel pen, especially if these areas have been too fiddly to mask off at the preparatory stage or lift out during the painting session.

Of course, these techniques needn't be reserved for painting a backdrop. Try using them to create sections of the birds themselves. In this piece, 'Eric In Flight', much of the movement was created by blowing the excess paint across the paper with a straw.

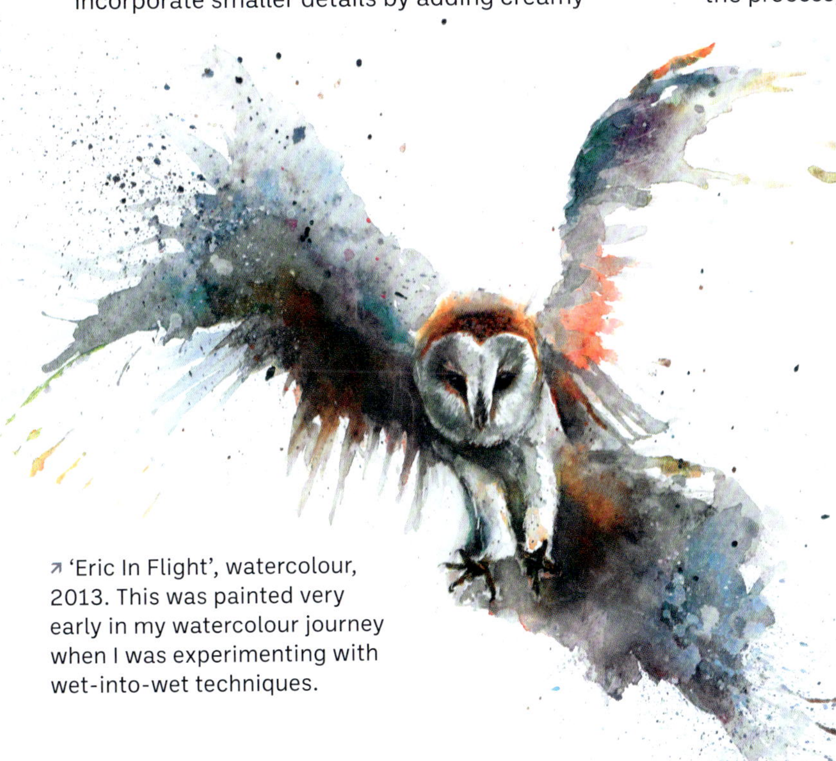

↗ 'Eric In Flight', watercolour, 2013. This was painted very early in my watercolour journey when I was experimenting with wet-into-wet techniques.

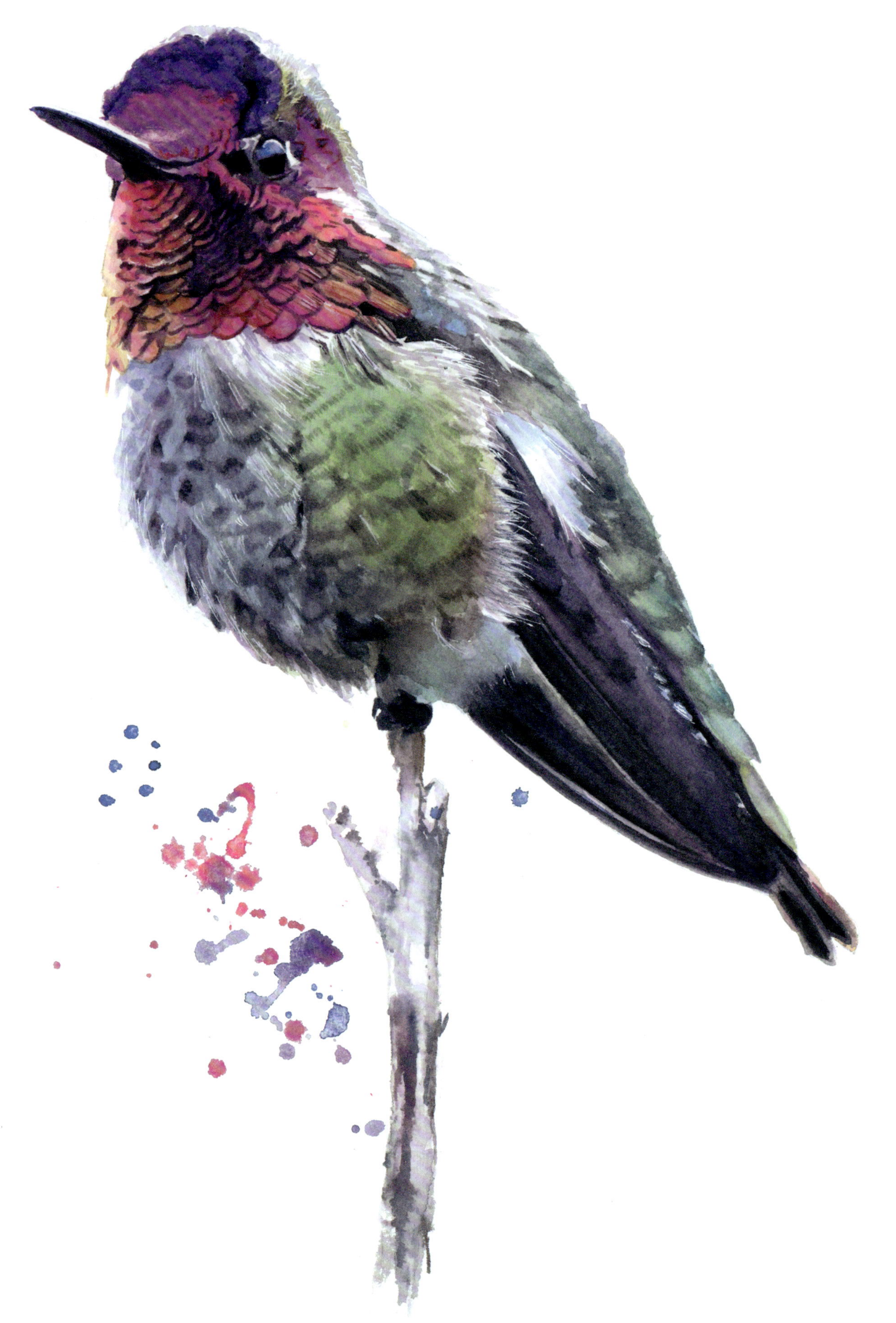

CHAPTER

4

Introduction to Colour

Understanding colour and how to mix it is key to depicting the wealth of birds available to paint. When I first discovered watercolour, I was in awe of its luminosity. I loved how the colours mixed and merged on the paper to create the most wonderful hues.

When I first started painting in 2012, I learnt a lot about colour theory by just playing with colour. In fact, I only started researching the science behind it in recent years. Colour theory can seem a dry subject, but it can be so helpful in providing shortcuts to creating harmonious compositions, beautiful neutral shades, effective shadows and a multitude of other things. Bright chromas can easily get drowned out if we inadvertently neutralise some of our vibrant colours in the painting process. It's also worth remembering that you can achieve many of your desired colours in a number of different ways, and you will learn most of this through trial and error.

Over the next couple of chapters, I'm going to show you how to see colour and replicate it on the paper. Once you've mastered the art of colour mixing, you will be able to paint a beautiful peacock using just four or five pigments. I rarely prescribe set colours unless they're particularly handy as you can mix them yourself from just four primary pigments.

PROJECT 4

Exploring a limited colour palette

THE COLOUR WHEEL RETHOUGHT

I can almost hear you groan as you turn the page to see yet another colour wheel! Although the subject of the colour wheel may appear a little boring, if your paintings have been suffering from a lack of dynamism, read on! Admittedly, I muddled through OK in the early years of my painting career, without even knowing of the existence of colour wheels. However, if I had known and understood their importance, I could have worked out why some of my paintings were more successful than others.

You may have noticed that I have referred to the subject of colour wheels using the plural. That is because there are a multitude of colour wheels, dating back from the earliest known wheel of Isaac Newton in the 1660s to more contemporary wheels. Such developments have come about as the result of scientific breakthroughs in our understanding of colour, and the multitude of different industries that rely on colour theory, from print and film to artistic creation.

← The complementary nature of a hummingbird's colours makes it a joy to paint.

Colour wheel theory is useful in terms of learning about how to make dynamic shadows and colour choices that work. However, some of the theory behind it can be problematic, especially when considering the primary colours. What might be true scientifically can often fall short in practice when it comes to the realities involved in the manufacturing of pigments.

Primary colours: A contemporary take

At its core, the colour wheel is made up of three primary colours. With traditional theory, we are taught that these are red, blue and yellow; something along the lines of cadmium red, ultramarine blue and cadmium yellow. We are led to believe that these are colours that cannot be created by mixing other colours together and that, moreover, these three colours will create any other colours desired.

I always found this theory troublesome. Try as I might, I could not create fresh magentas for my florals and zingy turquoises for my kingfishers using this system. For example, if I used my starting point as red, I simply couldn't create a dynamic pink or magenta, whether I added another colour or watered it down: rather I would end up with pale reds, pinks, or peach or purple hues at best. Conversely, I could make a red by mixing yellow and magenta, despite the fact that I had read that this was not theoretically possible!

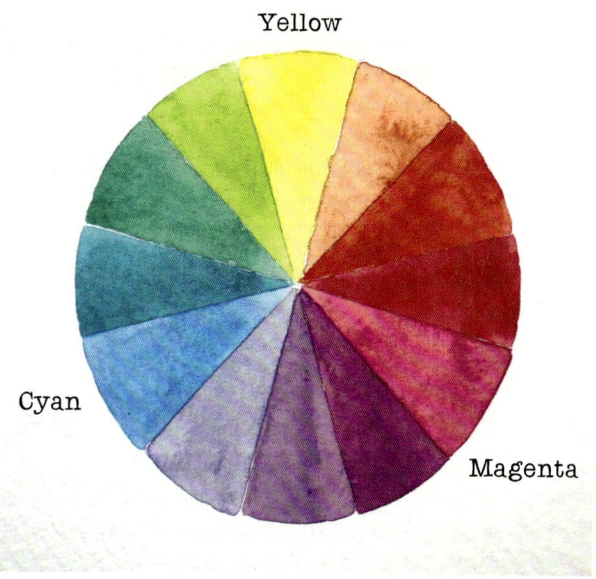

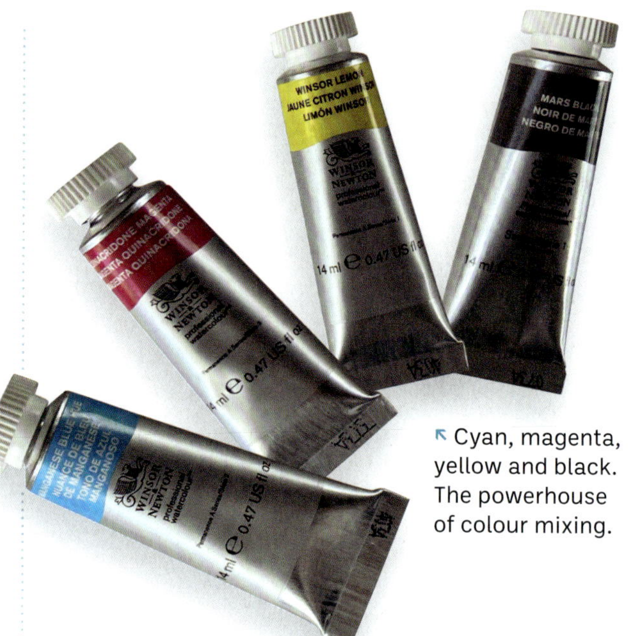

↖ Cyan, magenta, yellow and black. The powerhouse of colour mixing.

I eventually found my own solution by purchasing pinks and cyans to help my watercolours pop! For many years I relied on two colours in particular: Opera Pink and Cobalt Turquoise by Winsor & Newton (professional range). I rarely used these colours in their pure state; rather I mixed them with other colours as a means of making the most beautiful pale lilacs and rich, vibrant oranges.

More recently, inspired by the CMYK colour wheel, I have limited my primary palette to just four colours: Manganese Blue Hue, Quinacridone Magenta, Winsor Lemon and Mars Black.

I find that this range of colours, plus a black, can help me make most of the colours that I need for a piece. All of the exercises in the book have been created with these four colours. Some specific premixed colours such as French Ultramarine blue and Quinacridone Gold, however, can be problematic to replicate at speed in sufficient quantity and with the desired translucency. So, with each of the following exercise pieces, I will recommend supplementary colours if you have them to hand. I'd like to stress that they are not the be all and end all to a good painting; you can still achieve the most beautiful artwork using just these four pigments.

← Cyan, magenta and yellow watercolour pigments have created the beautiful colours in this wheel, most notably red. This disproves the myth that red is a primary colour that can't be mixed – here it has been made with a magenta/yellow mix.

Secondary colours

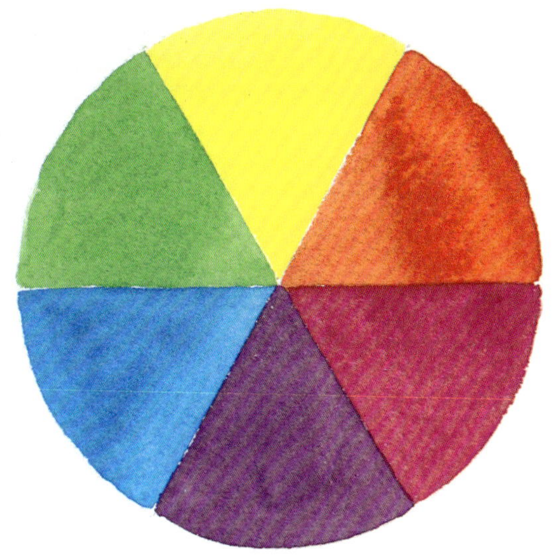

↑ Orange, green and purple are secondary colours created by mixing equal proportions of two primaries: magenta + yellow = orange; cyan + yellow = green; magenta + cyan = purple.

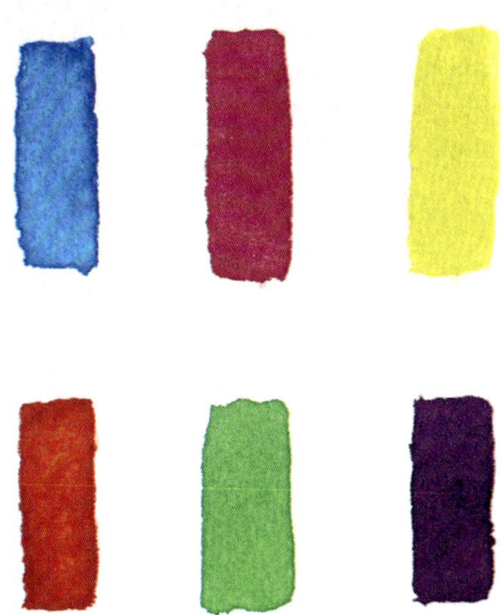

↑ The most commonly referred to complementary colours are: cyan and orange; magenta and green; and yellow and purple.

One of the wonderful things about watercolour is its ability to mix with other colours on the page to make an infinite number of other colours. It is a magical experience to see the colours merge on the paper, but it can be frustrating if you're not getting the colours you want to achieve. Learning about the principles of the colour wheel takes out some of the guesswork and, with play and practice, colour mixing will become second nature.

Secondary colours are a good place to start. These are colours which are created by mixing equal quantities of two primary colours.

Complementary colours

Complementary colours are the colours that sit opposite each other on the colour wheel.

Complementary colours are useful in three major ways:

1. To neutralise a colour

Mixing two complementary colours helps you to achieve beautifully muted colours. Desaturated colours, or neutrals, are easily achieved by adding the complement. You can turn a vivid green into a beautiful olive by adding its complement, red. Likewise, a bright yellow can be turned into a mustard by adding a touch of purple.

→ Using complementary colours to create neutral colours (also commonly referred to as 'greys' or desaturated colours). The neutral shades are most notable towards the middle of each swatch as the two complementary colours counteract each other.

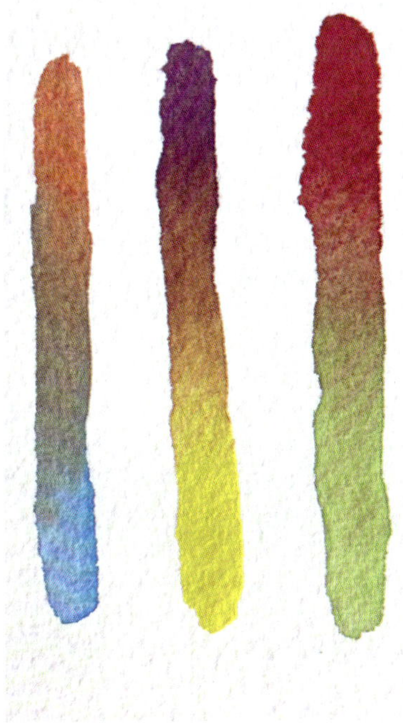

Using these pared-back colours is an invaluable aid to making the more saturated colours pop on your page. In this painting of the siskin, many of the colours are desaturated, even in the main body of the bird, where much of the pure yellow has been overlaid with desaturated hues. These neutral colours help the small sections of pure yellow to shine.

↓ 'Siskin', 2018, watercolour.

From a technical point of view, it's worth noting that although colours can theoretically be neutralised by their complement, the issue can be complicated when taking into account the natural chroma, tone and brightness of a colour. It would be difficult, if not impossible, to effectively desaturate a dark vivid purple with light yellow, as purple is naturally darker than yellow on the colour wheel. In such a case, for speed and simplicity, I would therefore add Cadmium Orange or Burnt Sienna to neutralise a vivid purple, as they have a similar tonal value.

A note of caution when it comes to colour mixing: once a colour is neutralised, you won't be able to regain the pure saturation of its previous state. Only desaturate it once you are sure that you need a more muted tone.

2. To make shadow colours

As we discovered in Chapter 1, shadows are an essential way of giving your birds depth and form. This is the case whether painting in monochrome or colour. Our natural inclination is to paint shadows in black or just to add more of the same colour to a section. However, to make a more convincing shadow, add the complement of the local colour (the colour that the shadow falls on). If the shadow needs to be darkened, I often find that adding a little indigo does the trick.

3. To help inform colour choices

When I first started out in painting, I hadn't heard of the phrase 'complementary colours'. However, I do remember going to my local art club one evening and marvelling at a member's painting of an orangutan. She had teamed up the beautiful bronze oranges in his fur with gorgeously rich blues and turquoises in his face, and I

↖ 'Whaoooo!', 2019, watercolour. The desaturated, muted tones in the underside of the puffin allow the saturated oranges of the feet to sing.

remember thinking 'Wow, how did she even know that that would work, when an orangutan's face is grey?' Complementary colours hold the key to this and many other tricks of the trade!

The phenomenon known as 'simultaneous contrast' means that a complementary colour will enhance and exaggerate the effects of its counterpart. This was used to excellent effect by painters such as Monet. In his *Impression Sunrise*, the orange sunset is striking against the predominantly blue colour palette. See how your eye is drawn to it, as well as to the man on the gondola, where a difference in tonal contrast is used to attract your attention.

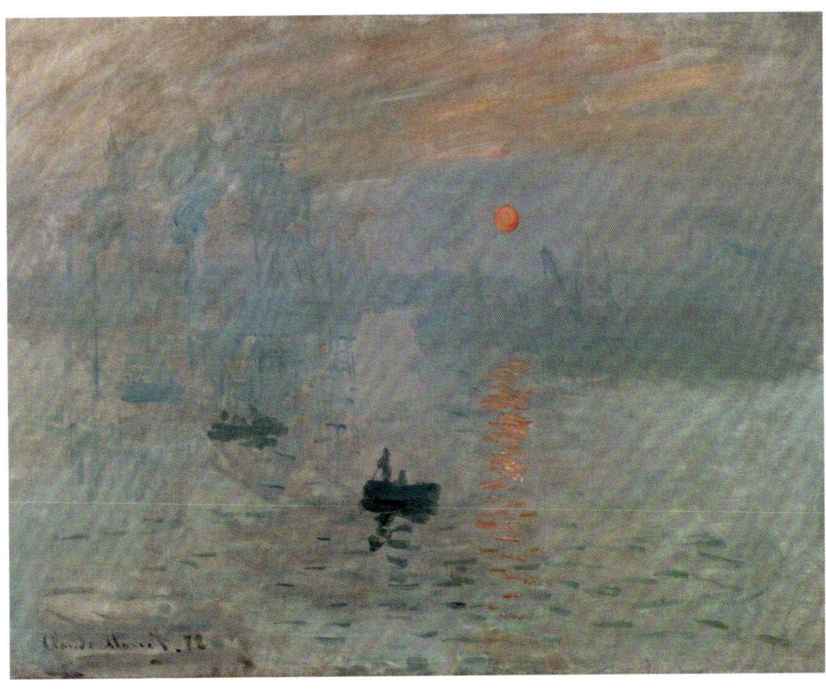

↑ *Impression Sunrise*, Claude Monet, 1872.

Similarly, and on the subject of bird paintings, look at how the red of the turkeys' snoods contrasts vividly with the greens in Monet's *The Turkeys*. In the desaturated version, you can see that the dark red and green tones are very similar. It is their colour combination that helps them to pop. The redness of the snoods helps lead the viewer's eye up and around the piece. If these had been a desaturated mid blue, for instance, they would not have had the same visual interest.

A working knowledge of colour and its effect on the composition and overall look of your painting is essential. Are there any pieces that you would revisit and perhaps tweak with this in mind?

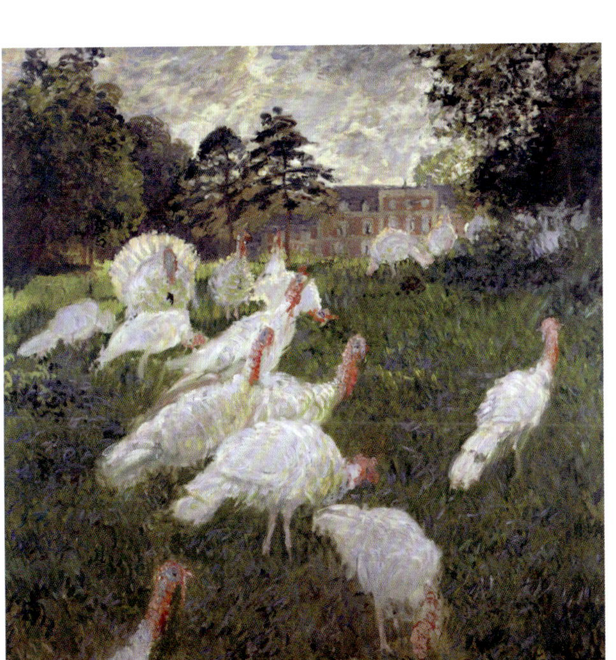

↑ *The Turkeys*, Claude Monet, 1876.

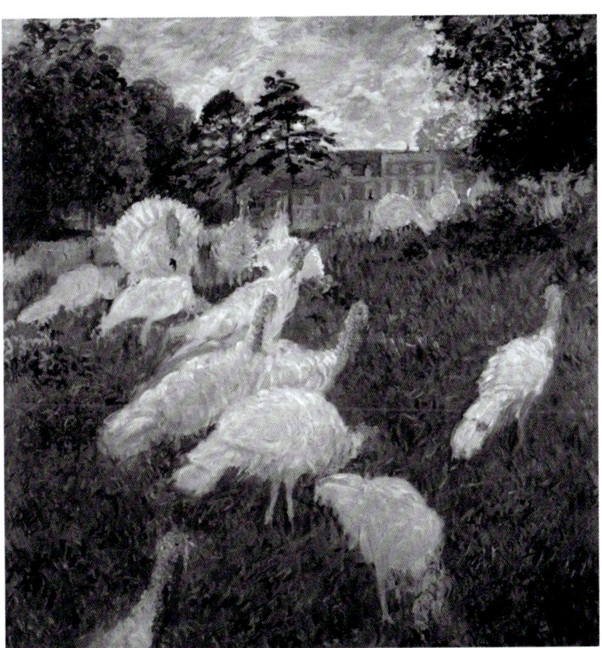

↑ In this desaturated version of *The Turkeys*, you can see that the dark red and green tones are similar.

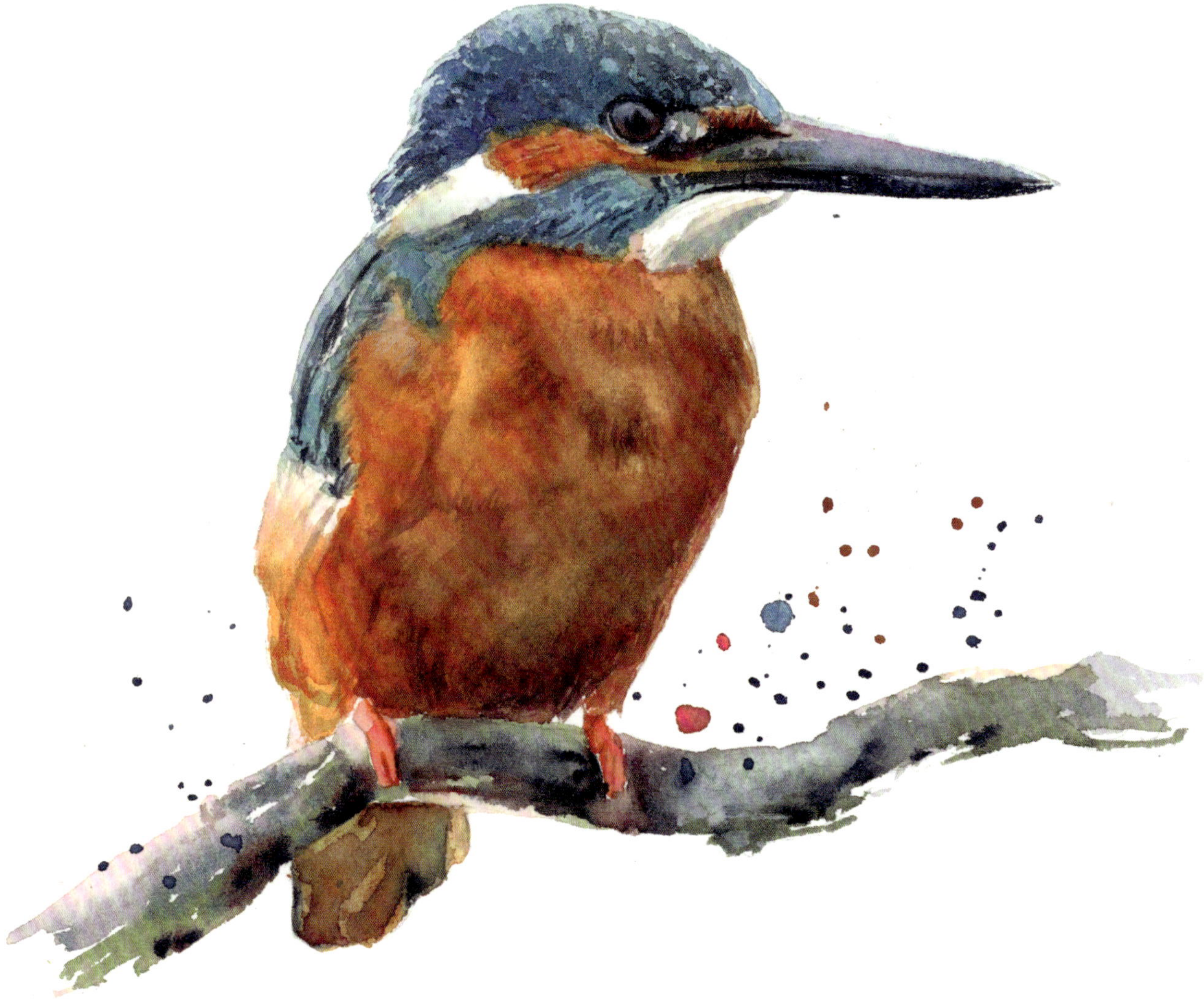

↑ 'Kingfisher', 2020, watercolour.

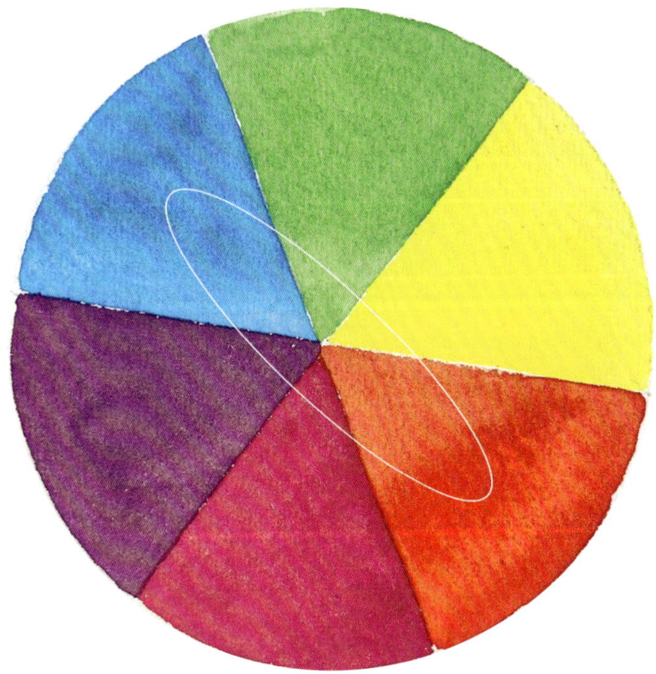

← The cyan/orange combination seen in the kingfisher.

EXERCISE 1: CREATE A RANGE OF COLOURS USING THREE COLOURS AND BLACK

This is a wonderfully calming exercise and an invaluable lesson in colour mixing that many of my students enjoy.

My pigments are from the Winsor & Newton Professional range, but other makes will be fine to use. I have chosen the pigments as the magenta, yellow and blue are either transparent or semi-transparent in nature. This will allow for some beautiful colour mixing when they merge, blend and overlap each other. Transparent colours, especially when applied lightly, can almost glow on the paper.

Although I use some opaque colours in my professional work, they need to be handled with care as they can have a tendency to overpower and muddy the more transparent colours. Having said that, they are perfect for adding finishing touches to a piece or for creating interesting effects when playing around with abstract sections of the work.

You will need

- Paint: CMYK colour palette (p.62), either watercolour pan or tube:
  - Manganese Blue Hue
  - Quinacridone Magenta
  - Winsor Lemon
  - Mars Black
- Paper: 300 gsm, student-grade watercolour paper
- Brushes: synthetic round size 6 or 12 brush
- Stationery: pencil, ruler, eraser and pen
- Palette or dish with adequate mixing space, water container

Top tip

Look for the transparent symbol on the back of your paint tube or check on the manufacturer's website. Watercolour pigments can be transparent, semi-transparent, opaque or semi-opaque.

↓ The transparency of each Winsor & Newton Professional pigment is shown on their chart and the back of each tube. The square blocks of black, white, and mixed black and white indicate the transparent, semi-transparent, semi-opaque and opaque properties of each pigment.

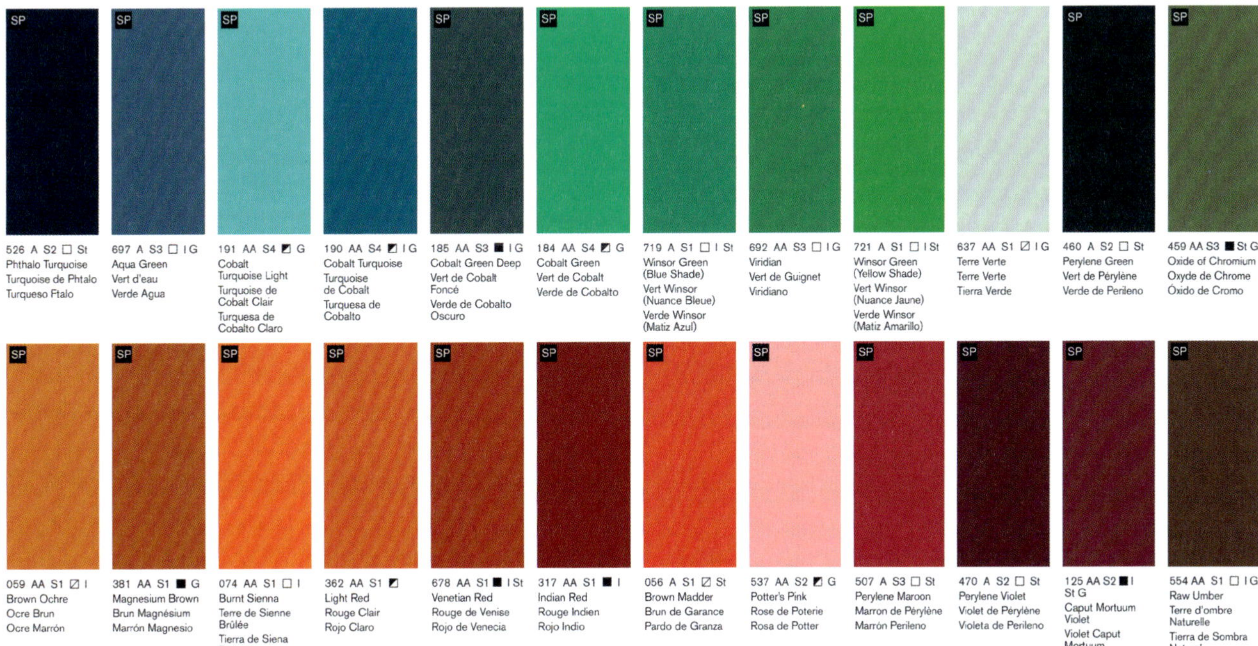

1 Mark out three sheets of watercolour paper, as shown, to form blank colour charts.

→ This is only a suggested chart. Make as many boxes as you like and have fun filling them with colour.

2 The first sheet will be full of colours mixed where the main pigments used are cyan and yellow. If using tube paint, squeeze equal measures of each colour onto a palette. If using pan paints, just activate the four colours by adding water via an atomiser or wet brush.

You will only be adding a touch of magenta and black to the swatches towards the end of the exercise. The four boxes in the bottom left-hand corner of the sheet indicate the amount of pigment used in proportion to each other. This is to give you a visual reminder of the colours that will predominate the page. For example, in sheet 1, where cyan and yellow predominate, the boxes will be completed as follows:

Yellow Cyan Magenta Black

↑ Yellow and cyan will predominate the first sheet to help you create a page of yellows, blues and greens. The large and small boxes are a visual reminder to keep you on track while you are mixing, so fill these boxes in first.

3 Mix a pale wash of cyan and yellow, using just a little cyan, a larger quantity of yellow and a lot of water. This will give you a pale green hue. Apply the paint to your first swatch. Now start adding more cyan to the mix and watch how the colour turns bluer in shade. Add this paint to the next swatch. Continue adjusting the quantities of paint to create a variety of blue/green shades until you complete the first row.

4 When completing the second row, add more pigment to the mix, so that it is less watery. Your colour will start to darken. Again, continue creating swatches across the page. At this stage, whether your colours are light or dark, they are saturated. They are clean, pure and sometimes vivid in appearance because you have only used the two primaries.

5 Now for your third row. It is time to introduce a very small amount of magenta into the mix. Suddenly you will see your fresh colours become desaturated in appearance. Your fresh greens will become olives, your clear blues will become greys.

6 Finally for your fourth row, experiment with just a touch of black to see how this darkens and desaturates your colours. I also created three longer strips on each page to demonstrate the impactful nature of water. Quite often I will 'bleed' a colour out on a spare piece of paper to double-check its hue.

7 Alter the quantities of the primary colours as per the colour key at the bottom of each sheet opposite. By the end of this exercise you will have created a beautiful range of colours from just four pigments!

Note: where magenta and cyan predominate, you will create the most beautiful lilacs and purples, right down to desaturated mauves.

Where the magenta and yellow predominate, you will create rich saturated golds down to their desaturated brown counterparts.

Challenge yourself to create at least twenty-eight different shades of blues/greens/yellows, as shown.

→ These colours will range from zesty lemon, sky blue and bright green to olive and dark emerald.

→ These colours will contain a range of warm blue, plum, damson, lavender, lilac and muted grey.

→ To help you keep on track, think of warm golden autumnal tones, golds, rusts and browns.

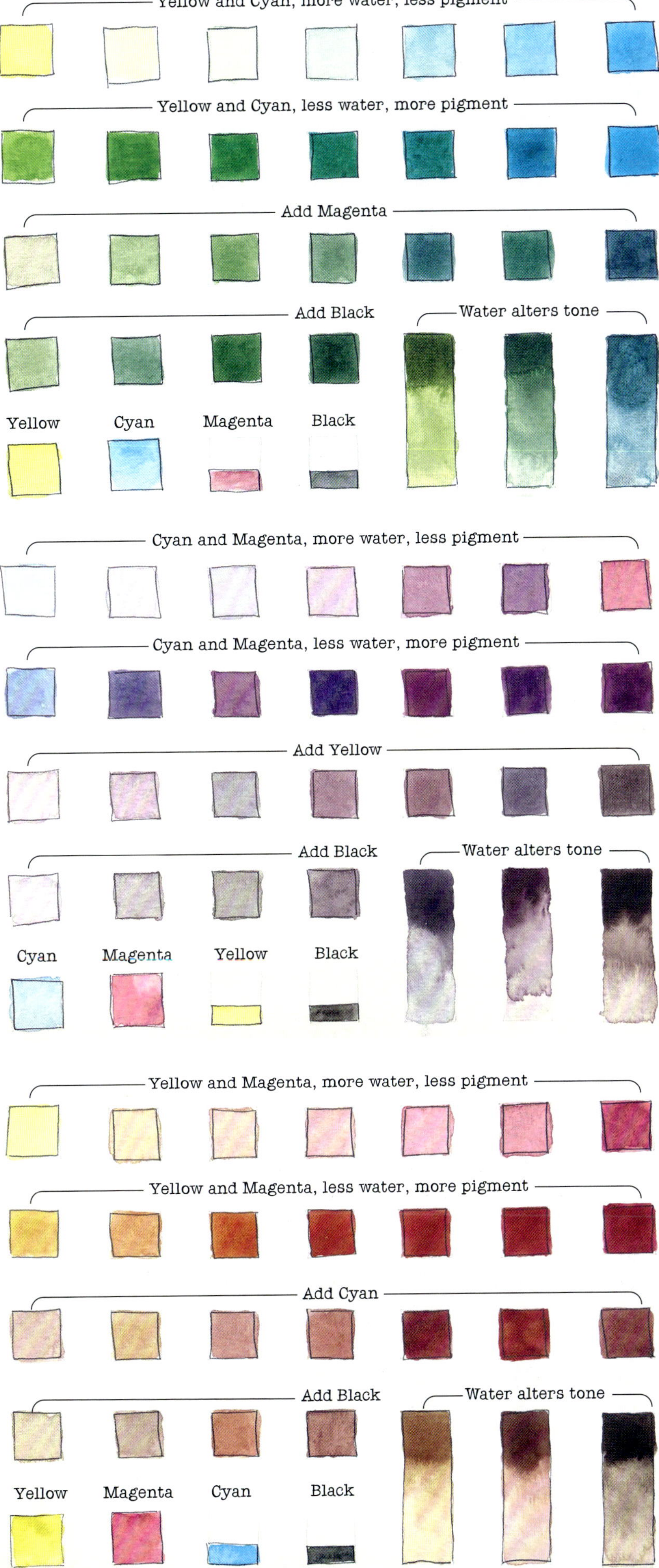

EXERCISE 2: CREATE A SPECIFIC COLOUR

'This is great', I hear you say, 'but what about when I want to create a specific colour?' The previous exercise was just guesswork with no written notes as to quantities used. It is to this particular area of colour mixing that we will turn next.

You will need

- Paints and equipment as on page 67
- Viewing aperture, homemade (made using copier paper and hole punches)

If you are an experienced painter, use the four CMYK colours for this exercise. If you are more inexperienced, I would recommend using the four CMYK colours but also having to hand a palette containing some basic premixed colours, including a red, mid green, orange and dark blue, for speed.

In the previous exercise you made a variety of colours from just four pigments, but what happens when you want to mix a specific colour? I am not a proponent of creating meticulous charts where I prescribe a percentage of each pigment to make a particular colour. While this makes for an interesting academic exercise, it is an unrealistic way to work in the real world, especially when you are up against time with watercolour. I use a more intuitive-based way of making colour, whether on the palette or on the paper, using a mixture of common sense and the information outlined previously. My method can be broken down into four main stages.

1. See the colour

This might sound obvious, but over time you will need to train your eyes to *see* colour. You may have experienced the problem in the past when you have tried, for instance, to match up grey accessories or emulsion paint for the home, only to discover that not all greys are the same. Some may be 'greenish' in hue while others can have a distinctly purple undertone. This problem applies, of course, to all colours, not just grey. Here are my hints to help you *see* the colours of a photo reference.

Finding and preparing the right photo reference

Whether you are painting for fun or as a commission, getting the right photograph to work from is crucial. You want to feel inspired and fired up to paint when you look at it, not have a sinking feeling in the pit of your stomach! I have turned down several pieces of work when I've not been happy with the photograph as I want to enjoy the process and allow the paint to sing. For me, a successful watercolour painting is the perfect merge of both subject and medium, where they complement each other in harmony.

Generally speaking, I will look for a high-resolution photo that has a good range of tones so that it doesn't look 'flat'. Even though my paintings may appear loose, I also look for detail in the

← Homemade viewing aperture made using hole punches and white copier paper.

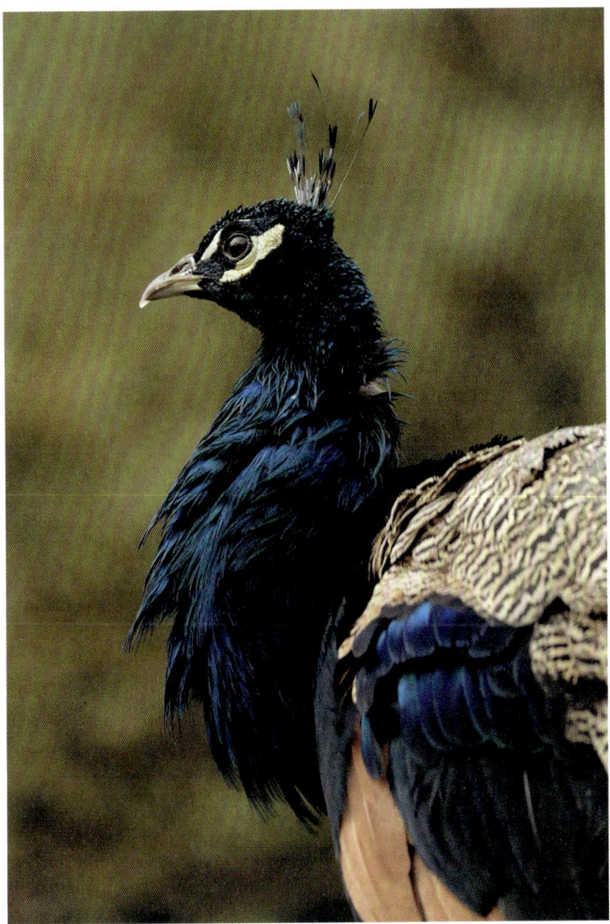

↑ The original peacock photograph.

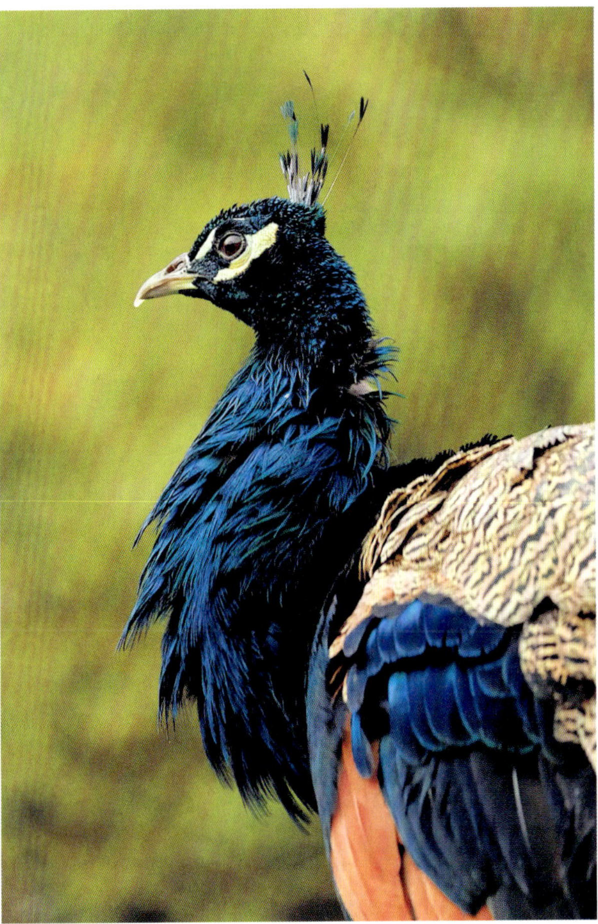

↑ For the purposes of painting, I have adjusted the level of contrast, brightness and saturation to help me see the colours more clearly.

photograph as I can then choose which information I want to paint and what to leave out.

Once I have a photograph in mind, I will often tweak it in apps such as Snapseed, Photoshop or Procreate in order to exaggerate the colours and tones. Most smartphones have a photo manipulation tool that is more than adequate for this task. This helps me see and depict the colours when painting the subject.

The photographs above show a 'before and after' image of a peacock. The original photo is beautiful as it is, but the more saturated version will help to inspire my choice of colours, as I will demonstrate later in Chapter 5.

I always work from images printed at the highest quality setting on photo-quality paper. It's much easier to work with a sharp, highly saturated image than one of draft quality printed on standard copier paper. If you don't have a printer available, you may wish to paint directly from the display on your device, such as an iPad, phone or computer.

Using a viewing aperture

One of the problems we have with identifying colour is due to a phenomenon called simultaneous contrast. The theory is that one colour can change how we perceive the tone and hue of another when the two are placed side by side. The actual colours themselves don't change, but we see them as altered.

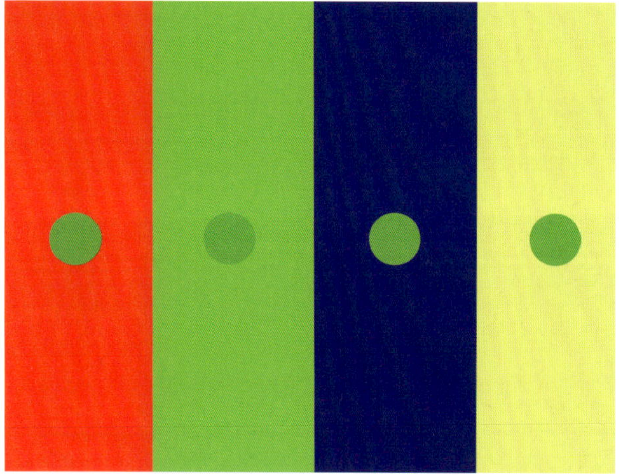

↑ In this example, one shade of green is laid over different colours. Look how much darker it appears when it's over the light green, compared to the red.

One of the easiest ways to overcome simultaneous contrast is to surround the problematic section of colour with white. Several of my students used a homemade viewing aperture when they were starting out to help them ascertain the hue and tone of a colour, until they eventually no longer needed it. If you place a piece of white paper with a viewing hole over the colour in question, it becomes much easier to work out its shade.

For those of you happier with digital apps, there are a variety of colour identifiers on the market, such as ColorSlurp. The image opposite shows how this app has magnified a small section of the photograph. When the colour is identified in such a way, it can make it easier to see.

→ The desaturated muted colours can be particularly difficult to work out when there are so many other colours in the photograph. In this example, we are going to isolate the colour of the peacock's eyelids.

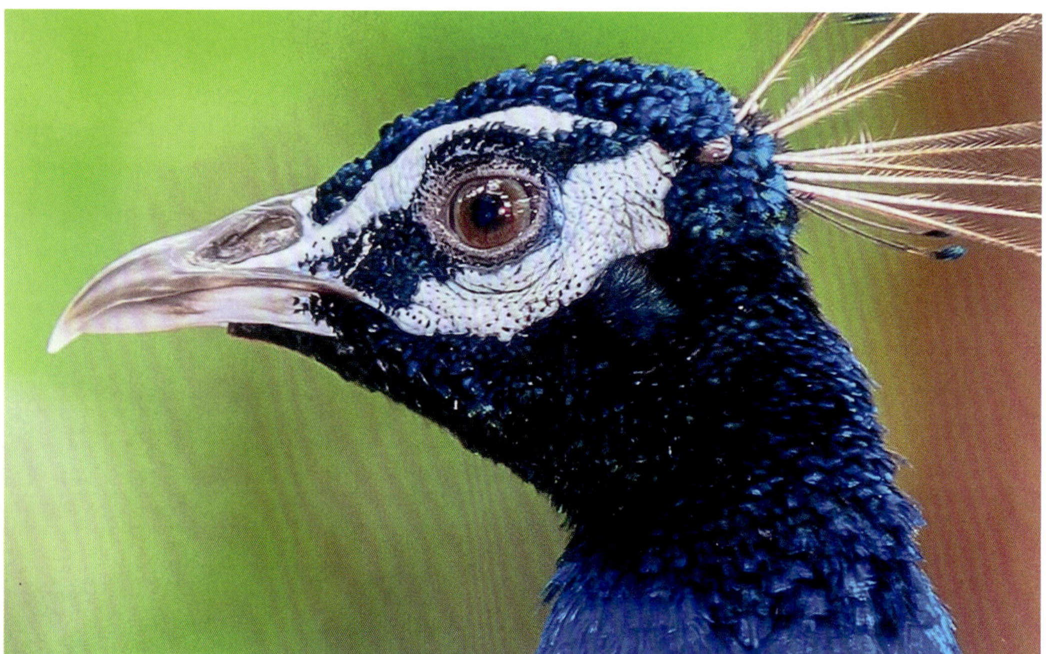

← A viewing aperture helps you to isolate the colour and identify it with surgical precision.

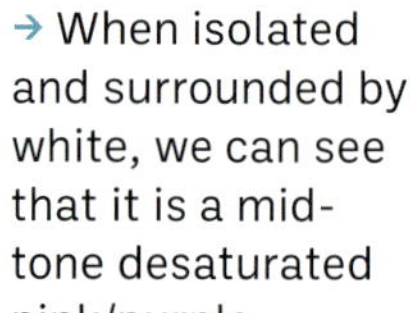

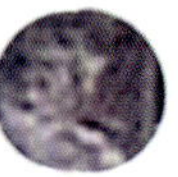

→ When isolated and surrounded by white, we can see that it is a mid-tone desaturated pink/purple.

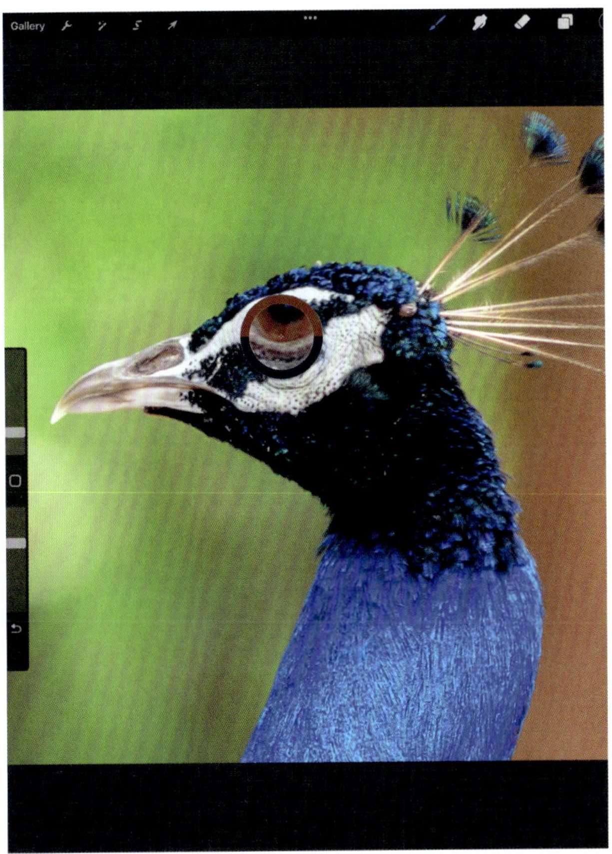

↑ Using a digital magnifying glass on an app to highlight the eye of the peacock and show one of the shades. ColorSlurp and Procreate are two of many apps that can help you distinguish colour.

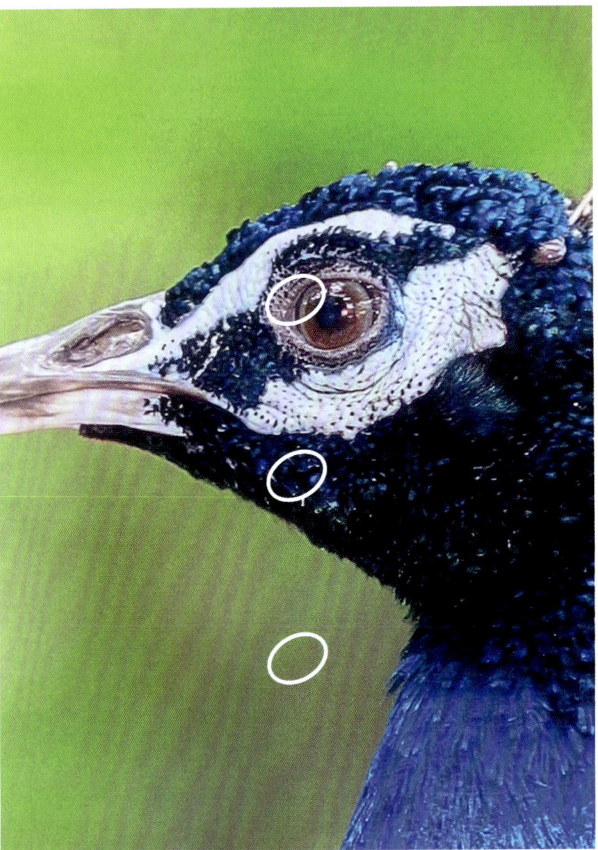

↑ The three white circles indicate the colours that we will make in this exercise.

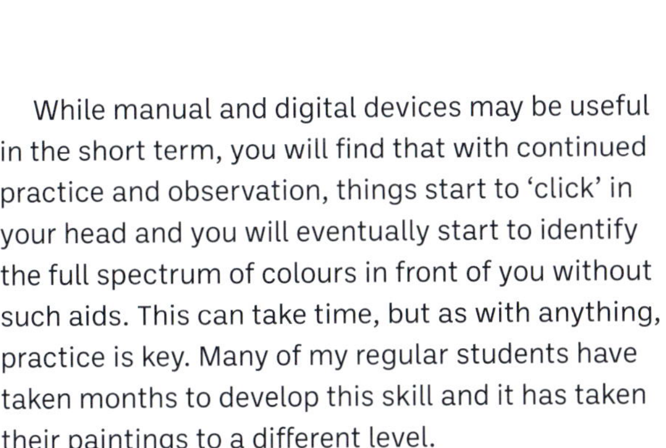

While manual and digital devices may be useful in the short term, you will find that with continued practice and observation, things start to 'click' in your head and you will eventually start to identify the full spectrum of colours in front of you without such aids. This can take time, but as with anything, practice is key. Many of my regular students have taken months to develop this skill and it has taken their paintings to a different level.

Now we are going to make some colour. For the purposes of this exercise, let's use the colours circled on the peacock photo as an example.

2. Family

The starting point for my colour mixing method is to establish what family a certain colour belongs to. Is it bluish, greenish, orangey, reddish or pinkish? This decision informs my choice of base colour.

3. Saturation

Next to ascertain is whether the colour is saturated or unsaturated. Is it pure or is it a neutral, grubbier version of the colour? If you need to desaturate it, remember the lessons learnt on pages 67–69 and how you were able to neutralise a colour by adding its complement.

4. Tone

Finally, establish the tone of the colour. Does it need to be lighter or darker? If lighter, try adding more water (not white paint, as that would simply make it a pastel-like shade and you would lose transparency); if darker, add darker pigment. Try a touch of dark blue or even a smidgen of black.

The following three examples demonstrate this method in practical terms, together with my notes on the process of mixing a particular colour.

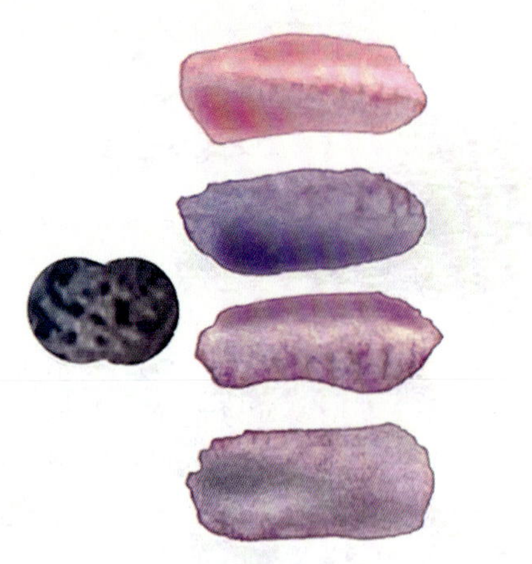

←

1 I wanted to create the lightest shade that I could see in the sample, which was a kind of light, neutral mauve. My starting point for this colour was pure magenta.
2 I added a little cyan to make it purple (its family colour).
3 I had made it a little too blue, so I dropped a little more magenta into it.
4 Finally, I wanted a slightly darker, desaturated version. If I had added yellow to the mix, it would have made it too 'warm' and brown in appearance, so instead I added a little black and I got the overall tone and colour that I was looking for. If I'd wanted it even darker, I would have added a blue/black mix with a touch of magenta.

Top tip

For the purposes of cool vs warm colours, think of premixed black as a very dark blue.

This example shows you that you can achieve a range of colours very quickly:

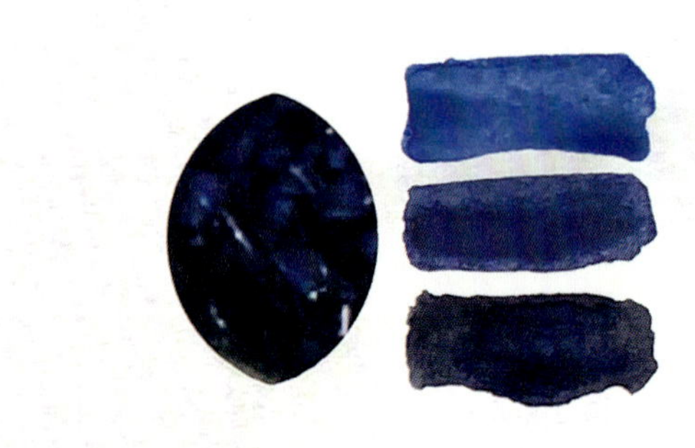

←

1 The first swatch is pure cyan.
2 A small amount of black darkens and neutralises it to an indigo shade.
3 Additional amounts of black darken it further.

Top tip

There are many ways to achieve the same colour. Practise creating the same colours using other colours as your starting point.

This example shows how you can get a chosen colour using more than one method:

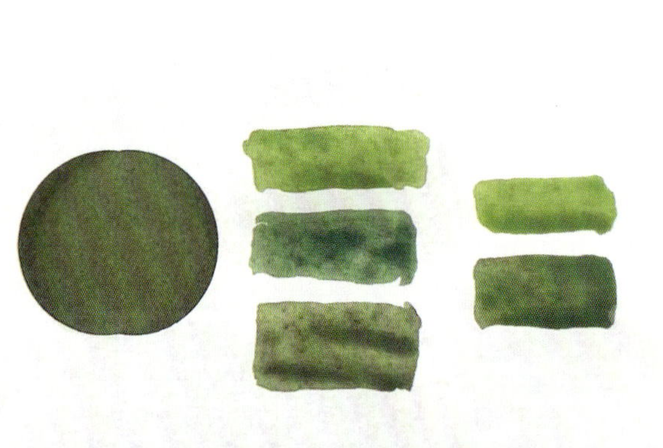

←

The left-hand set of swatches were made as follows:

1 Bright green made with cyan and yellow.
2 A little more cyan added to darken the tone.
3 A touch of magenta (the third primary) added to desaturate the green to make it an olive green.

The right-hand set of swatches were made as follows:

1 Bright green made with cyan and yellow as on the left.
2 A touch of black desaturates and darkens at the same time, so this is a quicker process.

All of these 'rules' sound like a protracted process that is a long way from expressive, intuitive painting, but rest assured that with practice, colour mixing takes only a few seconds, with colours created and adjusted on the page and on the palette as part of the painting process. Over time, colour mixing becomes second nature as you recognise how each pigment affects the other. Take heart in the fact that a good working knowledge of your palette will enable you to make the most wonderful colours which allow your painting to sing.

Time to play

Afford yourself the time and luxury of play as it is truly when most of your skills will develop. Use scrap watercolour paper and a viewing hole to challenge yourself to recreate some of the colours you see on the reference. Adjust and readjust until you get a similar hue and tone. This is time well-spent that will take your paintings to the next level. When your colours are correct, your tones will also fall into place, which will automatically add depth to your pieces.

In practice, seeing and creating colour takes a bit of getting used to, especially with the more muted, neutral shades that are really hard to describe. In the following photograph, a few colours can be problematic because we can't readily name them and we tend to generalise them as creams or greys. What we need to establish is what *value* and *hue* each colour is. Is it 'light peach', 'mid greenish-grey' or something else? Sometimes it is easier to establish what it isn't and go from there!

↓ Look at the dark emerald greens in this section of this peacock's plumage. A cursory glance at the peacock below would have suggested just taupes and browns.

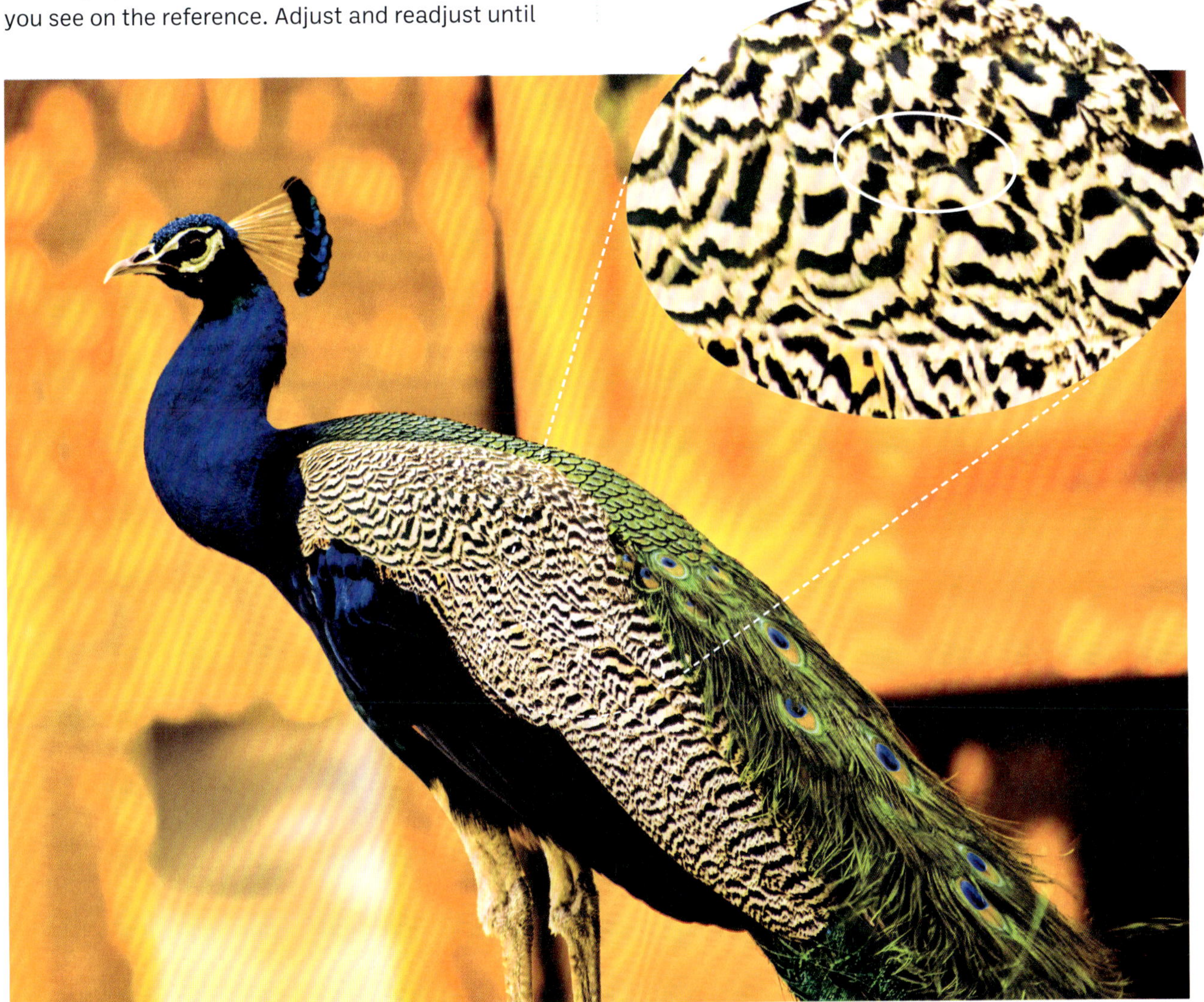

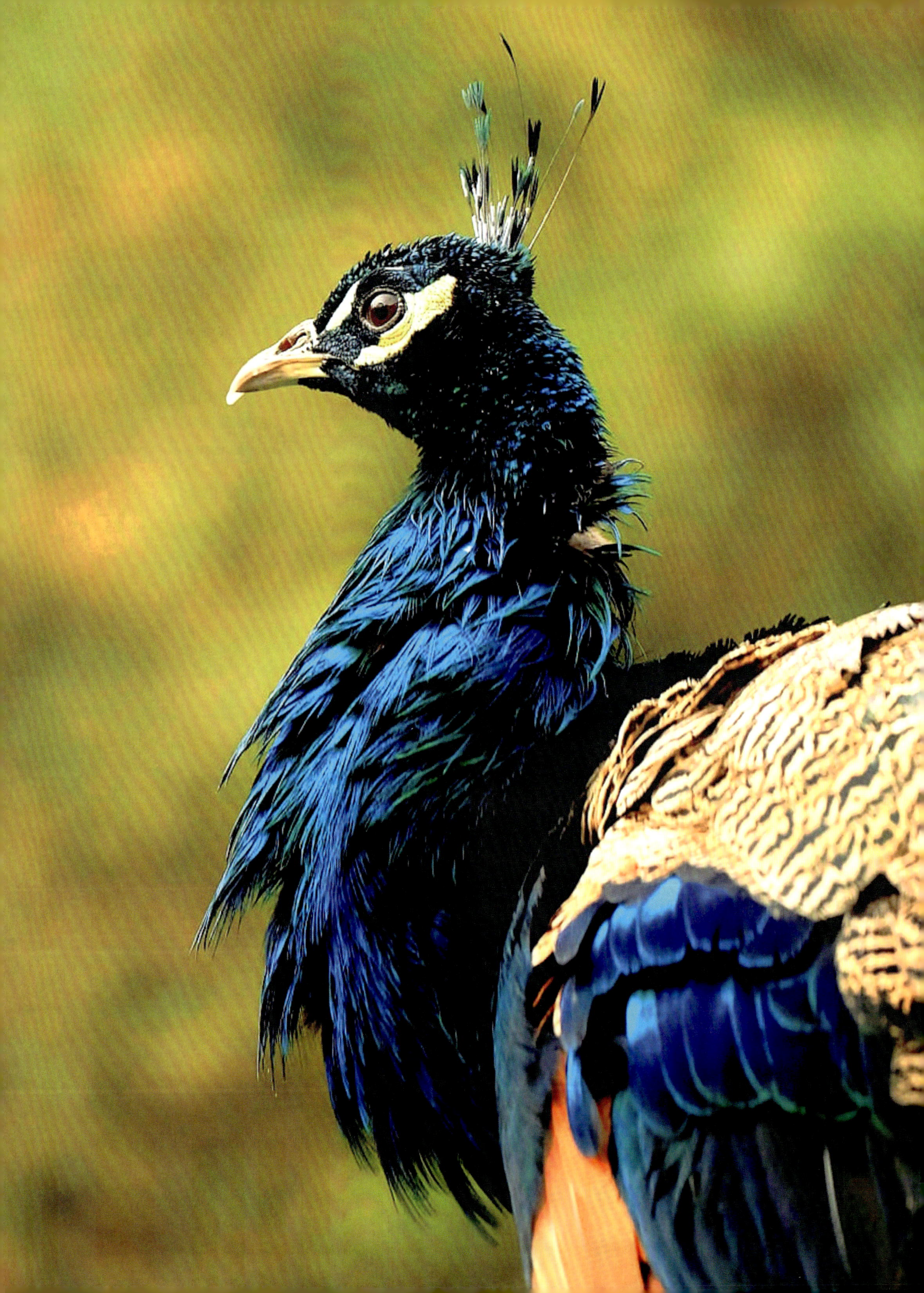

CHAPTER

5

Painting a Bird Using Three Colours and Black

We have spent the first part of this book looking at how to observe and render shape, tone and colour in watercolour. The beauty of learning these skills is that they are transferable. In many respects, if you can paint a bird, you can paint a variety of other animals. We will now commence our full-colour painting of a peacock using three primaries and a black. If you find it easier to paint from premixed colours, go for it!

PROJECT 5

Controlling colours – painting a peacock

For our first dive into controlling colours, I've chosen to study the peacock because of its limited colour palette of greens and blues, with just a couple of warmer notes for the eyes, beak and back.

If ever you feel overwhelmed when mixing colours, refer to the colour charts that you created on page 69. The chances are that you made up some of the colours inadvertently when you were playing around. So, have faith that you can do it!

Attention to detail with your colour choices will bring life to your piece and prevent it from looking flat and one-dimensional. By depicting tone through your colours, your subject will have depth, shape and interest.

You will need

- Photographic reference of a peacock
- Cutting mat and craft knife (optional)
- Paper: minimum 200 gsm, cold press, textured watercolour paper
- Paint: CMYK colour palette (p.158), either watercolour pan or tube, and French Ultramarine (optional)
- Brushes: synthetic round size 6 and size 12 brushes, size 0, 1 or 2 rigger brush and small detailer brush
- Wax-free transfer or tracing paper (optional)
- Palette, water container, paper towel
- Stationery: HB pencil, eraser, sharpener, white gel pen

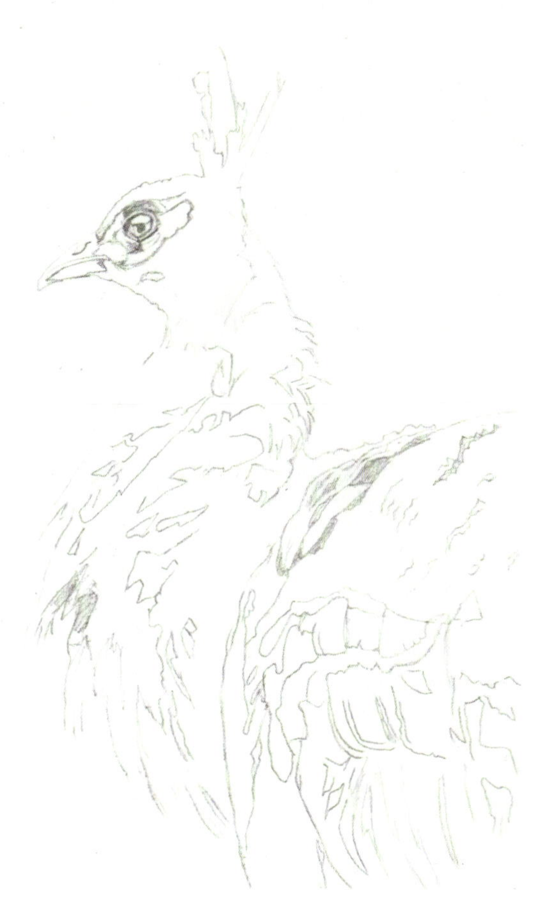

Top tip

To develop your drawing skills, I would thoroughly recommend *Drawing on the Right Side of the Brain* by Betty Edwards. It gives straightforward, scientifically backed advice and exercises on how to interpret the 3D world successfully on paper.

← Line drawing showing outline, major shapes and changes in tone.

DRAW THE OUTLINE

1 As with the previous projects, I start by creating a line drawing of the peacock, denoting both the outline of the bird and the changes in colour, tone and shape. With a watercolour piece I will normally trace or grid the image first to create a line drawing (see Chapters 1 and 3).

I think this is a good point at which to address one of the main issues I get in my mailbox. Many students get hung up on the idea of tracing, gridding or projecting their images when creating their underdrawing, as they think it's 'cheating'. My answer to this is simple. Freehand drawing is a joyful, meditative and skilful process, and one that I enjoy, especially when working on thumbnail sketches or exploring colour and style. However, when it comes to creating a large painting for a gallery, for me the drawing process is merely a means to an end. It is the foundation upon which the colour hangs, and for that reason it needs to be accurate. Once those colours drop on the page, most of your underdrawing all but disappears and you have to rely on traditional drawing methods, identifying shape, tone, texture, angles and proportion to create the piece.

In addition, many students feel embarrassed that they rely on photographs to depict their subject. They believe they aren't 'real artists' if they can't draw from memory in picture-perfect fashion. To put your mind at rest, I don't know many artists that can paint successful pieces without some type of reference, be it a life model, photograph or field study. I've even had students tell me that they had been told by old art teachers that erasing was cheating. Such advice can be debilitating, especially when given at a young age. Whatever your method for achieving that underdrawing – whether it be freehand or with the use of an aid – do it guilt-free and ignore the naysayers!

PRACTISE COLOUR MIXING

2 Experiment on spare watercolour paper, as you did in Chapter 4, to see what shades you can make. Royal blue is a particularly tricky colour to make in quantity and with speed, so I would recommend the addition of French Ultramarine for ease.

↑ This shows my attempts at making royal blue. After a couple of minutes I got there, but I was concerned that when it came to the painting process I wouldn't be able to make enough of it with sufficient speed and density. I opted to decant premixed French Ultramarine to make life easier!

Try not to jump to conclusions about a particular colour. It may take a while for you to adjust to seeing all these colours, but with the visual aids described in Chapter 4, and enough practice, this skill will develop over time.

PAINT THE PEACOCK

The peacock is almost a painting of two halves. Although it is tempting to wet the whole drawing and launch into applying both cool and warm colours, the chances are that they will all merge into each other and you'll end up with unwanted greys and greens in the wrong places. Therefore, when a bird, such as the peacock or kingfisher, has multiple sections of different colour temperatures, I will paint the various parts one at a time. With expressive painting, the trick is to make it look effortless even though a lot of thought has actually been put into the process and application.

First layer: Cool shades, light hues – head, neck and chest

3 Examine the lightest shades in the body and face. These are pale turquoise, yellow-greens and pale warm blues.

Activate your yellow, blue and black paints by adding a little water to part of the pigment just to loosen it up. Make up a few of the lighter colours in readiness so that you will be able to dip in and out of the colours with speed and without hesitation. This doesn't mean that the colours need to be spot on. Much of my process requires adjusting hues on the paper itself, as well as on the palette.

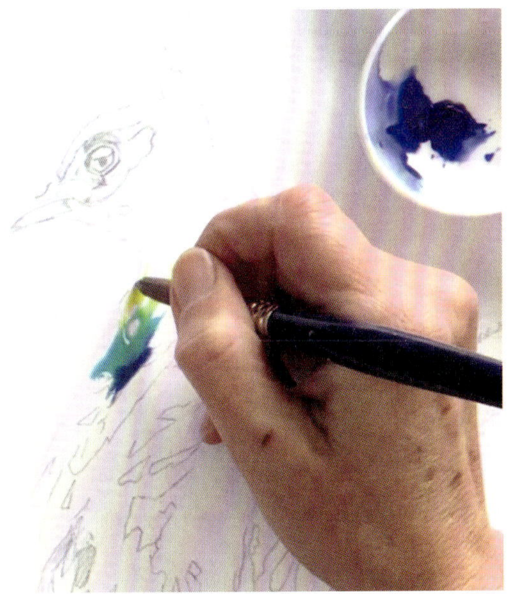

↑ Premixing a few colours allows you to drop one into the next with speed.

4 Working on dry paper, commence the process of laying down light swashes of paint, making sure each swipe of the brush links to the next one, continuously dipping into different hues to achieve a range of colours on the page.

Start with the neck of the peacock and then work up to the face. At this stage, it isn't important to have every hue spot on. Instead, look for an array of light colours that represent the hues that you're registering. In the cases where the lightest colour that you can see is 'black', go in with a very dark blue; using, for example, ultramarine and black at the base of the chest.

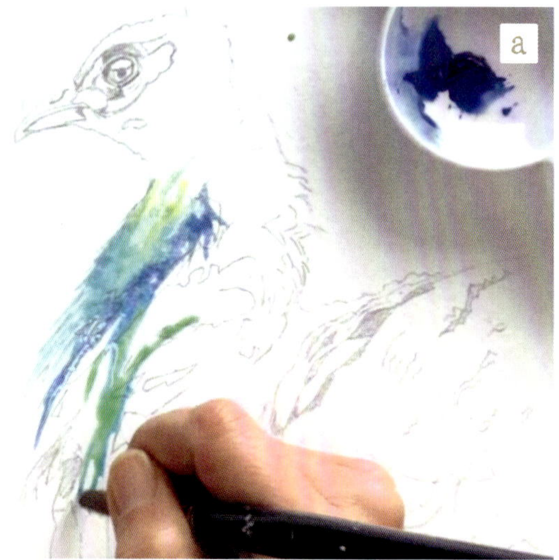

↑ Working wet-into-wet onto dry paper, using the tip of the brush in a fluid way to ensure the colours link up together and blend.

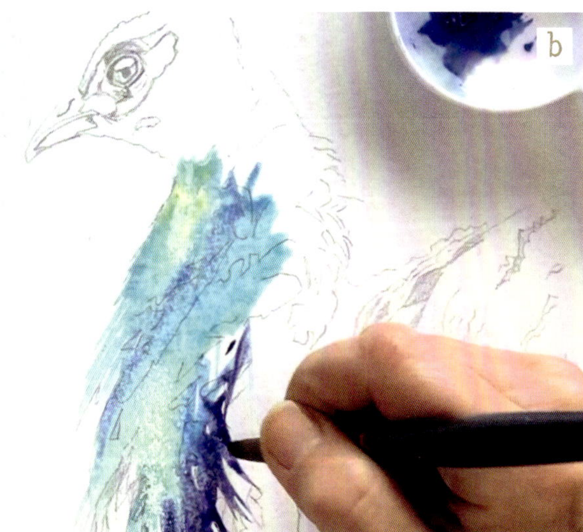

↑ Dropping thicker and darker tones into the mix with downward and upward swipes of the brush.

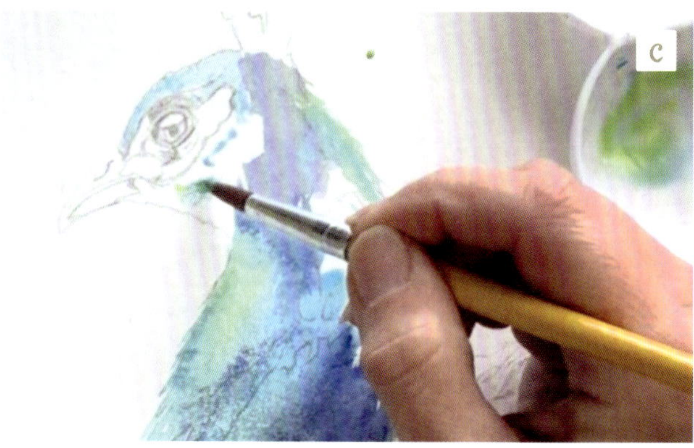

↑ A smaller size 6 synthetic brush was used for the facial features.

↓ Smaller feathers can be pulled out from the wet mix with a thin rigger brush.

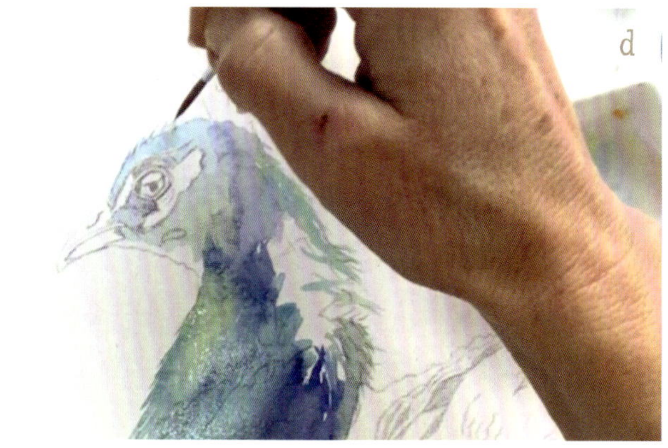

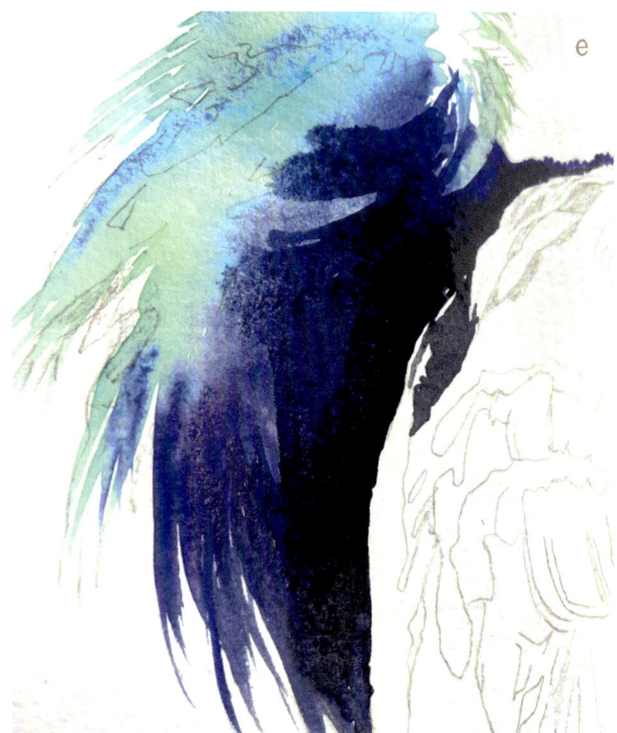

↑ Applying thicker paint into a damp (not wet) wash will give you soft, controlled edges.

5 Once I'd painted the majority of the head and chest, I decided to take a break and leave the back of the peacock's neck for another time. There was no logical reason for this; I simply needed my brain to reset. It's really important to take time out during the painting process to sit back and assess. When painting at full speed, you are making a quick succession of decisions about colour, tone, edge and shape, and it's easy to tire yourself out and get sloppy. I usually take this time out to clean my tools and make a cup of tea!

If you're painting along with me, once your piece has dried, take a good look at it. Examine the colour runs, the array of soft and hard edges and perhaps even the odd bloom. You will decide to keep some of these effects, some you may lift out, while others may eventually be buried under subsequent layers of paint. The main point is not to worry about them as this is your first layer, the 'ugly duckling' stage of the painting (see Chapter 6).

First layer: Cool shades, light hues – wings

6 Before starting this section, again study the photo, work out the lightest colours and make a couple of pools of turquoises and pale blues. Don't be overly concerned about the murkier pale shades showing on the photograph towards the base of the bird; you'll be able to desaturate these easily enough when you get to that point by dropping a little pink into the mix.

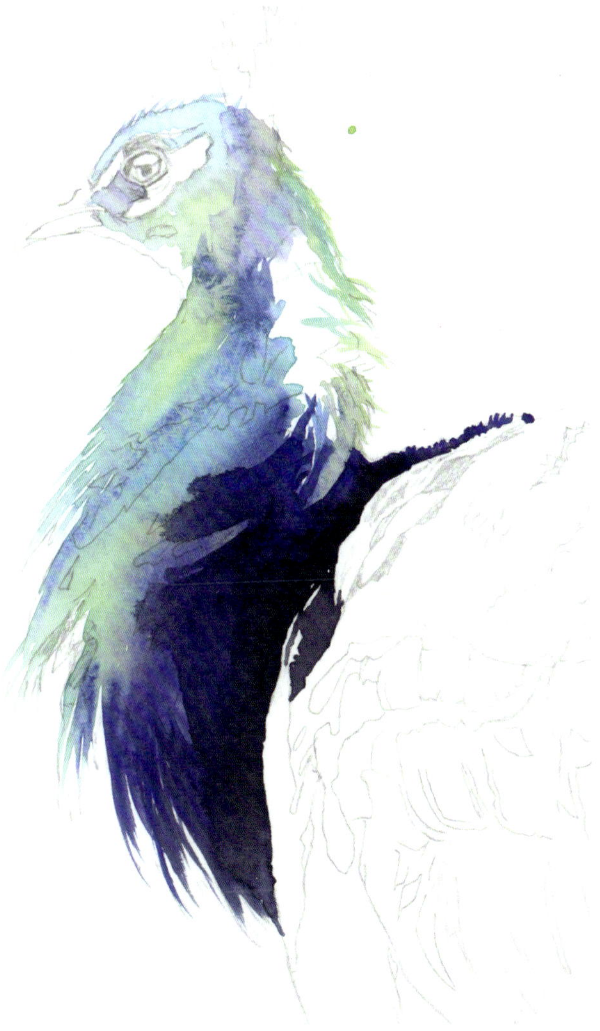

↑ The dried piece shows a mixture of blends with lost soft and hard edges. There are a number of blooms in the head and neck area, but these will be covered with subsequent marks.

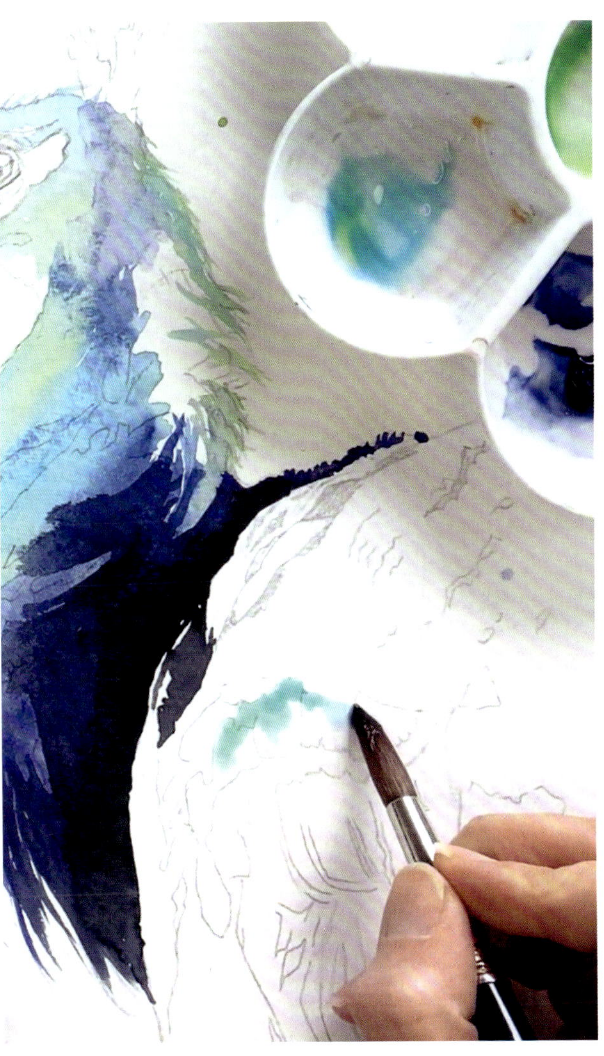

↑ Premix a variety of pale colours in your palette and let them blend on the paper.

7 Apply the light tones, making sure that the colours mingle and merge on the paper. As before, don't worry about being exact about the colours. Use the information on the photograph to give you some ideas as to the colours and tones you can use. At this stage, just concentrate on the lightest tones.

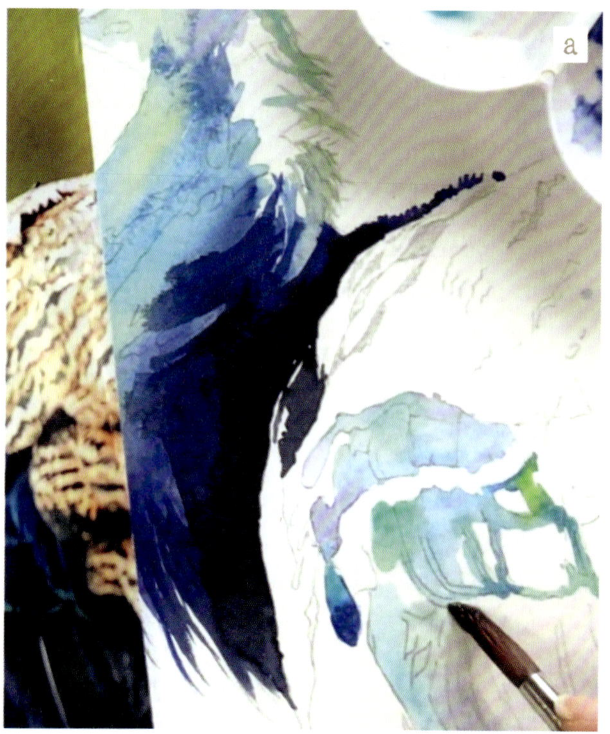

↑ There are some beautiful colours in the plumage. Cyan, yellow and ultramarine blue predominate in these sections.

By working with a variety of hues wet-into-wet, you will achieve some beautiful colours. Don't slavishly replicate the colours of the reference photo; just be inspired by them.

Once you have completed the light colours in this section, it's important to allow the paper to dry. Patience is key at this stage. The painting will start to make sense once the darker shades are applied, but if you apply them to the damp paper, they will completely obliterate the delicate, thin lines of light colour. By applying them to dry paper at a later stage, you will have maximum control and can soften the edges with clean water.

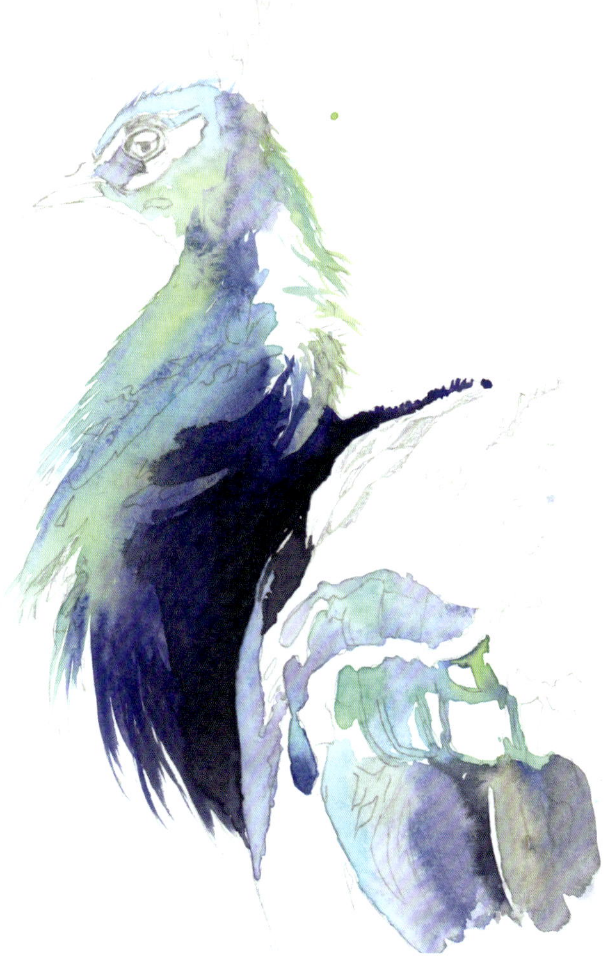

↑ Here you can see a bloom appearing between the lilac and blue section. This won't be noticeable once other layers have been added. Darker shades can be applied to the wings at a later stage, directly onto dry paper, with their edges softened with clean water.

Paint the eye

At this stage, it can be useful to complete the eye. This may seem inconvenient, as the eye is warm in tone and you most likely have cool colours on your palette and dirty water. However, painting the eye can help bring the piece to life, as well as creating some dark tones that will help inform your subsequent colour choices.

8 Make the warm, rich brown of the iris by mixing all three primaries, with an emphasis on magenta and yellow. If in doubt, look back to the autumnal colours you made in Chapter 4. Note that the reflected white is a very pale neutral colour tending towards a grey-brown hue.

On dry paper, start by painting the dark brown iris and then use a very diluted form of this colour, mixed with a little grey, for the reflected lights in the eye.

You may find it easier to turn the page and reference photo upside down to make it easier to paint the eye. Not only does this technique help you see shape more easily, it also makes practical sense so you don't drop your arm onto your damp work!

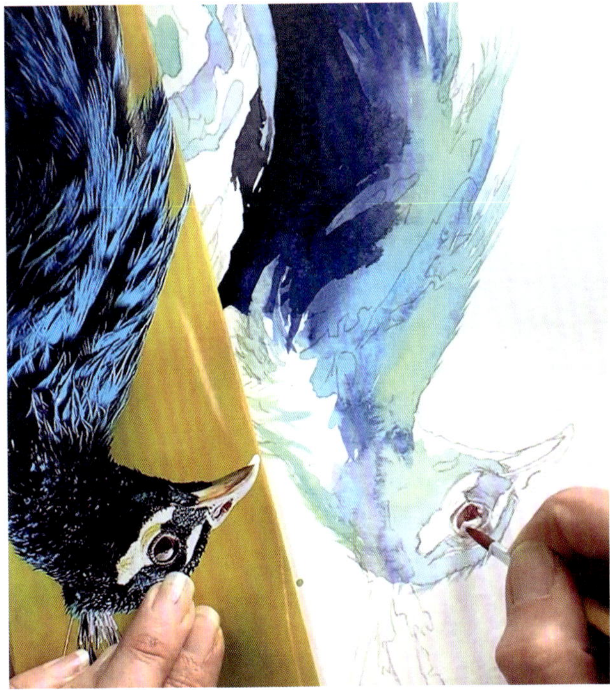

↑ Painting something upside down can help you to judge shapes and their relationships with each other more clearly.

9 Once dry, create the pupil by using a dense black, using more black just above the eyeball and around the eyelid. Do not paint a rigid solid line of black; instead, lightly dab black paint on the paper to mimic the shape of the lid's shadow. Needless to say, a thin brush and steady hand are useful!

Top tip

If your hands are shaky, rest your working arm and hand firmly on the table and apply pressure to that arm with your free hand. This has the effect of stabilising it. Also, make sure you have eaten!

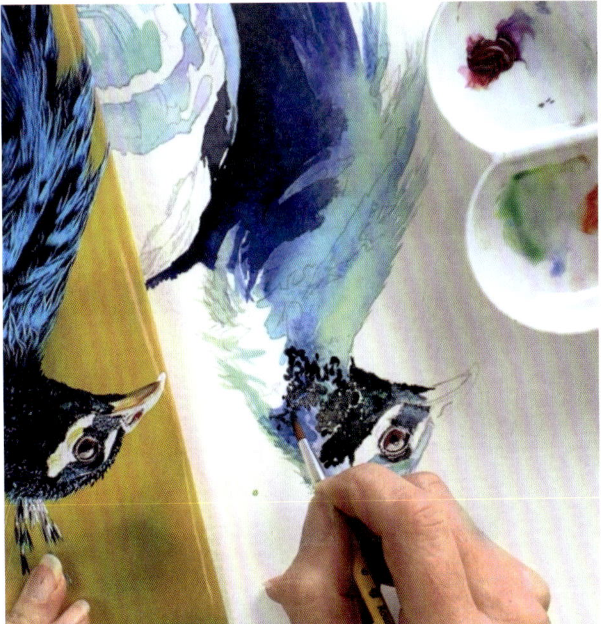

↑ Use a fast-paced dabbing motion when applying paint to this section. This will help you to maintain pockets of light and thus prevents the undercolours being completely swamped by the new layer of darker pigment.

10 When the eye is complete, you may need to reapply some punchier greens and blues on the face. Once done, drop thicker black pigment around these colours so they gently merge and blend without overpowering the lighter shades. This is where practice in terms of pigment control and timing is essential.

If your colours or paper are too watery, you can end up with colours bleeding excessively into each other. Ensure that your thicker pigments are applied to the wetter ones underneath just as the latter are beginning to dry out, to avoid this problem. Damp paper, as opposed to sodden paper, is great for achieving soft edges and blends.

Second layer: Add depth and detail to the face, neck and wings

11 Use a rigger or detailer brush to pull out some of the finer wisps of feathers as you work around the head and neck.

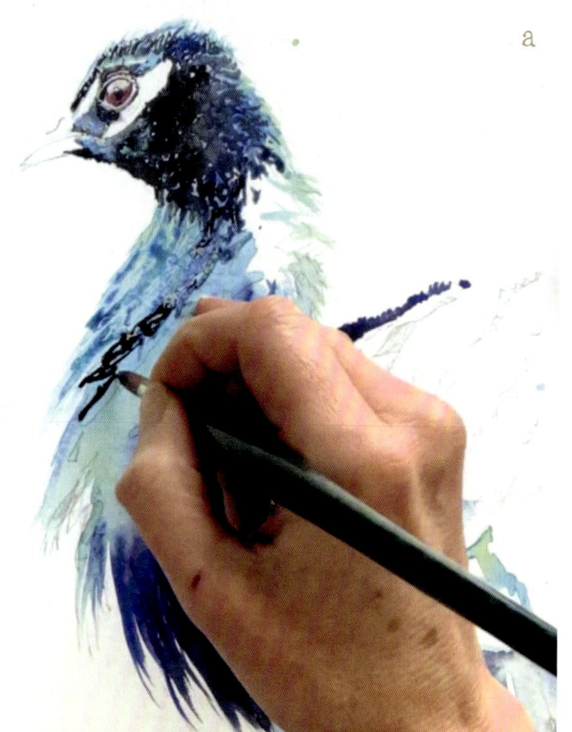

↑ Use the photo as a guide only to replicate the sweep of the feathers. You won't have time to meticulously depict every section. It's more important to get the paint moving on the page, ensuring that multiple colours run into each other and merge. This is where the magic of watercolour happens!

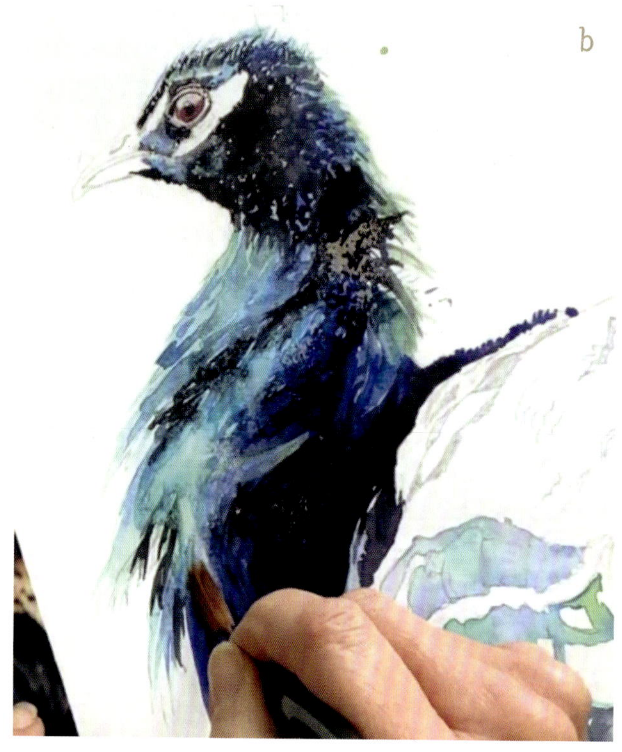

↑ Firm swipes down with a damp brush, and excess moisture absorbed with a paper towel, can help lift overworked sections.

12 Once the head and face are complete, move on to the neck and chest. As with the face, lay another thin wash of transparent pigment over the brighter colours to make them pop. I tend to do this in a fairly haphazard manner to allow pockets of undercolours to show through the newly applied paint. Once these have settled down, apply a blue/ black paint mix, sweeping up and down with a rigger brush and size 12 round brush in the general direction of the feathers. Lift any overworked sections with a thirsty brush. Allow any lifted areas to dry before adding more pigment.

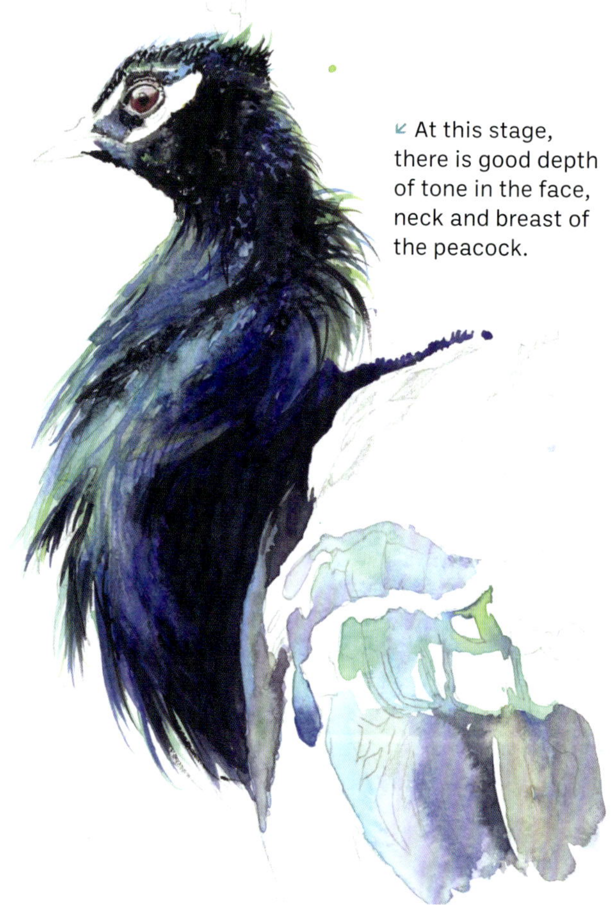

↙ At this stage, there is good depth of tone in the face, neck and breast of the peacock.

13 Turn your attention to the feathered regions on the side of the body. Make up some pools of bright and very dark blues. Ensure this section is completely dry before carefully cutting in shapes with the mixture of bright and dark blues, allowing slithers of the light undercolours to show through.

With the paper being dry underneath, you will have complete control over this area, enabling you to carve out hard edges. (The importance of edge control will be covered in the next chapter, but suffice it to say that much of the shadow work in this area will contain hard, dark edges that are best achieved by painting on dry paper.)

↑ The brighter and darker blues pull the piece together so it starts to make sense. If the slithers of light are too bright in the wing section and their edges too hard, you can 'knock them back' towards the end of the painting process with a mixture of blending, softening and colour application.

The transparent nature of the watercolour will allow you to eventually glaze over the larger sections of the feathers with the darker blues, but hold back from completely obliterating the beautiful pale green/turquoise undercolours that were created on the first layer.

Paint warm colours on the beak, face and body

14 When changing from cool to warm colours, I always make a point of changing my water and cleaning my palette. This is especially important if you are going to be applying pure, fresh colours. A little blue in your magenta-yellow mixes and those beautiful pale peaches will turn into a desaturated taupe – still a lovely colour, but unnecessary just yet.

15 Mix up a range of warm, autumnal colours in your palette; some runny, with the darker ones being creamier in consistency. Apply your warm colours onto dry paper, starting with your lightest tones and then dropping in the thicker, darker colours while still wet. This will help you to achieve soft blends.

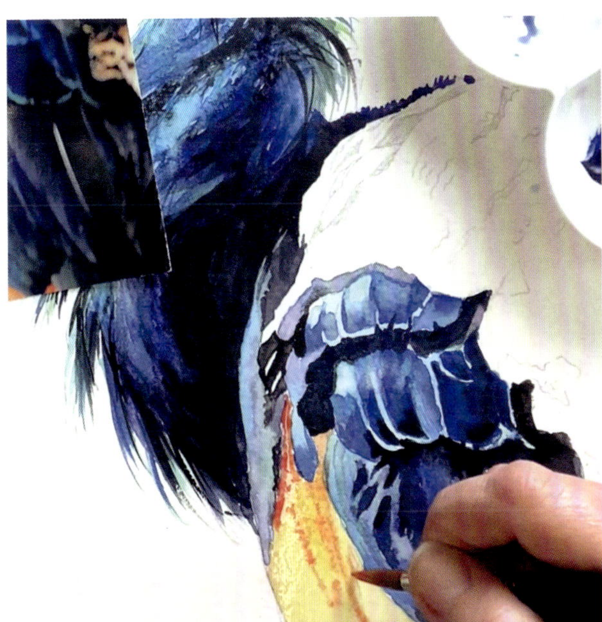

↑ Dropping creamier darker paint into a lighter wash will give you beautiful soft edges and great colour combinations.

16 Continue to add warm tones to the peacock's body and back, making sure that you alter your strokes and depth of colour according to the information in the photograph. Working on dry paper will give you maximum control, but it will lead to lots of hard edges. To overcome this, soften edges by introducing water to the colour on the paper and dragging the brush, side-on, across the page.

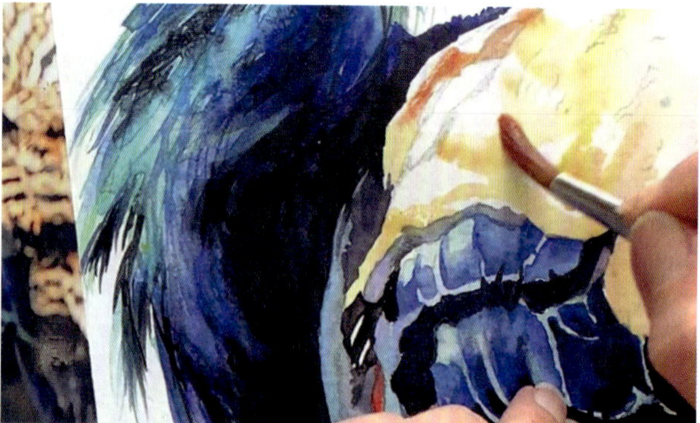

↑ Ensure you leave pockets of paper showing through for maximum light.

17 When adding the smaller details, it's important that this section doesn't get too busy and that you don't get bogged down in minutiae. Apply a variety of shapes to the back of the peacock using a range of paint consistencies. The shapes don't need to be replicated exactly; be inventive with your mark making.

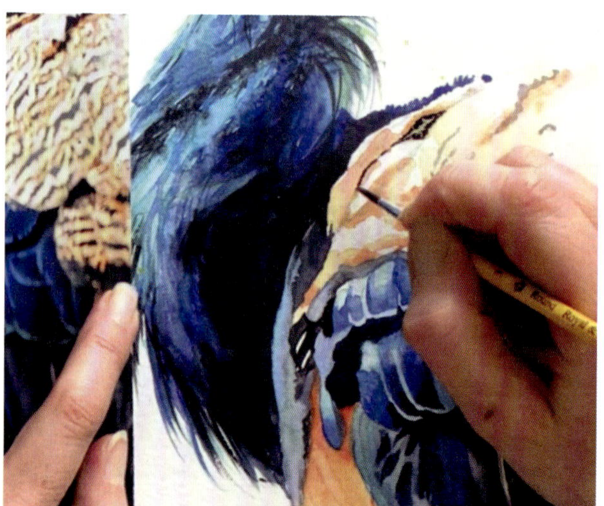

↑ I used a smaller size 3 round brush for this part of the process as it was what I had to hand, but the tip of a size 6 will also suffice. Sometimes I used the point of the brush and other times I simply swept the brush side-on to create more abstract shapes.

Finishing touches: Adjust the tones and add gel pen work

18 As a finishing touch, you may find that the light slithers in the blue wing section need to be pared back a little. If this is the case, just drop a light glaze of blue over any areas that are too bright and the sections will settle into place visually.

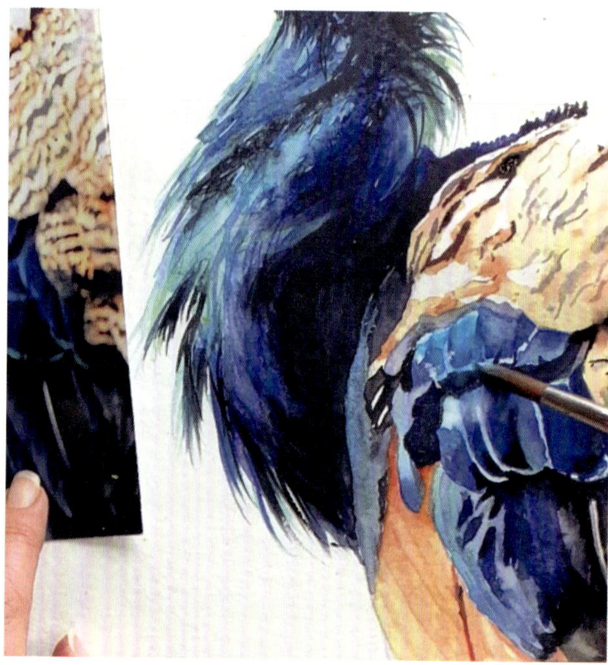

↑ Knocking back the light colours in this section means that they won't stand out so much. This is important as they would otherwise have been a distraction in the overall composition.

19 I added just a few squiggly lines with a white gel pen to break up the dark shapes in the neck. It wasn't risky because it lifts pretty easily off the paint that I use. I also added splashes to the piece. I normally use just a couple of colours for these and am mindful that they need to aid – and not ruin – the composition. I always have a clean pot of water and tissue ready, just in case they end up falling in the wrong place.

How much is too much detail?

There is no right or wrong answer to this; it really is a matter of personal preference and your natural style as an artist. Get creative with your finishing touches and you'll be pleasantly surprised by the results.

I hope that you enjoyed painting this peacock. Chickens, together with pheasants and turkeys, are amongst the peacock's many feathered cousins and they give us the ideal opportunity of going to town with expressive strokes for the dramatic tail feathers, and making the most of their stunning iridescent plumage. In 'Cock-a-hoot', you can see that the palette was made up of cool greys and warm golds and reds, in much the same way as the peacock balanced warm and cool colours.

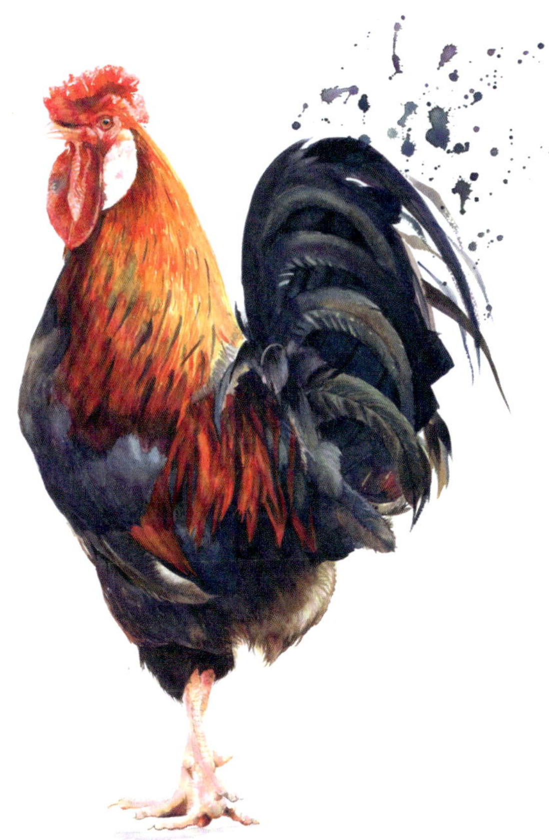

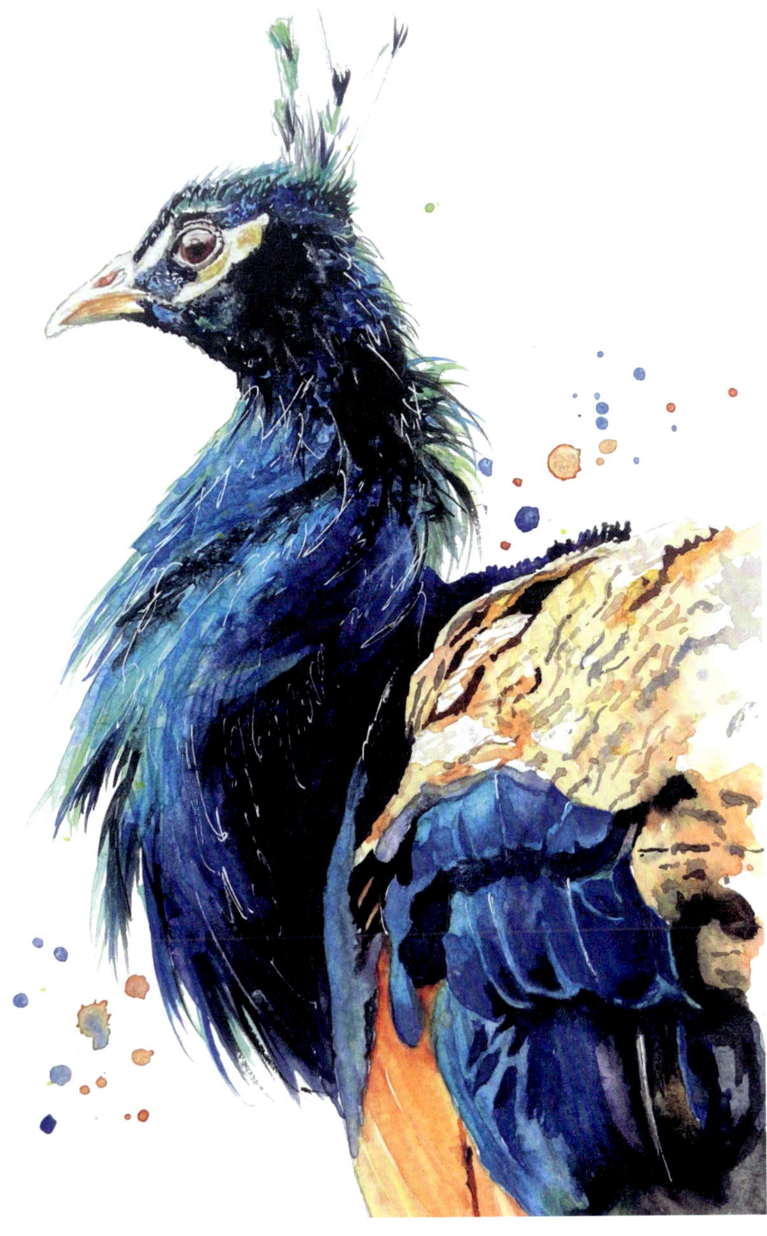

↑ 'Cock-a-hoot', 2018, watercolour. Don't be intimidated by abstract concepts such as iridescence or shininess. Replicating these factors is down to the colour, tone, shape and edge.

← The finished peacock.

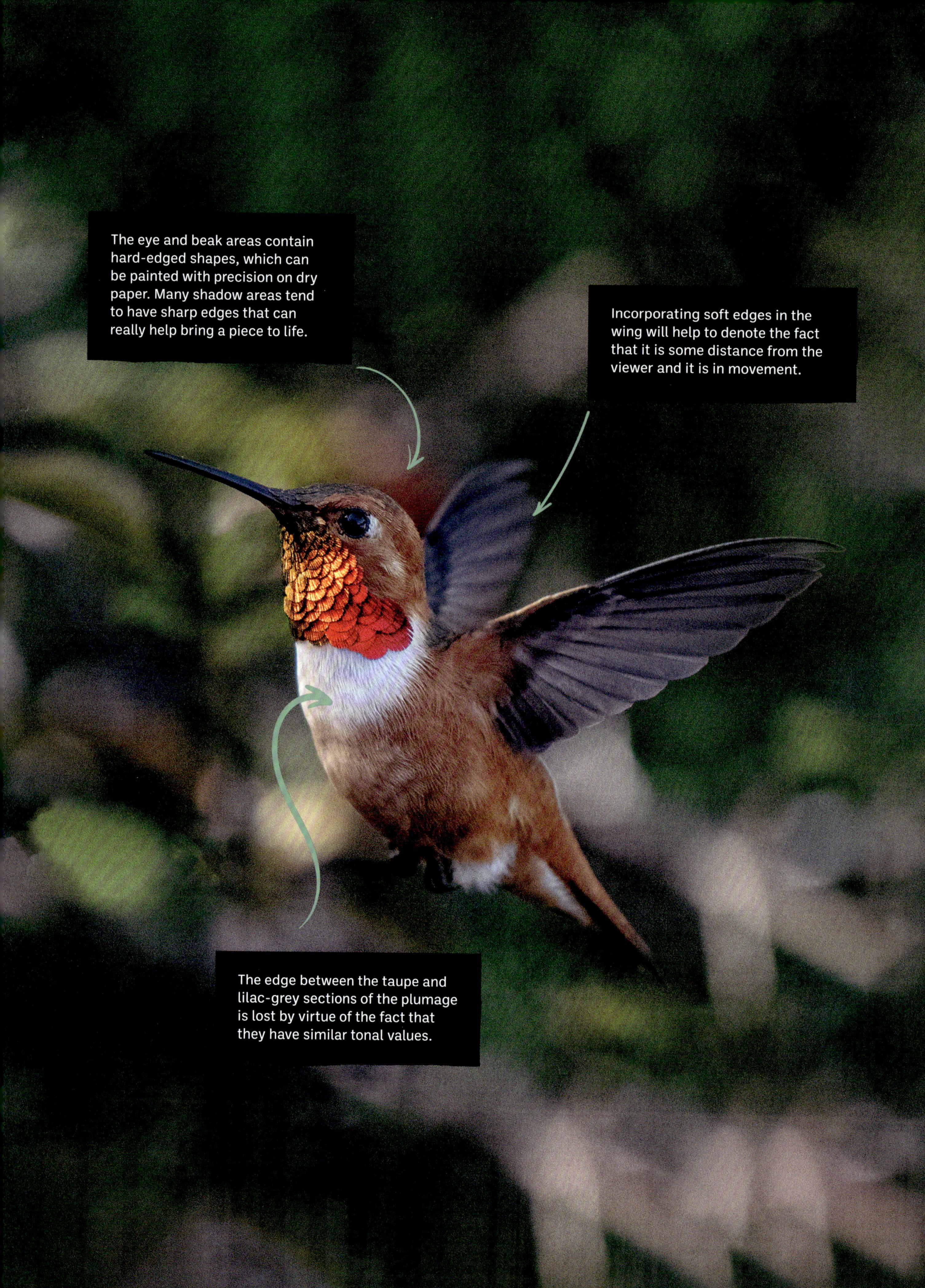
The eye and beak areas contain hard-edged shapes, which can be painted with precision on dry paper. Many shadow areas tend to have sharp edges that can really help bring a piece to life.
Incorporating soft edges in the wing will help to denote the fact that it is some distance from the viewer and it is in movement.
The edge between the taupe and lilac-grey sections of the plumage is lost by virtue of the fact that they have similar tonal values.

The Importance of Edges

I remember coming across the concept of edges just a few years ago and it hadn't previously been an aspect of painting I'd given much thought to. It transpires that it's an incredibly important consideration. Edges in art refer to the transition between two shapes of colour. These could be the edges revealed around the perimeter of your subject as well as those found within its features. There is a full range of edges, from hard to soft to lost.

What is an edge?

Generally speaking, a harsh edge, defined by a change in colour, tone or line, will attract the eye. Too many hard edges in a piece can make the painting look flat and lifeless. Adding lost edges in your piece, created through careful application of colour and tone, lifting and blending, is critical in so many respects. Lost edges can aid composition and help denote textures such as feathers and markings, as well as more abstract concepts such as transparency. What better bird to practise edge control with than a hummingbird?

I will be referring to edges extensively in the book until they become second nature. I'll show you how to lose or achieve edges, predominantly through moisture control and brushwork. The concept of edges can be demonstrated in photographic format using this hummingbird photograph as an example.

Hard edges

This close-up of the hummingbird's head shows examples of hard edges that can be found around the eye, beak and throat on a bird. They can be suggested in a painting by:

- Creating definitive line work
- Applying marks of opposing colour and tone

Soft edges

This section of the hummingbird's wing shows a range of soft edges. They can be suggested in a painting by:

- Creating lost and found lines
- Graduating washes
- Blending and softening with a brush
- Working on wet and damp paper

Lost edges

Lost edges can be found in certain sections of the plumage. They can be achieved by:

- Removing harsh lines through lifting, blending and bleeding out techniques with brushwork and water
- Applying colours of similar chroma and/or tone to neighbouring shapes

PROJECT 6

Depicting feathers, capturing light and movement – painting a hummingbird

I have chosen a beautiful ruby-throated hummingbird as the basis of this study because it incorporates a multitude of challenging features. During the process you'll get to practise creating the outstretched transparent wings through paint and edge control; the off-white shades of the chest through correct colour mixing; the illusion of iridescence in the plumage through shadow colour placement; and the general fluffiness of the bird through lifting and blending techniques.

DRAW THE HUMMINGBIRD

Draw out the shape of the bird (see Chapters 1 and 3).

↑ The drawing indicates changes of colour and tone in both the larger and smaller areas of the bird.

You will need

- Photographic reference of a hummingbird
- Cutting mat and craft knife (optional)
- Paper: minimum 200 gsm, cold press, textured watercolour paper
- Paint: CMYK colour palette (p.158), either watercolour pan or tube, and Burnt Sienna and Indigo premixed paints (optional)
- Brushes: synthetic round size 6 and small detailer brushes
- Wax-free transfer or tracing paper (optional)
- Palette, water container, paper towel
- Stationery: HB pencil, eraser, sharpener, white gel pen

SEE THE LIGHTEST COLOURS AND SHAPES AND PLAN THE FIRST WASH

1 At this planning stage, look at what shades are going to form the first wash of the bird, starting with the lightest areas at the top of the chest and the base of the body. These are pale lilacs and blues, with similar hues in the vast majority of the outstretched wings. I used blues and pinks to make these colours, but you can experiment with a viewing aperture (see Chapter 4) and your own colours to come up with suitable shades. Create a variety of shades so that you are not applying a wash of just one shade of lilac. I tend to have three pools of colour to hand on my palette for each section.

Mix some slightly thicker pools of rich golden-brown pigments using Burnt Sienna and Indigo in varying ratios for the head and body. By premixing these, you will have them to hand to drop onto the lilac wash at its damp stage, which will then create soft blends. Allow this section to dry.

Significantly, I wouldn't do anything with the iridescent throat area at this stage as the colours are so vastly different from the rest of the bird. I wouldn't want to risk desaturating any of those beautifully bright colours by inadvertently neutralising them with other colours.

APPLY THE FIRST WASH: WET ONTO DRY AND CREAMY INTO DAMP

2 With your pools of colours already to hand, paint the very pale lilacs and blues onto the dry paper with precision and speed, using a round size 6 brush, or similar. Wait until the paper loses its sheen a little. As soon as it is damp, drop on the warm browns of the body.

Look at how the paint moves, and adjust accordingly. If paint drifts into lighter areas, remove it with a thirsty brush. If it needs darkening, create a thicker, denser pool of rich brown and spot these colours onto the still-damp underlayer, being sure to leave small gaps between each colour to give them space to move and merge. Allow the piece to dry to avoid overworking it.

PAINT THE REMAINDER OF THE FIRST LAYER

3 Mix up a selection of pale and darker warm blues for the wings. Working on dry paper and starting with the nearest outstretched wing, apply a wash of pale blue to the whole area, followed by a darker smattering of paint along the top edge. Allow the colours to merge on the page. This is a bird in flight, so you don't want to be over-detailed in this section – a rough approximation is fine. Remember how you created the egret in flight (Chapter 3) and keep it as loose as possible.

4 Keep things interesting by altering your shade of blue with colours that inspire you in the photo. I added a little magenta at the base of the wing. Be careful not to overwork this area; it can always be returned to at a later stage. Allow it to dry and add pale shades to the base of the bird and the other wing.

↗ This layer contains beautiful soft edges but also unwanted hard edges between the lilac throat and brown body. These can be blended out at a later stage. Remember this is only the first layer, so many of the problematic areas can be fixed or painted over in later stages.

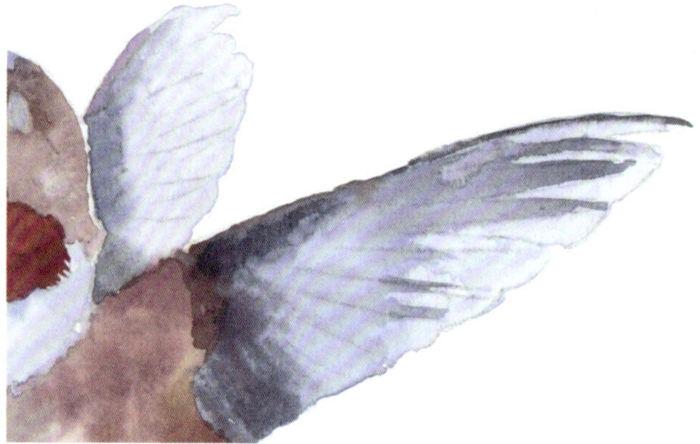

↑ Creamier, darker blue has been dropped onto the damp pale blue underneath, where the wing meets the body, to ensure soft edges and blends.

5 Now for the head. Study the lighter shades in the photographic reference and make sure that you have some preliminary colours made up in your palette. Now drop in the pale blues and warm browns accordingly, avoiding the throat areas, which will be reserved for pure yellow and red.

6 Create greyer, darker tones for the lower half of the beak. This is a similar shade to that of the feet, so they can also be completed at this stage while the paint is on your brush.

7 For the throat itself, establish the lightest yellow (using a very watery mix of yellow paint) and the lightest crimson and apply them to the dry section of the paper. A mixture of magenta and yellow in varying amounts will make you some beautiful reds. A tiny touch of blue or black will make them more crimson in appearance.

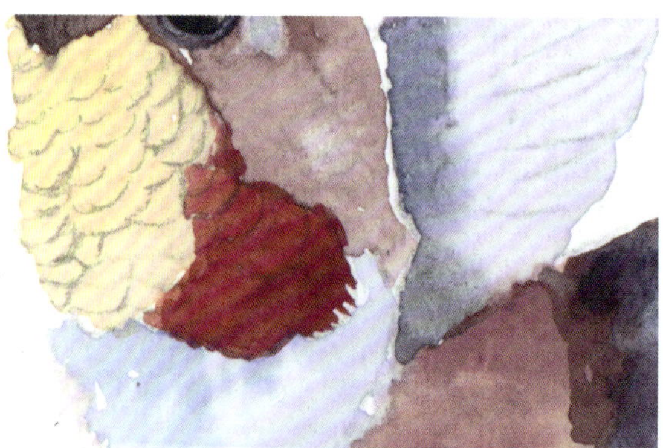

↑ There is no rushing the iridescent stage. It will take a mixture of colours and edges to make it look convincing. The best place to start is by dropping in the lightest colours you can see first.

PAINT THE EYE

8 At this point, I enjoy painting the eye in its totality. As it normally features some of the darkest darks, it can help me to gauge the tonal values for the rest of the piece. It can also quickly bring life to a painting, giving me the encouragement and energy to continue the process. You may find it easier to spin your painting and reference photo around to a more comfortable angle at this stage.

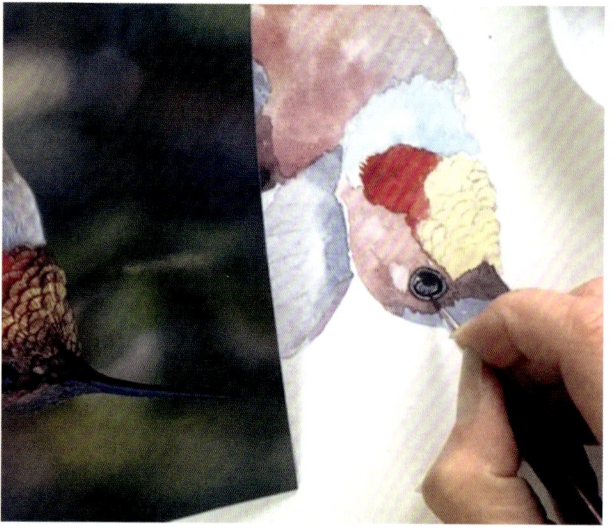

↑ I often turn my paintings upside down when it comes to painting faces. This is a comfortable position and means that I'm not in danger of dropping my arm into wet paint.

9 Painting eyes can sometimes intimidate students but if you work slowly, methodically and logically, it can be one of the most rewarding parts to complete. As with every other section, identify and paint the lightest section of the eye first. In this case it is the crescent of reflected light. Using a fine detailer brush, apply light blue/magenta mixes to the dry paper and, while damp, drop in darker blues to create the softness in the top half of the iris.

10 Once dry, add black to indicate the pupil and shadow area around the iris. This part of the process is quite fiddly and not at all loose or expressive, but I love the sense of reality that a well-painted eye can give to a piece.

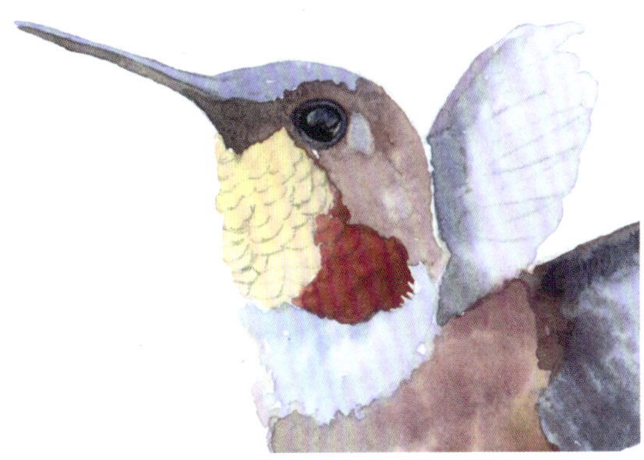

↑ The eye is made up of an array of edges and tones. Painting it with accuracy will lead to a convincing, spherical, shiny eye.

11 Allow your painting to dry, ready for the all-important final layers.

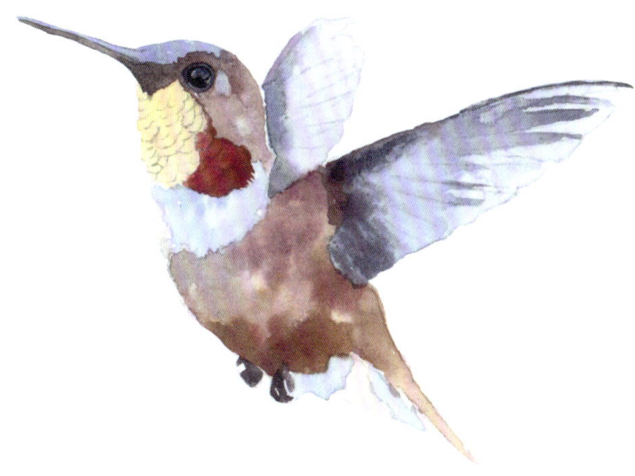

↑ The painting will now be at the 'ugly duckling' stage, looking like a wishy-washy patchwork of shapes. Take heart in the fact that it will pull together in the next stage.

APPLY SUBSEQUENT LAYERS

12 Once the first layers have dried, work around the piece in an order of your choice. As with the peacock (see Chapter 5), your second layer is concerned with adding brighter glazes, depth of tone and more defined shapes, as well as correcting overworked areas and softening unwanted edges.

Generally speaking, work wet (paint) onto dry (paper), allowing the multiple colours of paint to blend on the page, while coaxing them gently into the right direction with both the tip and, occasionally, with a side sweep of the brush. Soften edges by 'bleeding' out the pigment with pure water.

As sections start to dry, continue to assess and react. Ask yourself: 'Do I need to add pops of colour or darker shades, or to lift paint with a thirsty brush?' This damp stage is an ideal time to do any or all of these things. Throughout the process, constantly check your tones, colours and edges. As I mentioned before, they can all look so different when they are sitting next to new neighbours.

Don't completely paint over the first layer. Rather, ensure that sections of the previous layer pop through to create depth and interest. Also try to resist the temptation of overworking a layer. I understand the feeling of wanting to get a section completely finished, but if the paper becomes too wet with marks, any further work becomes counterproductive. Let the section dry and continue to work on another portion of the painting. Knowing when to stop and when to allow the paper to dry comes with experience, but hopefully the scanned images of my stages will help give you an idea.

I'm often asked how many layers to apply, but I'm wary of prescribing a fixed number as everyone will have their own techniques. In my particular case, I apply around two or three layers, depending on the level of complexity of any given section.

The 'ugly duckling to swan' phenomenon in art

It's amazing how layers bring depth to a painting. So many students give up halfway through a piece, when it's just a question of strengthening tones and shape. I thought it might be useful to lay the images side by side so you can see the magic that happens through the layering process.

Body

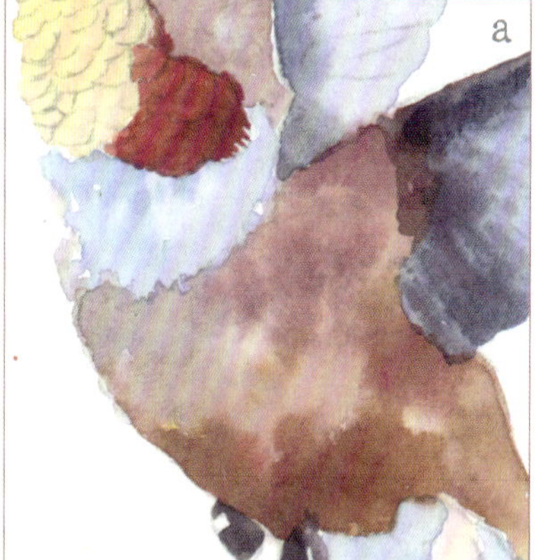

↑ The blue throat and brown body contain a multitude of colours, achieved by adding creamy paint into light washes.

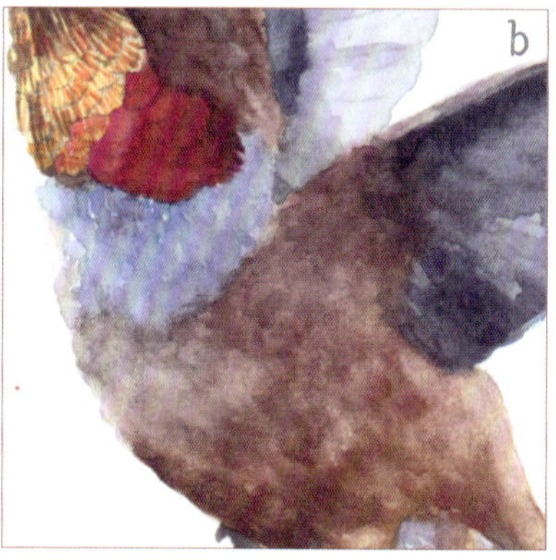

↑ The harsh edge that lay between the cool and warm colours is no longer apparent with the application of the next layer.

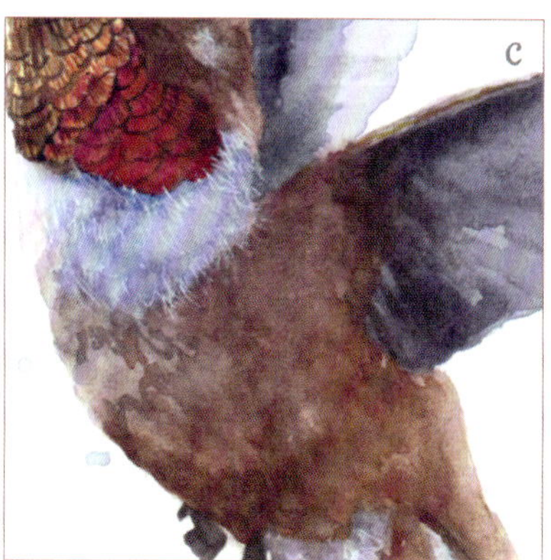

↑ Gel pen has been added to the throat area for texture and interest.

Throat

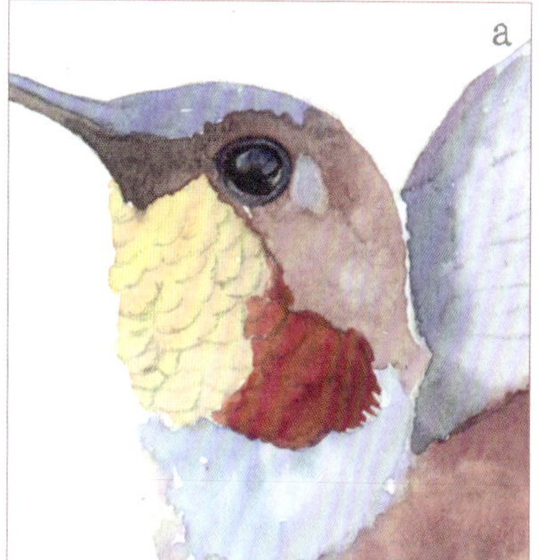

↑ Pale yellow and red are the lightest shades within the throat area, so it is with these that the first layer is painted.

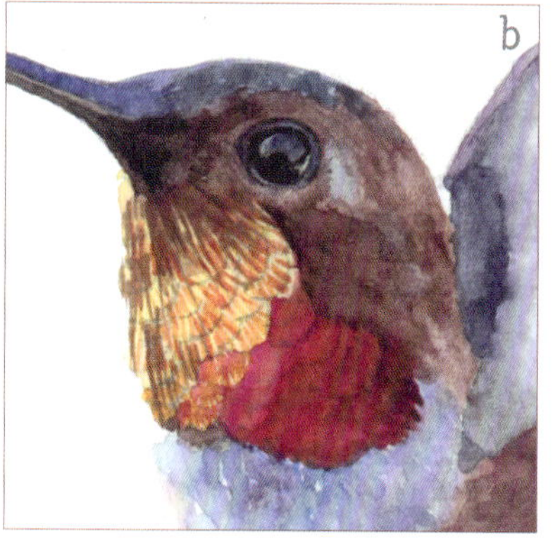

↑ By the time you've overlaid a variety of colours on top of the pale yellow, very little of the original yellow actually shows.

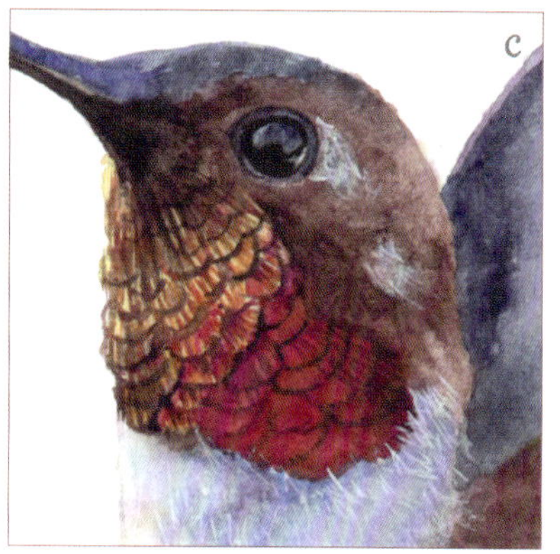

↑ Even the hard-edged shadow areas contain a multitude of colours and tones. They are not simply black.

Wings

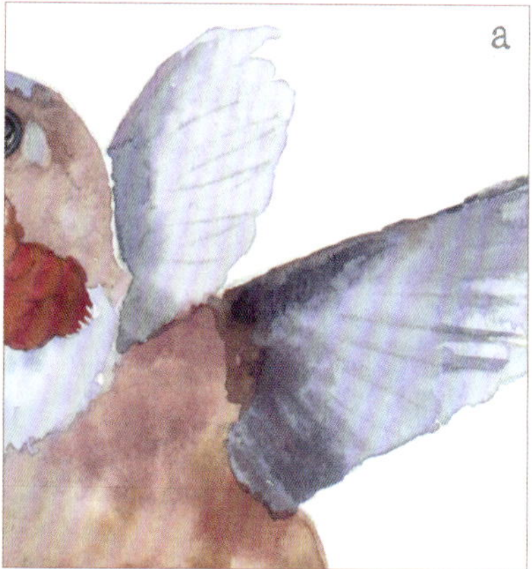

↑ Crimsons and blues were added to the wings in the first layer for depth and interest.

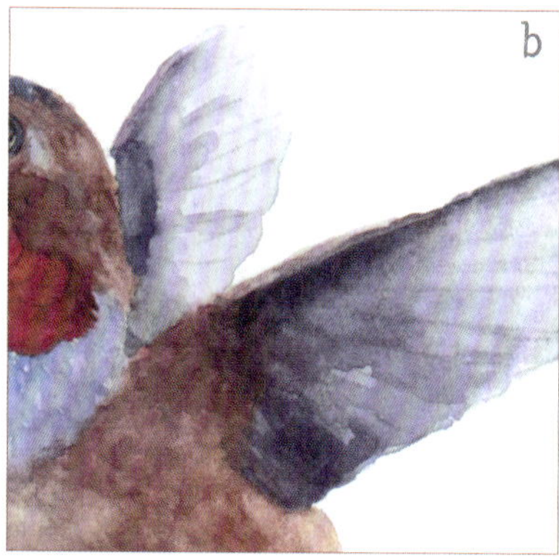

↑ Some of the marks originally made in the front wing were subsequently lifted out with a damp brush, as I wanted to get a sense of movement in the wing.

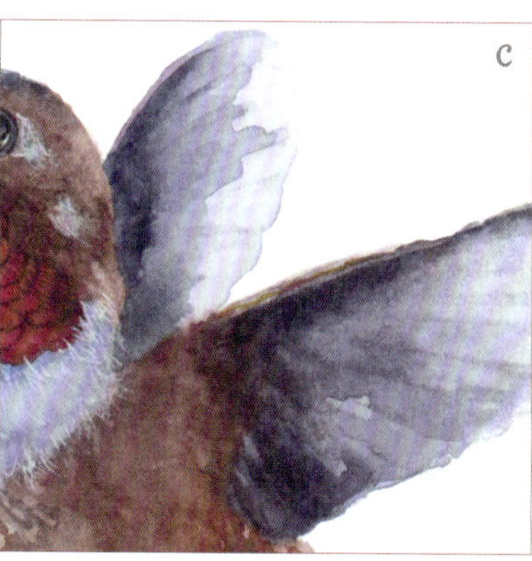

↑ Some of the marks on the back wing were altered and strengthened on the second layer.

Whole piece

→ The 'ugly duckling' stage of a painting is enough to dishearten even a seasoned painter!

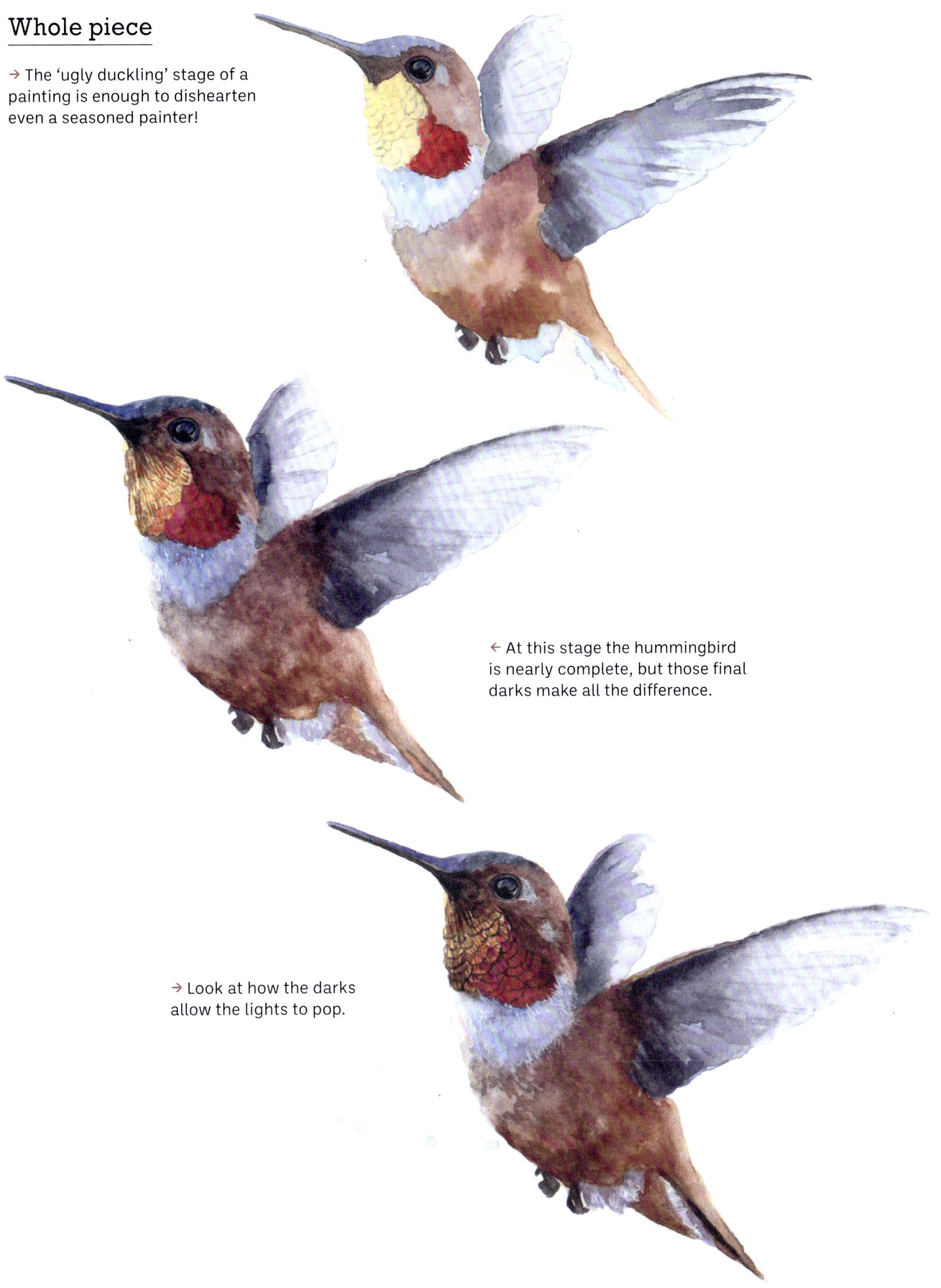

← At this stage the hummingbird is nearly complete, but those final darks make all the difference.

→ Look at how the darks allow the lights to pop.

Iridescence

It's easy to be intimidated by areas that are iridescent or shiny. It's important to remind ourselves that this is just colour, tone and edge applied in the right shape.

Conversely, like a magpie drawn to a bright, shiny object, I have sometimes launched in too quickly painting with myriad colours, with little thought to the process, and ended up with a disappointingly shapeless, oversaturated mess on the page, with little definition or form. We often put unrealistic expectations on ourselves, thinking we can achieve such luminosity with just a few swift, intuitive, joyful strokes of the brush. However, I have rarely found this to be the case. This doesn't sound very expressive, I know, but as I said in my introduction, not every section of your painting needs to be painted in a loose, whimsical fashion.

MY GOLDEN TIPS FOR IRIDESCENCE AND FEATHERS

- Paint what you see, not what you think you see.
- Embracing the darks and neutrals will help your saturated colours pop.
- Take your time.
- Paint with a degree of precision, even if you choose to loosen up or omit certain sections completely.
- Lift paint if necessary to regain lights and give an air of transparency.
- Pay close attention to your edges, blending and lifting them to create softer, lost edges to denote fluffiness.

Fine-tuning and troubleshooting a piece

Sometimes when you have completed a piece, something bothers you about it that you just can't put your finger on. In my experience, it can be down to a combination of the following factors.

A LACK OF OVERALL HARMONY OR PIZZAZZ

Sometimes a piece just doesn't gel. It lacks flow, harmony or punch. It could be that the colours chosen are too disparate. A viewer's eyes seek harmony and balance. Try to replicate certain colours in different parts of the bird, the background or splashes. In my hummingbird, I used the same pale lilac colours in the chest as I did in the tail. The indigo that I used in the wings is also replicated in the beak and feet.

On occasion, I have found that adding a very light transparent glaze to a key area is enough to tie in different sections. Another aspect to check is your colour temperature: it may be that your piece is too warm or cool overall. I prefer a painting that has a mixture of both types of colour hue. Even this predominantly warm hummingbird has the cooler shades of indigo and alizarin crimson in addition to the warmer yellow, orange and red shades. Try modifying some of the sections by lifting and then adding paint of the desired temperature.

AN OVERWORKED AREA

Sometimes, I inadvertently overwork a section of a bird, quite often in the breast or belly area. This normally happens when I've applied too many layers, or too thick a consistency, or used a pigment that is too opaque for the job; the whole section looks flat and uninspiring and I lose the luminosity.

If this is the case, I use a small scrubbing brush to lightly agitate the area. As the paint starts to lift, I remove it with a scrunched-up piece of kitchen roll. The underlying damp paper is normally stained with

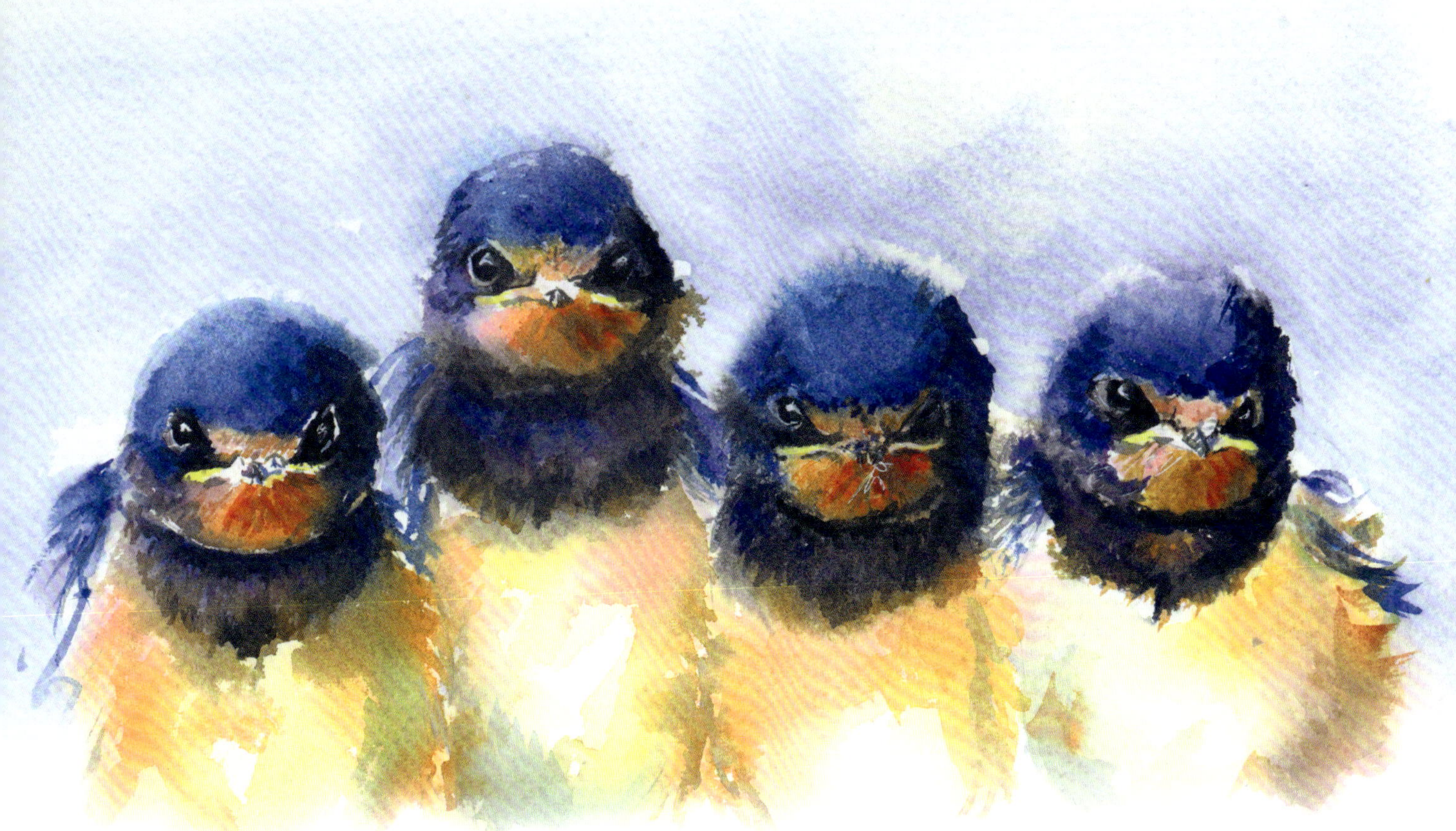

the previous paint, which I then go on to treat as if it was the first wash. I add thicker pigment, as usual, but this time, being mindful of going a bit steadier, I leave larger gaps between the blossoming colours and use transparent colours in my lightest section.

Only once I'm confident that the lightness has been regained do I cautiously go back in and place the necessary darker tones in the right spots. This normally resolves the issue.

THE PROPORTIONS ARE OUT

When something looks 'off' we assume that it is our drawing that is wrong, but quite often it's a tonal issue. If you are happy that your drawing is correct, check whether you have gone in dark enough with the shadow areas.

The easiest way to check this is to take a shot of the painting and the reference photograph side by side, view the image and spot the differences. Desaturating the photograph will show you any differences in tone even more clearly, enabling you to make the correct adjustments.

DARKER SHADOWS OR LINES ARE OVERWHELMING THE PIECE

The chances are that the shadows have either been created with too few colours or changes of tone, or you've been a little heavy-handed with the brush.

If this is the case, closely examine the areas of concern on the photograph and compare them to the ones on your painting. Are they similar in terms of shape and tone? You may recall the peacock from Chapter 5 and how the colours of the wing markings were discernibly different in tone and colour at the bottom of the photograph compared to the ones in shadow.

If you find any discrepancies, lift the colour with a scrubbing brush and reapply the correct tone while the paper is damp or dry, depending upon whether you want to create a soft or hard edge.

↑ 'Waiting For Mum', 2020, watercolour.

IT LACKS SOFTER AREAS

If your painting lacks 'fluffiness', it may be that some of your edges are too harsh or much harder that the ones in the photograph. To rectify this, gently blend and/or lift the edge in question with a short bristly brush until the edges soften. Reapply a light wash of paint, if necessary.

→ (*Opposite*) 'Nuthatch', 2017, watercolour.

↘ 'Tweedle Dee, Tweedle Dum', 2020, watercolour. Much of the 'fluffiness' in these two birds has been implied by creating subtle soft and lost edges, particularly in the chest areas where most of the tones are similar. Conversely, the majority of the hard edges are in the wings, tails, eyes and beaks.

The importance of taking a break during painting

This might seem an odd stage to add to the painting process, but it's necessary. Make sure that you build in regular breaks.

Painting isn't necessarily the cathartic, meditative process that people think it is or think it should be. It is often frustrating, exasperating and tiring! There are so many things that you are thinking about throughout the process: colour, tone, texture, shape, consistency... it's no wonder that it's exhausting! Take time away from the piece; make a cup of tea, phone a friend, take a walk! When you go back to your work, you'll have a fresh set of eyes and will make better choices as a result.

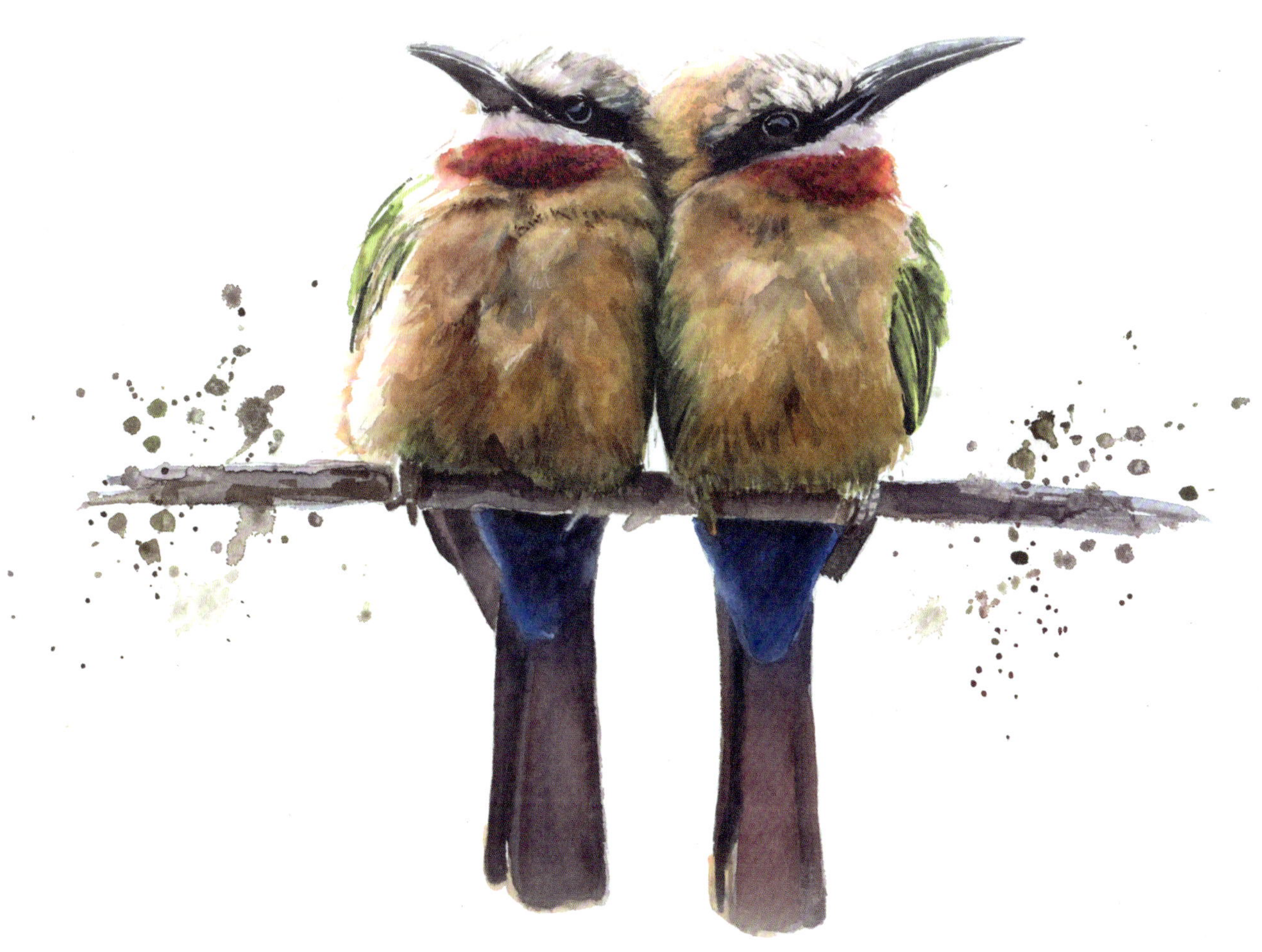

PART TWO

Advanced Techniques

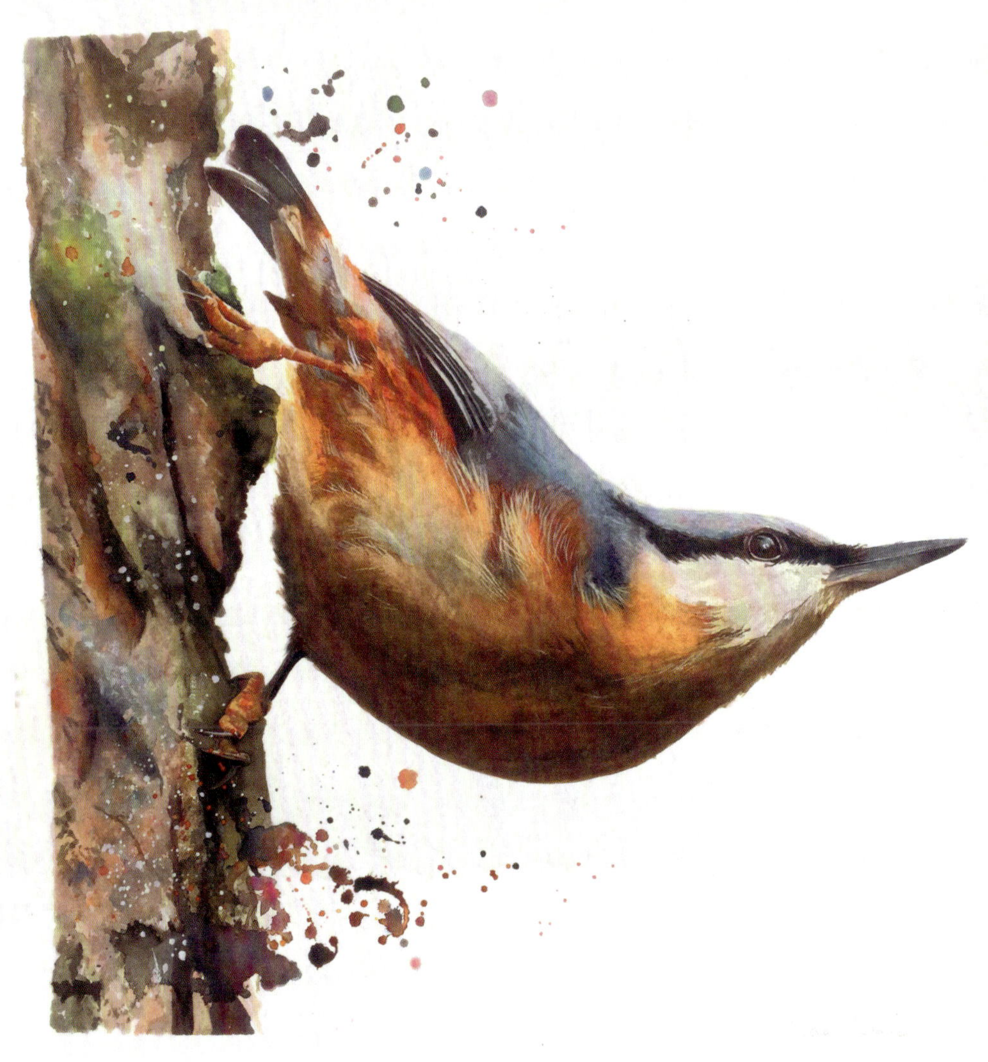

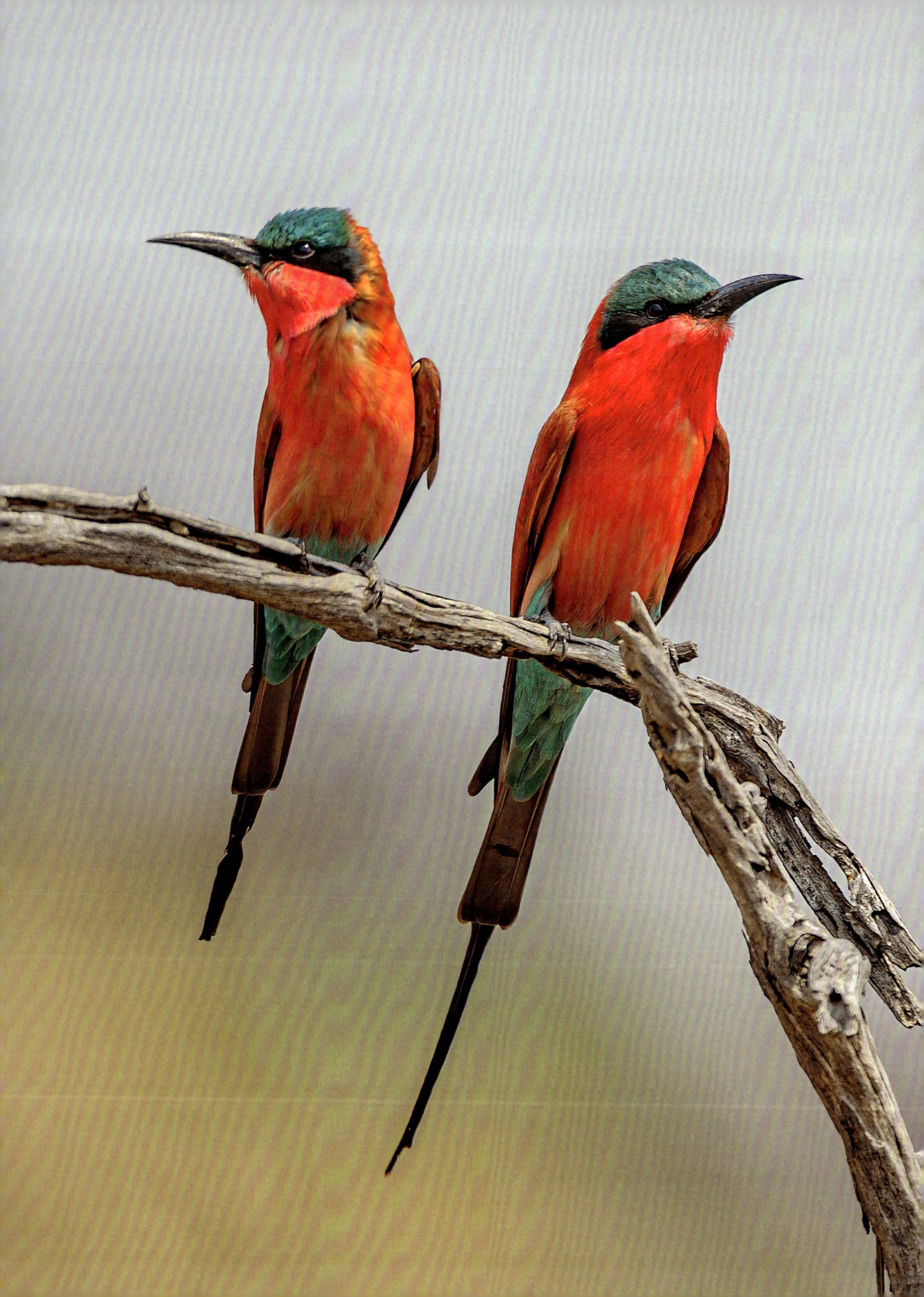

CHAPTER 7

Developing a Loose, Intuitive Style

When it comes to painting in a loose, dynamic style, how far you take the concept is up to you. With my work, not all of a piece is painted expressively. Some of it is rendered in a tight, more realistic way – usually the facial features, but sometimes, as in the case of the hummingbird in Chapter 6, even the plumage is described tightly and accurately. This is an artistic choice, so you can decide how much of any given subject you paint intuitively.

In Chapter 2, you got to experiment with a range of tools and movements, which enabled you to create a loose expressive backdrop for the great egret piece. In Chapter 5, I encouraged you to use the colours and shape of the peacock's chest feathers to influence the colour and brushwork in your process. Hopefully you found the experience in each case exhilarating, fast paced, even a bit scary.

This chapter delves deeper into developing your own individual style. The reason that I have left it until this stage in the book is that it is a more difficult technique to achieve than a tighter, more precise style. It relies as much upon a working knowledge of shape, tone and colour as it does the willingness to make mistakes and embrace the unknown. I often hear students express concern about how they would love to 'loosen up', so these next two chapters are devoted to exploring the issue of how to create an intuitive style, personal to you.

PROJECT 7

Using watercolour pencils – 'painting' carmine bee-eaters

I have chosen watercolour pencils as the medium of choice for the final exercise in this chapter as they give a gentle introduction into mark making. They can produce beautifully vibrant effects, without the many challenges associated with watercolour in tube or pan form.

Some of the exercises will appear easy at first sight, but you may be surprised by how much they challenge you and move you outside of your comfort zone. We will also be looking at how to make abstract marks that represent features, without adhering doggedly to the reference photo.

DISCOVER YOUR RHYTHM AND COLOUR PALETTE

Like many of us, when I first started painting, I copied the work of artists that inspired me in terms of their style, colours and mediums. I had read somewhere that I would eventually gain my own style and I found this hard to believe... and yet it happened.

There is nothing more rewarding to me than instantly recognising one of my student's pieces, to see them break away from zealously copying a class demonstration and make it their own. To encourage this, I carry out a series of warm-up exercises with my students to free up their minds and hands.

EXERCISE 1: MAKE YOUR MARK

You will need

- Drawing or photocopier paper
- Soft pencil (B grade or softer)

You'd think that it would be easy to scribble or doodle like a child, but it is actually a lot harder than it sounds! Shut the door on the outside world, pop some music on and relax into the process. The point of this exercise is to explore how the spirit of music can affect the direction and pressure of your hand movements, freeing you up to make loose, intuitive marks that you might otherwise struggle to make. At first you may feel a little silly, but try and put those negative voices to the back of your mind and enjoy the experience.

On a plain sheet of paper, use a soft pencil to create a series of varied marks.

How to achieve different marks

1. Hold the pencil in different ways: close to the tip, at the end, in a pointed fashion and from the side.
2. Use your right and left hand to make different marks.
3. Don't just move your fingers or hand when drawing; move your whole arm in large gestural strokes. Stand at the table if this energises you more.
4. Create lost and found lines as well as continual lines.
5. Think beyond linear shapes to include circles, zigzags, waves and so on.
6. Don't compartmentalise sections; instead overlap lines and shapes.
7. Change the weight and speed of your hand on the pencil to affect the depth of tone.
8. Close your eyes as you make marks.
9. Try the exercise with coloured pencils, even holding two at a time.

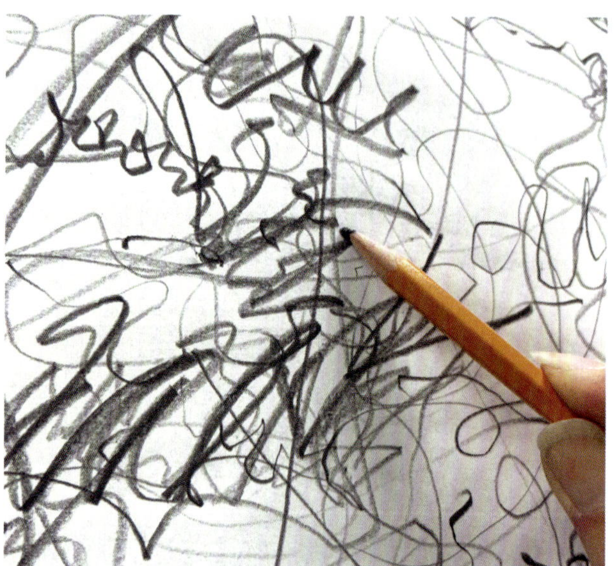

↑ This particular exercise was drawn while listening to 'Time' by Hans Zimmer, which builds up to a beautiful and moving crescendo of sound. Experiment with your favourite music to achieve a whole variety of marks.

Once completed, look at the sheet and see which marks you like. Was there a regular movement that you returned to again and again? What do these marks convey: excitement, calmness, beauty? Which marks were unexpected and which would you like to replicate?

This is a meditative process, whereby your pencil becomes an extension of your hand. It will help you get into the frame of mind for creating looser interpretations when it comes to drawing and painting.

EXERCISE 2: CREATE A LOOSE TONAL DRAWING

You will need

- Photographic reference
- Drawing or photocopier paper
- Soft pencil (B grade or softer)

For this exercise, use the emu below or a photograph of your choice that has plenty of texture and contrast. You may wish to desaturate the image first to make it easier to render a tonal drawing.

In Chapter 1, we created a tonal drawing of a coal tit in a very precise style. This time, try to be more creative with your mark making. To draw my emu, I used a soft 2B pencil to create a series of marks. I applied different pressure to the pencil at various times to achieve discontinuity of line. I made sure that my tones and shapes were roughly in the right spots and my marks tended to go in the direction of the feathers. I gave myself just 30 minutes to complete the exercise so that I would avoid over-fussing with any areas.

This is a useful exercise, because it allows you to relax into the drawing at your own pace, without the worries that watercolour can cause, such as issues with timing and pigment control. The observations, rhythm and mark making that you lay down with the pencil will help you get into the swing of things when

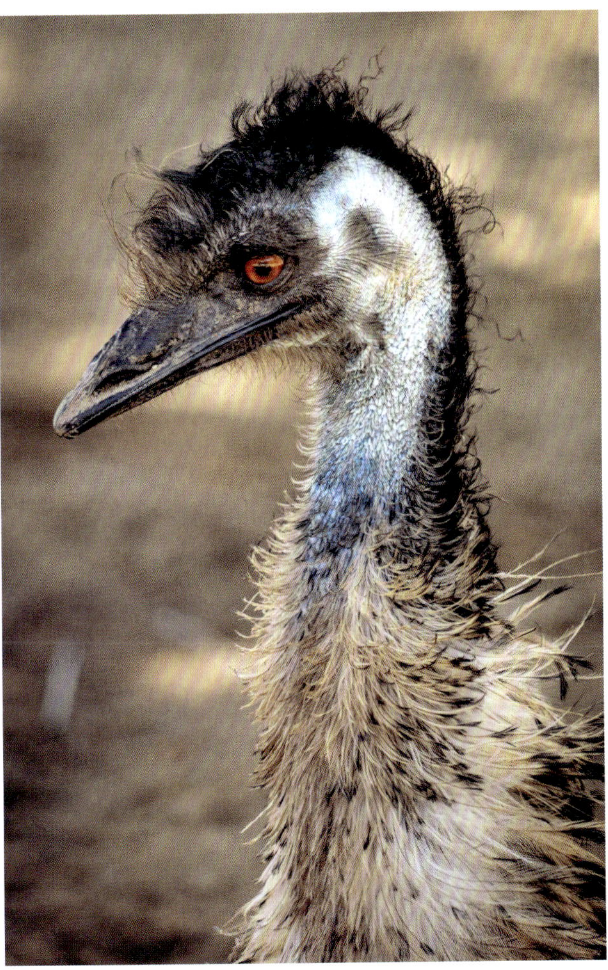

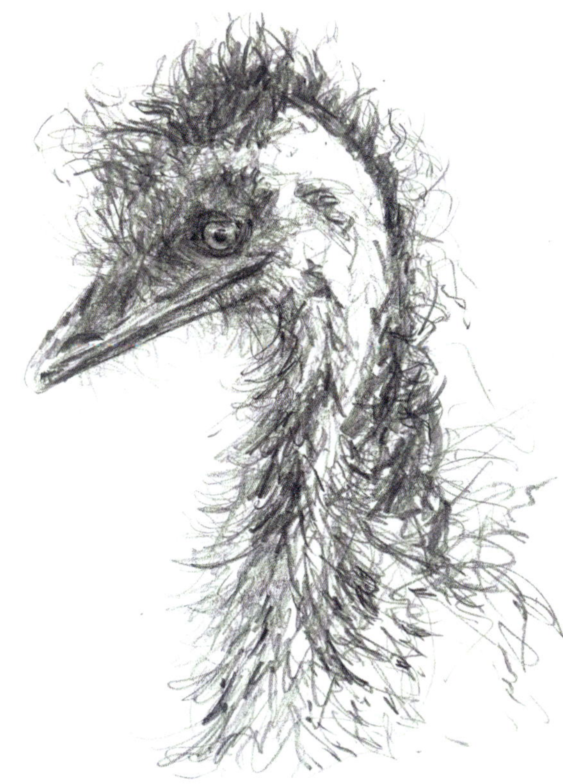

↑ Here, only the eye has been rendered with any accuracy. The rest of the marks were made intuitively using the reference photo just as a guide to the direction of the feathers and tones. I rarely lifted the pencil off the page, which added to the sense of fluidity and movement.

you come to start working with watercolour expressively.

The subject of building up tones and texture through monochromatic mark making is fascinating. Whether you prefer to shade a piece precisely and smoothly like the charcoal coal tit piece in Chapter 1 or create more gestural marks, as in the emu study, is a personal choice. I created the swan piece below using micron pens, building up tone and shape using the cross-hatch system of shading.

↓ 'Grace', 2020, micron pen, designed for the vocalist and songwriter Robert Plant for his band, Saving Grace.

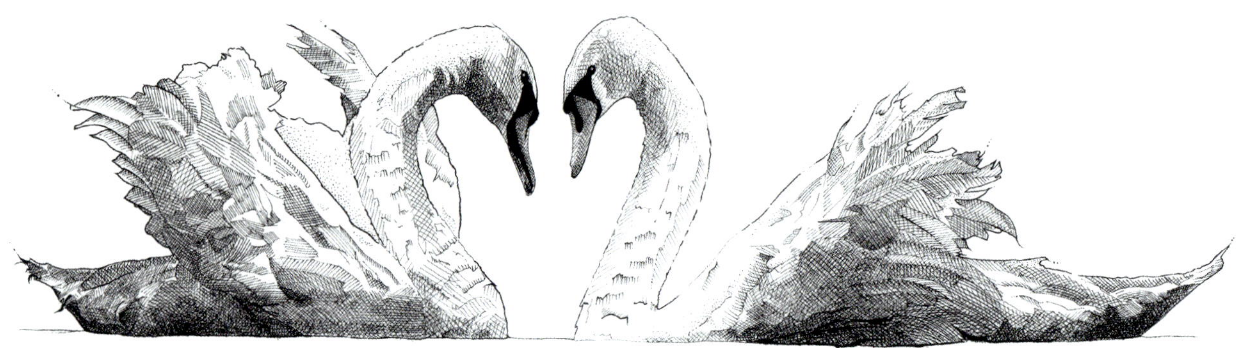

You will need

- Photographic reference of the carmine bee-eaters
- Paper: 200 gsm, cold press, textured student-grade watercolour paper
- Watercolour pencils (p.158)
- Paint: CMYK colour palette (p.158), Alizarin Crimson, Cobalt Turquoise Light, Opera Pink, either watercolour pan or tube (optional)
- Gouache paints (optional)
- Brushes: synthetic round size 6 and small detailer brushes
- Palette, water container, paper towel
- Stationery: soft B pencil, eraser, sharpener, black micron pen, white gel pen

EXERCISE 3: PAINT A PAIR OF CARMINE BEE-EATERS IN A LOOSE, INTUITIVE STYLE

Draw out the bee-eaters

1 The reference photograph shows the two carmine bee-eaters at an angle (see p.100). Draw out the birds from the reference photo at less of an angle, so they look like they are sitting at the same height. I found that the painted piece was more successful this way.

↗ Line drawing of the bee-eaters with the angle of the branch adjusted.

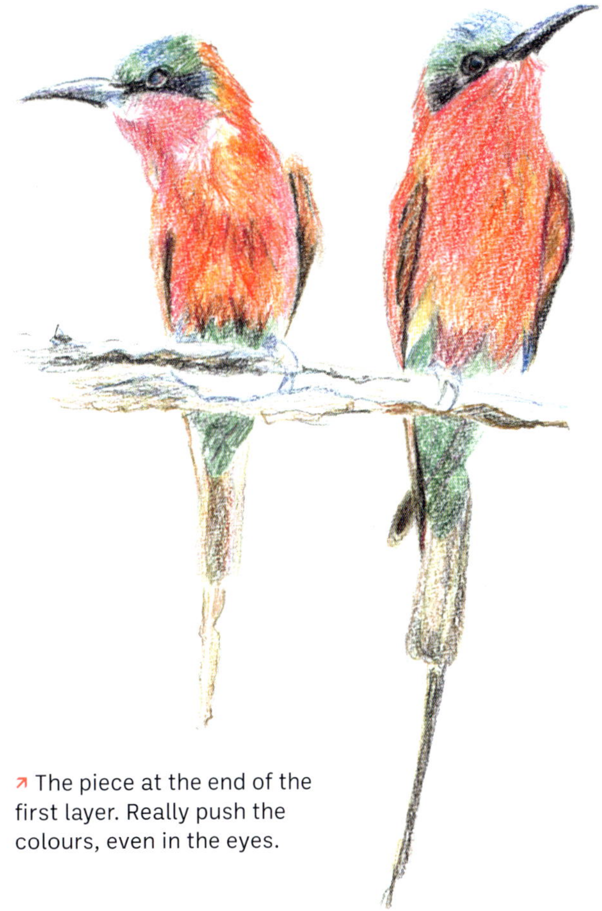

↗ The piece at the end of the first layer. Really push the colours, even in the eyes.

Apply the first layer of watercolour pencil

2 Examine the photograph and ascertain the lightest shades, just as you would with a normal watercolour piece. As with traditional watercolour, apply your lightest tones first, then gradually build up your darkest colours. I applied my warm colours first – from yellows to oranges, pinks to deeper reds – before moving on to the turquoises and blues in the head and tail.

Go steady and light at first, as there is a limit to the layering that you can achieve. The pencils eventually build up a waxy resistance that makes subsequent layers difficult. Bear in mind that watercolour pencils work in a similar way to traditional paint in that the colours will blend once water is added. Reserve your darkest tones for the bark, tail and shadow areas where the wings meet the breasts.

The cold press paper will give you a great texture, allowing you to achieve interesting marks as your pencils bob over the top. You won't be using much water, so the paper doesn't need to be thick. Apply the colour in a loose, almost impatient, way. It's best not to overthink the process – go with your gut feeling and see what emerges. Look at those beautiful colours in the heads, for instance. Exaggerate and push these aspects to their limit.

3 As you work your way around the piece, revisit areas in need of more depth or colour.

Apply water to the watercolour pencil

4 Once you're happy that you've applied sufficient pigment to the paper, apply water sparingly using a small round synthetic brush. Use your brush to lift and soften colour in the same way as you did in previous chapters. I applied water using a dabbing motion with my size 6 brush, applying it in small patches and encouraging the colours to flow and mingle with each other.

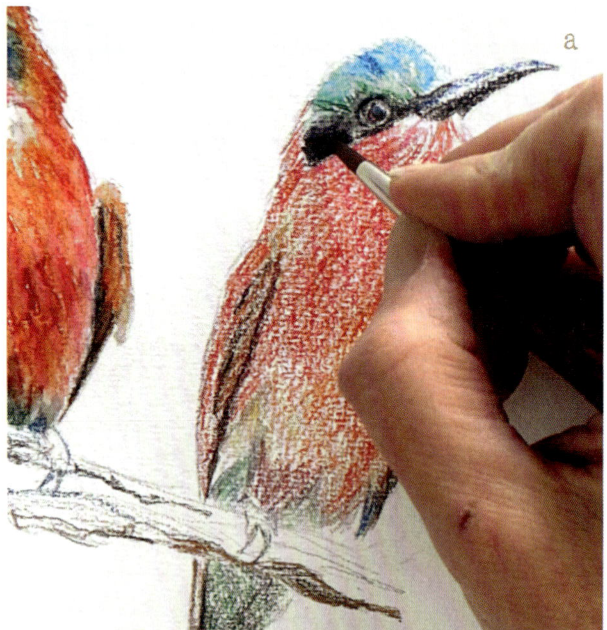

↑ Applying water to activate the pigment in the facial area.

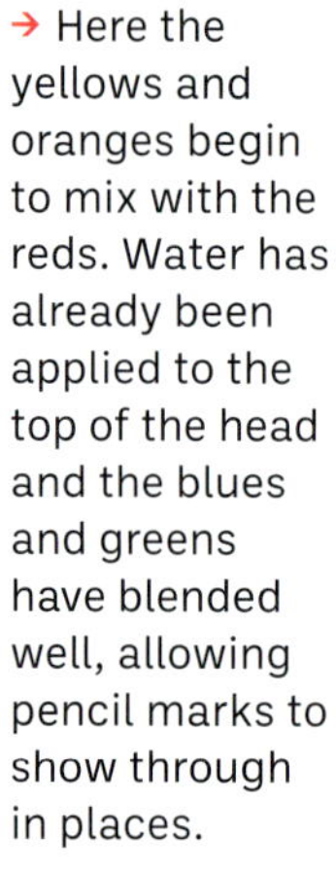

→ Here the yellows and oranges begin to mix with the reds. Water has already been applied to the top of the head and the blues and greens have blended well, allowing pencil marks to show through in places.

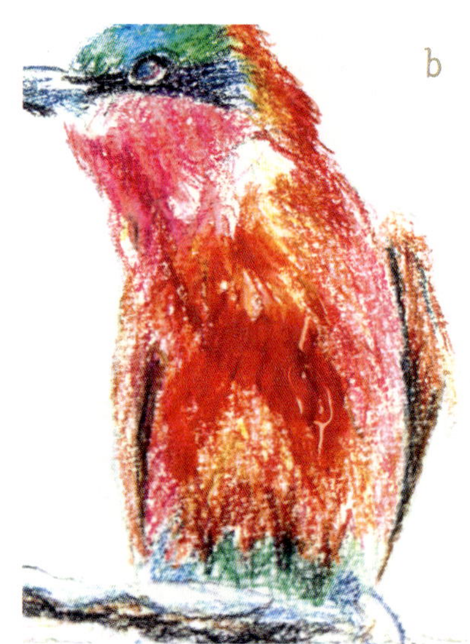

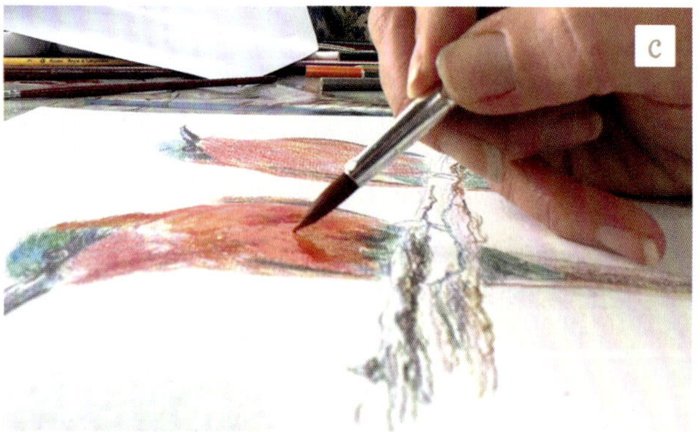

↑ The tip of the brush encourages the colours to mix gently together in a dabbing motion.

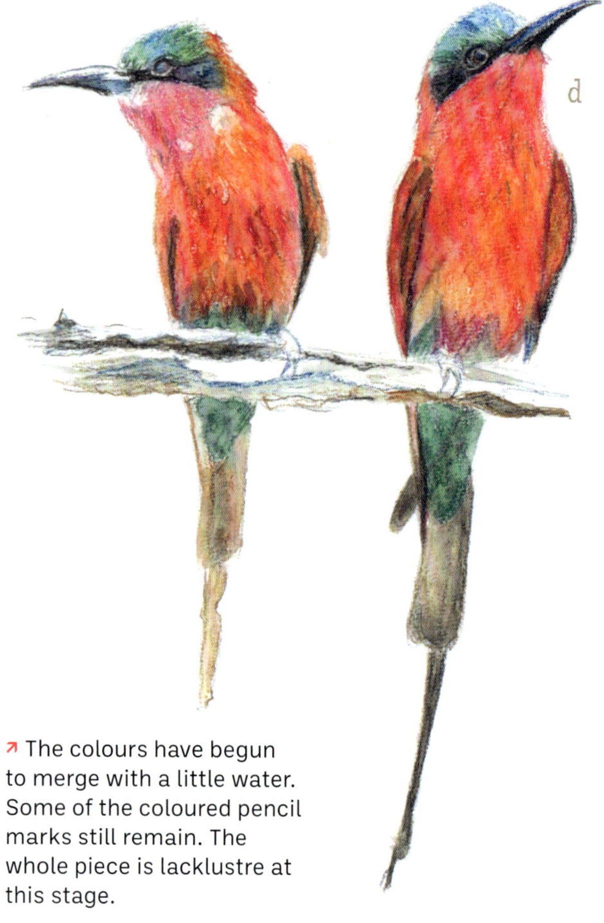

↗ The colours have begun to merge with a little water. Some of the coloured pencil marks still remain. The whole piece is lacklustre at this stage.

5 Once you have activated the pigments, allow the piece to dry.

Add another layer of watercolour pencil work

6 Continue to work on the piece, adding another layer of coloured pencil. As before, blend some of the marks together with water and allow others to remain rough on the paper. Allow the piece to dry.

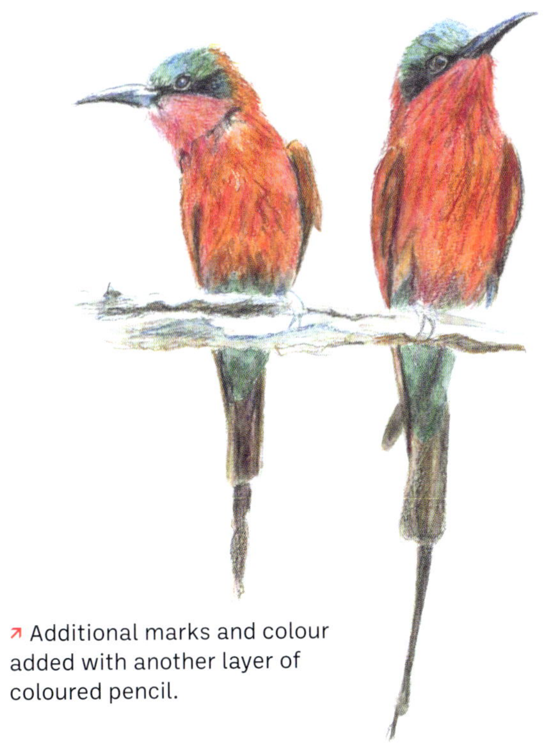

↗ Additional marks and colour added with another layer of coloured pencil.

Create tonal variation

Now you can add more tonal variation to the piece. This is crucial to make the piece pop! There are two ways to do this:

Using watercolour pigment

Using a little watercolour pigment from your traditional set of pan or tube paints can add useful spots of colour and a deeper tone. I applied paint to a couple of areas on my birds with creamy pigment.

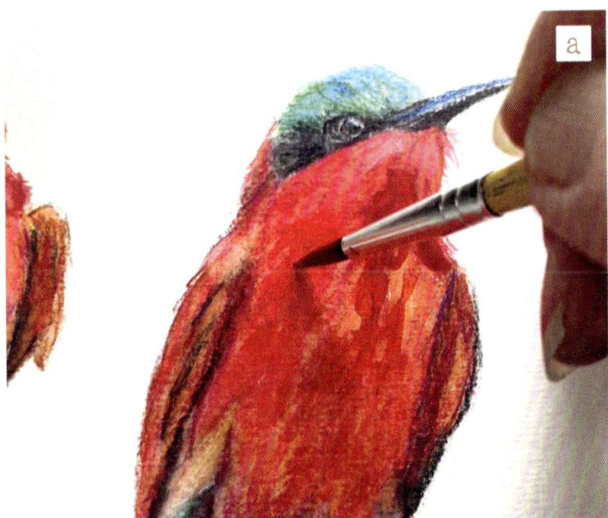

↑ Adding Opera Pink and a little Alizarin Crimson to deepen the tones.

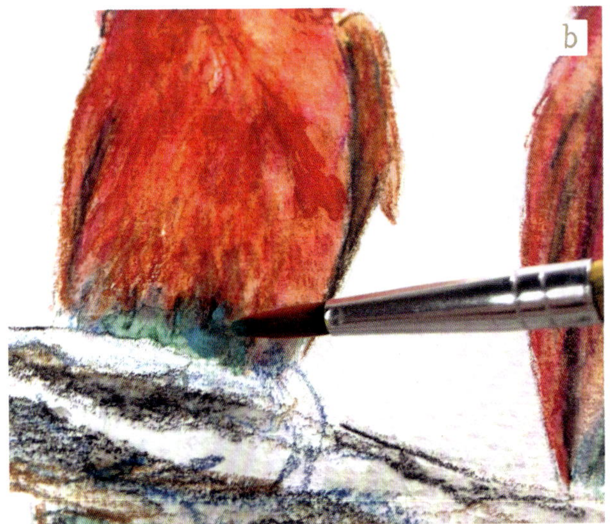

↑ Adding Cobalt Turquoise Light to the base.

Using gouache

If you've never tried gouache before, this is an excellent time to experiment with it. Gouache is an opaque, water-medium paint. It can be used as a medium in its own right or in conjunction with traditional watercolours to beautiful effect. It can be applied, reactivated and lifted in much the same way as watercolour; however, due to the size of its particles, it is opaque in nature. This can be great if you want to add light shades to your piece. If you have a full set of coloured gouaches to hand, great; if not, don't worry. I tend to stain a little white gouache with the watercolour pigment of my choice, which gives me an acceptable alternative.

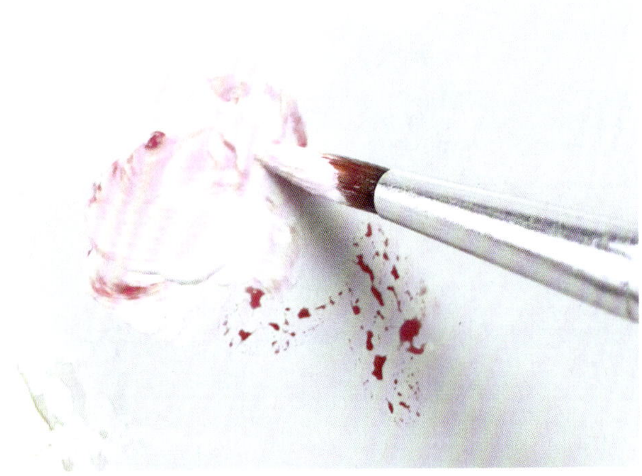

↑ Mixing white gouache with a little Opera Pink water-colour pigment to achieve a pale pink opaque paint.

Apply the gouache sparingly on the piece, as it can easily take out the luminosity of your carefully applied watercolour. Keep gouache away from the watercolour paints on your palette as, if mixed with them, it will affect the opacity of your watercolour pigments.

The image below shows how colour and light have been added to the piece using both water-colour paint and a touch of gouache.

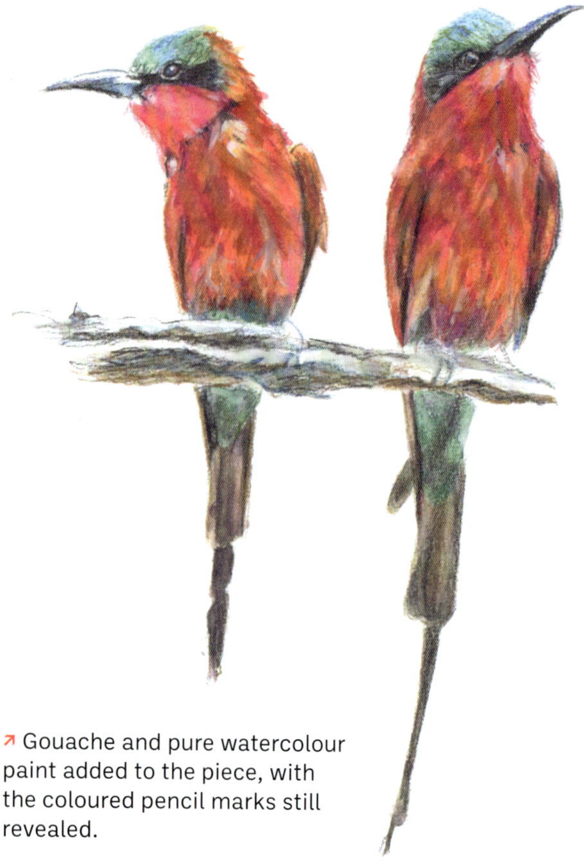

↗ Gouache and pure watercolour paint added to the piece, with the coloured pencil marks still revealed.

Finishing touches

8 Apply white gel pen to regain some of the lights and return to the watercolour pencils to build up interesting marks in the chest area.

9 I used a micron pen to draw some loose lines around the perimeters of the birds and the bark. These lost and found lines were applied in a scribbled fashion. A close-up of this bird reveals a series of marks that makes for an interesting interpretation of the original photograph.

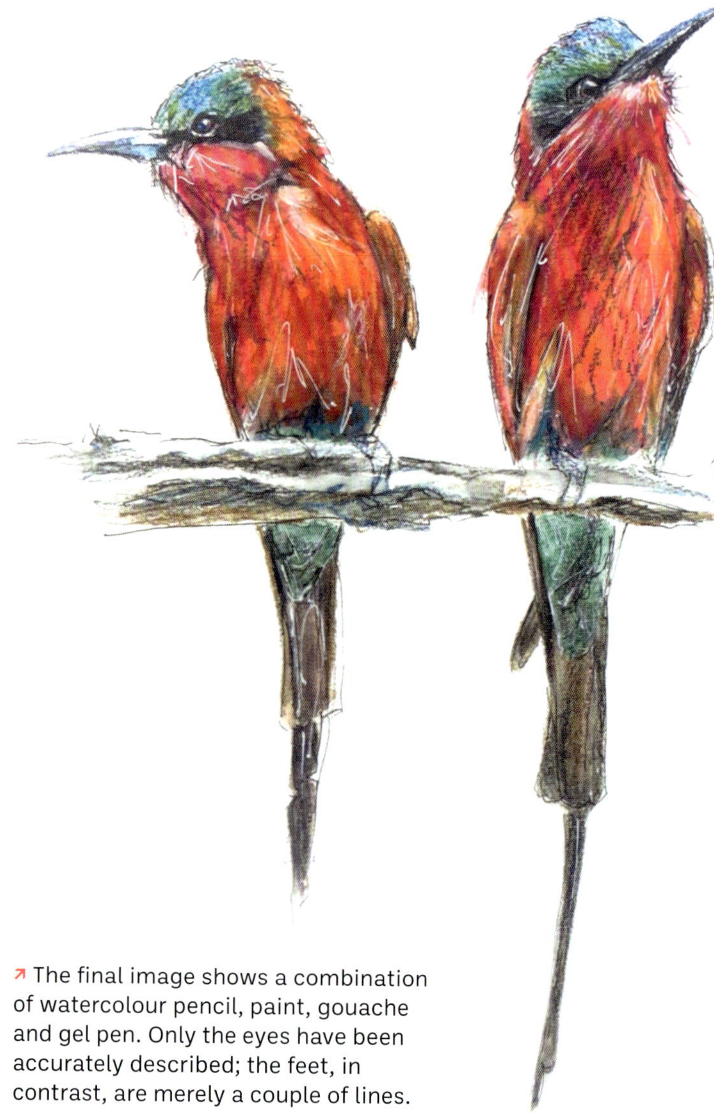

↗ The final image shows a combination of watercolour pencil, paint, gouache and gel pen. Only the eyes have been accurately described; the feet, in contrast, are merely a couple of lines.

The apparent randomness of the finished look belies the difficulty of expressive mark making. The process involves a whole series of decisions in which you may find yourself going backwards and forwards, applying and lifting colour and marks. However, let shape, tone and texture be your guides through this journey of discovery.

WHAT DID YOU DISCOVER DURING THESE EXERCISES?

Was there a particular movement or medium you kept coming back to or liked the results of? Over time, your mark making, colour choices and mediums will be what define your signature style. I hope this chapter has helped you in that journey.

These techniques are ideal for the more illustrative nature of art journaling entries, as seen in the southern carmine bee-eater pieces below.

↓ Journal page: 'Southern Carmine Bee-eaters'. The versatility of watercolour crayons coupled with water-filled brush pens makes them invaluable tools for use outdoors, as well as in the studio.

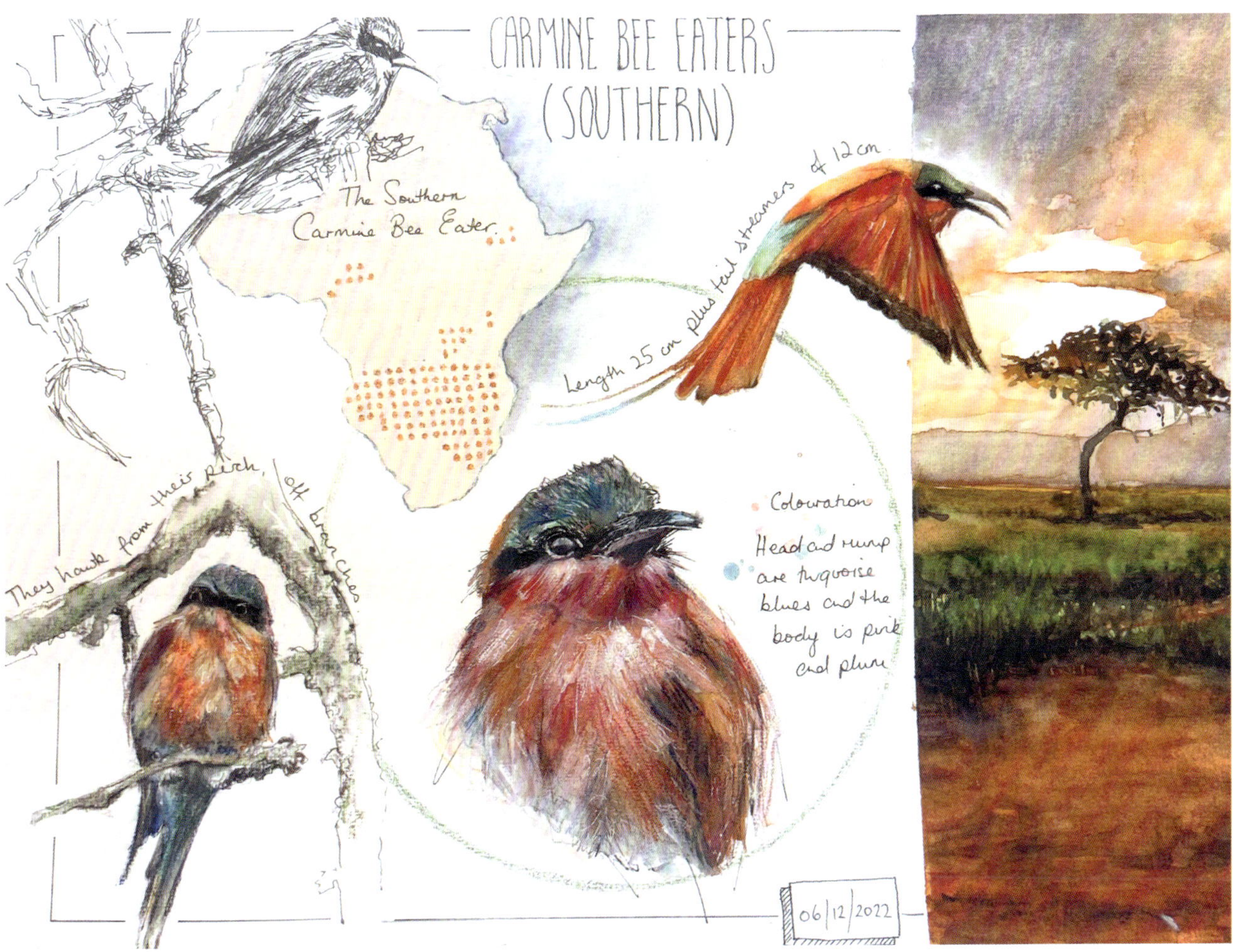

↑ Bee-eater, watercolour crayon and pastel. Push the textures and colours to their limit.

↑ Detail of a bee-eater head, made using watercolour crayons and gouache. Note how I have added a couple of orange and pink shapes to the head for balance. Likewise, I have added a few cooler shades to the body, even though my photograph reference was predominantly warm in tone.

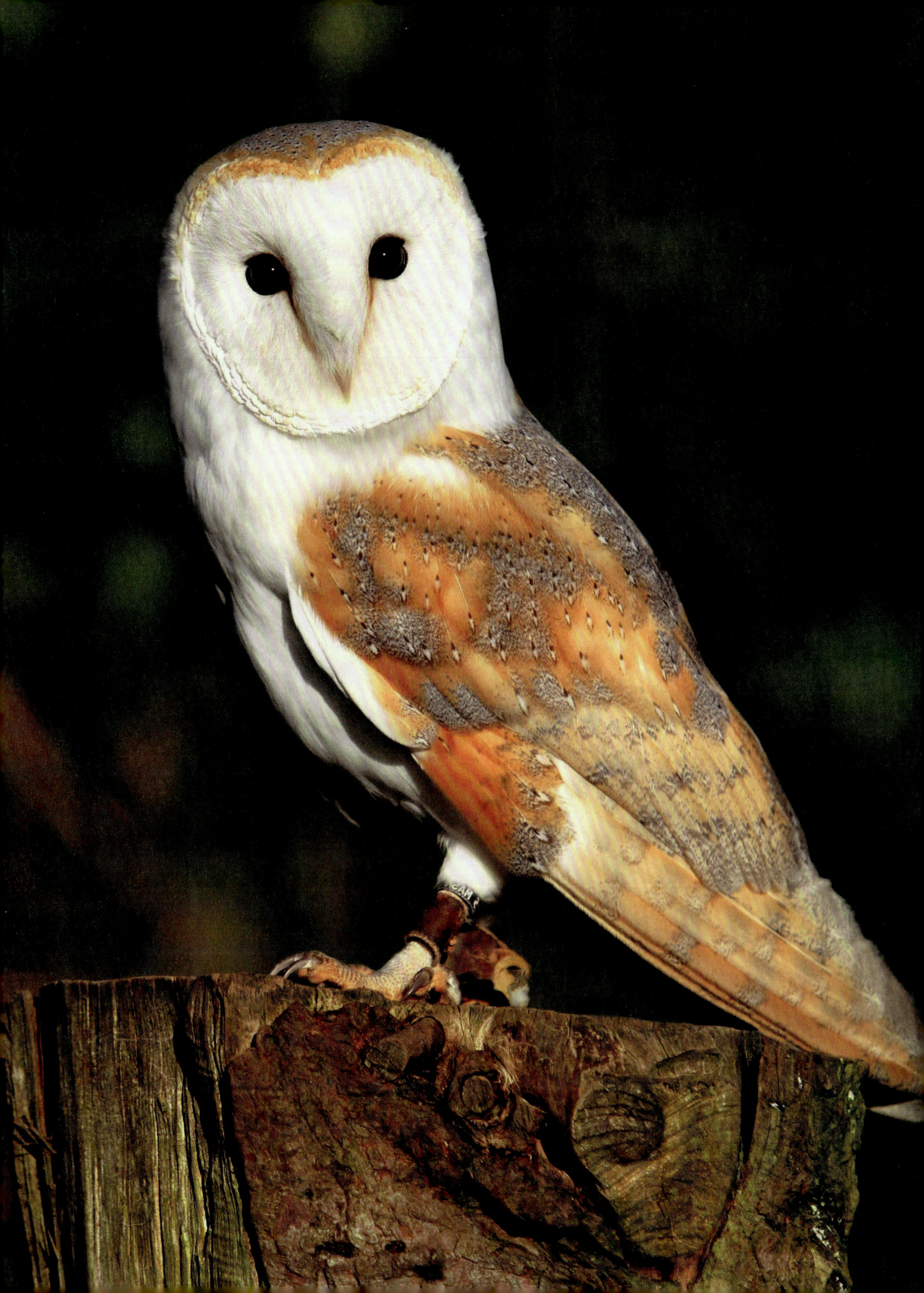

CHAPTER 8

Rendering Details in an Expressive Fashion

Meet Oscar, a beautiful barn owl who is incredibly photogenic! I had the pleasure of meeting him at a local sanctuary and was blown away by his beauty and grace. During this chapter we will learn how to abstract large sections of Oscar's wing detail, relying on his key facial features and the beauty of the paint itself to support the final painting. I want the colours to sing and for his beautiful face to be the star of the show. Therefore, I don't want to create overly fussy wing detail. This will make a far more impressionistic painting than that of the hummingbird in Chapter 6.

With this expressive method of painting, be prepared to take risks and experiment! There is less planning involved in this piece and you will need to react quickly to what is happening on the page. As a result, some attempts will work better than others, so don't be hard on yourself if a few end up pushed to one side. Each one will have been a learning experience.

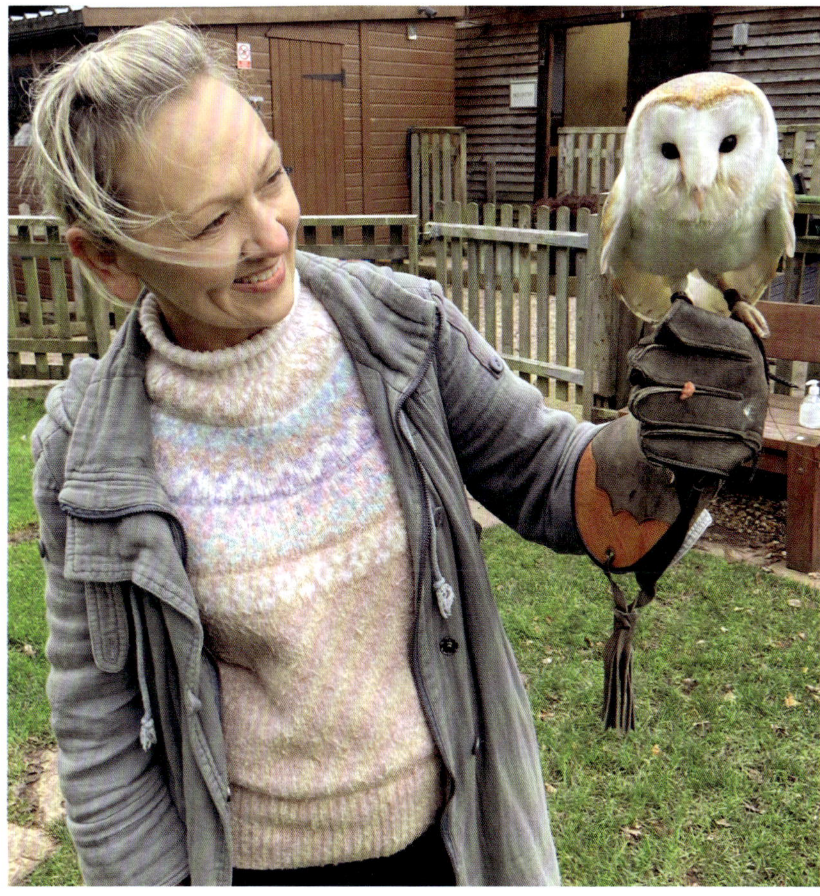

→ It was a real pleasure to meet the devilishly handsome Oscar.

TIPS FOR PAINTING EXPRESSIVELY

- Get into the habit of using a larger brush as it will help you to loosen up. Hold the brush further up the handle to lose a little control.
- Use your arm, not just your hand, to paint. Stand if this makes the process easier and more dynamic.
- Think shape and colour, not detail!
- Be prepared to experiment. Use colours and paper that will allow for lifting – this will help to remove the fear of 'messing up'. Lifting will also allow you to regain lights, which are imperative in creating a piece with a full range of values.
- Take your time choosing your reference, whether it be from life or photographic. Try to foresee and resolve any compositional issues prior to starting the painting.
- Keep your initial sketch to the bare minimum, simply outlining the main shapes.
- Remember that no one is going to be comparing your painting to the original photograph. Allow yourself the freedom of artistic interpretation, as long as the bird doesn't end up with three legs!
- Embrace a rhythm that is as natural to you as your handwriting. If it helps, pop on some music that will relax you and help you go with the flow.

PROJECT 8

Creating wing markings intuitively – painting a barn owl

COMPOSE, SKETCH AND THINK ABOUT COLOUR

1 I have chosen this particular image as I want to make the most of the yellow/purple colour combination. It also gives me an opportunity to address the issues of markings and detail.

Sketch the owl onto an A4 sheet of watercolour paper. You may decide to trace, grid up, freehand draw or totally omit an underdrawing (see Chapters 1 and 3). Whatever method you decide on when preparing your piece, make sure that the proportions and symmetry are correct by the end of the painting process, as there is nothing worse than a wonky owl!

Use a minimum of 250 gsm, cold press paper as we will be applying a quantity of watery paint to the wing area. For this particular piece I used 638 gsm Saunders Waterford 100% cotton, CP (NOT), textured, high white paper because the paint settles so beautifully on it, in the way it granulates and blends. Keep your markings fairly light, as some papers don't allow for erasing once water has been applied.

You will need

- Photographic reference of an owl
- Paper: minimum 250 gsm, cold press, textured watercolour paper
- Paint: CMYK colour palette (p.158), either watercolour pan or tube, Burnt Sienna or Burnt Umber premixed paint and white gouache (optional)
- Brushes: synthetic round size 12 and small detailer brushes
- Palette, water container, paper towel
- Stationery: HB pencil, eraser, white gel pen

I decided to place the owl in a position that reads top left to bottom right, and I wanted to make sure that the base of the owl faded into nothing to allow a flow, as opposed to an abrupt end. I allowed sufficient space around the owl to allow it to 'breathe' and to prevent it from feeling too hemmed in.

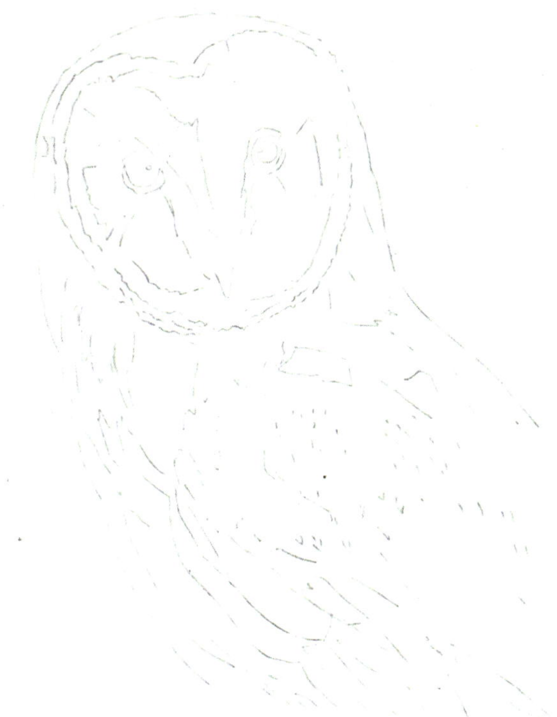

↑ My initial sketch. It is important to draw only the pertinent features and not go into too much detail with intricate wing markings.

2 Set your finished drawing aside and give yourself a chance to work out your colour palette. Study the shades of blue, purple, orange and brown and make three or four light and mid-tone pools of colour, just to get you started. I mixed up a neutral lilac-grey, an orange-brown and a thicker, darker crimson-brown. I'd like you to think about the colours that draw you to the piece. What stands out for you? This will help you to define your style.

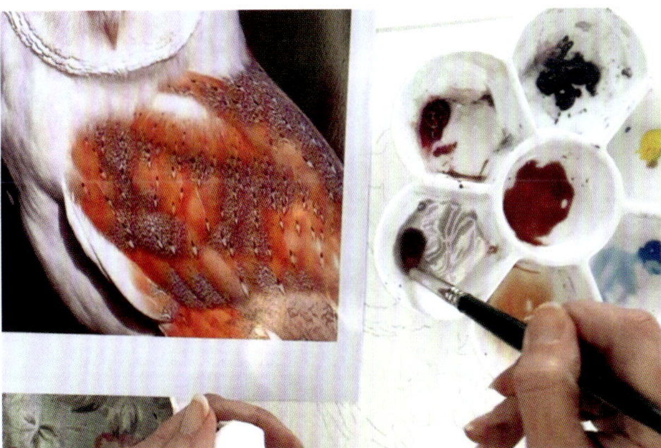

↑ Premix your chosen colours for the head so that you can work quickly and intuitively.

The photograph has a lovely balance of warm and cool shades. How much you want to push the saturation and contrast in this piece is a stylistic decision. I have painted this photograph a few times and explored both muted and more zingy colour palettes with varying degrees of success. For this project, my demonstration piece incorporates a more subdued and restrained colour palette, which I felt represented the calmness and serenity that Oscar exuded when I met him.

Applying the first layer to the face

3 Apply your first wash of colour onto dry paper. If your brush has a good point to it and your hand is steady, you may find that the size 12 is the only brush you need. If this isn't the case, you may want to use a smaller detailer brush for the precision areas, such as the eyes.

I started with the head, but, wherever you start, ensure that you vary your colours throughout this first layer with different water/pigment ratios and strokes, much as I did with the peacock (see Chapter 5).

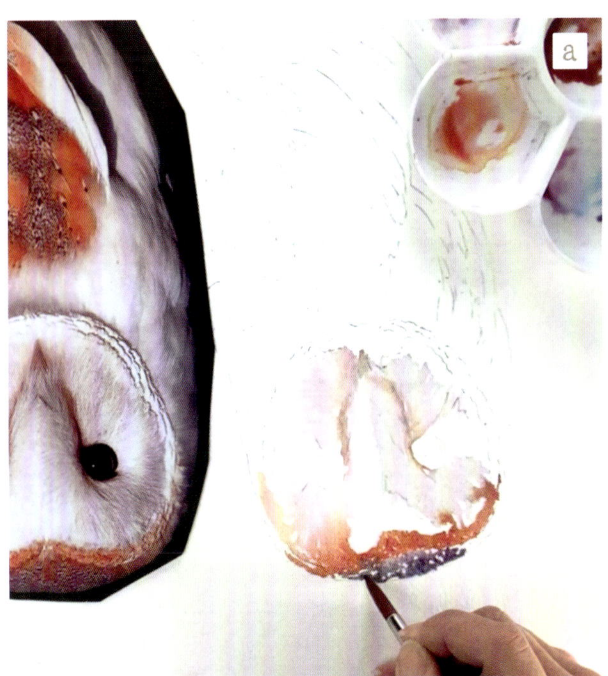

↑ I loved the way that the purple hues bled into the warm tones. I quickly dabbed the paint onto dry paper with a loaded brush, making sure to leave pockets of paper completely clear of paint. I could decide at a later stage whether I wanted to remove some or all of the lights if they didn't work.

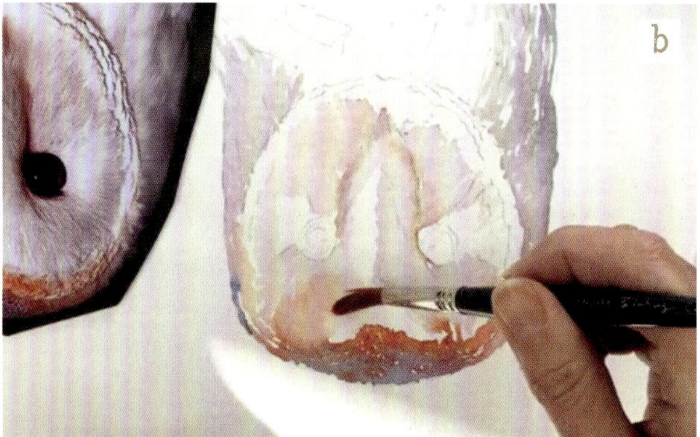

↑ Here I am removing a hard edge by sweeping a damp brush across the paint and lifting it out with tissue.

One of the reasons that I started with the head was because it is a smaller area to deal with, which gave me the chance to find my rhythm and flow before tackling the wing. There are a lot of markings in the wing and I wanted to make sure that I was in the right frame of mind to describe them loosely, without getting bogged down in detail. Painting expressively is as much about a confident state of mind as it is about technique.

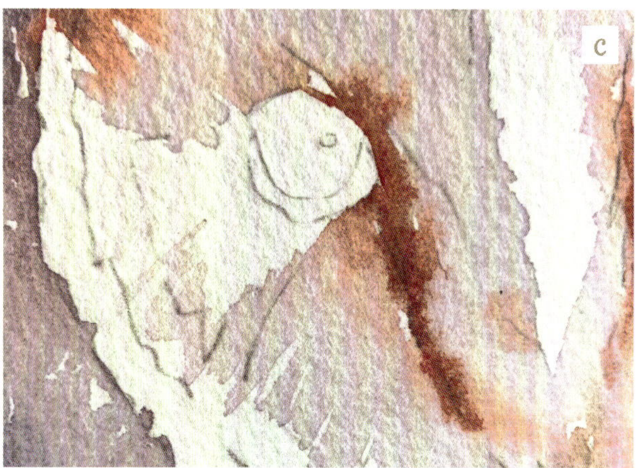

↑ Soft brown edges upon which harder edged shapes can be applied with the next layer.

→ While painting the face upside down, I am resting my little finger on the paper. This helps to keep my hand steady for delicate brushwork.

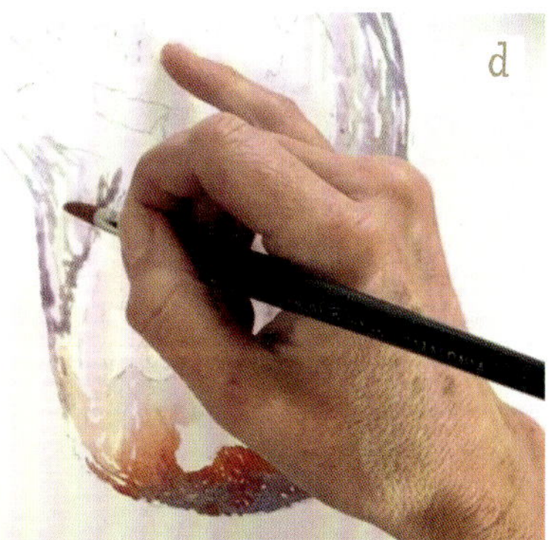

Applying the first layer to the body and wing

4 Preparation is key, so when you are ready to start the wing, create both runny light and darker rich pools of paint. This will help you to paint quickly and intuitively.

5 Ease yourself in by starting on the right-hand side of the neck and start travelling down and across the wing. Ensure that your colours mix and mingle as you paint. Use a variety of strokes and pigment/water ratios to drop, spread, merge and dilute the colour.

→ Easing myself into the wing, finding a rhythm and flow and enjoying the colour runs.

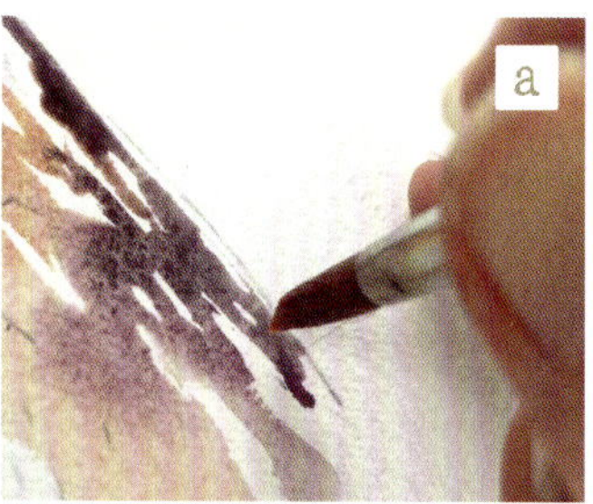

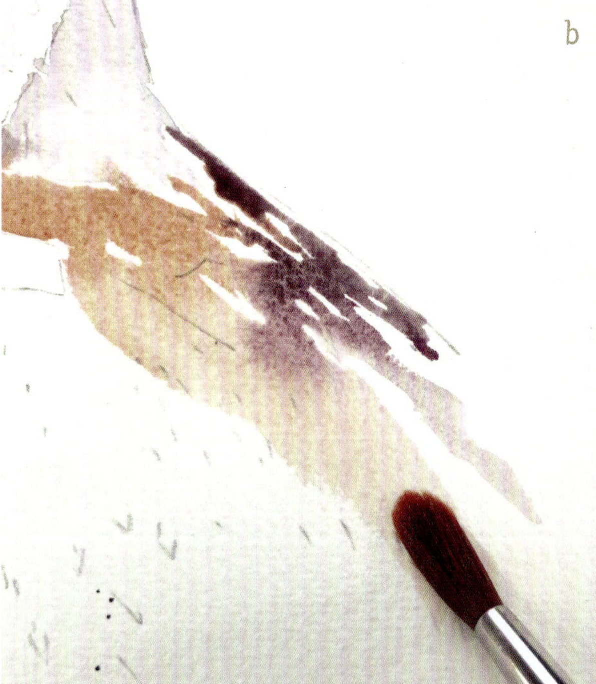

↑ Still working on the right-hand side of Oscar's body, I am dragging paint down to spread the lighter pigment around a little. A few minutes after this, I was able to come in from the left with a darker wash to create a lovely blend. Not much of this process is planned; it's about reacting to what is happening on the paper and seeing what effects you can achieve.

6 Build up the tones and shapes to suggest the markings and shape of the wings.

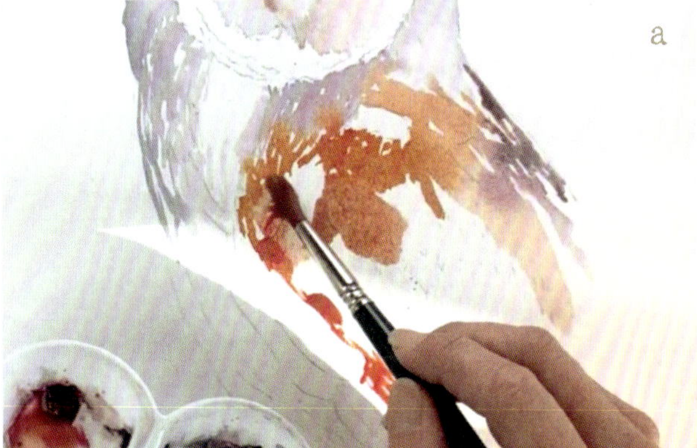

↑ Dragging paint to the side to join sections together.

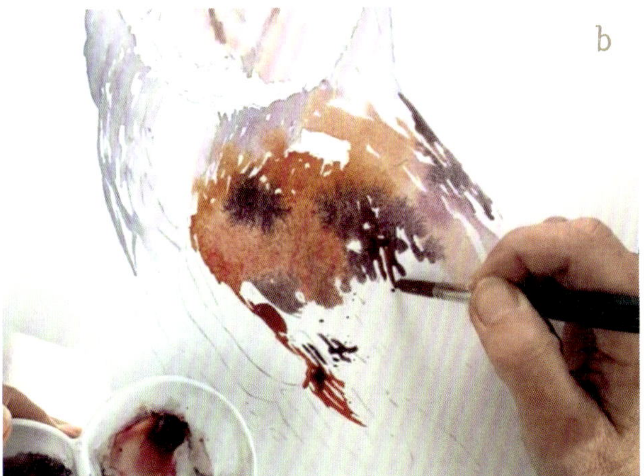

↑ Delicate downward strokes of the brush tip filled with purple paint. Leave pockets of light by using the pointed tip of your brush in places to create delicate shards, allowing the paper to pop through. Some will stay and some will be painted over.

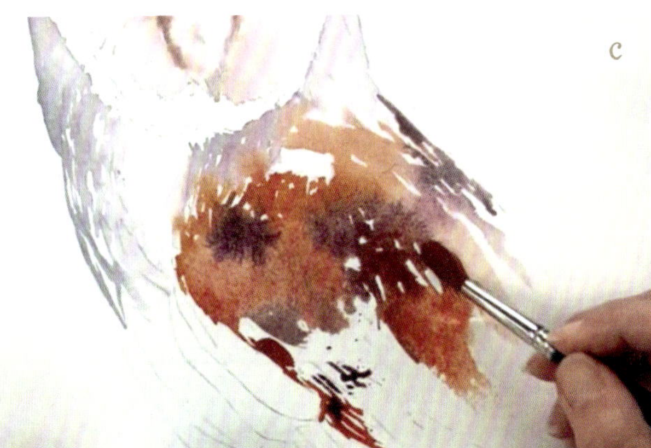

↑ Upward side swipes with a flattened brush to join areas of paint.

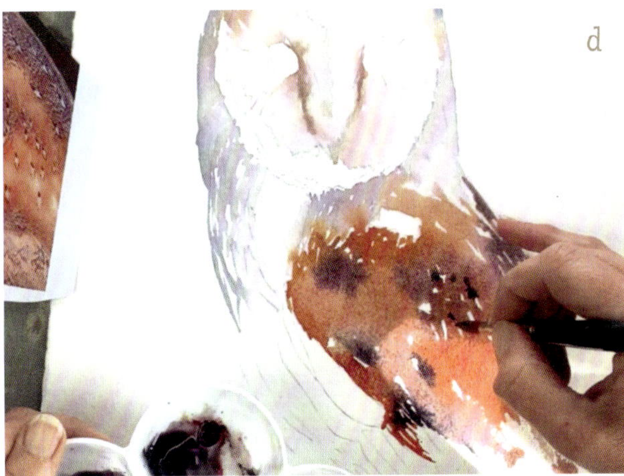

↑ Use this golden opportunity of damp paint to add creamy dark pigments for soft edges. Remember that this paint must be thicker than the damp underlayer if you want to avoid blooms.

At this point I want to create a pop of light in the wing, so I added a drop of water on it to create a lovely bloom.

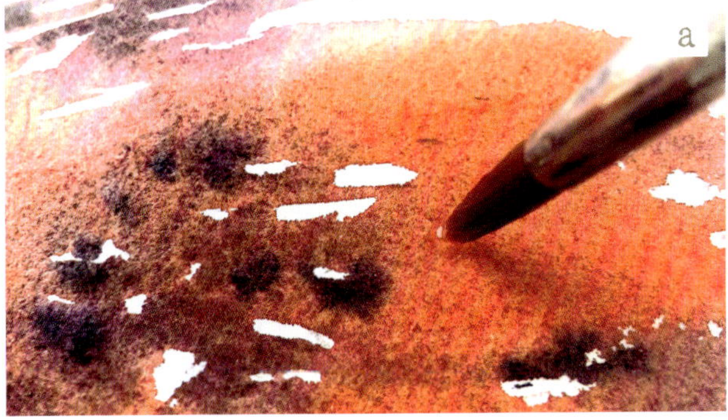

↑ Add water to the damp paper to dissipate pigment and create lighter tones. Be aware that a bloom will most likely appear, which you can either embrace or fix.

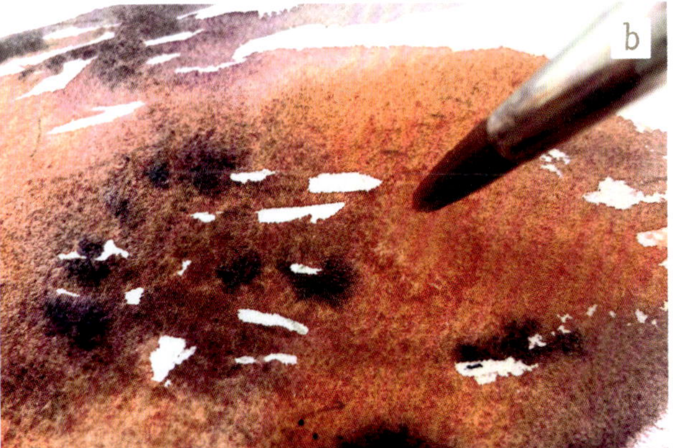

↑ The resultant bloom was kept in my final piece.

8 The edges of Oscar's face are created with a series of lost and found, thin, wiggly lines using the point of a brush. Throughout this line work, the colours are varied to prevent the piece looking flat and dull. Much of the owl can be completed in this first layer, even the eyes, which we will move on to next.

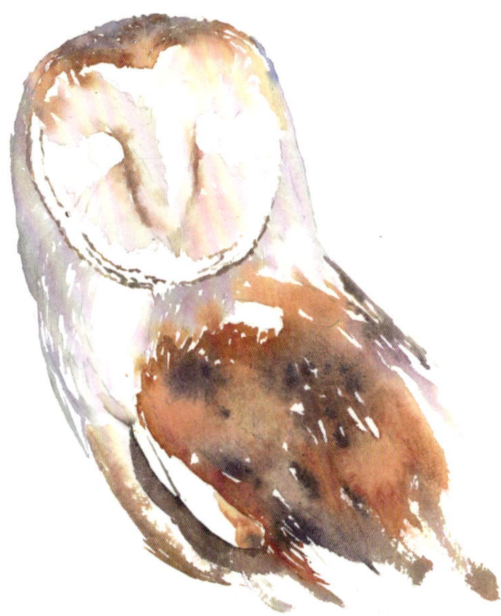

↑ Ensure that pockets of light are left in the appropriate places. I left patches of white at the top of the head and in the wings. I didn't plan to necessarily keep all of these areas free of paint, but it gave me time to think about my next moves without completely obliterating the white paper below.

Completing the eyes and adding depth of tone

9 It's now a good time to work on the eyes using a detailer brush. I find the slow, precise work of completing eyes to be a welcome break from the fast-paced decision-making process that goes into creating the larger, more abstract areas.

As with every section of the painting process, observe, identify and mix the colours in the eye and apply them onto dry paper, starting with your lightest tones. The eyes in the photograph are very dark, so exaggerate any mid tones that you see and ensure that the reflected light is carefully retained to add that touch of sparkle. I tend to cut around the reflected light shape carefully with black pigment, but if you lose it, don't worry. You can always add a dot of white gel pen or gouache at the end of the process to regain the light.

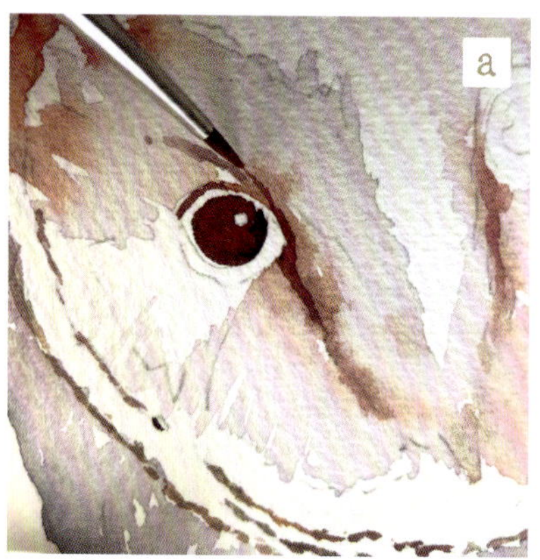

→ Painting in and around the eyes using a detailer brush.

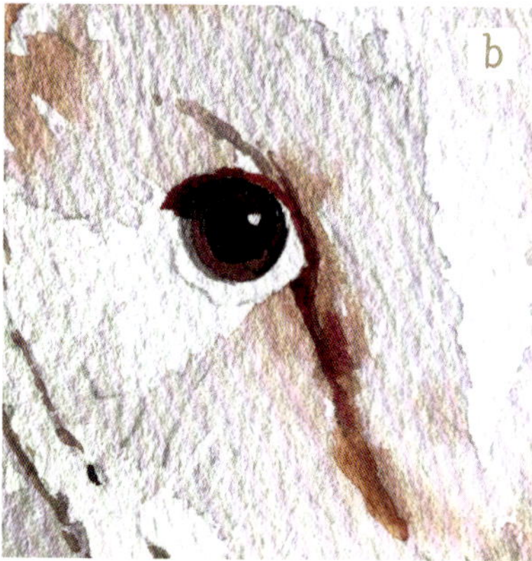

→ The finished eye with black pigment added to the pupil area.

10 Once the eyes have been completed, you will find it easier to gauge the rest of the tones in the face and beak. Take your time, building up marks around the face; chopping, changing and linking your colours. Use the direction of the facial feathers in the photo as your guide only, and be sure to allow gaps in the new paint to allow some of the undercolours to peep through.

11 Once the face is done, finish this stage by adding colour and tone to the body, which has most likely lost some of its vibrancy in the drying process. Reapply brighter pigments to areas that need it. Cut in and spread any darker shades, such as the shadow areas under the wings, again being mindful not to fill spaces with just one single colour.

Top tip

Always ensure that your painting has a good mix of light, mid and dark values for added impact.

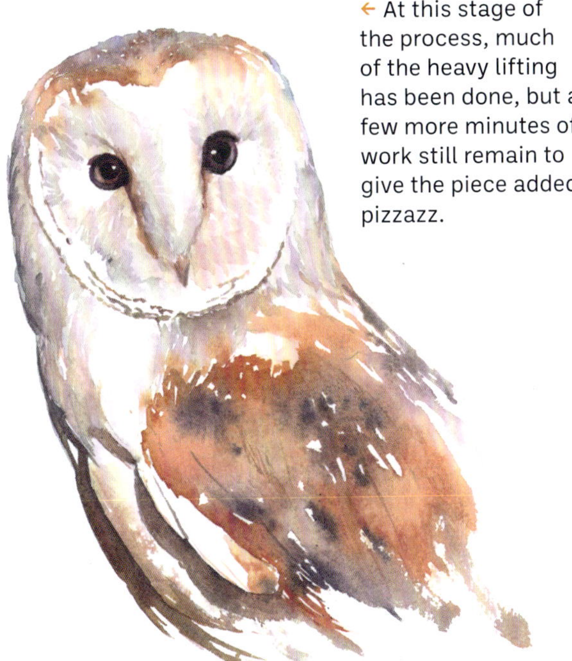

← At this stage of the process, much of the heavy lifting has been done, but a few more minutes of work still remain to give the piece added pizzazz.

Pushing tone and colour and adding finishing touches

The final stage of the process is one of the most important.

Things to look out for at this stage

1 Colour balance and harmony: Is there a section that jars with the rest? Does it need removing or repeating in another section of the piece? In my painting, I made a point of adding far more brown to the left-hand side of the body than the photograph indicated, to give the piece a sense of balance.
2 Add splashes: These are a great compositional tool, if used sparingly and in moderation. I always use just a couple of colours from the existing palette and often apply them at a diagonal to the body, with the largest of the splashes by the body.

← Sometimes I will deliberately place a bead of paint in a given place if it aids the composition. Yes, it feels like cheating, but I won't tell anyone if you don't!

3 Push colours and tones in key areas to allow chosen sections to pop: In my piece, I wanted the top of the head, the eyes and the top section of the right wing area to pull the viewer in.
4 Apply optional marks with gel pens or alternative mediums for added texture, if needed.

12 A word of caution: After every few additions or alterations, take a few seconds to think. It's easy for a piece to become overly busy and to lose sight of all those wonderful brush marks created in the early stages of the process.

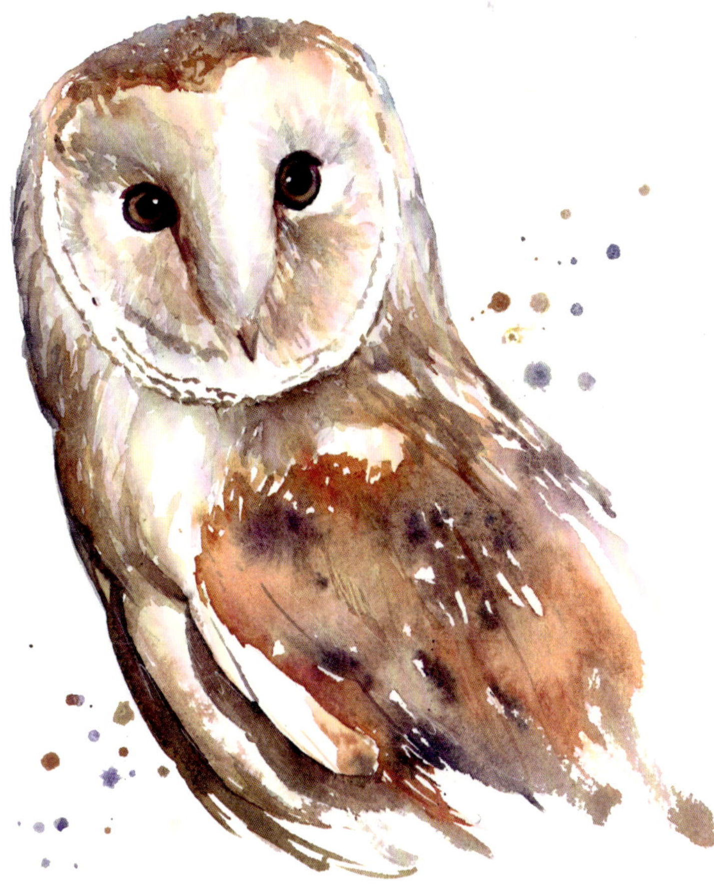

↑ My final piece. I did start to add more and more marks to the wings and then decided to remove them and call it a day. It was getting overly fussy, to the point that Oscar's face was no longer the main star of the show!

These two images show my previous attempts at painting Oscar with varying degrees of success. The importance of practice and experimentation cannot be overstated.

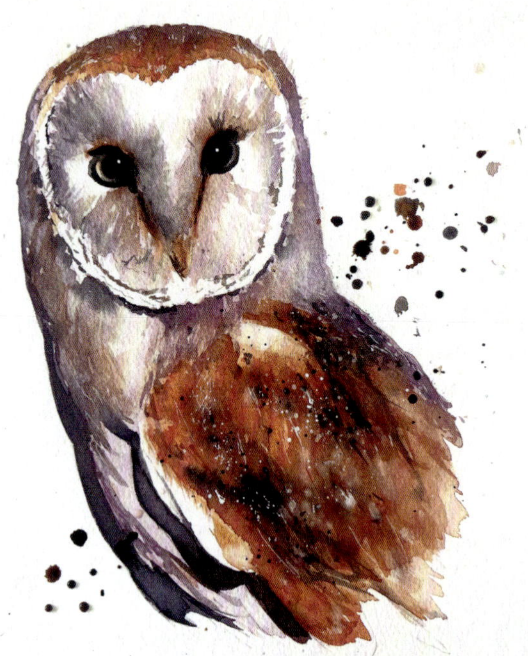

↑ Brighter colours, really pushing the purples with darker tones and more exaggerated contrasts. I felt that this was a less successful piece; it felt too 'loud'. Having said that, I prefer the markings on the wings in this piece.

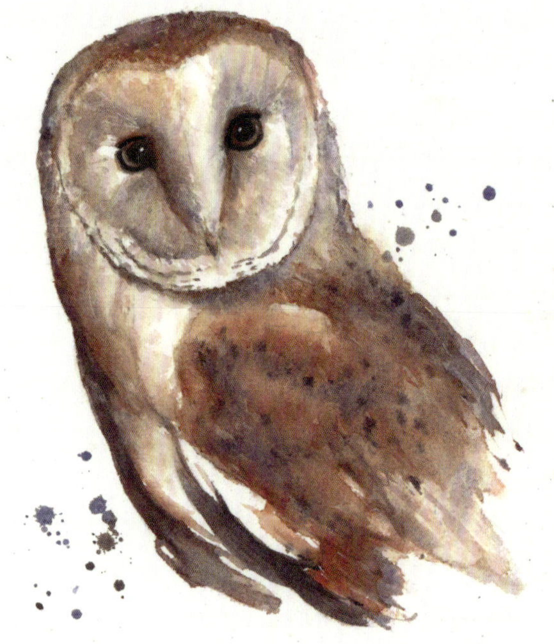

↑ This piece has a more subdued colour palette, which I preferred. I would have liked to have left a little of the white paper showing in the wing, however, for added contrast.

Studying owls: an evolution of my style

Owls have always been a favourite subject of mine to paint, although my style has developed and changed over the years, as shown by these four paintings, spanning eight years. Some are more detailed than others. Some have clearly rendered markings and others, like Oscar, are far more impressionistic. For me, the important factor is to make sure that both the beauty and colour of the subject marry in perfect harmony with those of the watercolour.

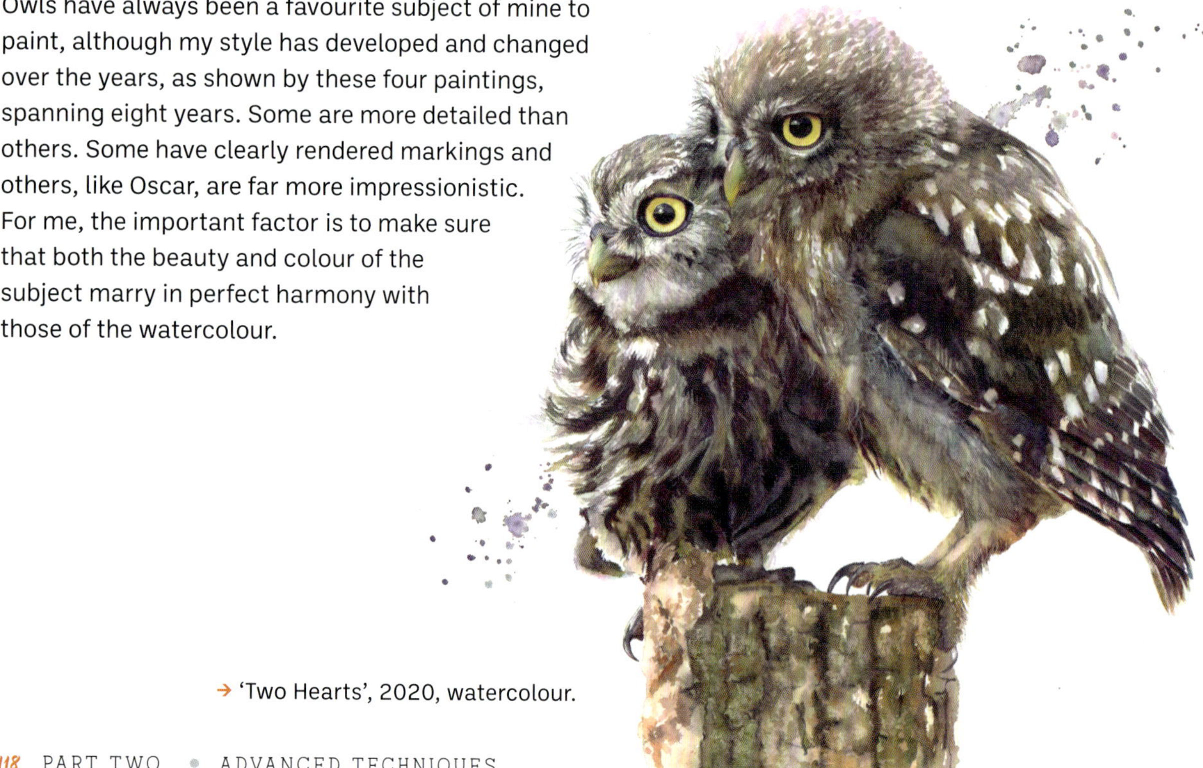

→ 'Two Hearts', 2020, watercolour.

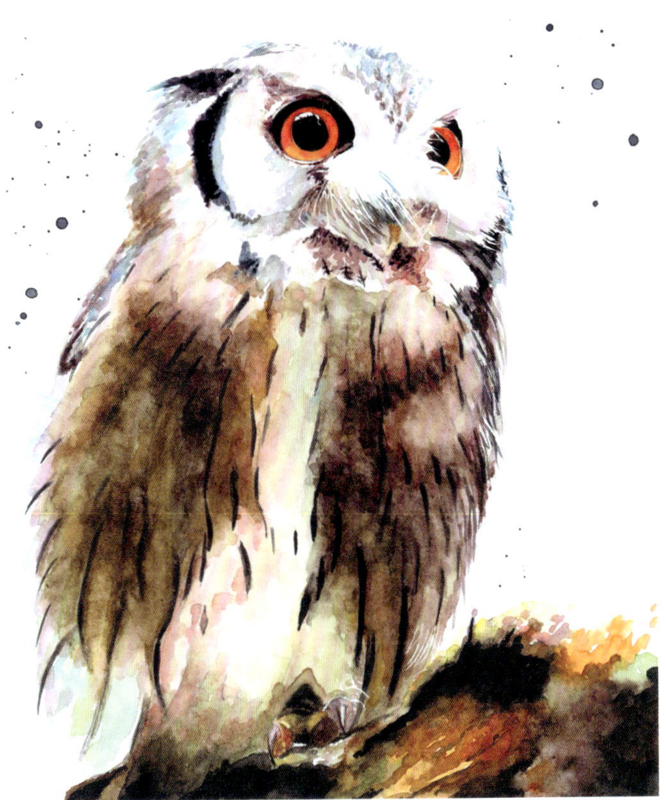

↑ 'Pools of Amber', 2017, watercolour.

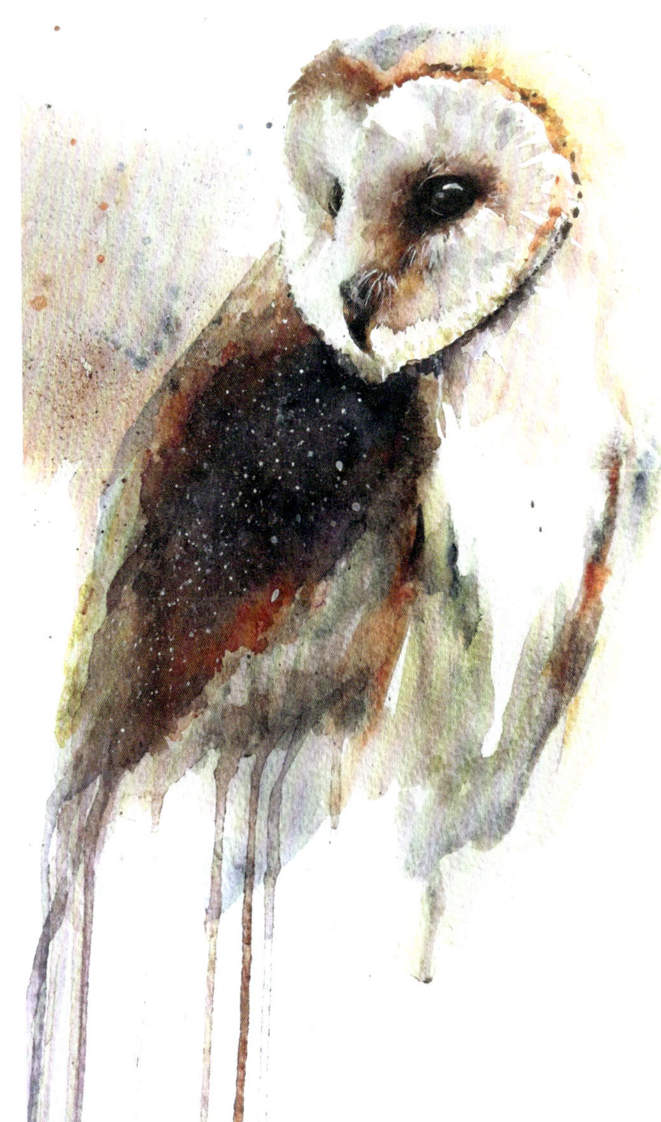

↑ 'Eric Sitting' was painted in 2012 and went on to become one of my best-selling prints.

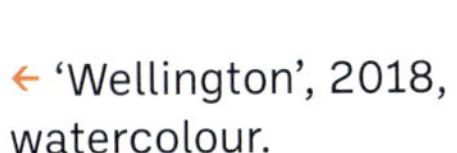

← 'Wellington', 2018, watercolour.

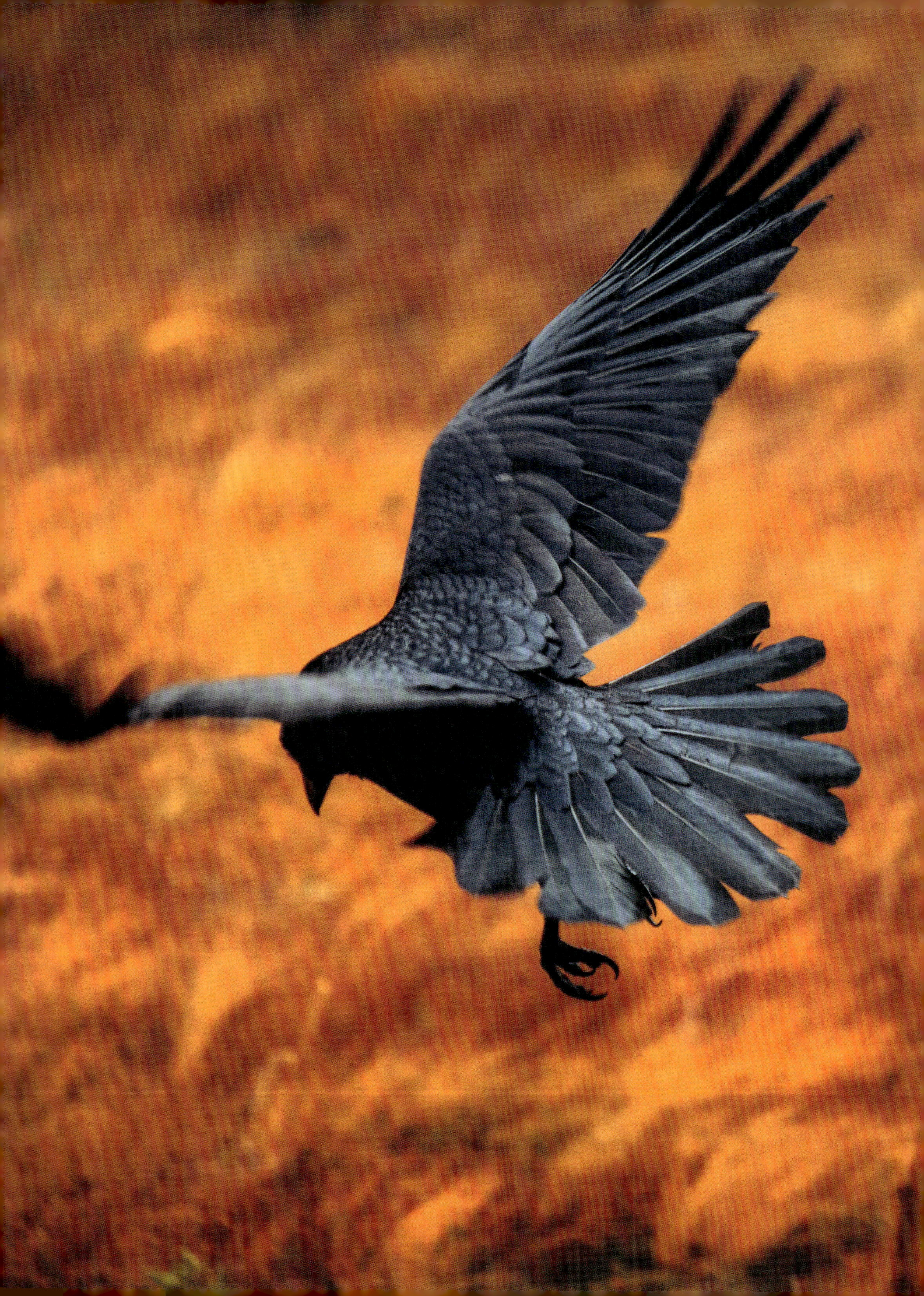

CHAPTER

9

Painting Black Birds and Incorporating Environmental Aspects

Painting black birds can be challenging, but in this chapter you will discover that black is not 'just black', and black birds can be created with a range of beautiful colours. This is also the first chapter in which we will be adding some foreground elements in full colour. This will give us additional opportunities to paint expressively and apply a number of different types of brush marks.

PROJECT 9

Utilising the blue/orange colour palette for a dynamic composition – painting a raven in flight

When I was researching photographs of black birds for this book, I came across a beautiful series of raven photographs.

Close inspection of the black bird revealed some beautiful shades of indigos and turquoises in the feathers. These can be saturated to take full advantage. If you can't see these shades easily, use your viewing aperture (see Chapter 4) to check out the blue tones.

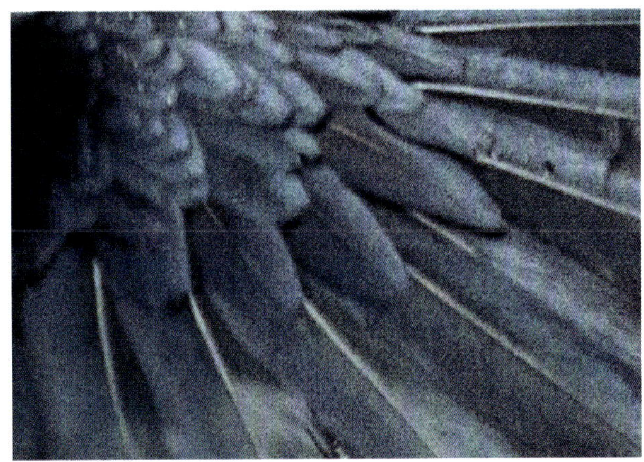

↑ If you are using the CMYK palette, the colours of these tail feathers can be made by combining cyan and black in different proportions.

← I loved the sense of movement conveyed by the shape of the raven as it swooped down.

Although the colours in the background of the first photograph offer a beautifully complementary blue/orange colour scheme, I thought these subsequent photos offered me the chance to explore a wider range of warm colours and textures, which incorporated mustards and olives.

You will need

- Photographic references of the raven and its environment
- Paper: minimum 200 gsm, cold press, textured watercolour paper
- Paints: CMYK colour palette (p.158), either watercolour pan or tube
- Premixed paints: Cadmium Orange, Sap Green, Indigo, Alizarin Crimson (optional)
- White gouache or acrylic ink (optional)
- Brushes: synthetic size 6 and 12 round pointed brushes, small detailer brush, slim rigger brush, 1 inch flat brush
- Palette, water container, paper towel
- Salt, crayon, pastel or cling film (optional)
- Stationery: HB pencil, eraser, white gel pen

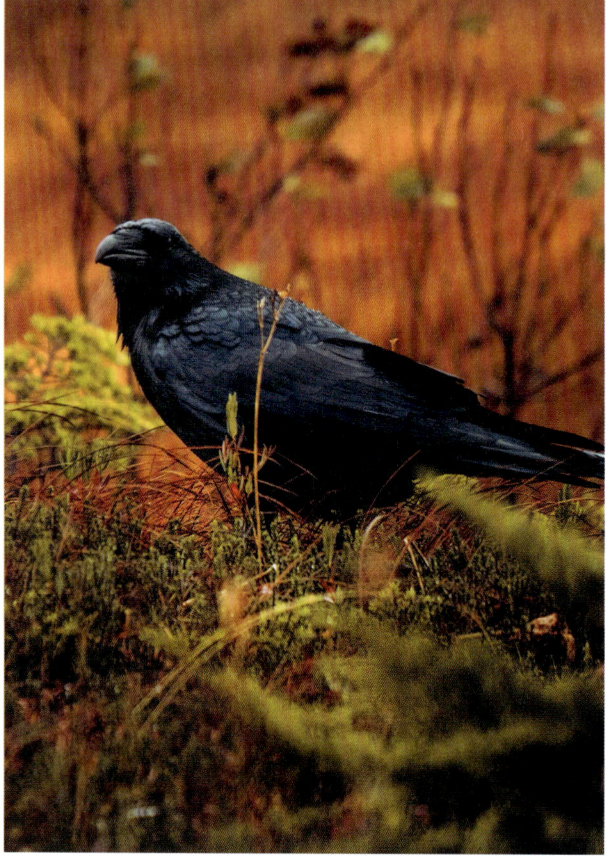

↑ Look at the colour charts you made in Chapter 4. How many of these yellows and oranges did you make? Many of the colours in the vegetation are desaturated. The olives, mustard and burnt orange colours are all made up of the three primaries in differing proportions. Very few of the colours in this photograph are pure saturated colour. Whether you would like to introduce some – for example, by way of bright zingy orange foliage or pale turquoise notes in the feathers – would be an artistic choice.

↓ The beautiful environment that the raven was situated in.

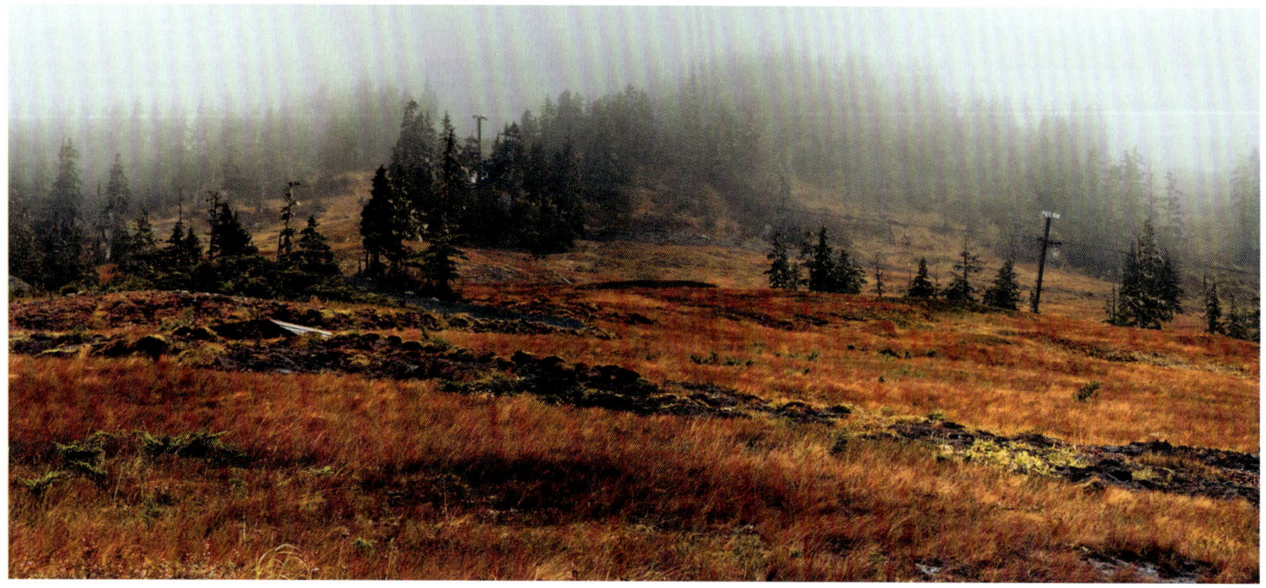

WORK OUT COMPOSITION BY CREATING A THUMBNAIL SKETCH

1 I created three thumbnail sketches, as shown below. One was portrait in orientation and the other two were landscape. These were really useful as they helped me decide on the placement of the raven and vegetation. I used the rule of thirds as my main compositional tool (see p.48), hence the gridlines on the sketches.

It's amazing how the placement of the subject alters the theme of the piece, even in quick sketches such as these. I decided to go with the first of the sketches, as it will help to push the wonderful colours in the raven's outstretched wings.

↘ Sketch 1: Here, the raven and its wingspan are the main feature, with the foliage as the supporting act.

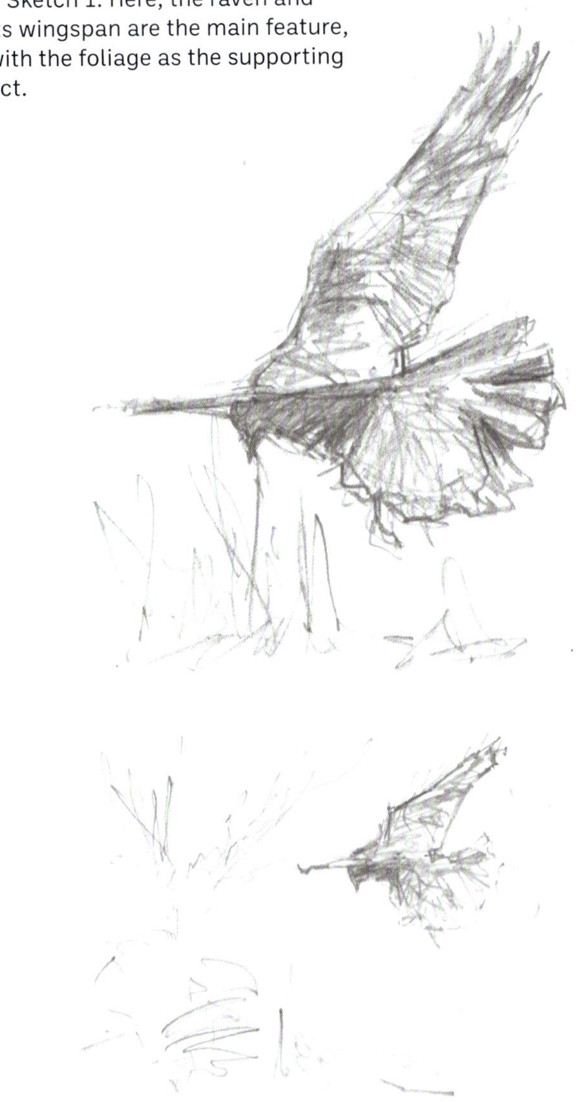

↑ Sketch 2: I was playing about with the idea of doing an abstract wash in the background and using some of the background features, such as the pine trees and power cable.

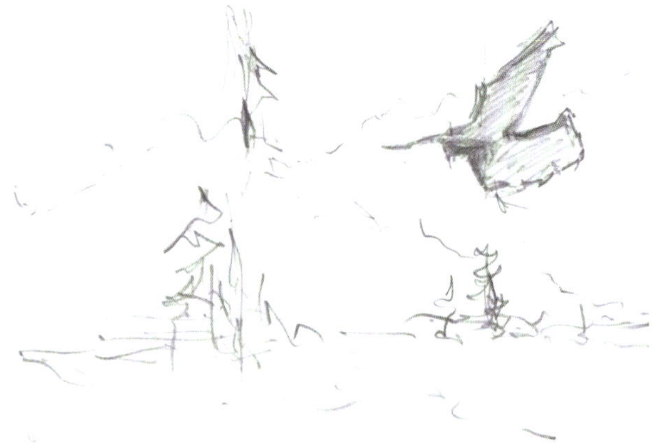

↑ Sketch 3: I wanted to incorporate more of the background features, taking inspiration from the landscape photograph.

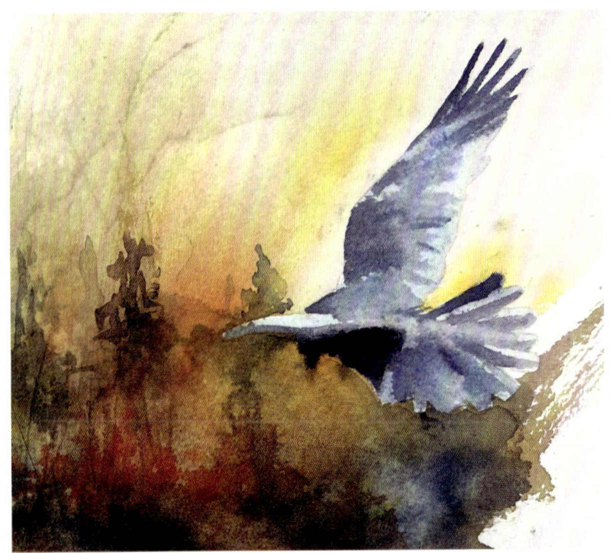

↑ This is the paint sketch developed from Sketch 2. The raven was first masked out with masking fluid while I painted the background, just as we did in Chapter 3. This was a playful piece, nothing serious, but I love the colours. It's definitely an idea that I'll be developing into a future painting.

DRAW OUT THE PIECE

2 For this piece, you will need an A4 sheet of watercolour paper. Draw or trace the raven out as below.

↑ This drawing contains a lot of details in the wings, many of which will eventually be abandoned once the paint goes on. They help keep me on track and ensure that even if my painting style is loose, at least the direction of the strokes and the tonal values are not out of place.

PAINT THE RAVEN: LAYER 1

3 Study the lightest shades in the bird and activate your cyan, magenta and black (if using the CMYK colour palette) by adding a touch of water to the pigments. This will enable you to add new colours to your first wash with ease.

4 Create a pool of light blue mix in your palette, tinged with a little pink and a hint of black. Apply the mix to dry paper, along and inside the wing area. As you spread paint across the wing, observe the colour changes and add a little magenta into your blue mix, allowing it to merge with the colour on the paper.

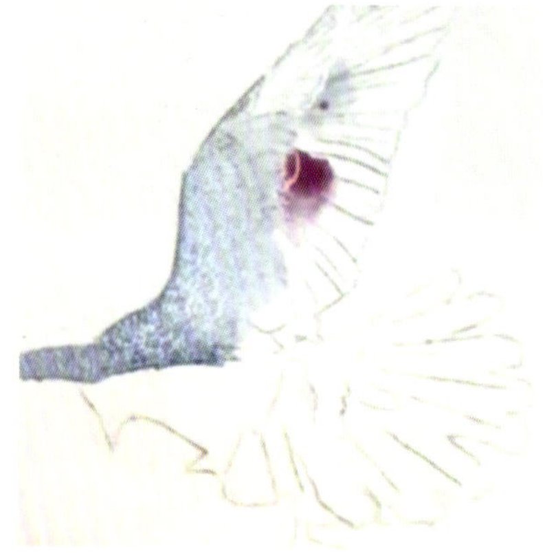

→ Drop new colour into existing colour, prior to dragging it over the rest of the wing.

5 Spread the magenta/blue over the centre and edges of the wing. When it comes to the individual tips of the wing, use the point of your brush to create the thin vertical shapes.

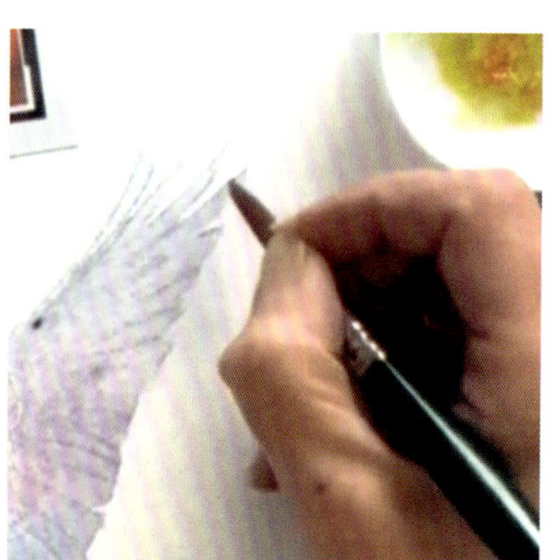

→ If your brush tip is sharp, you can use a size 10 or 12 round brush for the finer sections too.

6 Once this wash has been laid down, you will have an excellent opportunity to add darker, thicker shades to the end of the wing tips, while the paper is still damp. This will enable subtle blends and soft edges.

When you have added the thicker pigment, try not to fuss with it. Give the watercolour time to settle down and do its thing. Turn your attention to one of the other parts of the raven and build up colours and tones elsewhere, such as in the tail.

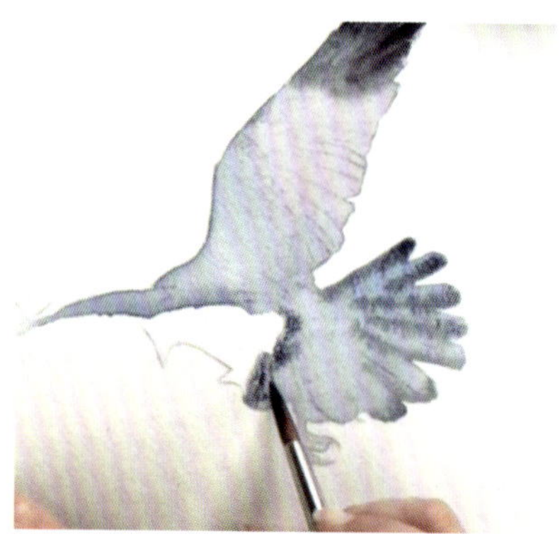

→ Thicker paint into a damp underlayer to create soft edges in the tail and wing.

7 If any areas are still damp, this is a really great time to build up colour and tone by using darker thicker paint. Apply it delicately with the tip of your brush. Just coax the paint and let the moisture carry it through the page.

Continue until paint covers the whole raven. Remember that this layer must be denser than the damp one underneath to avoid blooms and an ineffective wash.

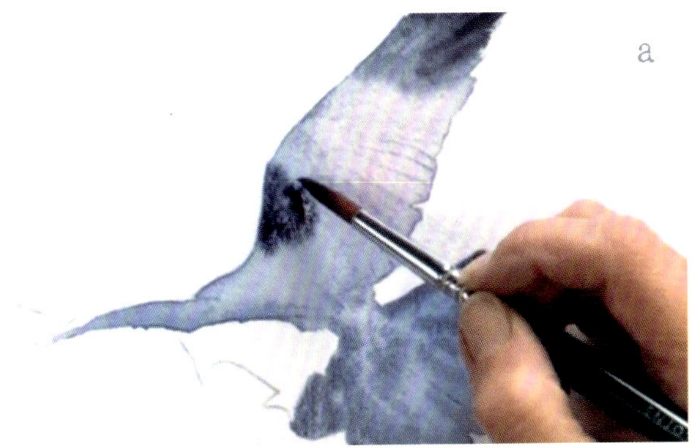

↑ Dabbing the paint onto the paper, allowing spaces between the dabs for the paint to spread.

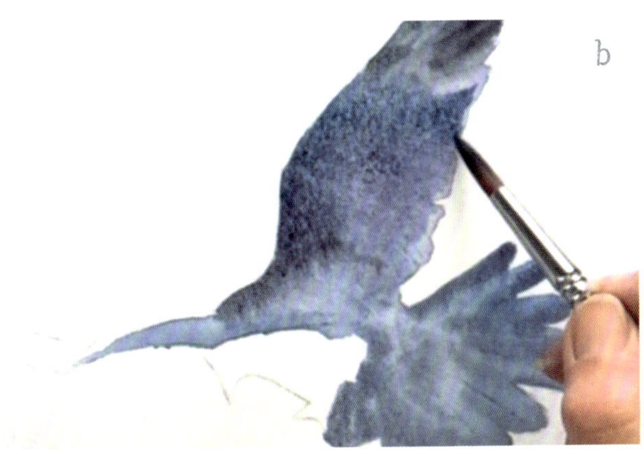

↑ Continuing to spread colour onto damp paper.

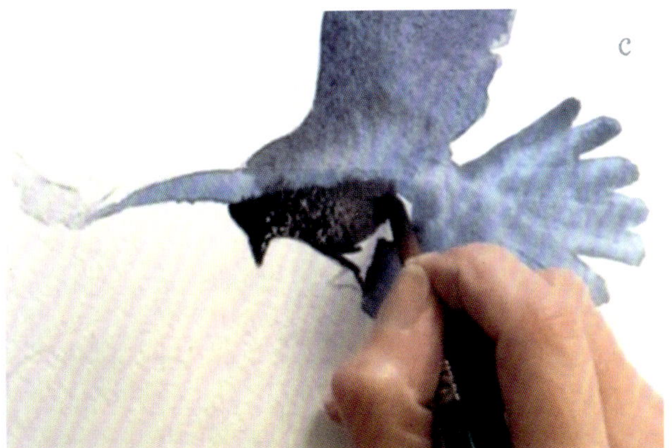

↑ Applying the darkest shade to the underside of the raven.

8 While leaving paint to do its thing is a great idea, sometimes you'll need to pull it back a little to regain light and form. I lifted paint from the wing areas with a damp brush.

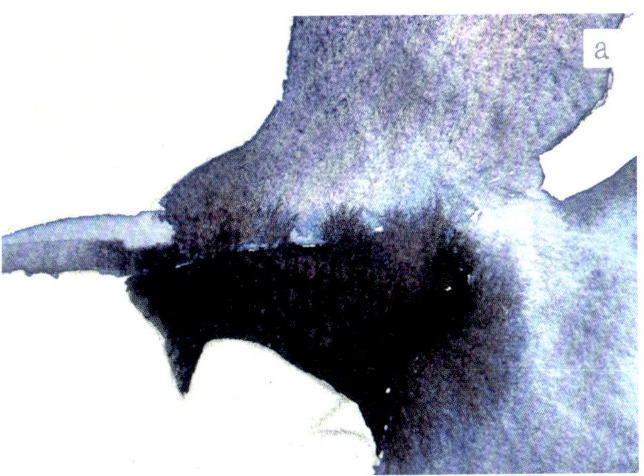

↑ The newly applied paint has spread into the wing area. I did consider leaving it, as I loved the soft blends, but then decided to lift it away to regain some definition.

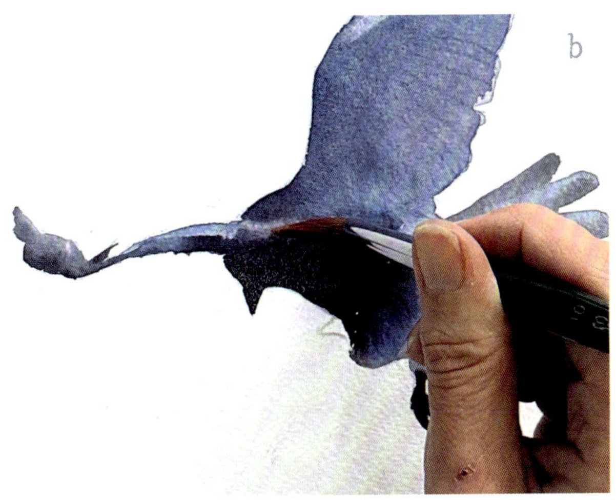

↑ Paint always manages to seep back into the newly cleared areas, so multiple sweeps using a damp brush to lift the paint are often needed.

↘ Allow the piece to dry thoroughly before the next stage.

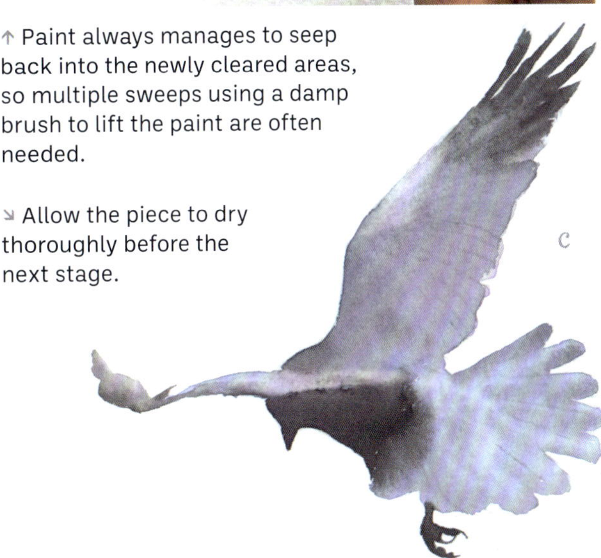

ADD DETAILS TO THE RAVEN: LAYER 2, SKETCHING THE FOLIAGE

9 Once the painting has dried, assess the piece. Are there parts you'd like to lift or darken? Are there beautiful sections that you'd like to retain where the watercolour has created fabulous shapes, colours and edges? These are decisions that only you can make, and much of it will be trial and error during your early stages as a painter.

In my painting, I loved the softness of the tail feathers and how the purples had dissipated gently into the cool blues. I felt the main wing needed more detail, in terms of brighter colours, darker tones and additional structure. I also wanted to add detail to the top of the head to define it more clearly from the wing nearest to the viewer.

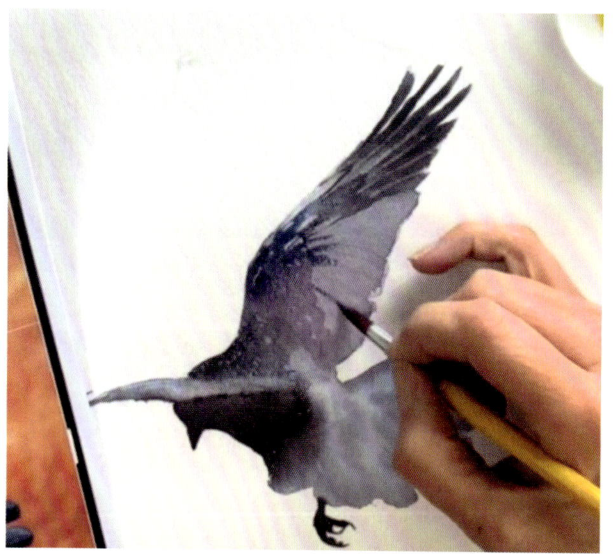

↑ Colours, tones and shapes emboldened but allowing some of the undercolours to show through.

At this stage, I always work on dry paper and apply more confident tones directly to the surface, bleeding them out with water and allowing the undercolours to peep through.

10 The image below shows how I've adjusted the areas of concern. I also found it useful at this point to sketch out the foliage in readiness for the next stage.

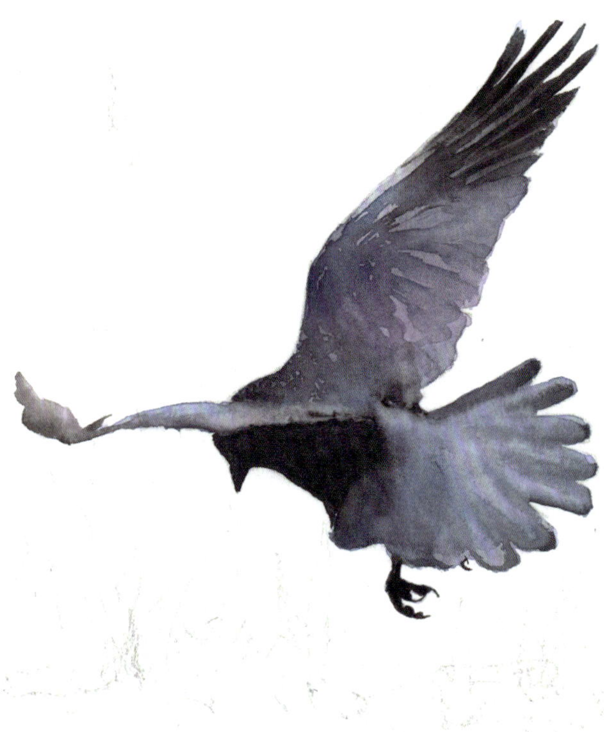

↑ The finished raven, ready for the foliage.

PAINT THE FOLIAGE

11 This is an exciting stage when you can let your imagination run wild. Look at the photograph and be inspired by the colours and shapes that you see. In readiness to paint the foliage, mix up some washes of mustard, olive, orange and burgundy.

12 Working on dry paper, use both the rigger brush and round brush to create loose wisps of grasses and foliage. You can achieve this by flicking your brush up the paper, making sure that the line tapers towards the end. Vary your strokes in terms of direction, length, colour and opacity. Start with your lighter colours first and then move on to thicker, darker colours. If you paint these wet-into-wet you will create some gorgeous blends.

The following images show the process of how I layered the foliage. Remember all the techniques that you employed in the previous projects, especially Chapter 2. If you want to add salt, crayon, pastel, cling film or anything else that you had success with, go for it!

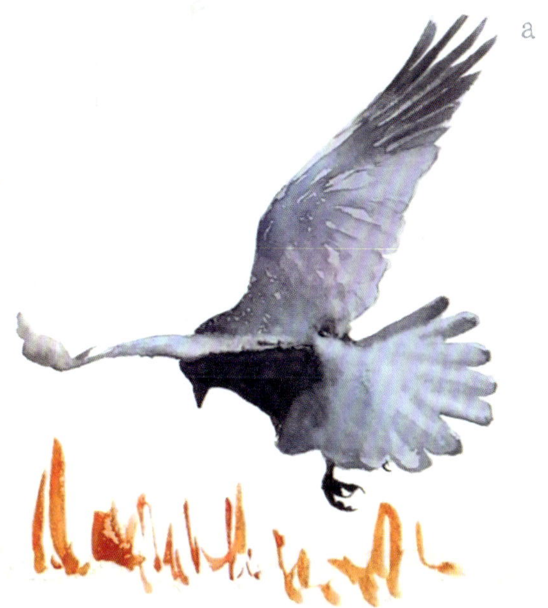

↑ Warm orange reds added to dry paper with the rigger brush.

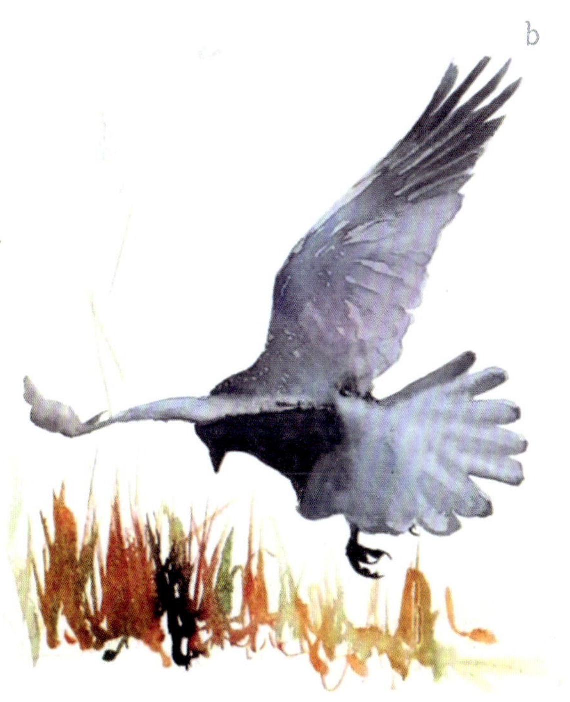

↑ Darker greens and browns flicked on, allowing colours to merge and blend.

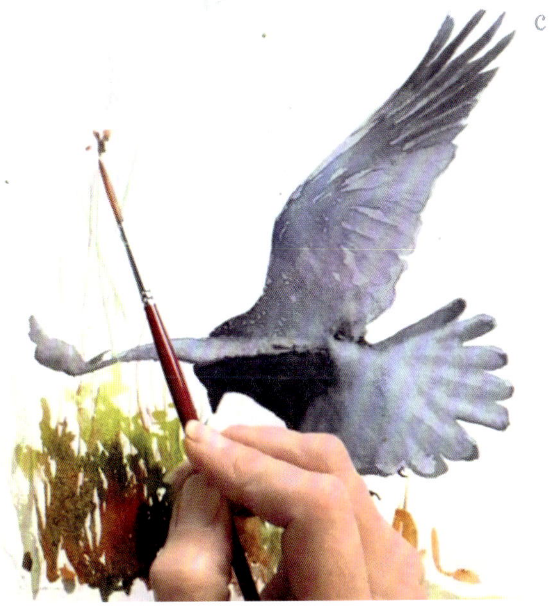

↑ The rigger was used to make light marks suggesting buds or flowers. This was in line with the composition.

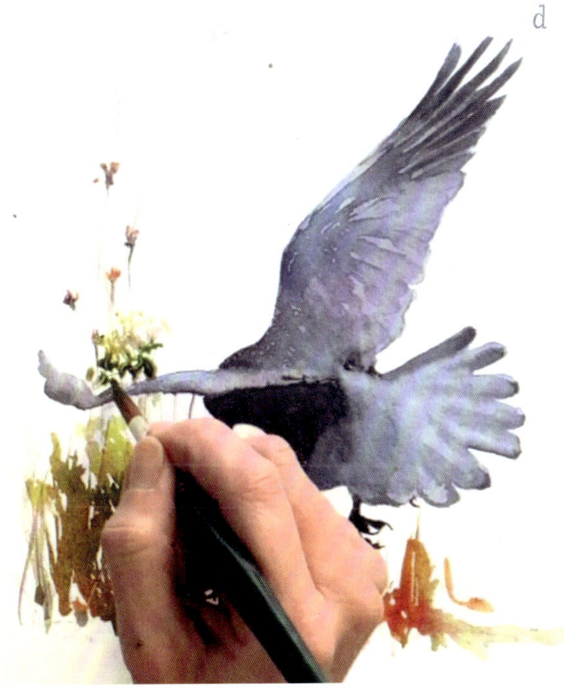

↑ Take advantage of the paint's wet state to drop other colours into it. Use any brush to dob colours onto the paper.

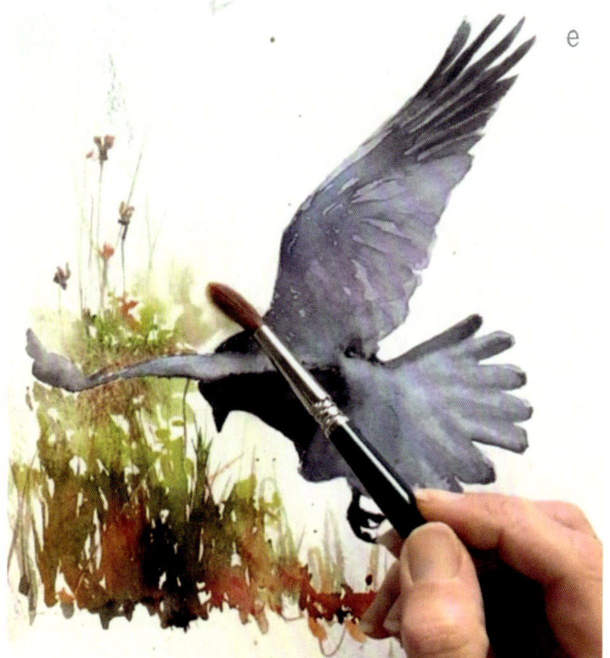

↑ Loosen sections up and create small background washes at the same time by dragging a large bead of water across setting paint.

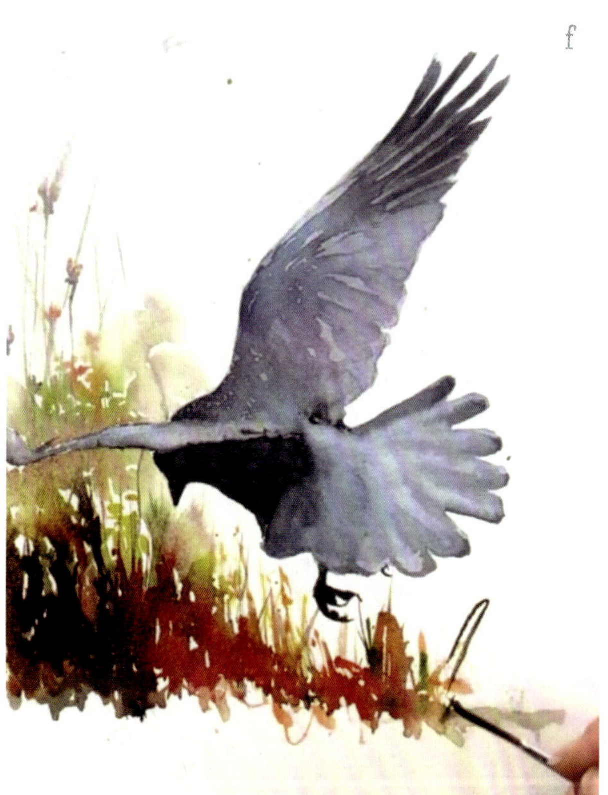

↑ Use a rigger brush to create calligraphic marks. Remember that nature is messy, so make sure that some of your grasses bend and loop.

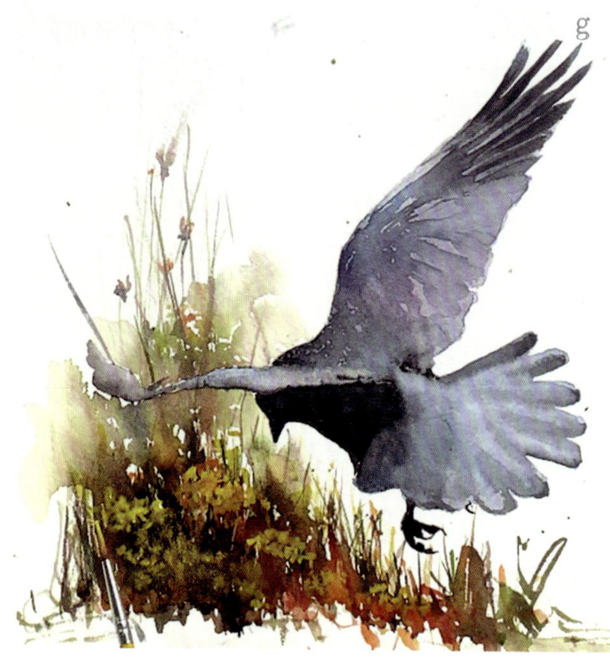

↑ Once you have got your darks established, you are ready to add some lighter notes. These can be pushed further at the next stage with gouache.

13 When the piece has dried, it may look rather flat. Brighter notes can bring life and energy back into the piece, so explore marks with pens, gouache and acrylic inks, as in the following images.

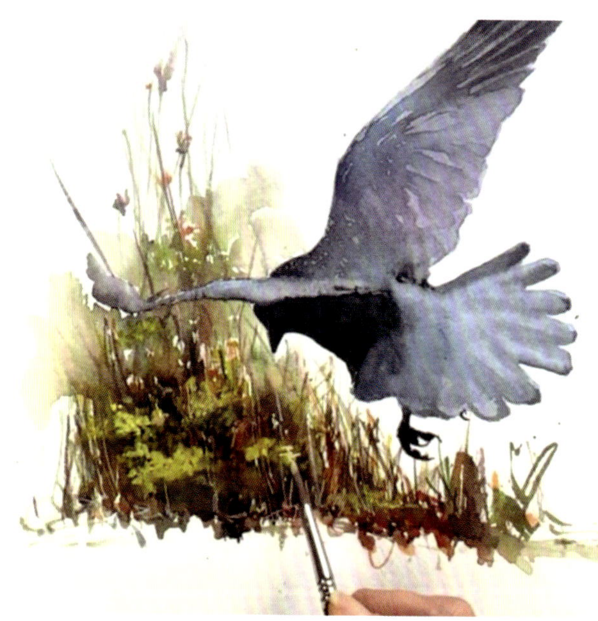

↑ Yellow or white gouache mixed with yellow watercolour can give you beautiful light colours. The addition of bright and pale oranges also works well at this stage, either brushed or splashed onto the page.

FINISHING TOUCHES

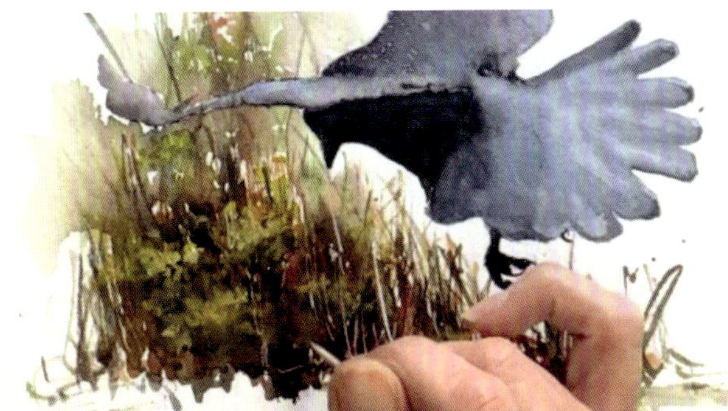

↑ I used white gel pen to scribble lines on top of the dark shapes. Line work with white acrylic ink can really break up those dark blocks of colour. If it's too bright, simply wipe off the excess with your finger. I find this more accurate than taking a tissue to it.

→ A close-up of the foliage, showing a whole range of marks applied with brushes, pens and splashes.

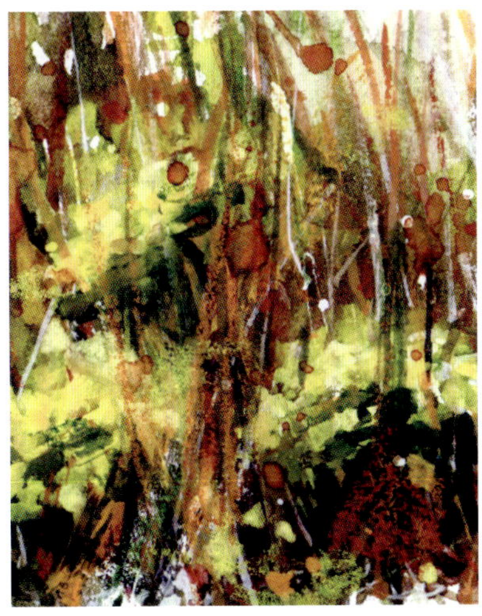

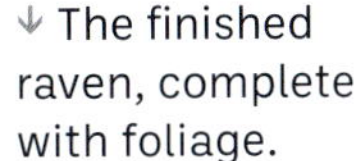

↓ The finished raven, complete with foliage.

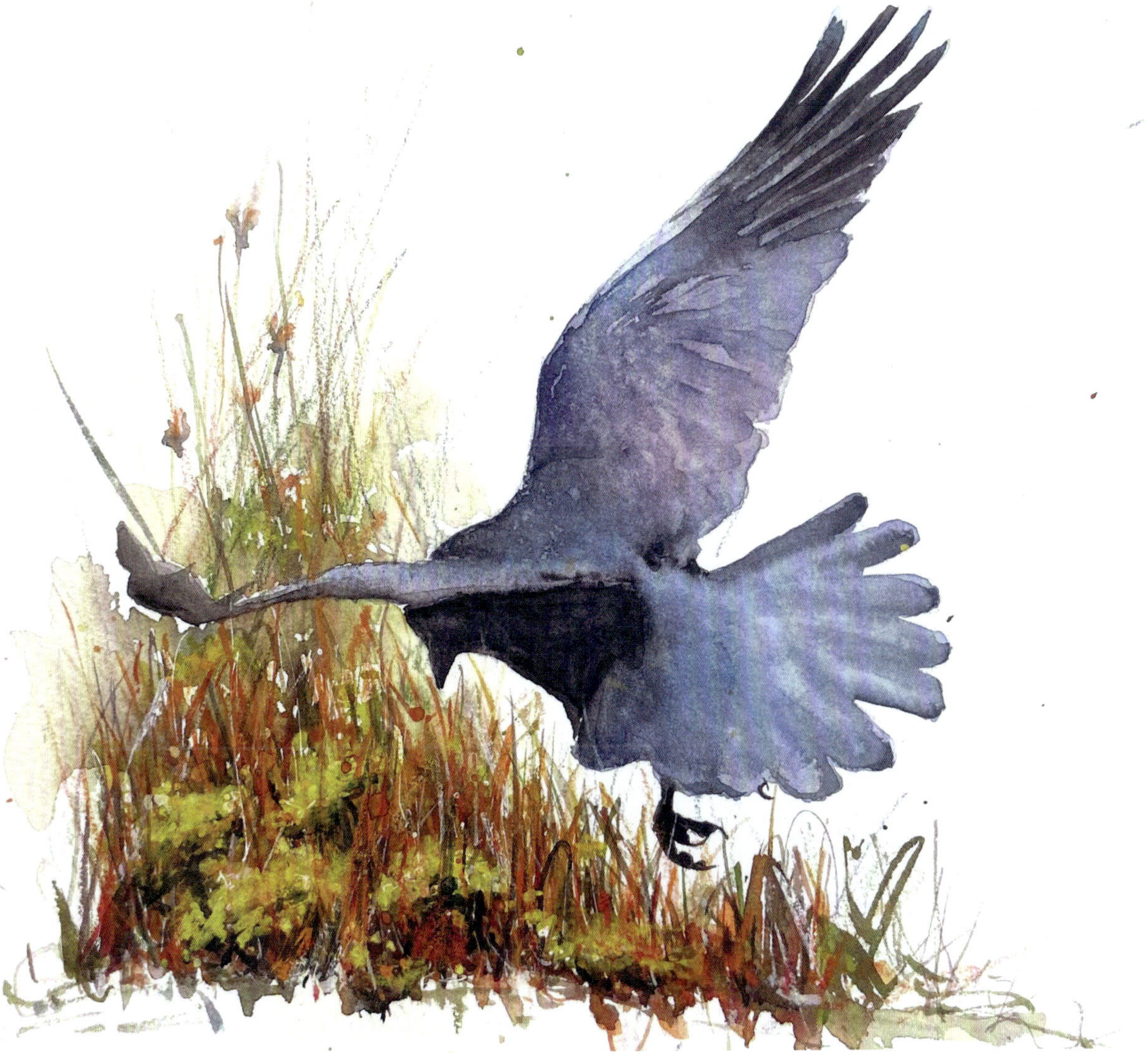

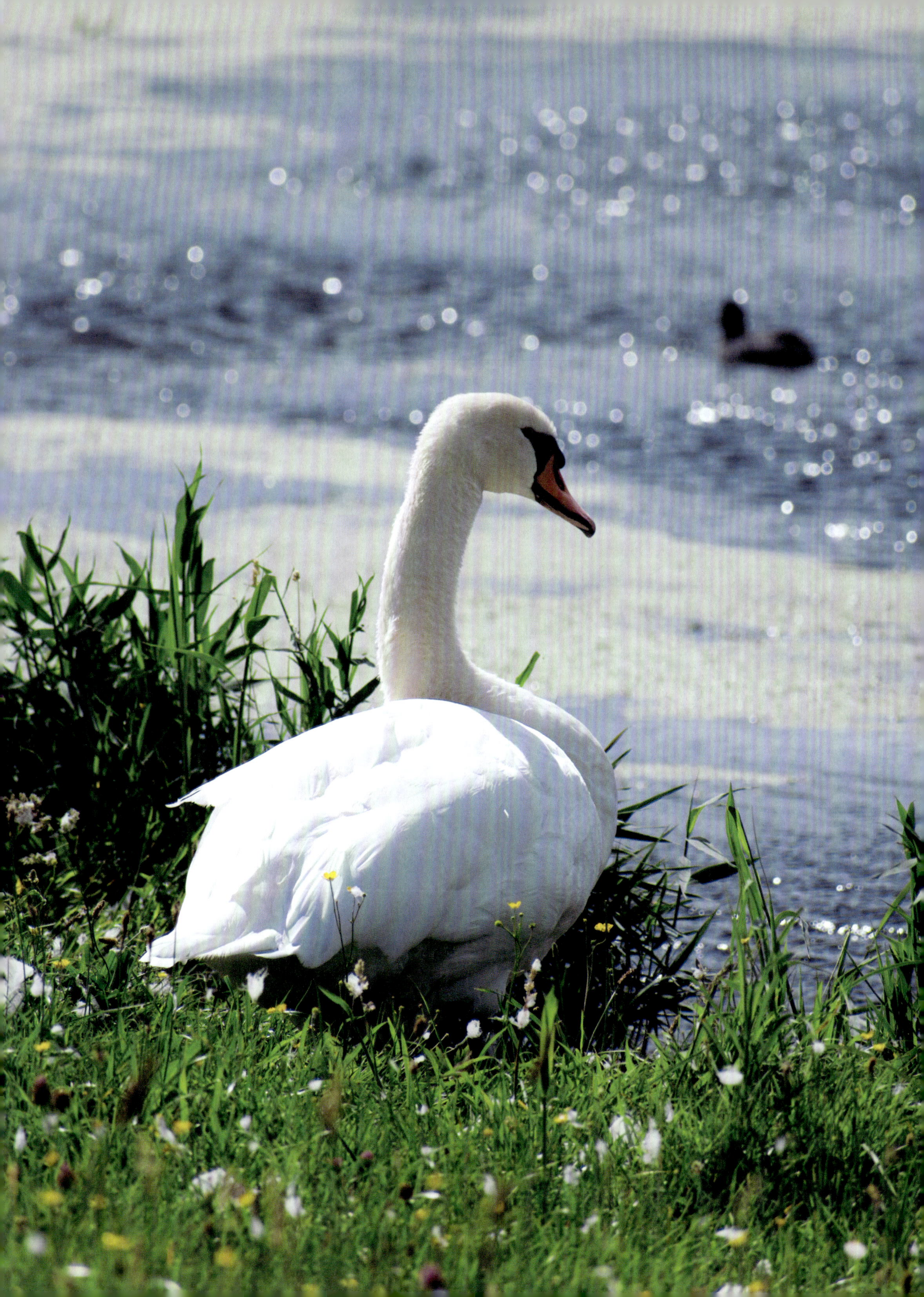

CHAPTER 10

Depicting White Birds and Creating Environmental Elements

Even the whitest of birds aren't actually 'white' when it comes to painting them; large sections of their bodies are often in shadow, creating a vast array of colours. This painting features one of our dear old rescue hens, who lived to the ripe old age of nine. Watching the chickens go about their daily business always gives me a sense of calm. When taking a photograph, try and capture the backlight for added impact.

One particularly effective way of enhancing the whites of a bird is to embed it in a background, whether it be a loose wash of sky or a garden scene, as in the case of 'Life Goes On'. The darks of the foliage serve to enhance the perceived lightness of the hen, even though closer inspection reveals that much of her body is painted with mid-tone neutrals. The brighter, more saturated tones are concentrated in the grass.

In this chapter we are going to paint a beautiful swan, but this time we will incorporate background washes and marks into the painting to suggest skies, water and vegetation.

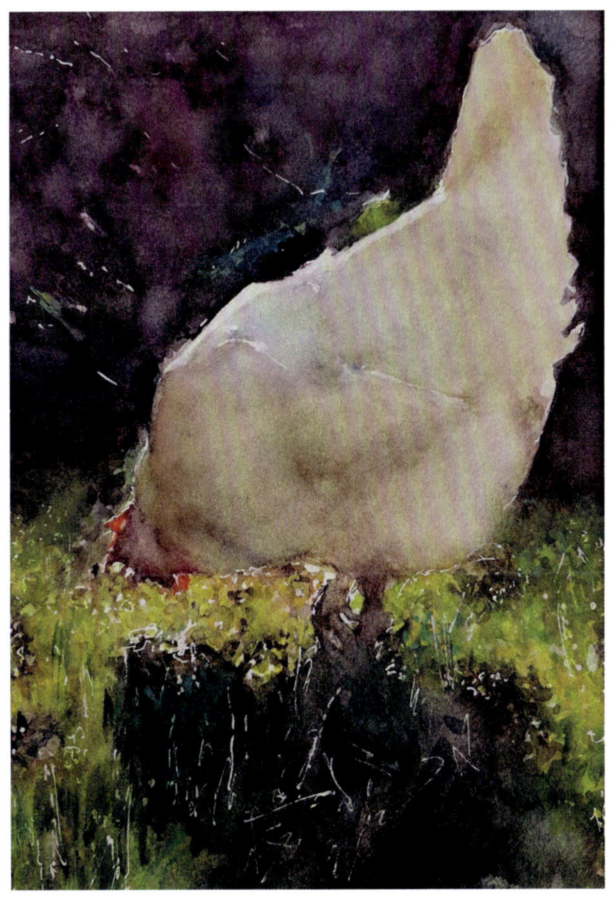

→ 'Life Goes On', 2020, watercolour and gel pen. Winner of the Felix Award 2021, Wolverhampton Society of Artists, Wolverhampton Public Art Gallery and Museum.

PROJECT 10

Exploiting shadow colours and supporting features – painting a swan

You will need

- Photographic references of the swan and its environment
- Paper: minimum 200 gsm, cold press, textured watercolour paper
- Paint: CMYK colour palette (p.158), either watercolour pan or tube
- Brushes: synthetic size 6 and 12 round pointed brushes, small detailer brush, size 0, 1 or 2 rigger brush, 1 inch flat brush
- Palette, water container, paper towel
- Wax-free transfer or tracing paper and washi tape (optional)
- Stationery: HB pencil and eraser

COMPOSE AND DRAFT OUT THE PIECE

It's really important that the addition of background and foreground features are not treated as afterthoughts. That's not to say you have to rigidly adhere to a preconceived composition, but take care not to inadvertently spoil a piece by creating outside elements that jar with or take the emphasis away from the main subject. Both the subject and supporting features need to work well together in harmony.

1 Give yourself permission to play about with a photograph to decide how you are going to make it work for you. Things that work well in a photograph won't necessarily translate well if copied meticulously in a painting. You are the artist. You get to decide what the emphasis of your painting is and how you will set about achieving your goal.

When I first came across this photograph of a swan by some water, I was drawn to the potential that the hues in the shadow areas gave me. However beautiful the photo though, I wanted to build up a composition that was more suitable for my purposes. In this case, I used Procreate, but you could just as easily make a thumbnail composition using a pencil and paper as we did in Chapter 9. My priorities were as follows:

1 Create a more subtle, desaturated palette.
2 Draw attention to the swan and away from the water.
3 Utilise the foliage to help silhouette the swan.
4 Use the rule of thirds (see p.48) to keep the major activity in the bottom two-thirds of the image, with the swan's face sitting near the top-right intersection and the light from its back hitting the lower-left intersection.

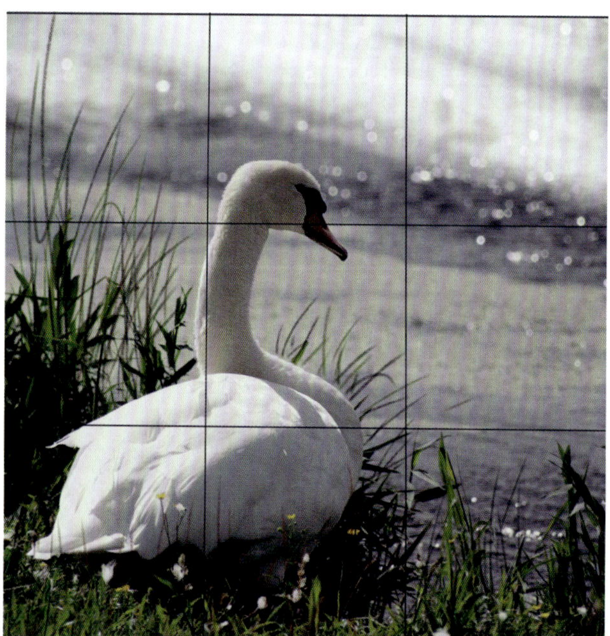

↑ My digital thumbnail composition: I felt this arrangement helped place emphasis on the main subject, the swan.

In my digital thumbnail composition, you can see that I have elongated the grasses to the left to help form a diagonal flow from top left to bottom right and to give me the chance to add expressive brush marks. I have also reduced the dominance of the water, as I felt it was competing for the viewer's attention with the swan.

There is still enough colour in the piece to create an effective halo of colour around the subject. You will also see that I decided to mute the colours a little to give the piece a sense of calm and tranquillity. I decided on some red/green colourways in the long grasses, and the river will most likely be an indigo/magenta mix.

Bear in mind that you will be applying this background wash when you select your paper. Depending on the thickness of your paper and the quantity of water that you apply to it, it may be advisable for you to 'stretch' your paper first (see Chapter 2). I used 350 gsm paper by Seawhite of Brighton and was reasonably restrained with the quantity of water that I applied at this stage. As a result, my paper didn't buckle too badly. If you have not created background washes before, I would recommend that you create a test piece first on spare paper to avoid any unexpected surprises midway through the painting.

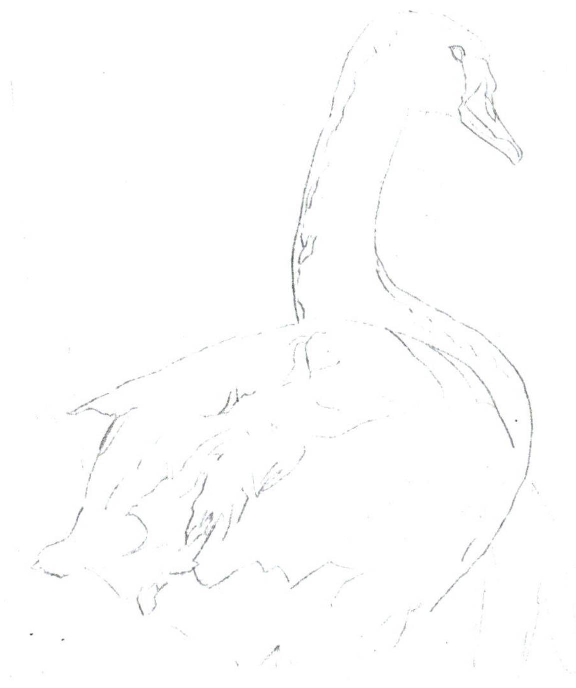

↑ My drawing of the swan.

PREPARE THE PIECE FOR PAINTING

2 Once you have designed your composition, draw or trace the swan onto a piece of watercolour paper.

3 Use washi tape to mask the edge of the page. This is a form of low-tack masking tape, ideal for masking off the edges of paintings, which allows for a lovely crisp edge on removal. Be aware that some brands are tackier than others, so always test a piece first.

Top tip

If you have purchased masking tape that is too sticky, remove some of the tackiness by lightly pressing it onto a piece of material until it has the right level of adhesion.

4 Study the photograph and decide which section of the swan you'd like to start painting. I started with the neck. Activate your palette with a little water and mix up varying thicknesses of some of the hues. When looking at the shadow colours in the face and neck, I saw mostly blues and lilacs, but you may wish to emphasise other colours.

PAINT THE FIRST LAYER

5 Starting with the neck and moving into the body, lay down your first wash on dry paper, ensuring that you chop and change your colours regularly to allow for variation of both hue and tone. This is where your activated mixes come in handy. The following photos show me working through the head and body, linking colours while still wet in that first wash.

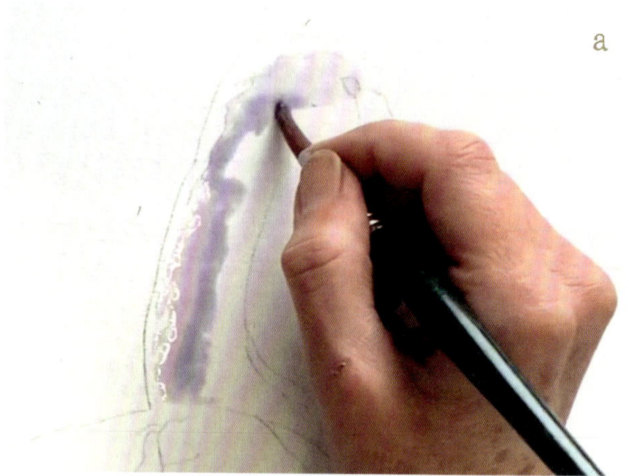

↑ Lilac and pink hues made with varying degrees of cyan and magenta.

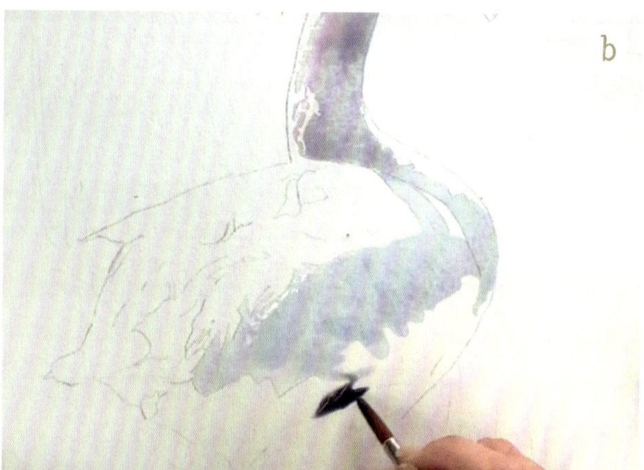

↑ Moving into darker shades by adding just a touch of black to a cyan mix.

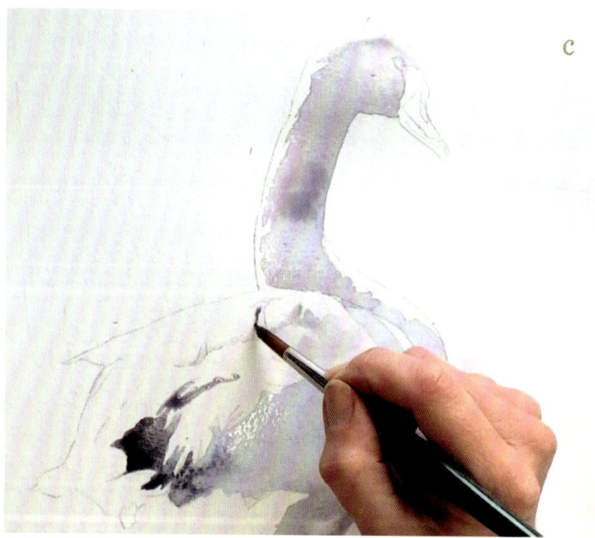

↑ If working on dry paper, be aware that your edges will be hard with a resultant tidemark around each shape on drying, so be sure to use plenty of water if you are recreating lighter shades.

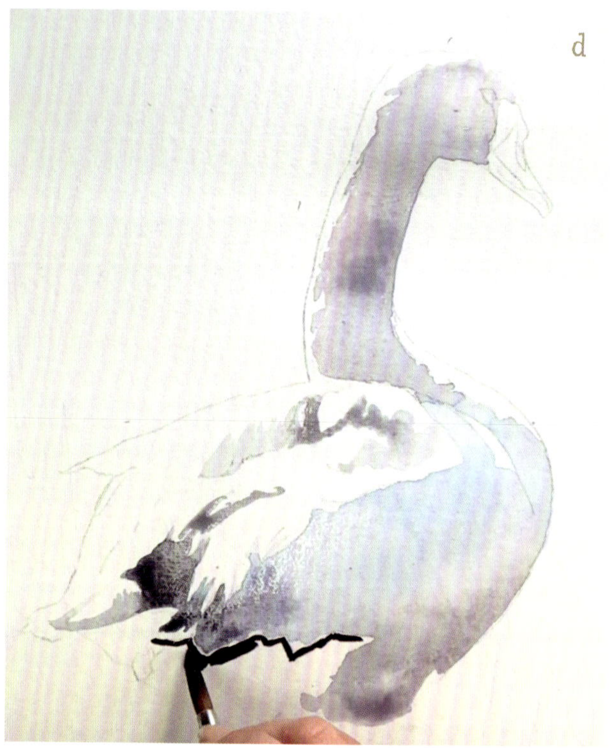

↑ Cutting in the dark shape at the base of the swan. I am careful not to touch the damp area above at this stage, as it will spread and overpower the lighter shades.

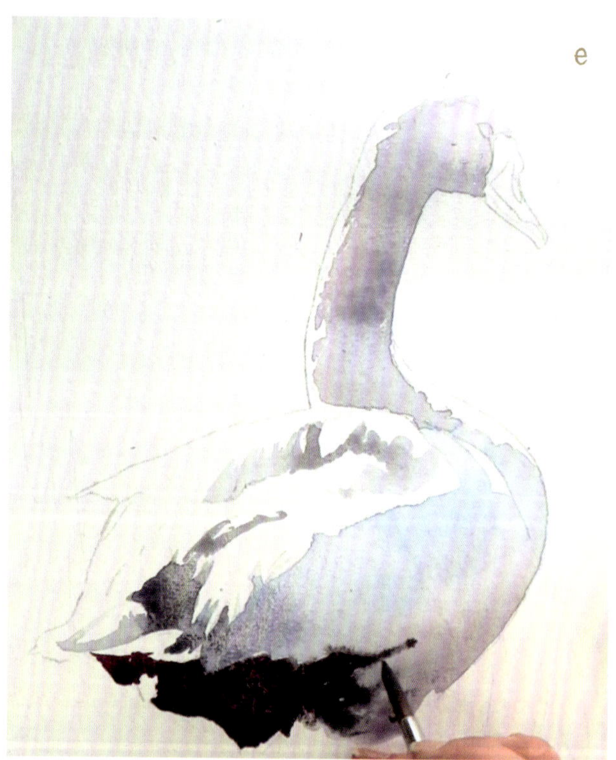

↑ The dark magenta/black mix is being gently coaxed into the lighter section at this stage, with the expectation that it will create some beautiful soft edges.

6 Note how I have treated the base of the swan and the vegetation almost as one, allowing the colours to bleed into each other. Do not worry about this first layer, as much of it will be overlaid or even lifted during the process.

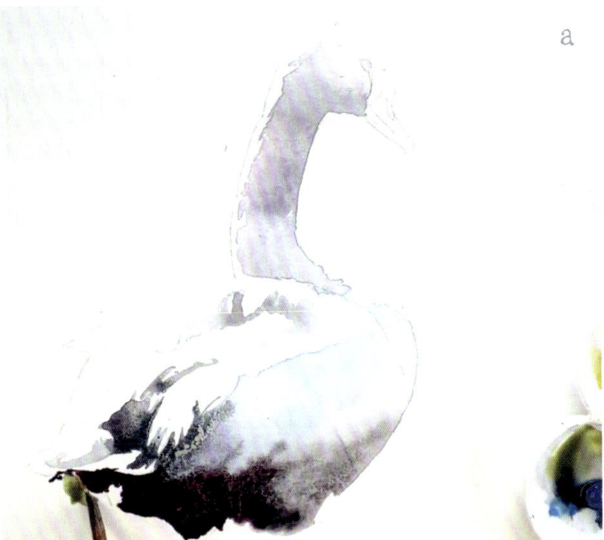

↑ Ensuring a seamless transition from vegetation to swan by joining the colours together. Timing and pigment control is key here to avoid a bland shape.

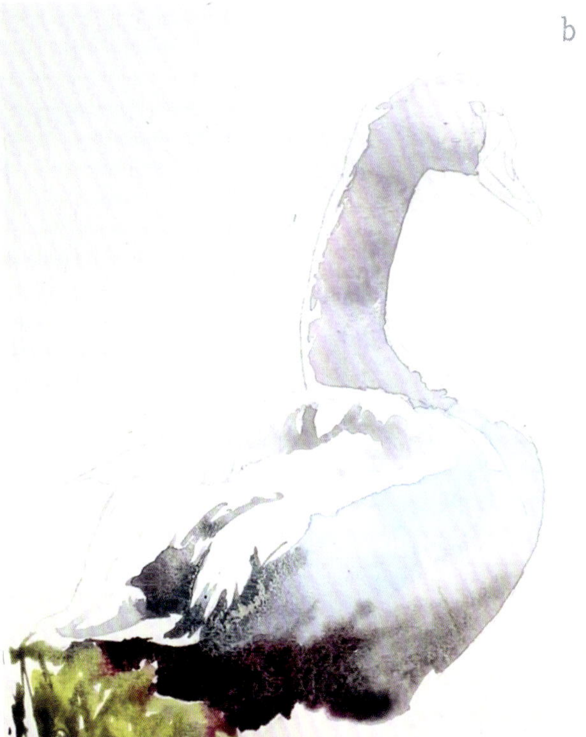

↑ The magenta is just beginning to bleed into the green to create beautiful tones. Much of this will most likely be covered with subsequent layers, but some may make the final cut.

7 Once you have laid down the first wash on the body, complete the face. I found it easier to turn the painting and reference photograph upside down. I completed the beak details with a detailer brush for precision.

→ Painting the facial features upside down for ease of painting. See how the colours at the base of the swan's neck have moved into each other. Some of the paint has granulated, which was an unexpected surprise.

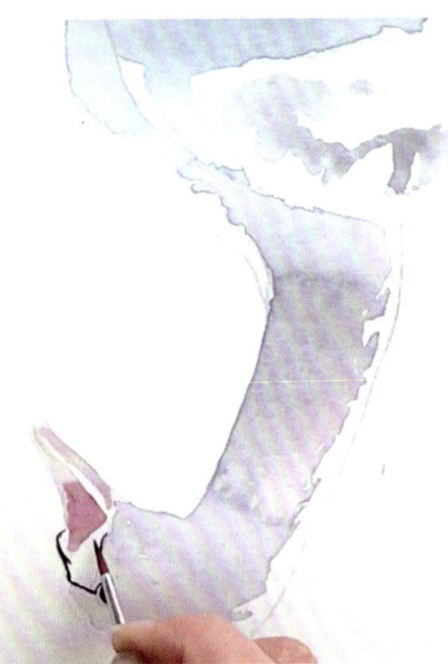

8 There comes a point when working on this stage becomes counterproductive as the paper becomes oversaturated. This is a good time to let it settle and dry.

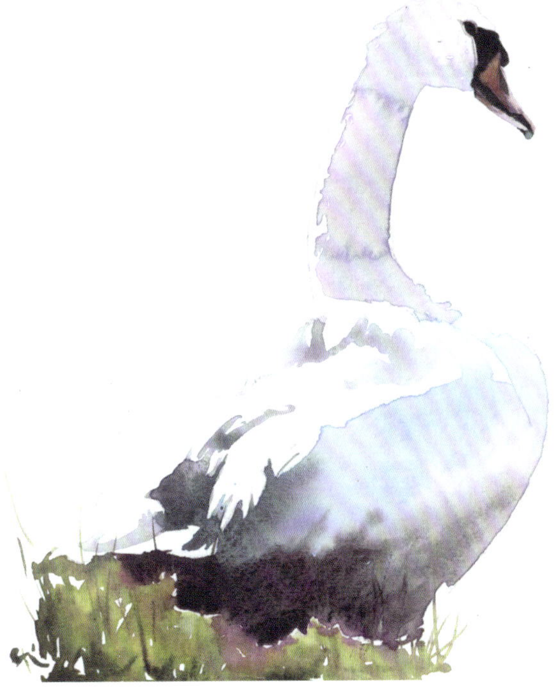

↑ A lot can be achieved in layer one. There is an unsightly bloom in the neck of the swan, but this can be fixed on subsequent layers.

CREATE THE FIRST LAYER OF THE BACKGROUND WASH AND DROP IN VEGETATION WET-INTO-WET

9 Background washes can be scary to do; however they can be less intimidating if you cover the selected area with water first. I tend to work flat, but you may find it helpful to tilt your board at a slight angle to facilitate the flow of the pigment. Using a 1 inch flat brush for speed, cover as much of the background as you can with water.

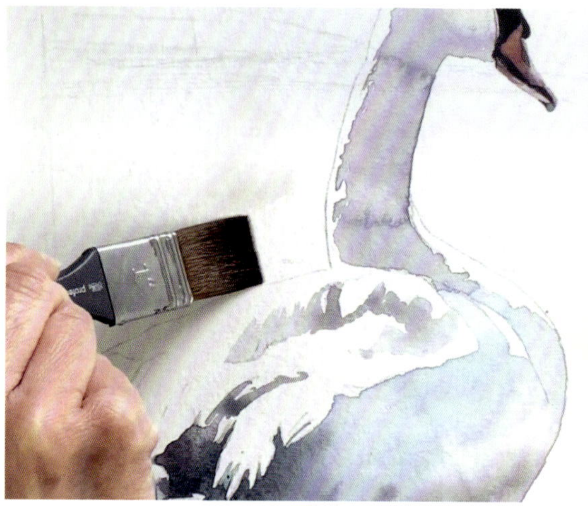

↑ A 1 inch flat brush is an excellent tool for laying down water or paint quickly. Applying water to the paper first makes the process of creating a sky or water less daunting.

10 Having applied water to the majority of your paper, cut in tighter to the swan itself using a smaller brush.

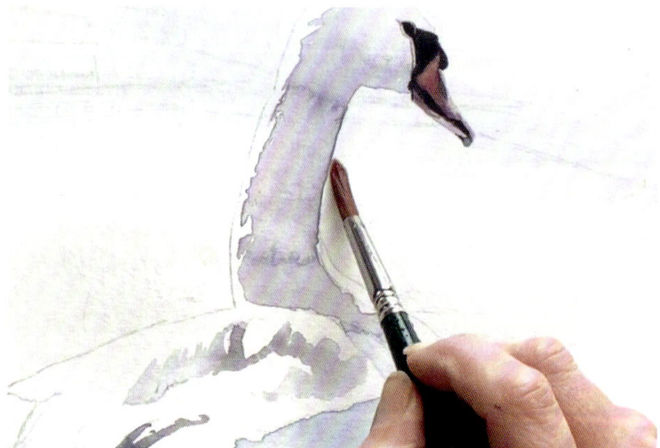

↑ A size 10 or 12 round brush with a sharp point is great for getting closer to the swan with water.

11 Using a cyan/black or indigo mix, use the 1 inch flat brush to swipe and spread blue hues in a variety of directions. By turning your brush around you can lay down and pull colour through wherever you wish. The clear water will help carry the pigment through.

Try not to overthink this process, but use your thumbnail to help guide the direction and spread of your pigment. Leave pockets of areas of paper to allow for light relief that might suggest clouds, waves and so on.

Although the photograph showed an expanse of water in front of the swan, I wanted to suggest that there was sky and water in the background, but that was just my interpretation.

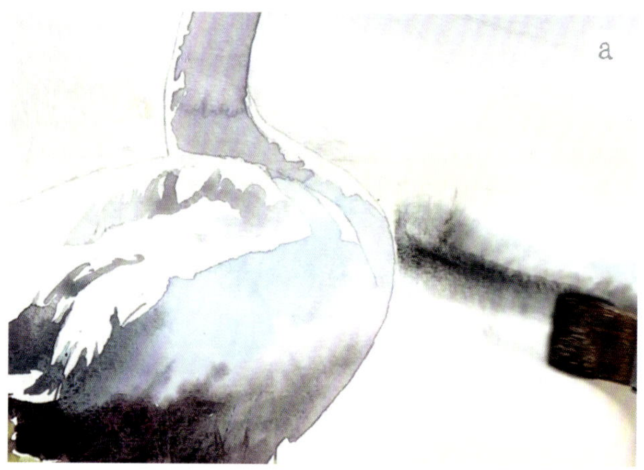

↑ Applying a cyan/black mix onto damp paper with a swift wide stroke. The black and cyan dissipate on the paper, which can lead to interesting results.

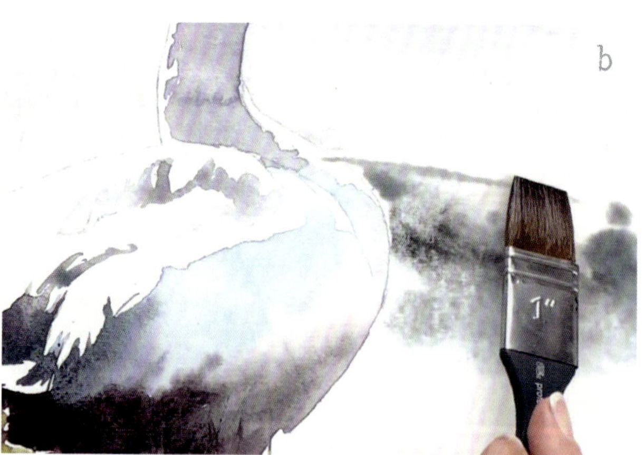

↑ Use the tip of the flat brush to create a linear shape. I'm always conscious of leaving unpainted sections too, so that the paint will have chance to spread of its own accord.

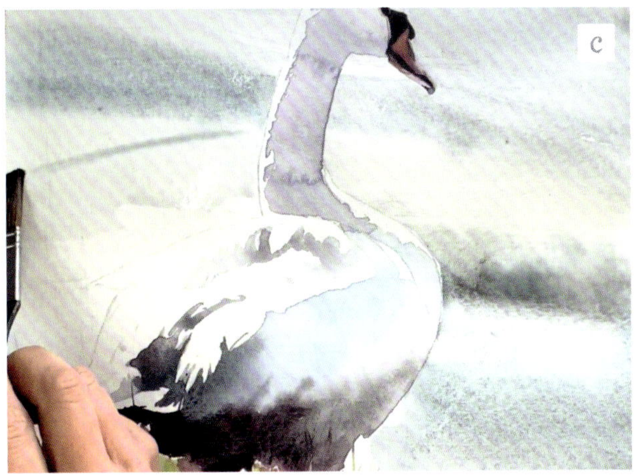

↑ Paint applied as a thinner line by sweeping the tip of the flat brush across the page. These strokes are intuitive and I'd encourage you to experiment with brushes and movements that come naturally to you.

BUILD UP TONE AND DETAIL

12 This is the all-important section where you get to add depth and interest through colour, tone and mark making, creating the beginnings of the vegetation. Try to avoid a sharp delineation between sky, water and grasses, otherwise the piece can look like two separate paintings cobbled together. Re-wet the paper in the sections where you want to accentuate the water or sky. Apply more pigment and spread as you did with the first layer.

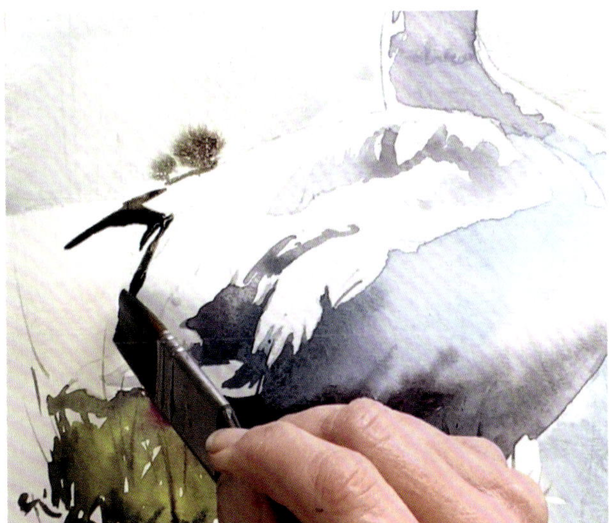

↑ Using the 1 inch flat brush to cut in the dark vegetation to the edge of the swan. A pointed brush could be used equally as well.

13 The damp stage of the drying process is the ideal time to start cutting in the edge of the swan and dropping in long strokes of pigment using the rigger brush. As long as the pigment on your rigger brush is thick enough, you'll create beautiful fuzzy marks that will end up being faraway wisps of grass.

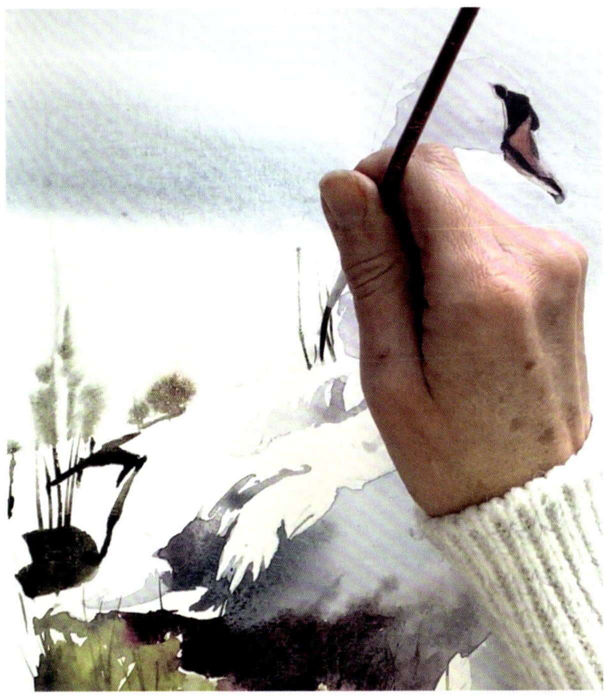

↑ Using a slim rigger to commence the grasses. See how that rigger brushwork has created fuzzy lines that will eventually be overlaid with tighter, hard-edged marks.

14 At this stage, it is worth mentioning the concept of aerial perspective. The further away something is from the viewer, the lighter, cooler (in terms of colour temperature) and less defined it is. So in order to paint a convincing background, it's good to have a mixture of shapes, some with soft and others hard edges, as well as ones that vary in tone and colour temperature. Reserve some lovely warm pigments for the vegetation at the front of your piece.

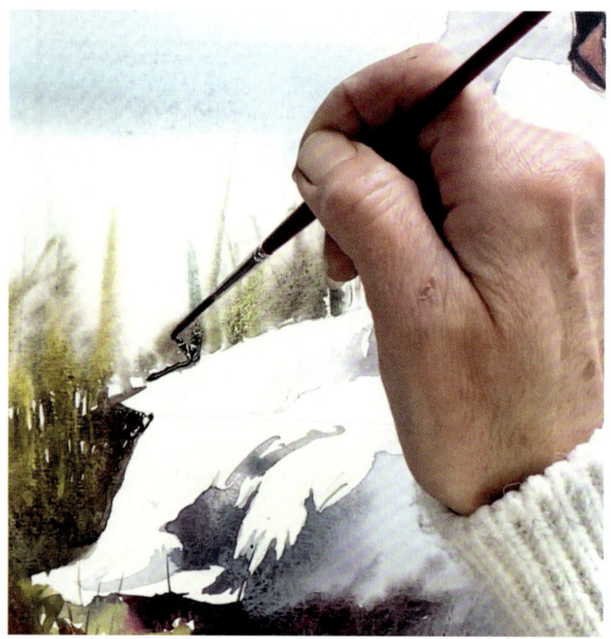

↑ The grasses are being painted, wet-into-wet to ensure soft edges. They are an excellent way of forming a silhouette around the white swan to create an area of strong tonal contrast. This will help create interest in the piece at a key grid intersection of the composition.

15 Don't worry about the odd bloom that may develop. The chances are it may work with the piece as it is, or it will be covered by subsequent layers, as in the case of my painting.

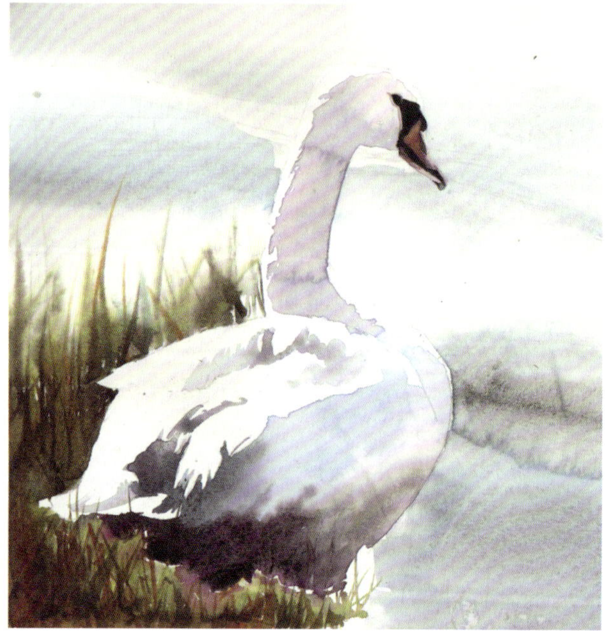

↑ I inadvertently created a bloom in the background. The paper had buckled slightly and water had pooled in it, creating a backwash.

Top tip

The artist John Lovett gives some really useful advice as to how blooms can be removed. He advocates gently working over the unwanted bloom, while it is still damp, with a dry hake brush to help remove it. If you keep the brush dry, and very gently and quickly feather it in different directions, it will smooth out the pigment.

SECOND LAYER AND FINISHING TOUCHES

16 Darken, lighten or brighten any areas that need adjustment on the swan and the grasses. I find it easier to work on dry paper at this stage, as it ensures more control over the shapes, colours and edges. If you need soft or lost edges, simply add water to the brush mark you've laid down on the page and bleed it out to the chosen endpoint. This also means that you can create some lovely sharp marks for the grasses.

I tend to work in a fairly random fashion at this point, switching between the swan and grasses. I'm constantly judging the piece and something might quickly catch my eye as I'm moving through it.

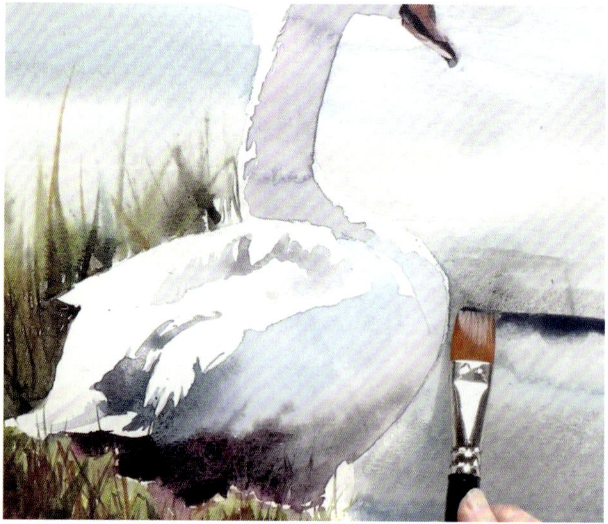

↑ Water has been applied to the paper with a smaller flat brush; then an additional layer of pigment is applied over the unwanted bloom.

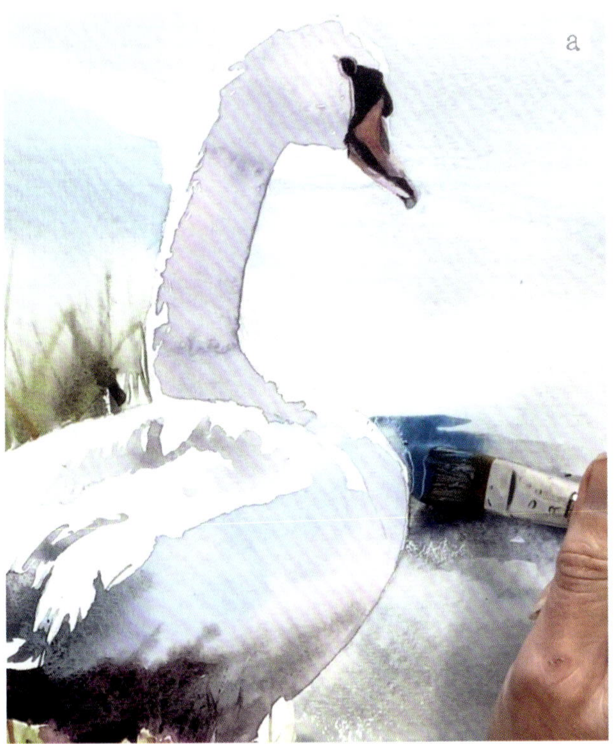

↑ Pigment being spread into the chosen area with the flat of the brush.

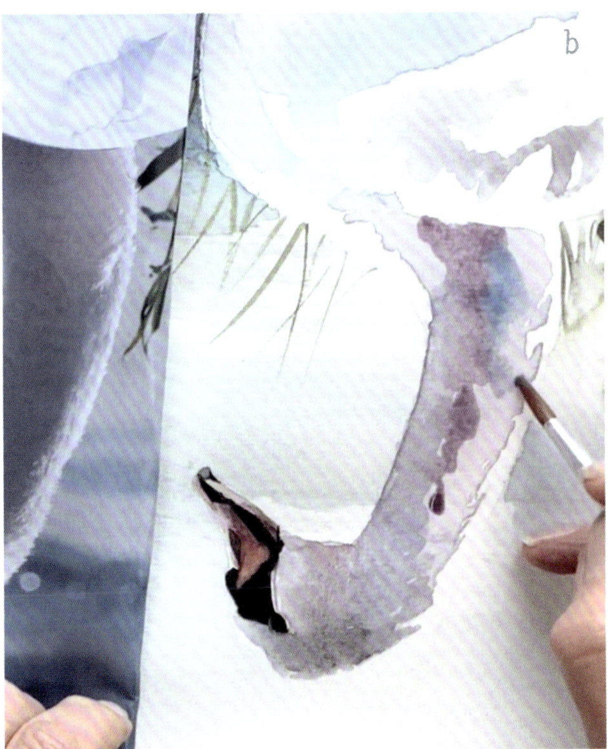

↑ Working with the photograph close to hand and upside down helps me to judge colour and value. As I darken areas on the second layer, I am still mindful of changing up the colours and encouraging them to blend.

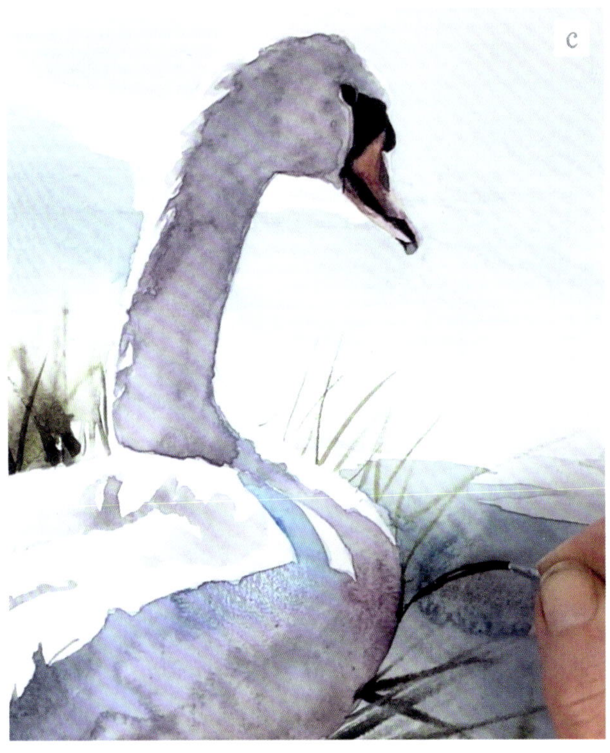

↑ Adding rigger brushwork to dry paper creates hard-edged lines. I am conscious of varying the direction of my strokes.

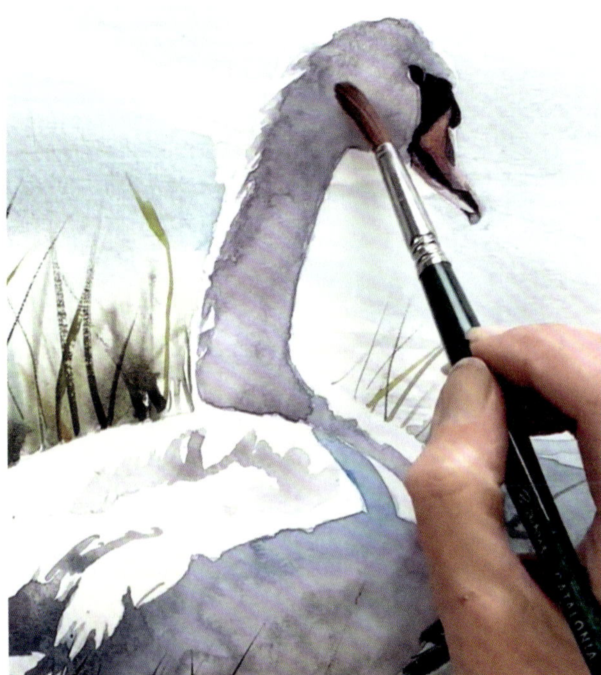

↑ Gently lifting out an area that was too dark by reactivating, agitating and swiping through with a thirsty brush. The residual paint can be dabbed away with a piece of kitchen towel, rolled into a point.

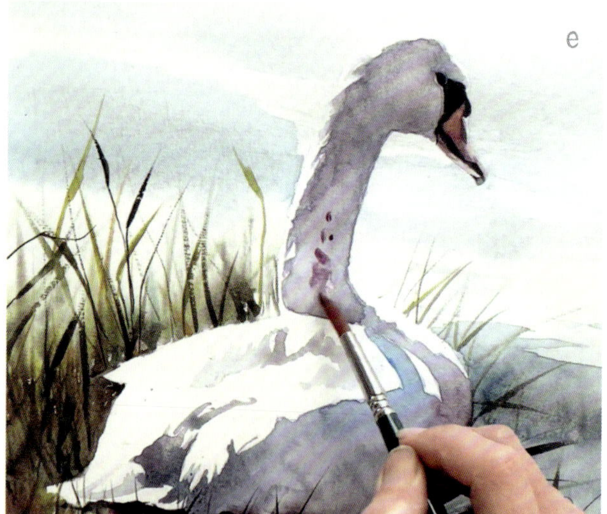

↑ Additional pops of magenta are added at the final stages.

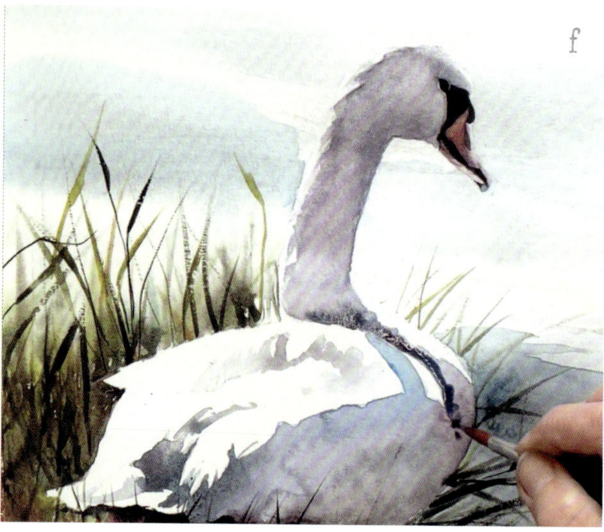

↑ An example of cyan/black tones being added to give form to the swan.

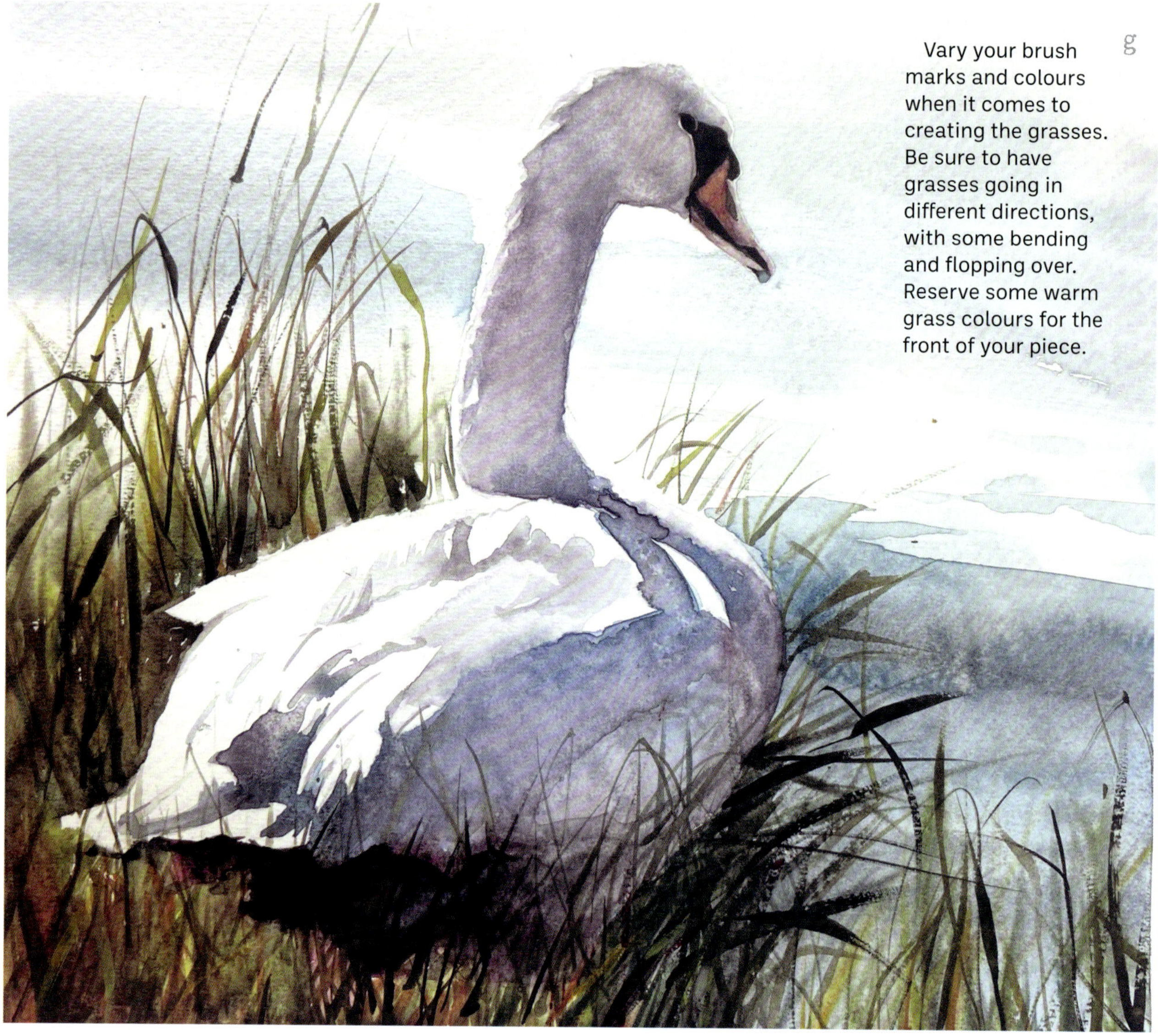

g

Vary your brush marks and colours when it comes to creating the grasses. Be sure to have grasses going in different directions, with some bending and flopping over. Reserve some warm grass colours for the front of your piece.

→ 'Me and My Shadow', 2019, watercolour. The 'whites' in the adult penguin are anything but white, as the penguin's body reflects its surroundings. Really push those colours to the max!

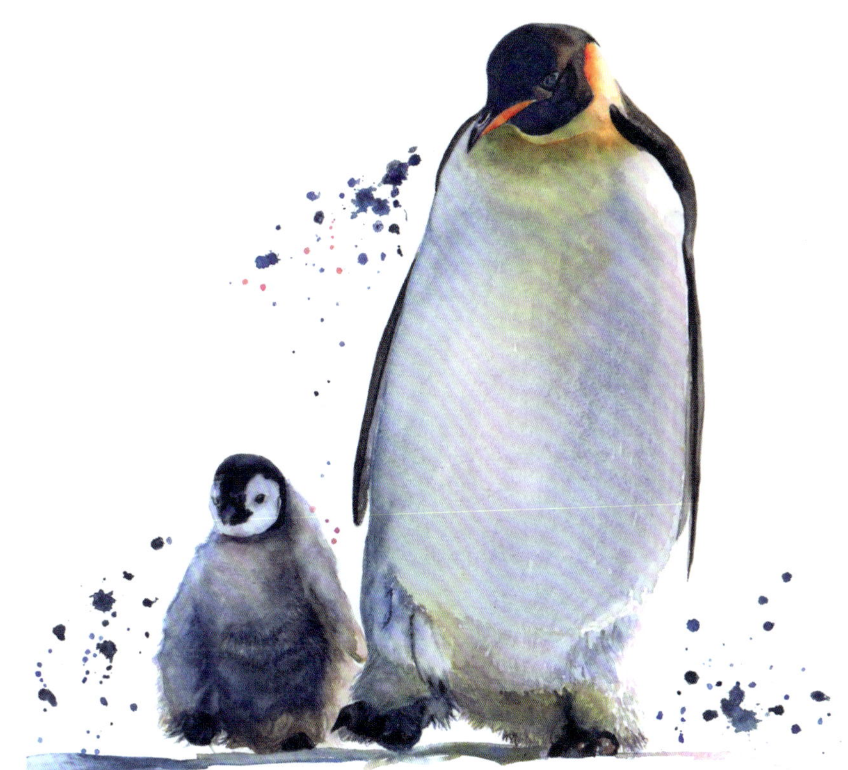

↓ 'Girls Night In', 2020, watercolour. White birds don't necessarily need to be surrounded by colour to allow them to shine. Look at the multitude of soft shades within the feathers of the white chicken.

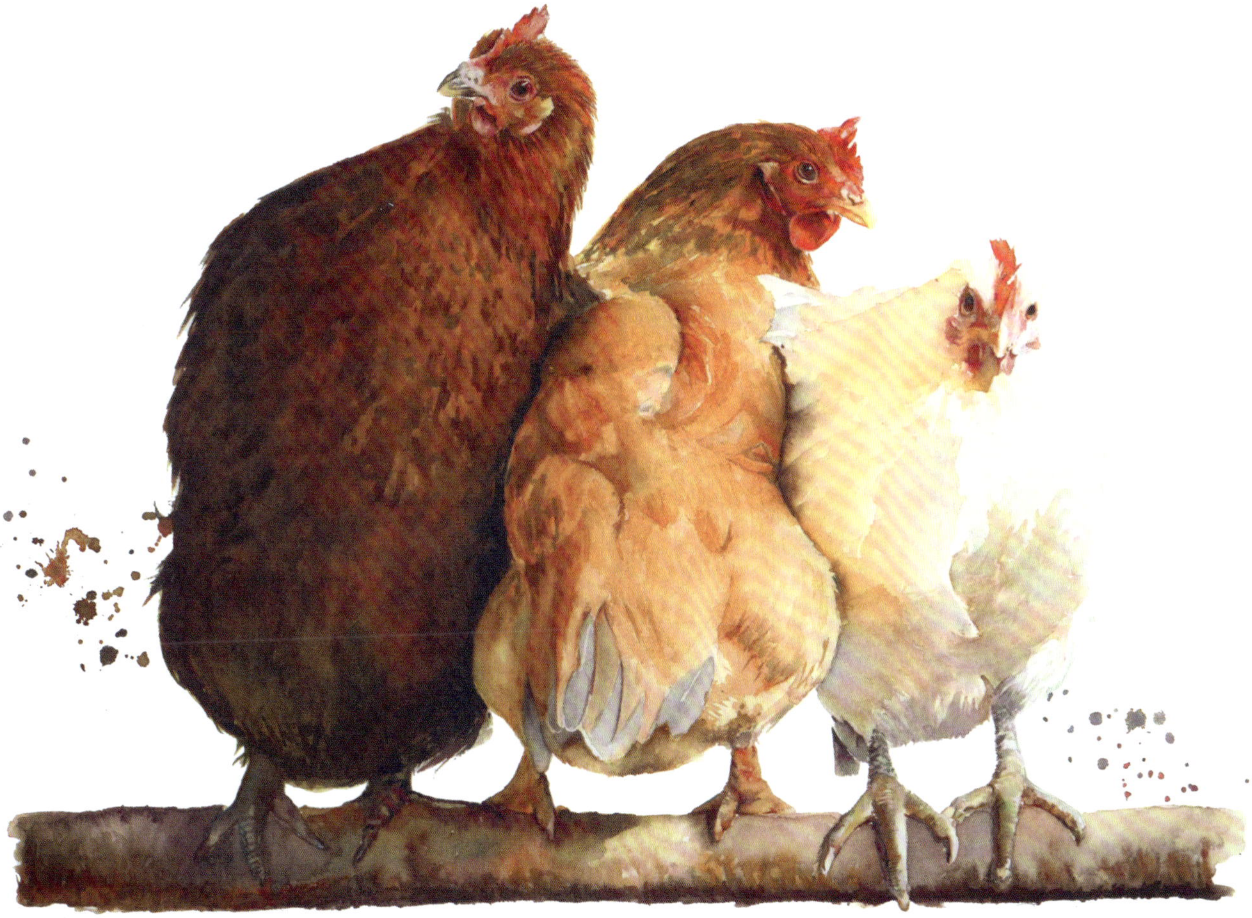

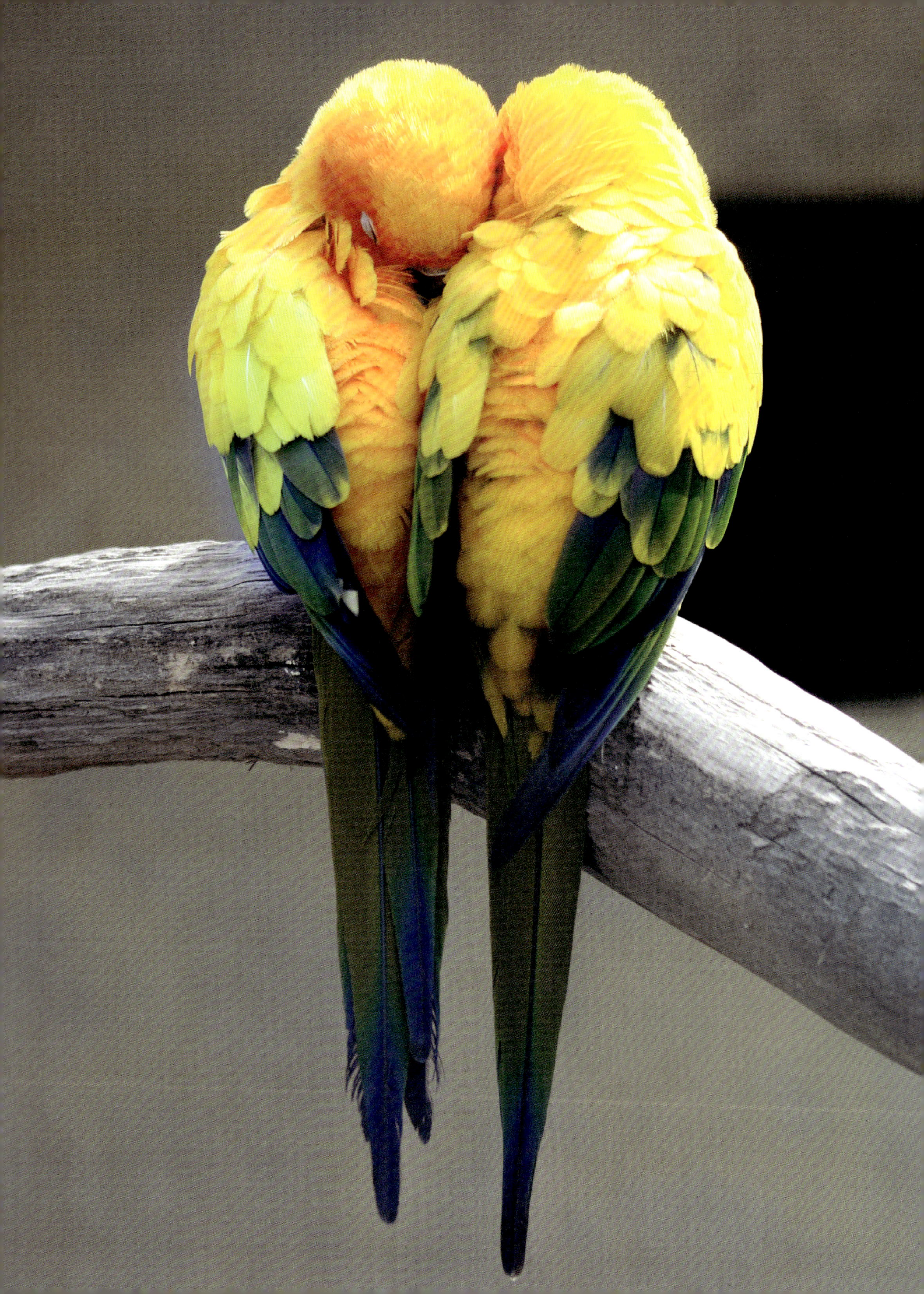

Making Your Mark and Finding Your Voice

I hope you've enjoyed reading this book and carrying out the exercises to help you discover and develop your own style. I've aimed to cover the majority of the topics that my students need help with and I hope that the methodical approach that I've demonstrated will enable you to take your paintings to the next level.

To recap the most important points:

- Look at a bird's features as simply tone, shape, colour and edge.
- Don't get distracted by the details of the bird's markings, or overwhelmed with their more abstract qualities such as luminosity. Spend more time laying down the larger shapes - light to dark - and less on those smaller details.
- Above all, have fun, practise hard, be patient with yourself and trust in the process.

Drawing and painting are learnt skills, similar to learning to play a musical instrument. Some people 'click' straight away, while others have to practise a little harder to get the results they want. None of us ever stop learning when it comes to artistic practice - in many ways, that is the joy of creativity. It really is the gift that keeps on giving.

For my final chapter, I want to leave you with a series of paintings that were all created using the techniques described in this book. This section contains some of my favourite photographs, so you can interpret them yourself. As I've painted them, I've taken some process shots of the more important aspects of my techniques. Unless otherwise stated, I've used cyan, magenta, yellow and black, as in previous exercises.

You will see after the first few paintings that my process follows a similar pattern. I paint the first layers wet-into-wet and creamy paint into damp. Once dry, I follow on with a second layer of paint to deepen tones, adjust edges and add colour. The finishing touches, such as random mark making, and a few well-placed details and splashes, are added on the third and final part of the process.

I hope you have as much fun recreating these beautiful birds as I did and that this book proves to be a useful reference guide for years to come.

The lovebirds

The sentiment, as well as the light hitting the edge of the birds, was the element that drew me to this image. Although the finished piece appears to have been painted in a photorealistic way, much of the first layer and the branch were painted in a loose manner to allow for beautiful blends and soft edges.

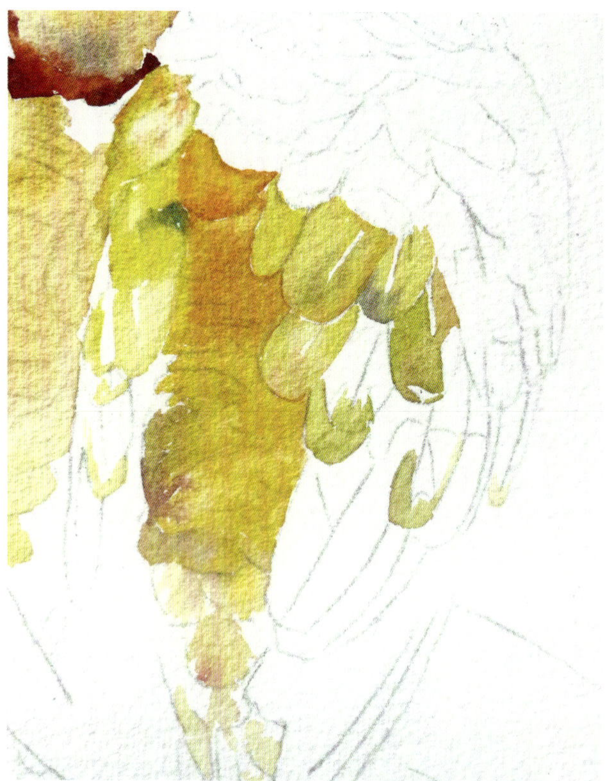

↑ Soft edges created by adding paint wet-into-wet onto dry paper at the first layer stage.

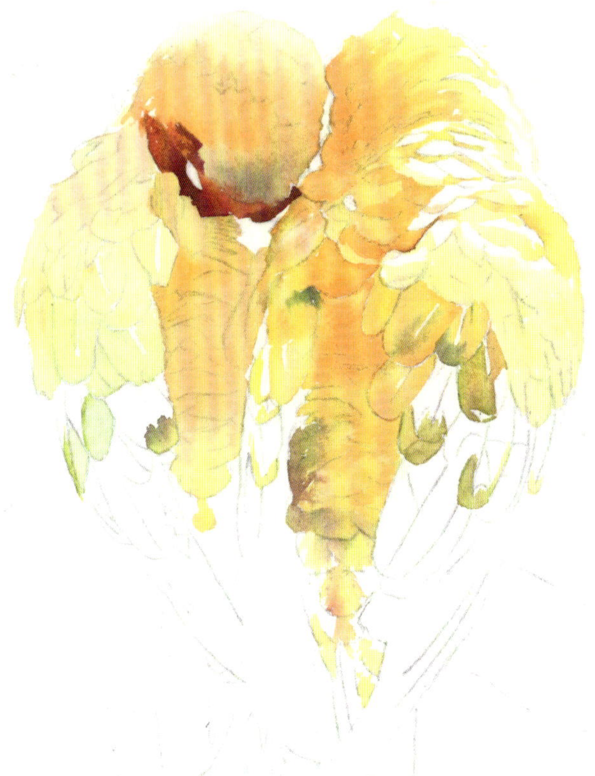

↑ The first layer of warm colours.

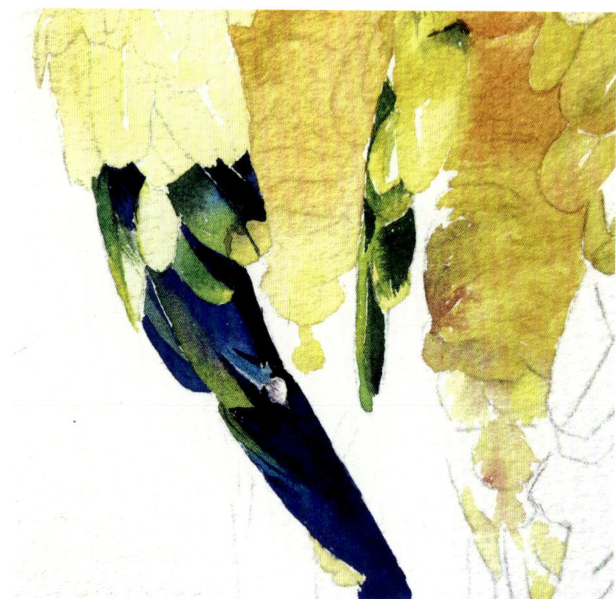

↑ A mixture of hard and soft edges. The soft blends of the greens contrast with the hard blue edges, the latter having been formed by painting onto dry paper.

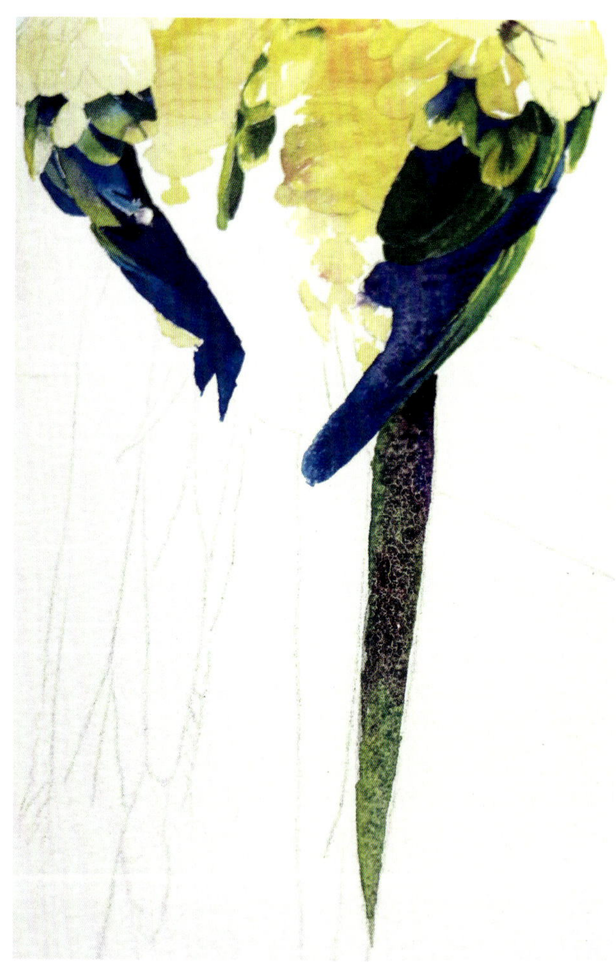

↑ Gorgeous merges of purples and greens as they mingle on the paper, wet-into-wet.

→ First layer of warm and cool colours completed.

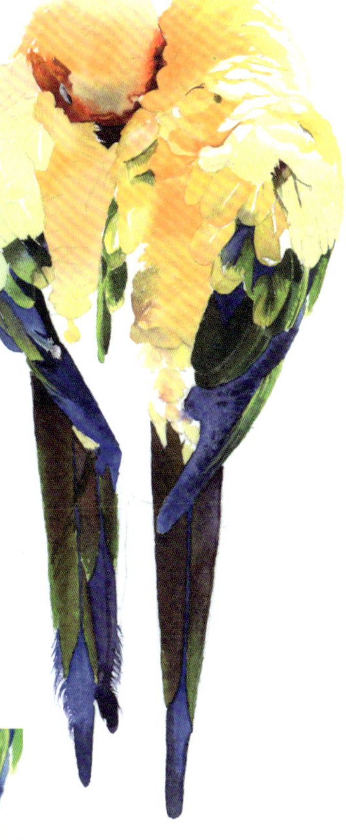

→ Happy accidents as two colours hit the same spot.

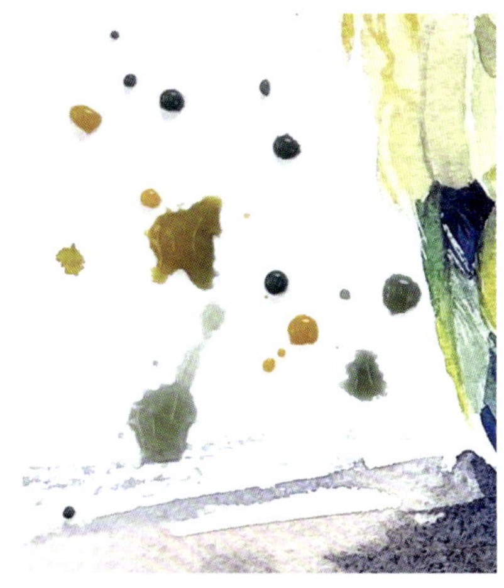

↓ Branch and splashes added to finish. The branch was a great opportunity to use the yellow/purple combination in a desaturated format. I really enjoyed watching the paint merge on the paper; it made some beautiful patterns and colours.

← Using a small detailer brush to get colours to merge into each other on the paper, wet-into-wet.

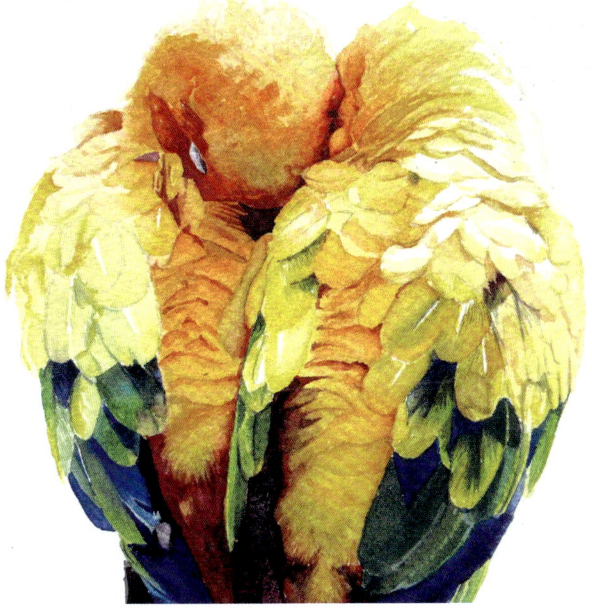

↑ Some of these sections contained a number of colours but most were achieved in just two layers.

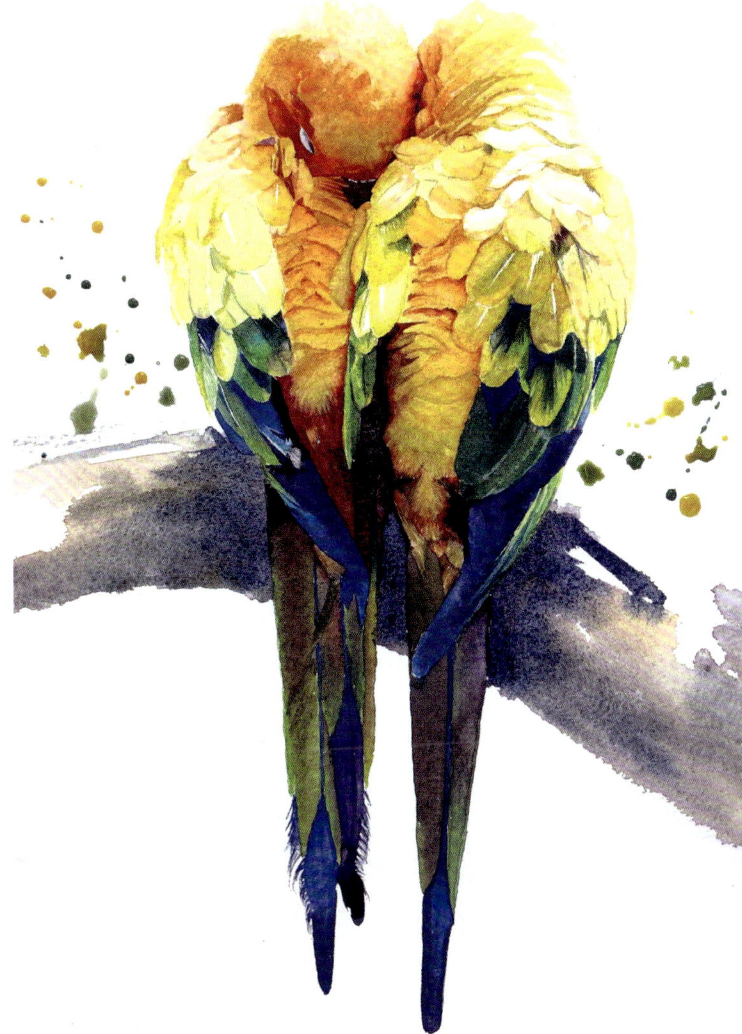

The puffins

The shadows in this photograph are beautiful and their hard edges contrast wonderfully with the softer blends in much of the rest of the piece. In the resultant painting, both the white and black of the birds were painted with a mixture of cyan and magenta.

The first layer of cool colours was painted before adding the first layer of warm colours. This avoided having to change the water too many times. Much of this first layer, with the exception of the shadows, was painted to create soft edges so that the blues drifted seamlessly into the other colours.

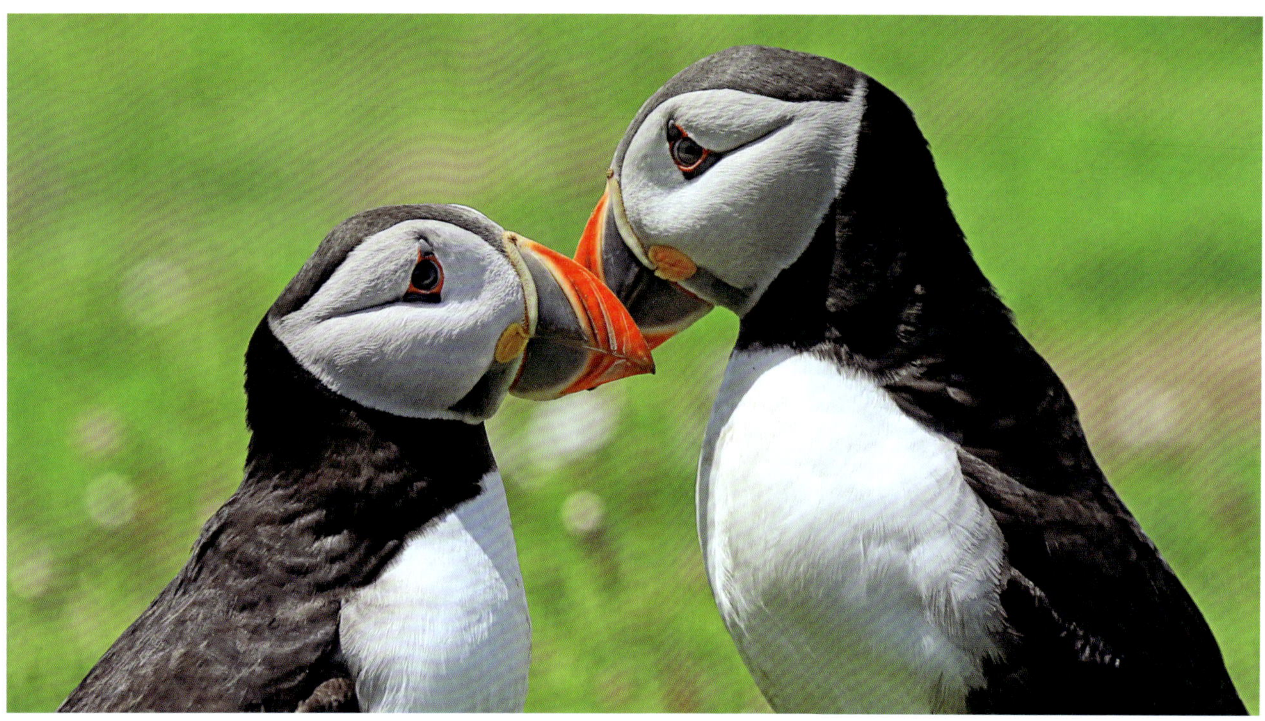

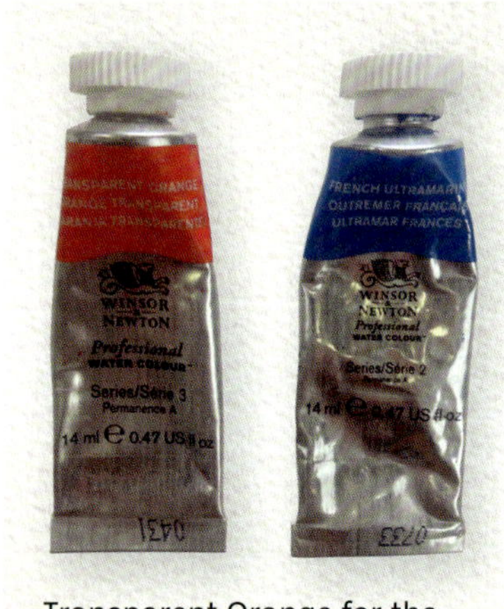

Transparent Orange for the beak and French Ultramarine for the blues in the feathers helped this piece to pop.

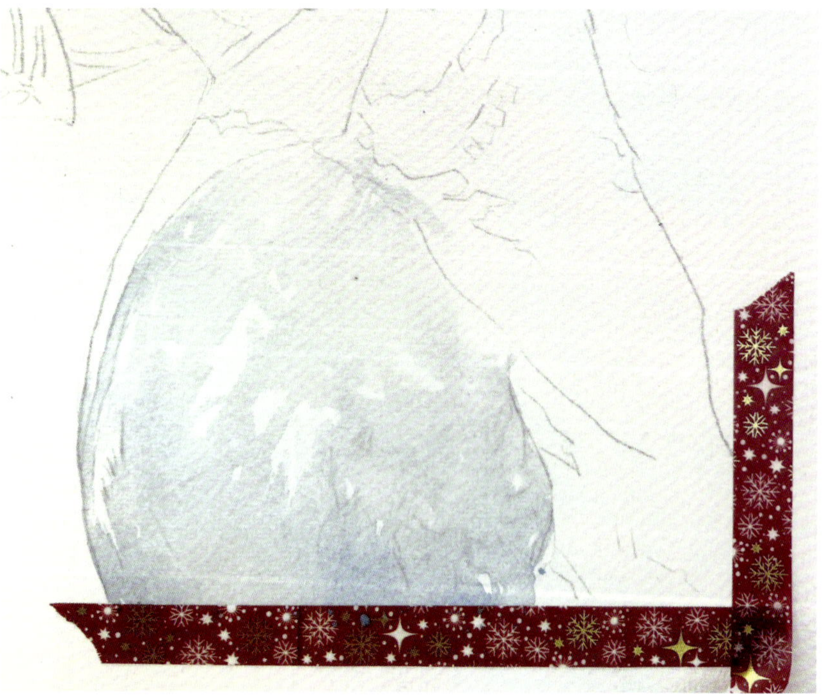

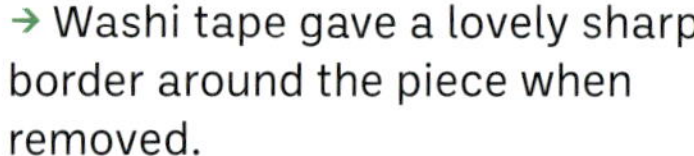

→ Washi tape gave a lovely sharp border around the piece when removed.

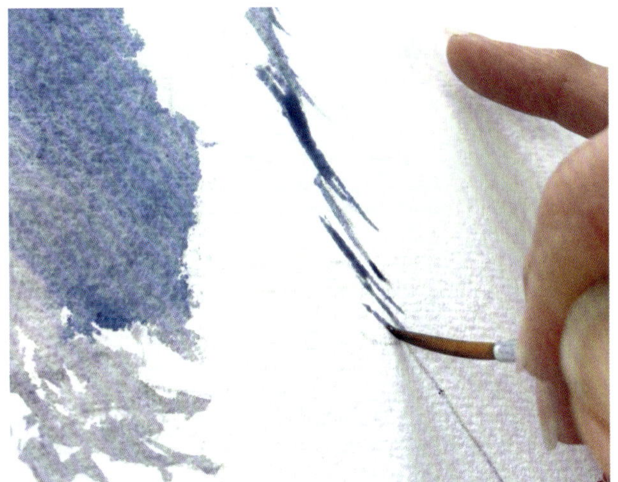

↑ The rigger brush was ideal for flicking the feathery textures outwards.

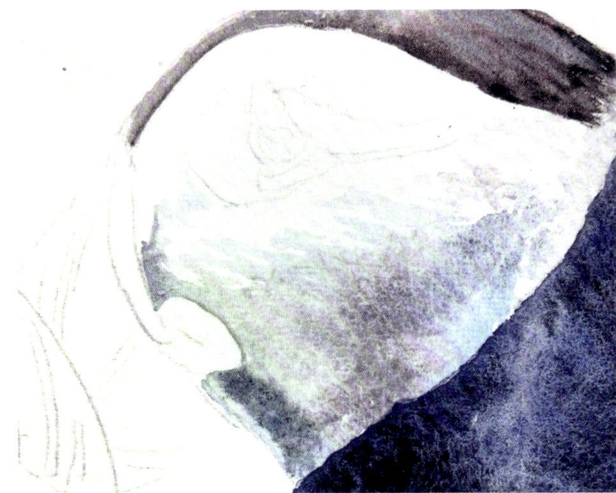

↑ The face contained green, purple and blue hues, which merged on the page.

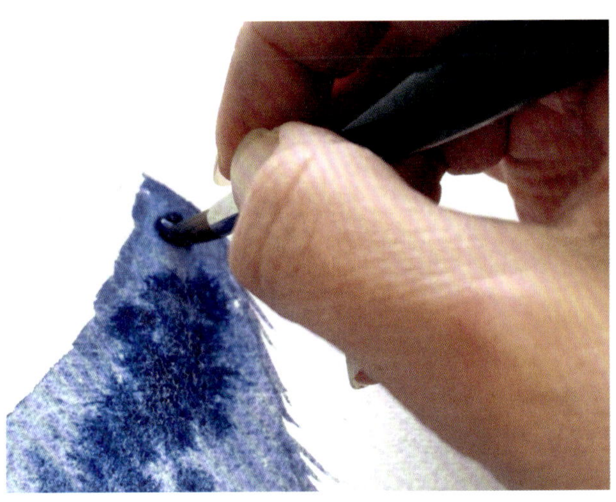

↑ The first layer involved dropping thicker beads of paint into the damp underlayer to create soft-edged darker colours. I was sure to leave spaces between the dabs of paint to allow new tones to develop.

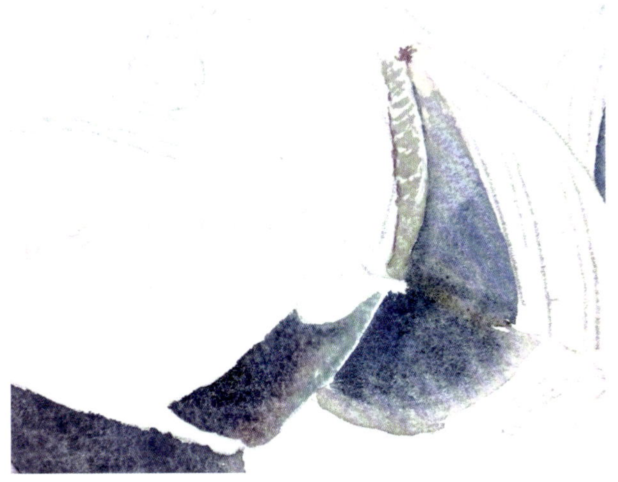

↑ The beak of the left puffin had an extensive range of cool colours, from turquoise and olive to purple.

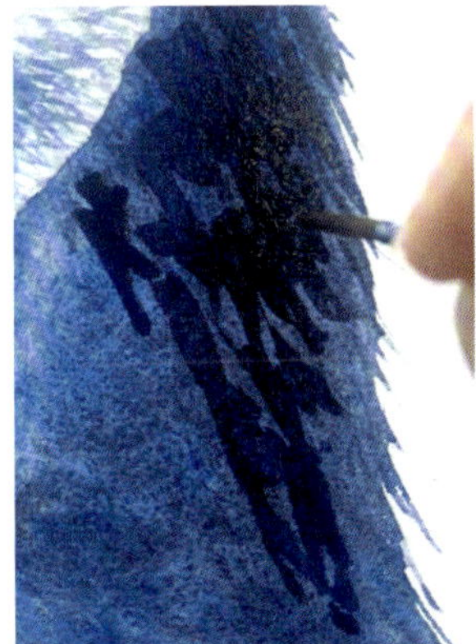

↑ Loose marks applied in the general direction of the feathers, occasionally loosened with water.

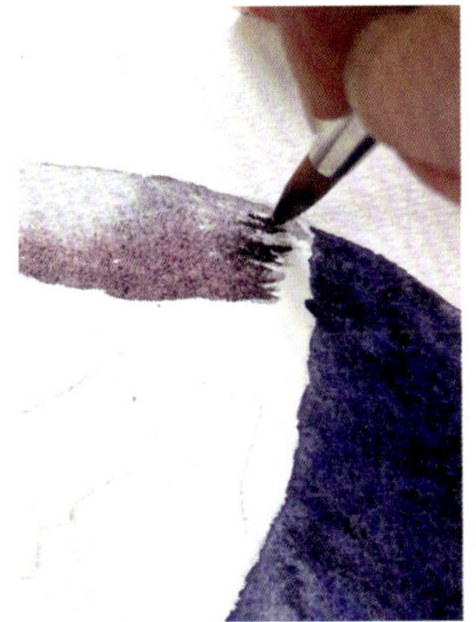

↑ The first layer of the head was created using a mixture of desaturated blue-purple tones.

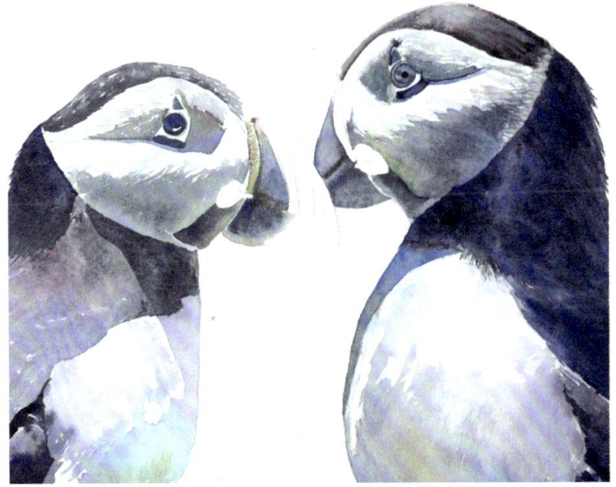

↑ First layer of cool colours completed.

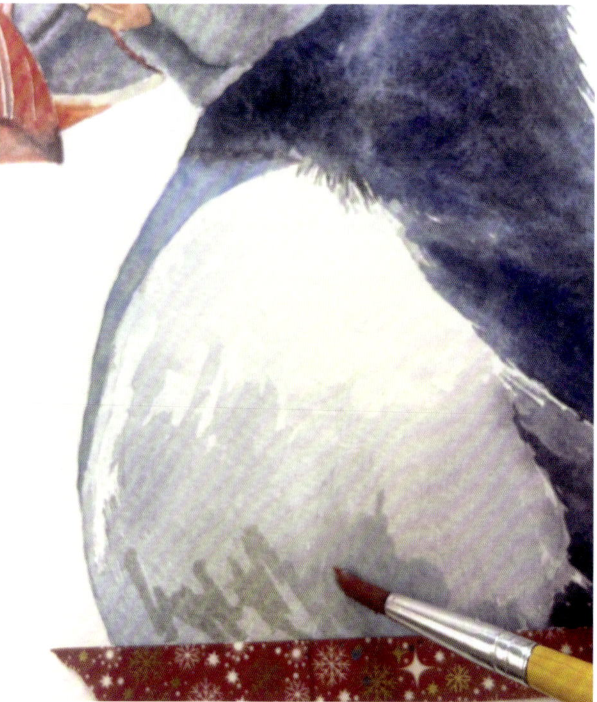

↑ I generally start my second layers by adding washes onto dry paper. This gives me hard edges. If I need to soften them, I simply add water. At this stage, as with the underlayer, I add a couple of different colours and encourage them to merge.

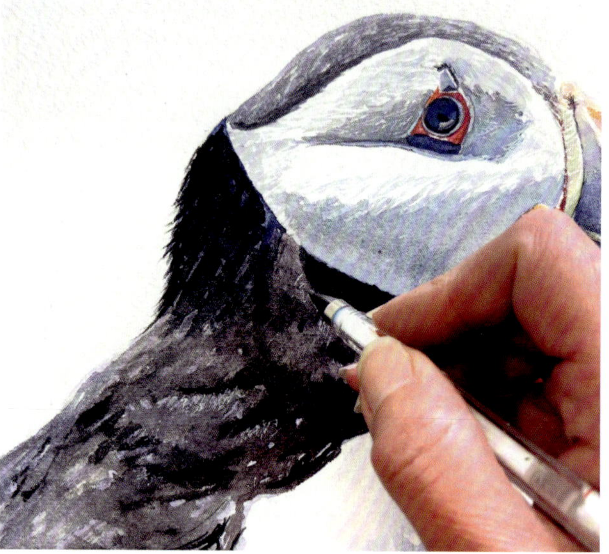

↑ Even the tuxedo-like appearance of a puffin's coat gives us the opportunity to apply loose calligraphic markings. A little white gel pen is scribbled on towards the end of the process to indicate bits of light.

↓ The finished piece, with splashes added. I chose to use the blues and oranges that had been so predominant in my painting.

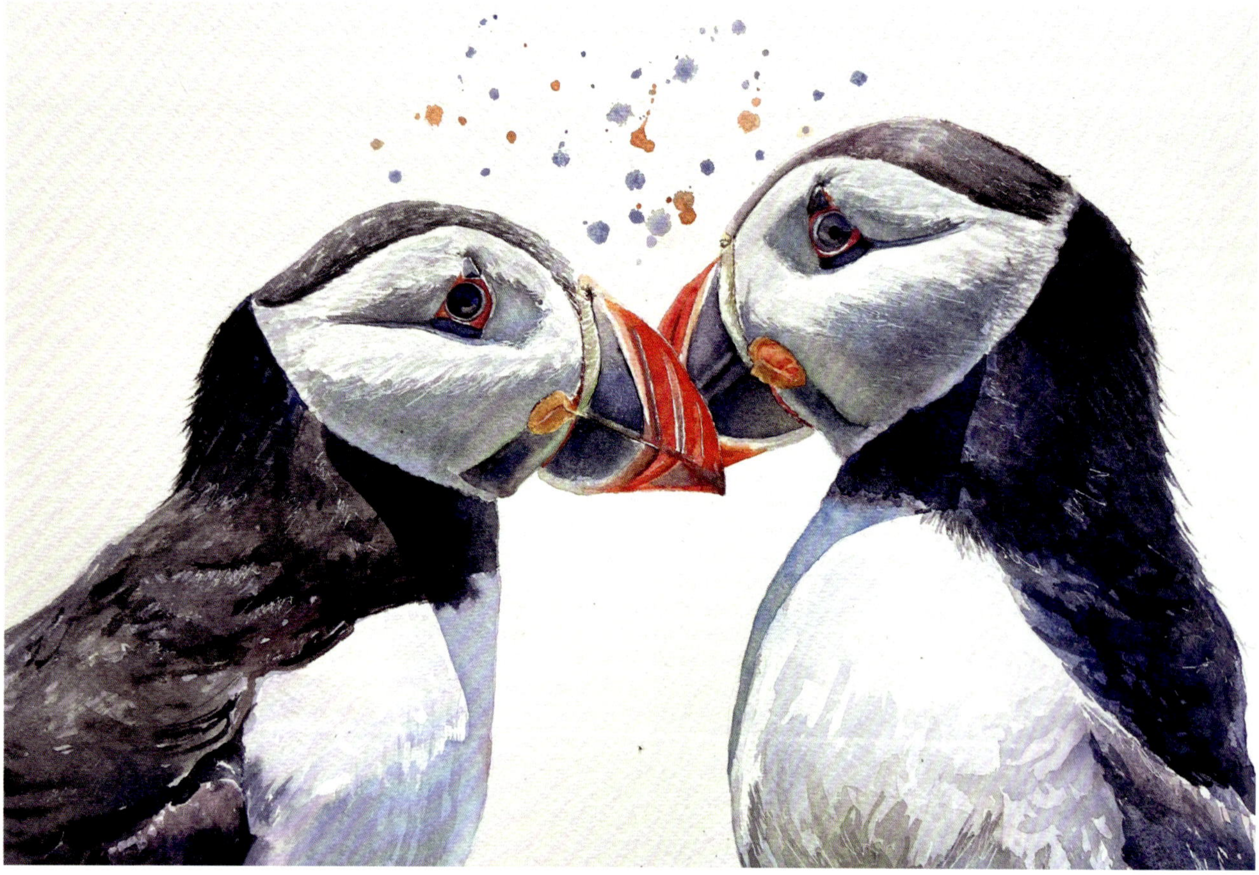

The eagle

I loved the vibrant golds in this eagle's beak and I thought they'd work so well with the blues in its 'white' feathers. The body of the eagle didn't interest me as much, so I wanted to keep this area fairly loose.

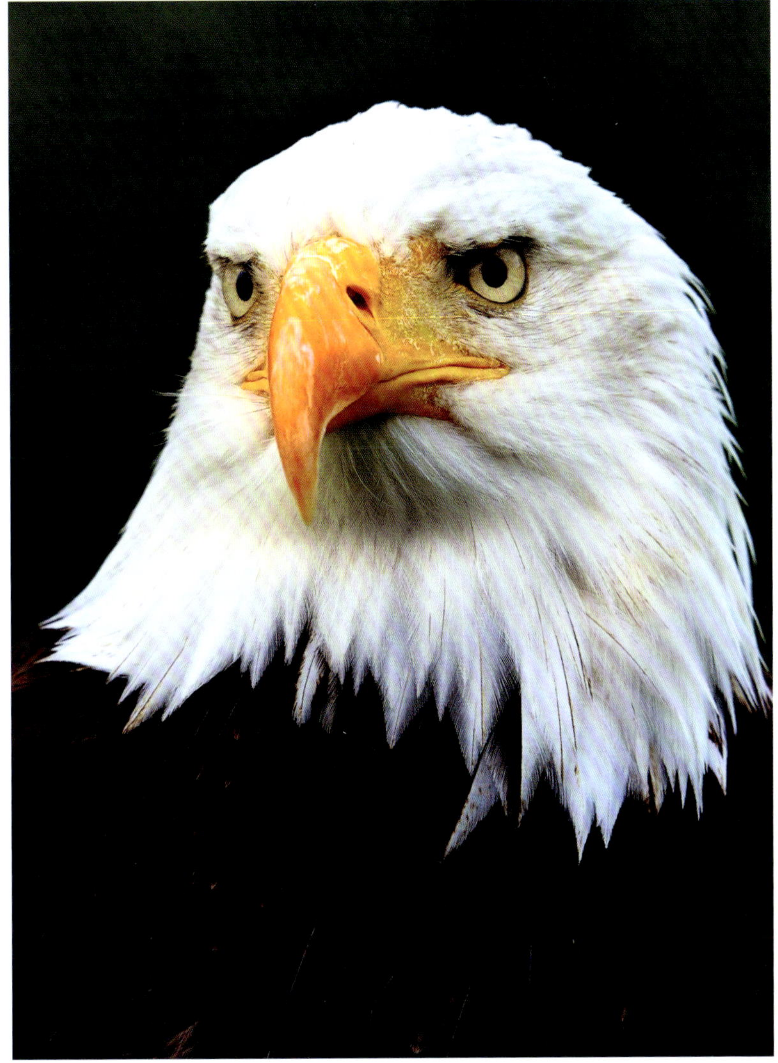

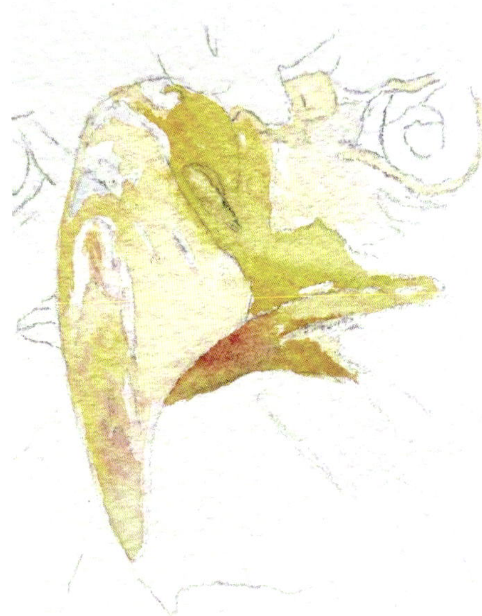

↑ The beak was built up gradually in a fairly tight, exact fashion.

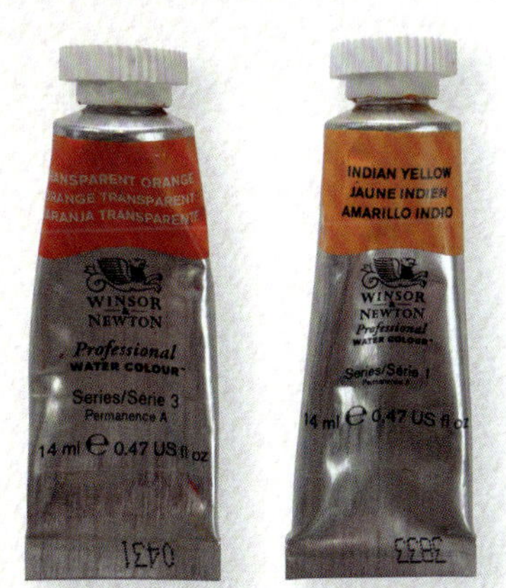

Transparent Orange and Indian Yellow were the perfect colours to give the beak a little extra vibrancy.

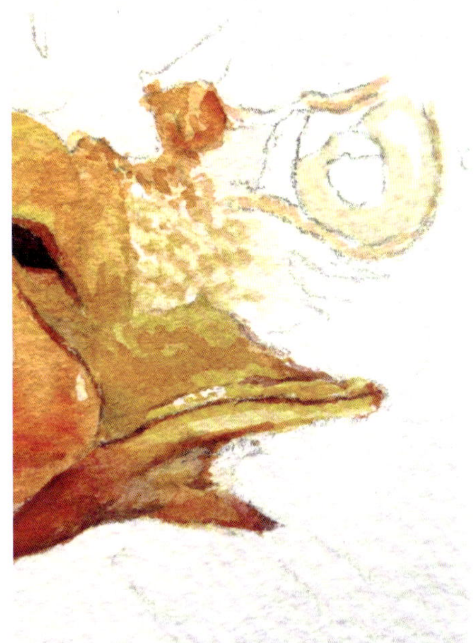

↑ I made up a desaturated yellow by adding a little black to yellow for the eye, then applied this to the paper.

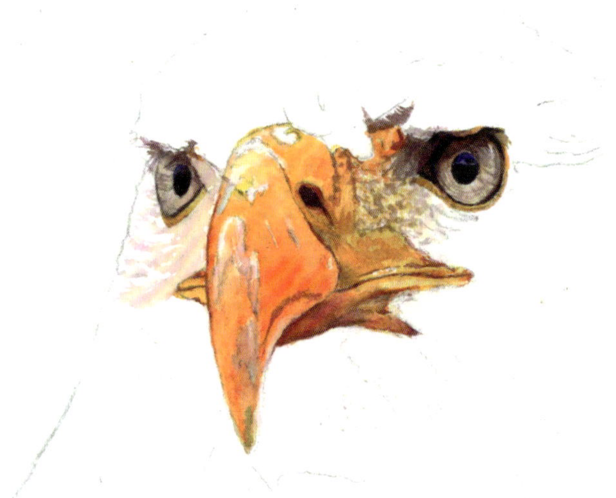

↑ At this stage, the facial features had all been painted.

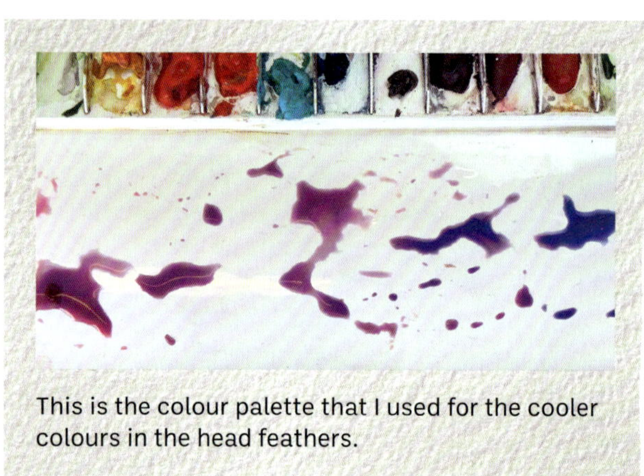

This is the colour palette that I used for the cooler colours in the head feathers.

↑ I used the tip of a size 12 round brush to loosely paint in the shadows. As usual, I intermingled a couple of colours on the page, allowing them to bleed into each other.

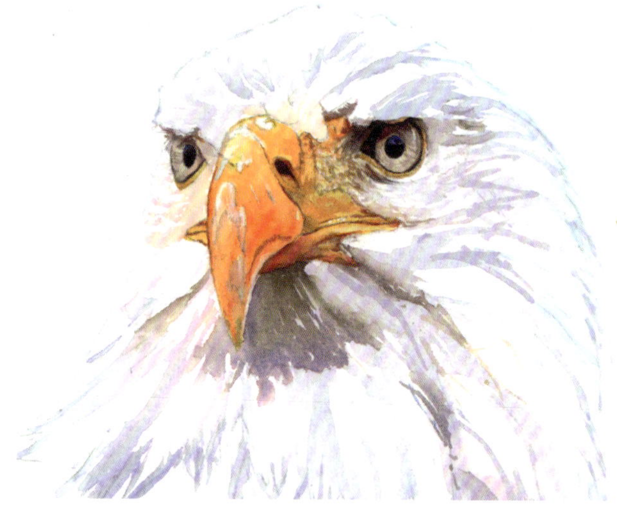

↑ The blue-lilac hues counterbalanced beautifully with the warmth of the beak and eyes.

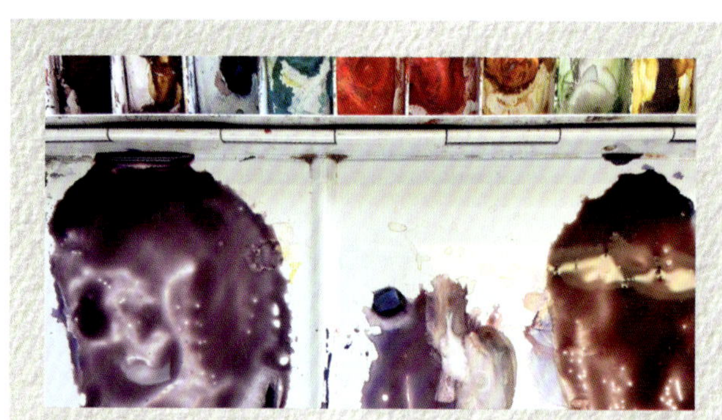

These are the colours that I made up for the body of the eagle: rich, warm plums and browns.

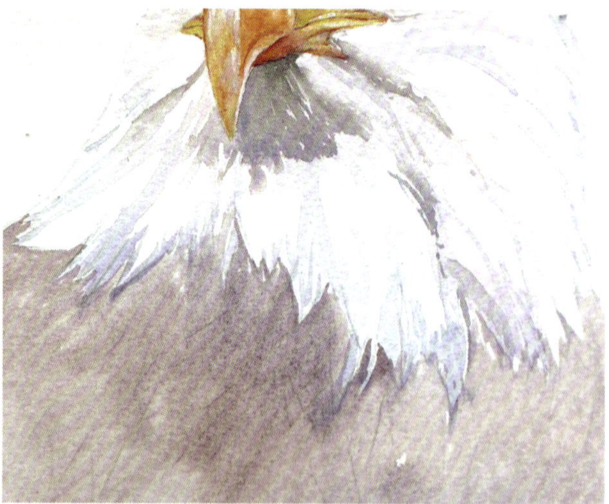

↑ I initially applied a wash of water to the body and then dropped in some of the rich darks, but to my disappointment, I'd misjudged the wetness of the paper. It was too wet so that when I applied the rich colours I had mixed, they all looked a little bland!

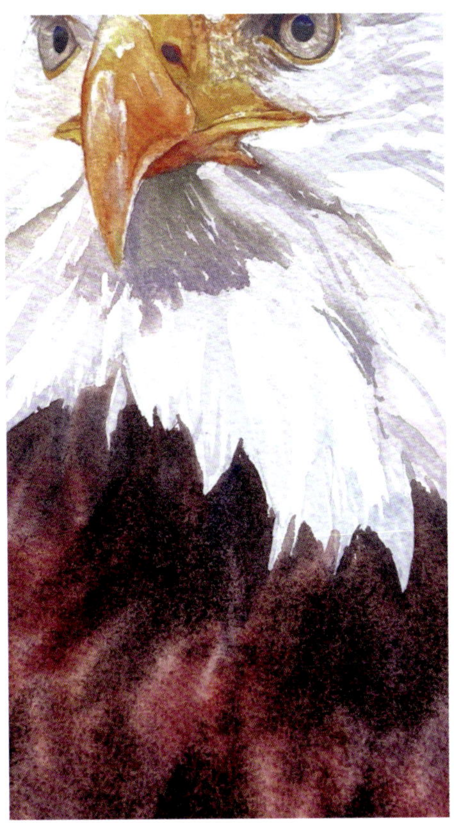

↑ While the paper started to dry, I mixed some more pools of rich colour and dobbed them on, chopping and changing my colours and leaving areas of clear spaces between brush marks, so pockets of light could peep through.

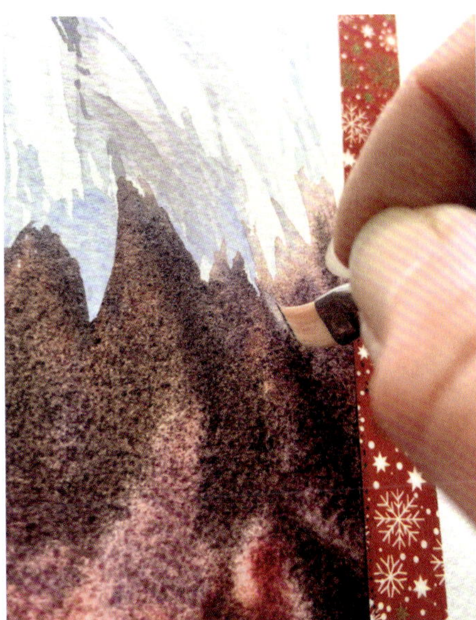

↑ I used a small flat brush to slice and lift through the damp paint to indicate the shafts of the feathers.

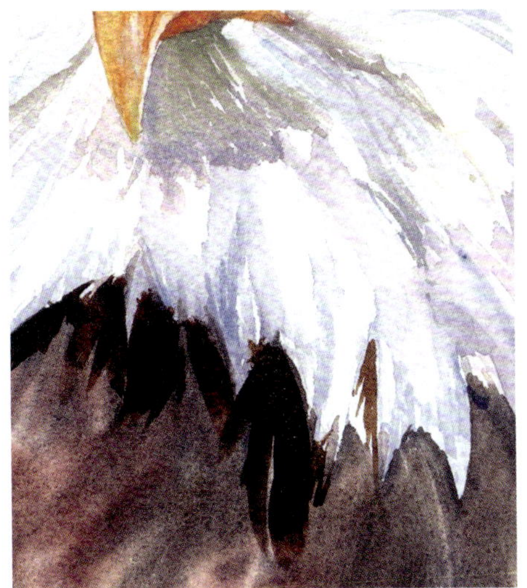

← When the paint dried, I was concerned that the head and body looked like two separate paintings and I wanted them to blend into each other. I therefore applied darker blues to the edge of the white feathers and allowed them to bleed into the crimson/brown body. I immediately added rich crimson/blue mixes to the bleeds and pulled them down to the base of the body in the direction of the feathers.

↓ Once the body had been covered with a second glaze, I strengthened some of the details in the face by adding fine black whiskers and subtle pops of desaturated golds in white sections with a rigger brush. I felt that the body still needed a little interest, so I broke it up by adding a quick intuitive mark with a stroke of white gouache. This had the added benefit of bringing balance to the piece, with a nod to the white of the eagle's head. A few scribbles with the white gel pen and I felt the piece was finished.

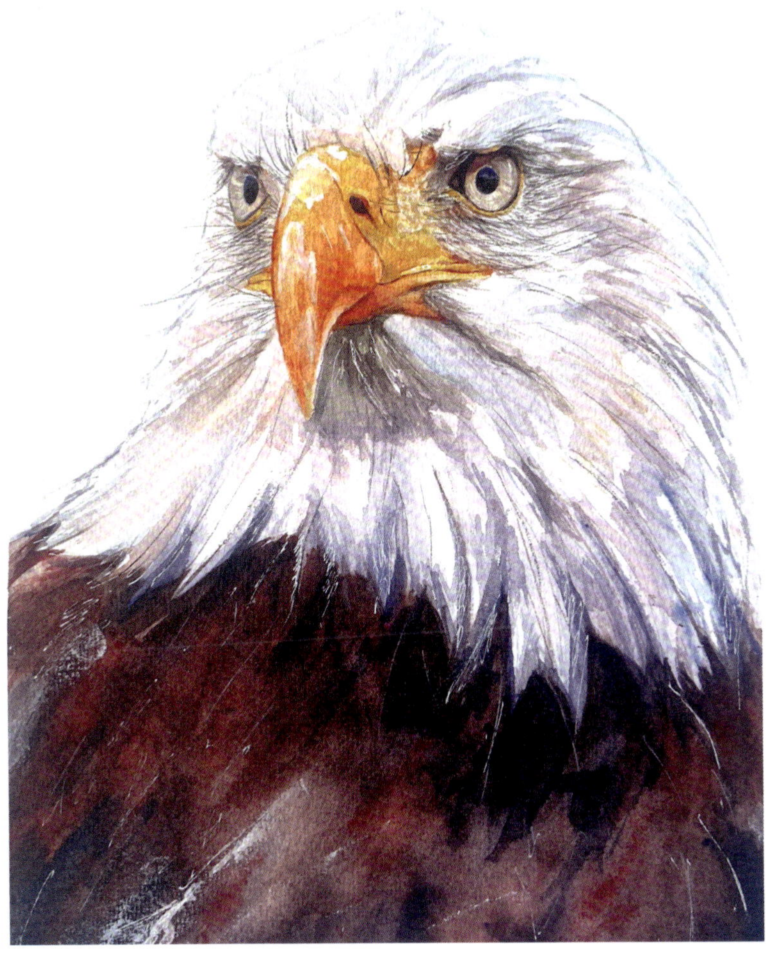

The kingfisher

I never tire of painting kingfishers and I really liked the composition of this reference photo. The fact that the kingfisher was photographed by a local photographer, Ian Gray, in my hometown of Bewdley, made it extra special.

Kingfishers are tricky birds to paint. Their chests are easy to overwork and the transition from orange to blue tones is tricky. If you're not careful, you can arrive at an unwanted shade of green. As a result, I often resort to lifting out and reapplying sections midway through the painting. This piece was no exception.

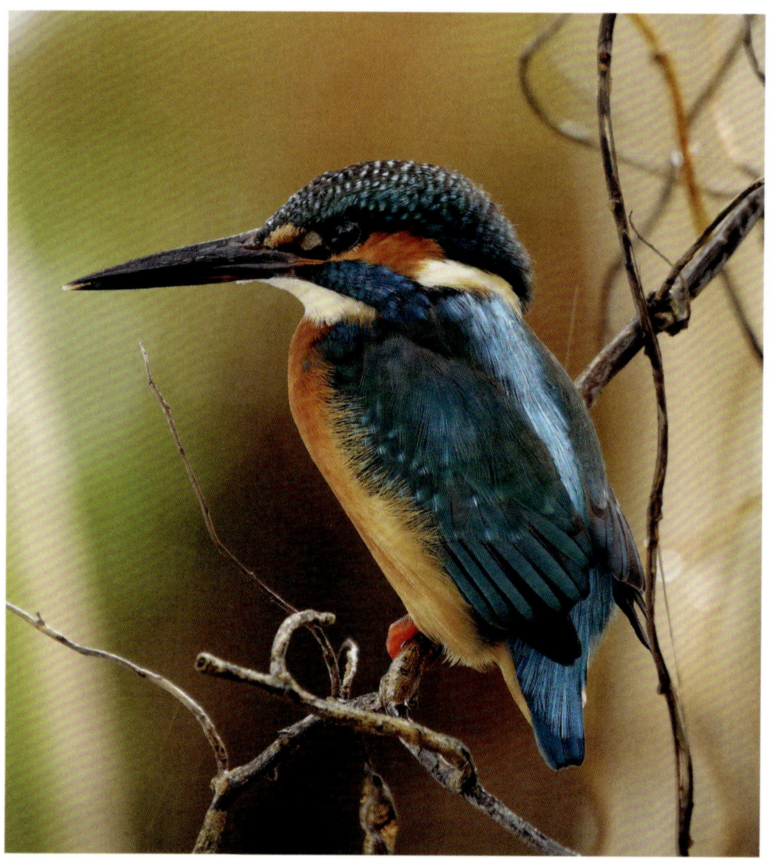

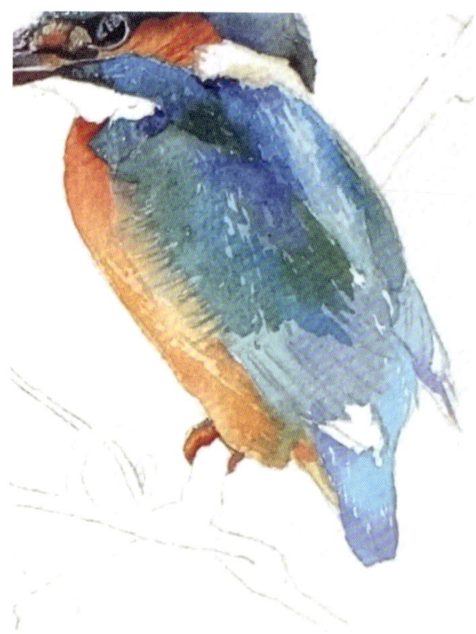

↑ At this stage I had started the second layer of paint but felt like I'd lost the flow and looseness in the piece. I didn't like the hard edge between the oranges and blues.

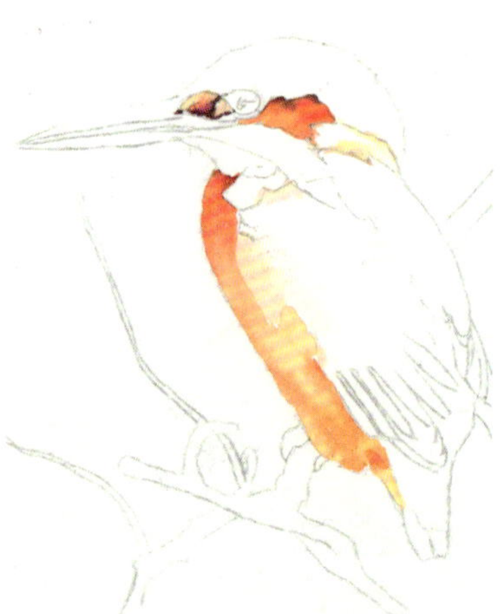

↑ First I laid down the warm tones.

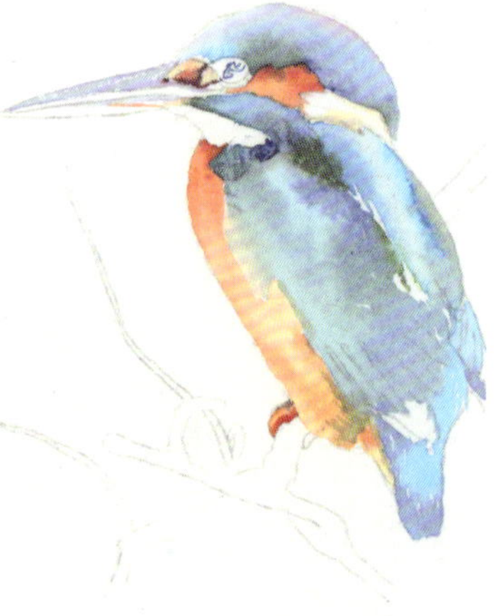

↑ Here, the first layer of warm and cool colours had been painted.

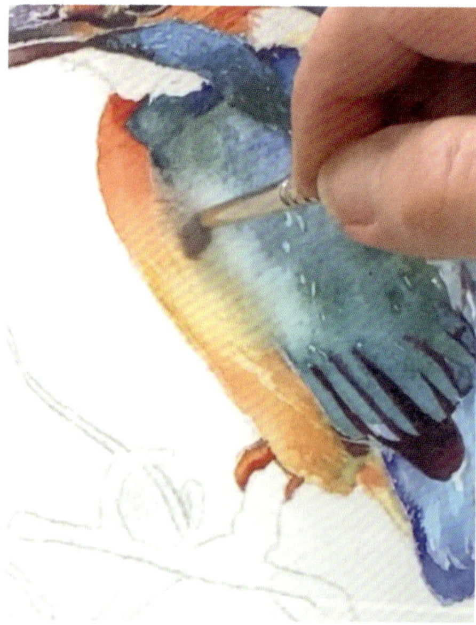

↑ I therefore lifted the dry paint away by gently scrubbing it with a damp brush.

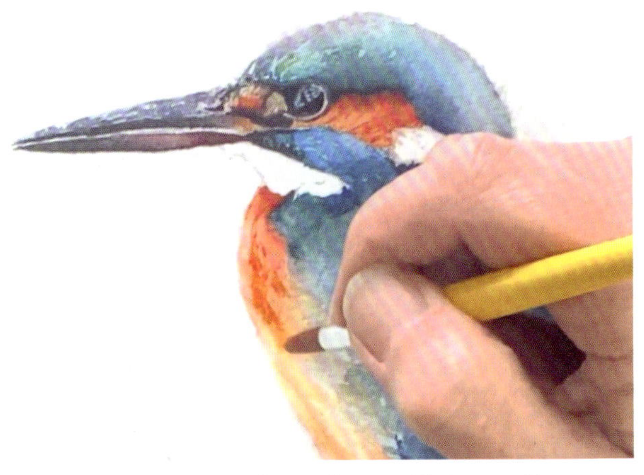

↑ I allowed the area to dry and was able to use the underlying stain as a base for additional colours.

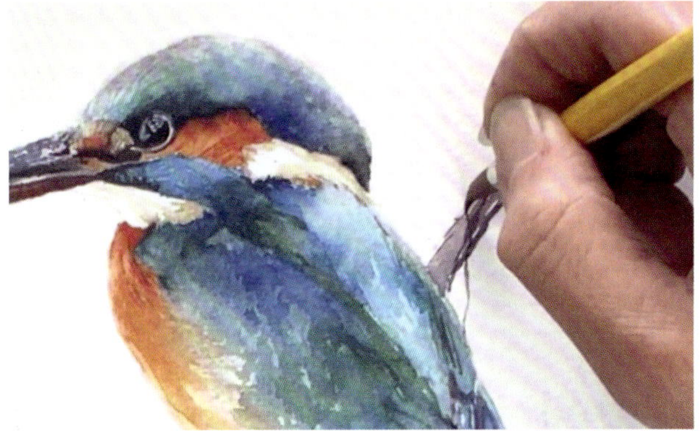

↑ I used a medium-sized brush at different angles and pressures to lay a series of twisted lines to represent branches and twigs. I didn't follow the reference photograph exactly; instead I used the shapes and colours to inspire the brushstrokes.

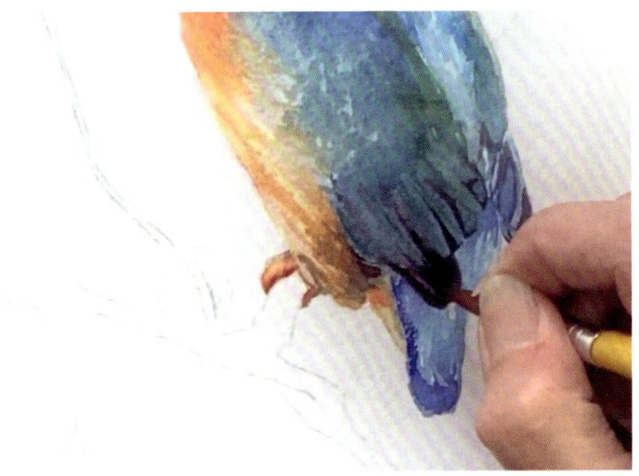

↑ I was then back on track to add warm and cool marks to the second, final layer.

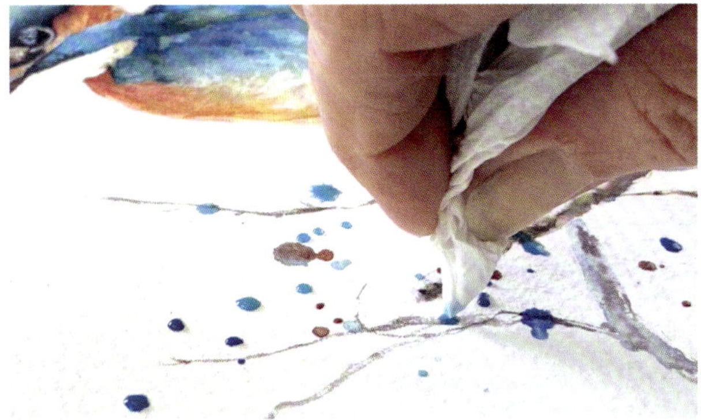

↑ I was careful where I laid the splashes. I lifted out a few that had fallen in the wrong places with tissue. If needs be, I 'cheat' by deliberately adding the odd spot to aid composition.

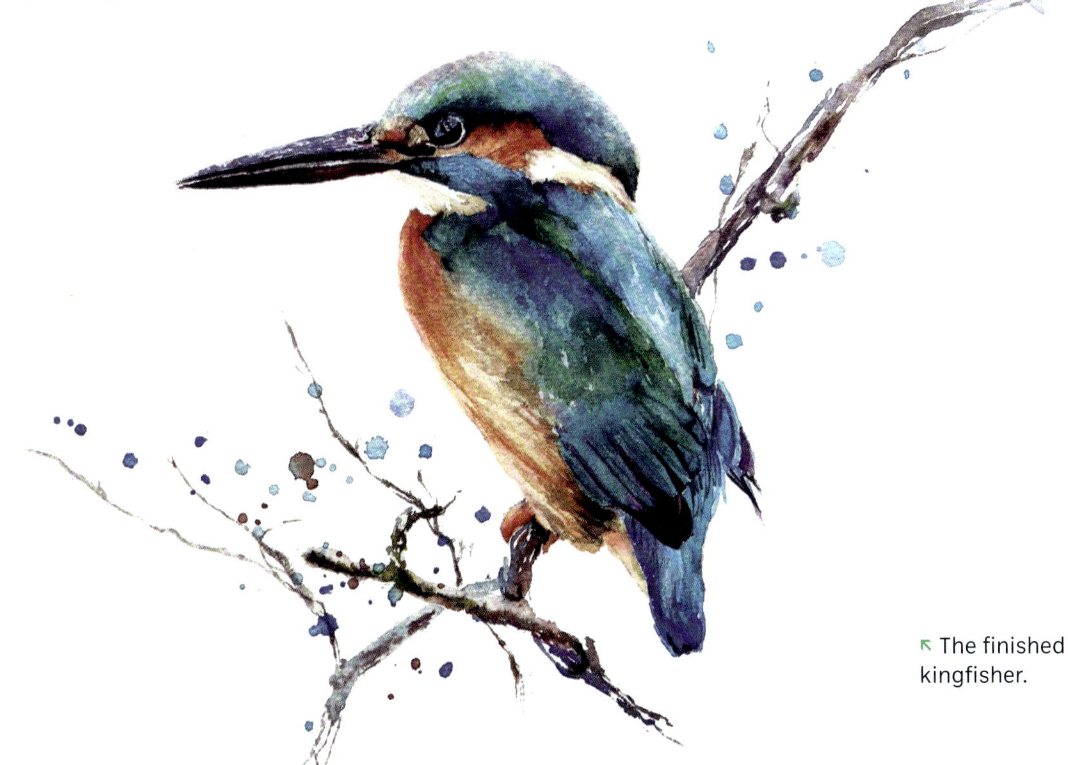

↖ The finished kingfisher.

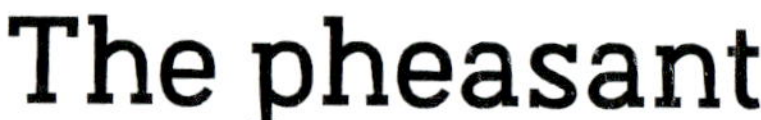

The pheasant

Pheasants are a common sight around the studio. Their feathers are beautifully iridescent. I wanted to capture their skittishness as well as their incredible markings in this piece, without painting every feather.

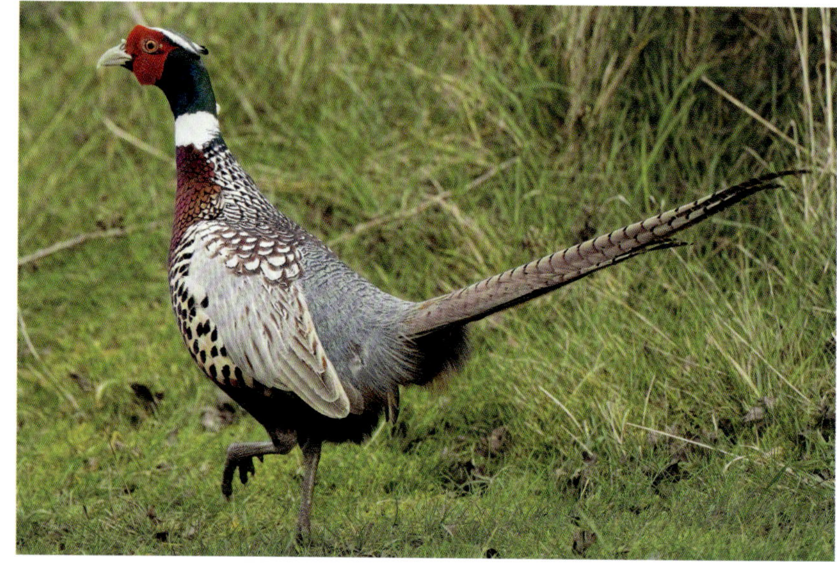

↘ The pheasant has a number of different sections and I tackled them on an individual basis. I was able to run some colours from the tail directly into the base of the back, but most of the other sections were painted separately. I chose not to mask off the white sections but to paint around them instead; masking them off is another option that I've used in the past when painting these birds.

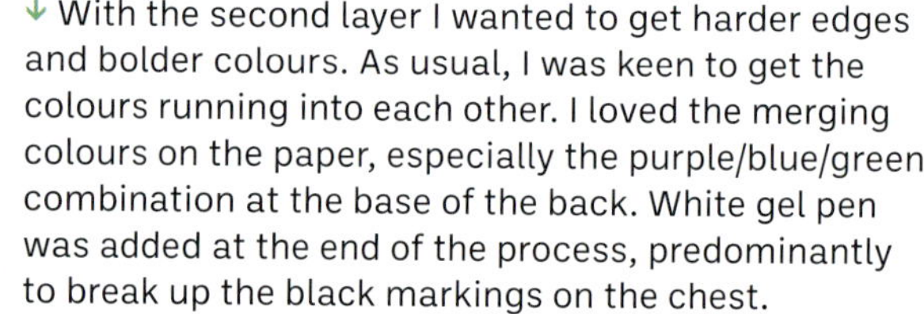

↓ With the second layer I wanted to get harder edges and bolder colours. As usual, I was keen to get the colours running into each other. I loved the merging colours on the paper, especially the purple/blue/green combination at the base of the back. White gel pen was added at the end of the process, predominantly to break up the black markings on the chest.

The blue tit

Blue tits are frequent visitors to our garden. They are fearless little characters, often ready to do battle with their rivals. I thought this wonderful photograph really summed up their sense of confidence and attitude.

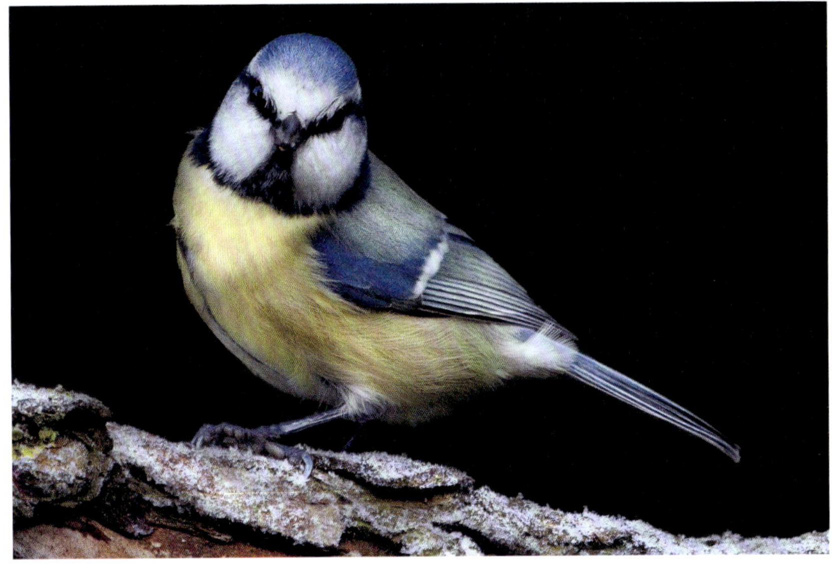

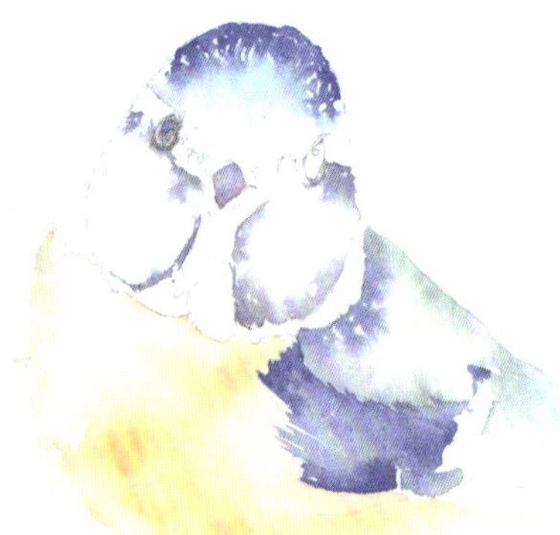

↑ I completed the blue and green sections before moving on to the yellow ones. The head and back were particularly fun to do. I was keen to keep the back as simple as possible and let the watercolours do their thing.

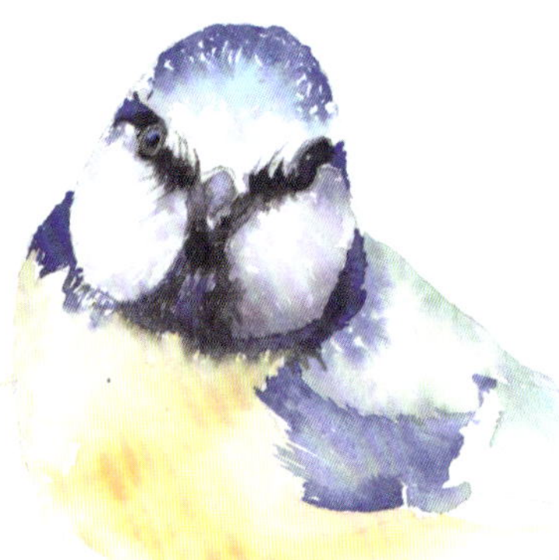

↑ I wanted to bring this little chap to life as quickly as possible, so I hopped on to complete the face. Note the blue in the eyes and the lilac of the beak. I achieved the white wispy areas over the eyes by cutting into the white with a fine brush loaded with black paint.

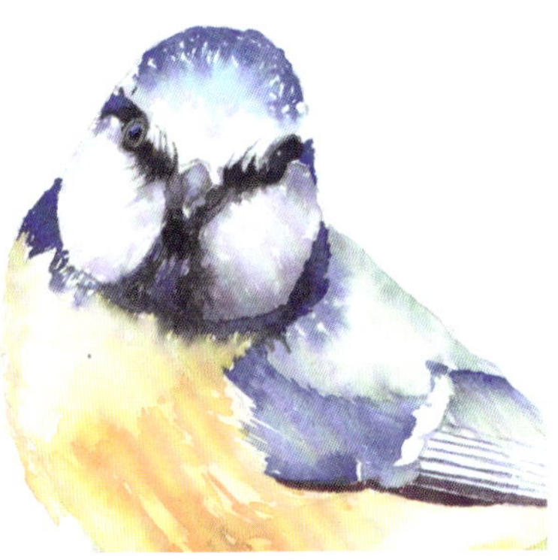

↑ Dark, warm shades of mustard, orange and olive were then added to the body to help give it depth and form.

→ I wanted to create a loose interpretation of the branch, so I only glanced at it every now and again for colour inspiration and shape. The branch was quite a large solid mass, so if I had painted it in its entirety I felt it would have overwhelmed the subject of the bird.

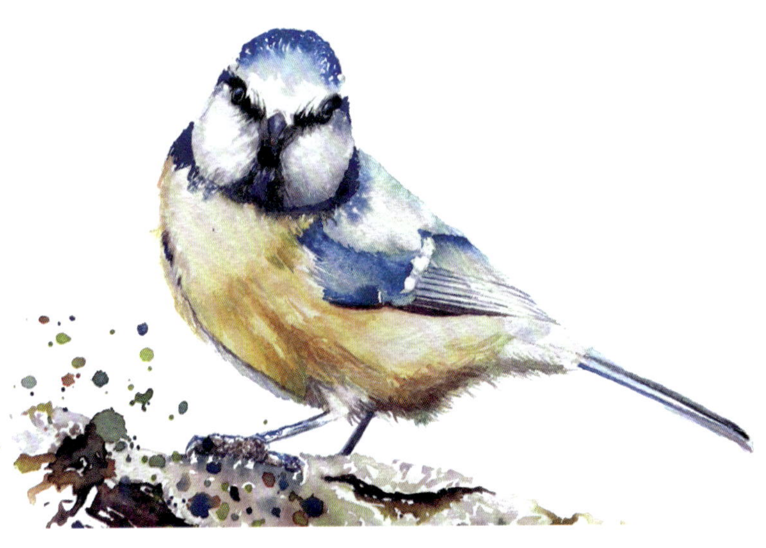

The cockerel

This cockerel attracted my eye due to his beautiful tail feathers. I started off painting them with accuracy but then decided to free up my strokes to create an abundance of imaginary tail feathers.

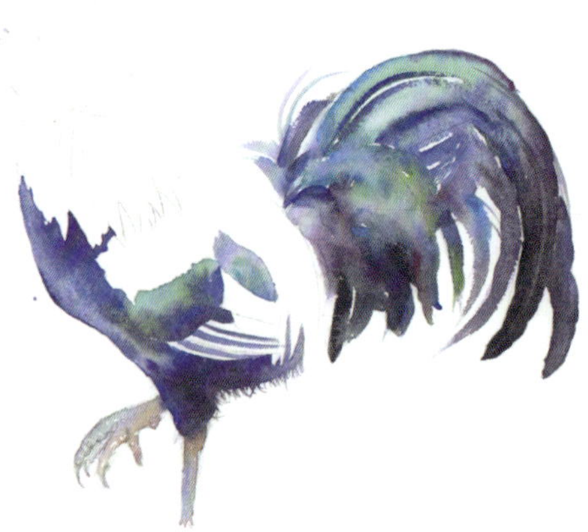

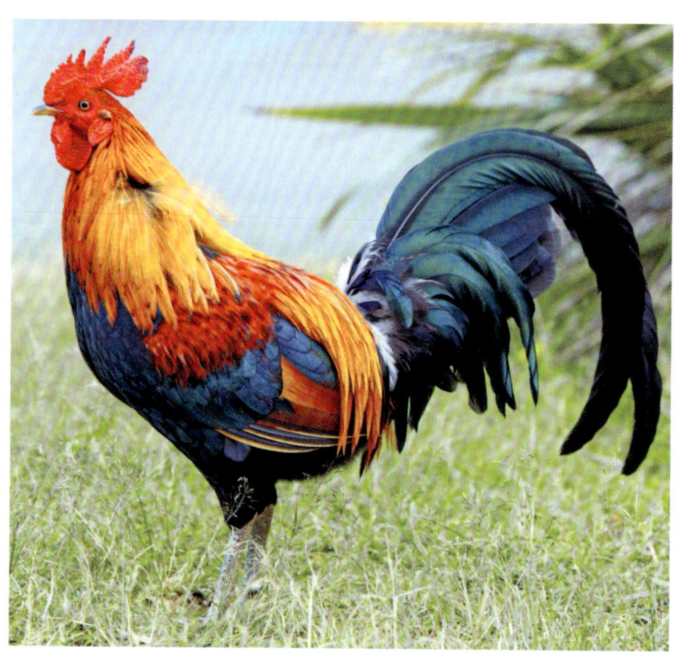

↑ I brought a little movement to the initial sketch by adding a foot in motion. I really enjoyed laying down those first layers of emerald and blue, especially in the tail feathers. However, they looked a little rigid and staid.

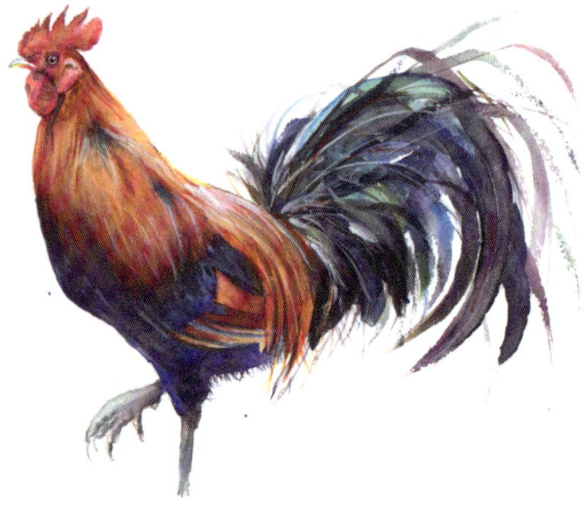

↑ I therefore decided to create my own feathers to break up the piece and add a little dynamism. I initially painted the gold and red sections of the body as separate chunks, but the piece lacked flow so I lifted and blended the areas together instead, much like I did with the kingfisher (p.152).

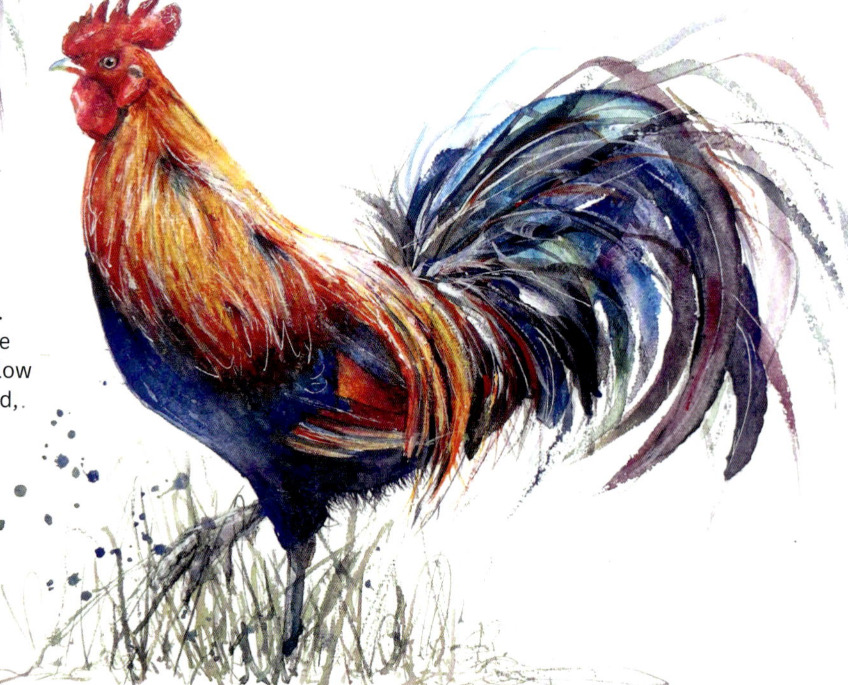

→ I finished the piece off by creating grass-like strokes with the rigger brush and some splashes with my size 12 brush. Finally, I added some white gel pen scribbles to increase the sense of movement about the piece.

The penguins

This was such a beautiful photograph; I loved the fluffiness of the baby penguin's coat. I used 638 gsm Saunders Waterford 100% cotton, CP (NOT), high white paper, which seemed to create the most beautiful textures of its own accord. It was ideal for this piece.

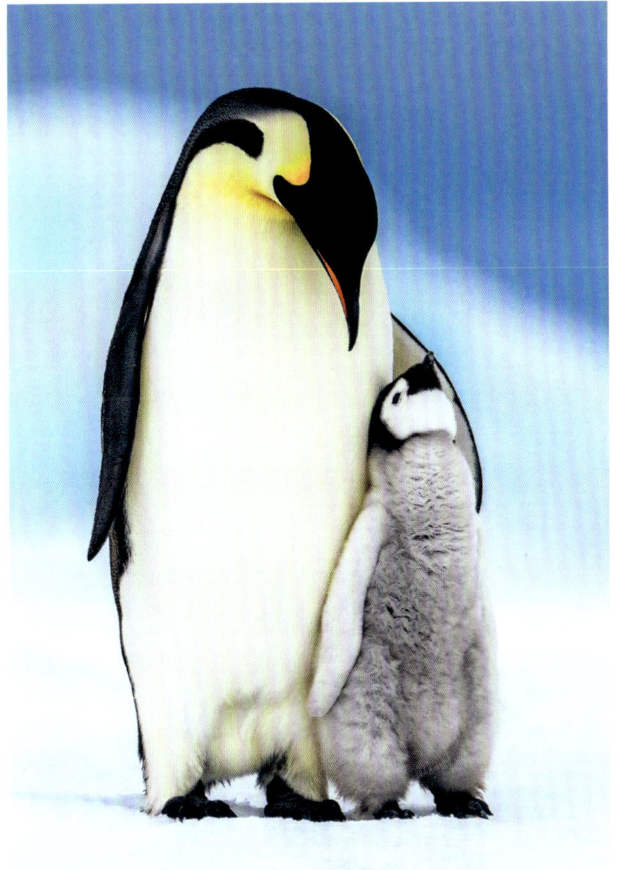

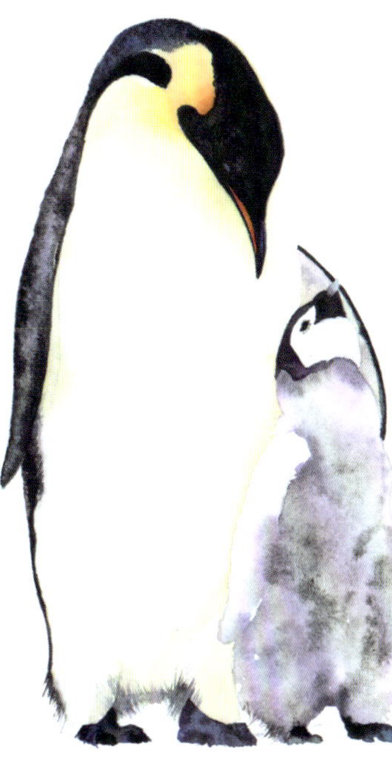

← The adult penguin was covered with a wash of pale, barely there desaturated yellow, with just a hint of pale cyan at the base of the left leg. I exaggerated the brightness of the eye as it was barely discernible in the photograph. The little penguin's coat was a dream to paint. I used a mix of magenta, cyan and black, and it spread and granulated beautifully on the page. It almost painted itself!

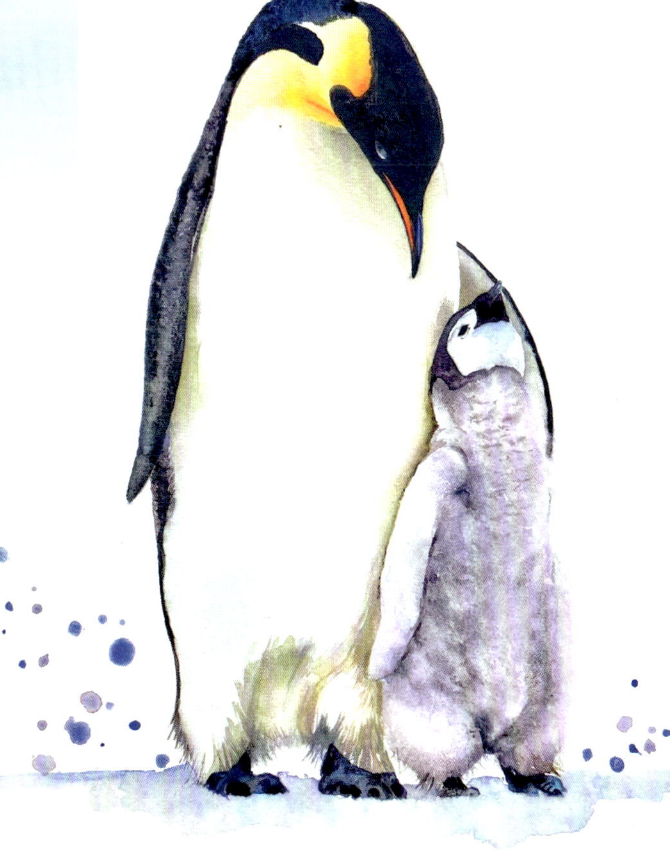

→ The second layer was just a question of enhancing the colour and dropping in the shadow areas under the chin and at the section where the two penguins meet. I added a drop shadow made up of cyan and a cyan/magenta mix to cool the piece down and to hint at a sense of place.

TOOL LIST

Core tools

- Synthetic brushes: size 12 round and size 6 round brushes, size 0, 1 or 2 rigger brush, small oval brush as a detailer brush, 1 inch flat brush (for the occasional background wash) and old bristle brush for lifting paint
- Minimum 200 gsm, cold press, textured watercolour paper
- HB or B pencil, ruler, eraser and sharpener
- Printer and gloss paper for photo references
- Palette, water container, paper towels

Other essentials

- Masking fluid, small brush and washing-up liquid
- White gel pen and a black micron pen or similar
- Salt, cling film, bubble wrap, feather, spatula
- Dark charcoal pencil, a slim stick of vine or willow charcoal, a blending stump and spray fixative
- Watercolour pencils and gouache paints
- Washi tape (for masking borders) and wax-free transfer or tracing paper
- Cutting mat and craft knife

Paints

The CMYK colour palette is core for this book: Cyan, Magenta, Yellow and Key (Black). I use tube and pan paints by Winsor & Newton and I have found that the colours closest to the CMYK palette are Manganese Blue Hue, Quinacridone Magenta, Winsor Lemon and Mars Black. Any other black or neutral tint can replace Mars Black, but be aware of any colour bias – Mars Black is cooler and bluer while Ivory Black is warmer and browner.

I find that the Cotman range suffices for other standard colours such as Indigo, Burnt Sienna, Sap Green, Burnt Umber, Alizarin Crimson and Cadmium Orange. Some colours mentioned in the book are only available in their professional range, such as French Ultramarine, Opera Rose, Cobalt Turquoise Light and Quinacridone Gold.

My preferred tools and materials are listed below, but any similar brands will work.

- Escoda round watercolour brushes
- Daler-Rowney line and wash board (fine) for charcoal pieces
- Derwent charcoal set
- Koh-I-Noor watercolour pencils
- Mono Zero eraser
- Saunders Waterford 638 gsm, CP (NOT) paper (luxury 100% cotton paper which does not require stretching)
- Seawhite 350 gsm watercolour paper
- Winsor & Newton watercolour paint (see p.62 for key colours)
- Winsor & Newton masking fluid

SUPPLIERS

Art materials and equipment

UK

I buy much of my art equipment from the online art supplier Jackson's Art Supplies: **www.jacksonsart.com**

If you'd prefer to have a good old mooch in a shop, then Cass Art are comprehensive stockists of many of the items used in the book, such as watercolour paints, palettes and charcoals. They have a number of stores all over the UK: **www.cassart.co.uk**

For general supplies, visit **www.hobbycraft.com**

Australia

jacksons.com.au
artpartsfinearts.com.au
artsuppliesaustralia.com.au

USA

www.jerrysartarama.com
www.dickblick.com
www.michaels.com

Canada

www.deserres.ca
canada.michaels.com
opusartsupplies.com
midoco.ca

Professional reference photos

For stock images I use the following websites as they carry a number of copyright-free images. Make sure that you always look for the CC Creative Commons symbol before using.

unsplash.com
pixabay.com
www.flickr.com
pmp-art.com

Exhibitions and workshops

For the chance to see inspirational watercolour artists at work, visit the International Watercolour Masters Exhibition, which takes place generally every couple of years in Shropshire, UK.
internationalwatercolourmasters.com

If you're interested in watching workshops involving a range of mediums, I would also recommend visiting the Patchings Festival in Nottinghamshire, UK.
www.patchingsartcentre.co.uk/patchings-festival

I hold retreats and workshops at my studios in Upper Arley, Worcestershire and further afield in Europe and South Africa. For more information, please click the subscribe button on my website:
www.sarahstokesartist.co.uk

Useful resources

Apps

If you're curious to know which birds are singing in your back garden, or even further afield, there is a fabulous app called Merlin which helps identify them. It's really magical knowing which birds are making those wonderful sounds.
merlin.allaboutbirds.org

Books

Colour and Light: A Guide for the Realist Painter by James Gurney (Andrews McMeel Publishing, 2010)
Drawing on the Right Side of the Brain by Betty Edwards (HarperCollins, 2001)

PICTURE CREDITS

P1, 3, 6, 7, 25, 66, 155 Rob Van Mourick
P8 agefotostock / Alamy Stock Photo
P9 GL Archive / Alamy Stock Photo
P10 Bonnie Taylor Barry via Shutterstock
P12 Erik Karits via Pixabay
P13, 23, 24 (right), 71, 76, 152, 154 Ian Gray
P24 (top) Paul Sawford
P24 (left) Hans Cornet
P43 (top) Barbara Wooldridge
P43 (bottom) Villager Jim
P44 Ray Purkiss
P46 John M Lund Photography Inc / DigitalVision via Getty Images
P64 (top), 97 Steve Ward
P65 (top) Wiki commons
P65 (bottom row) DEA / G. DAGLI ORTI / Contributor via Getty Images
P67 Winsor & Newton reference chart
P72 Kwanchai Chai-Udom / EyeEm via Getty Images
P73 Procreate screenshot
P75 Prasanta Seal via Unsplash
P88 Dan Plale
P98 Hawk Photography Namibia via Shutterstock
P99 Russ Bridges
P100 Gerald Corsi / E+ via Getty Images
P103 Grant Durr via Unsplash
P109 Trish Liggett (Freedom to Roam Adventures)
P110, 111 Gemma Atherton, The Falconry Centre, Hagley
P118 Zdenek Machacek via Unsplash
P120, 122 (both) Sonny Mauricio via Unsplash
P130 Shyam via Unsplash
P141 (top) David Yarrow
P141 (bottom) Johanna Ratia at Ratia Ranch
P142 Julia Kuznetsova via Shutterstock
P146 © Jackie Bale / Moment Open via Getty Images
P149 Ingo Doerrie via Unsplash
P156 Allan Baxter / DigitalVision via Getty Images
P157 David Merron Photography / Moment via Getty Images

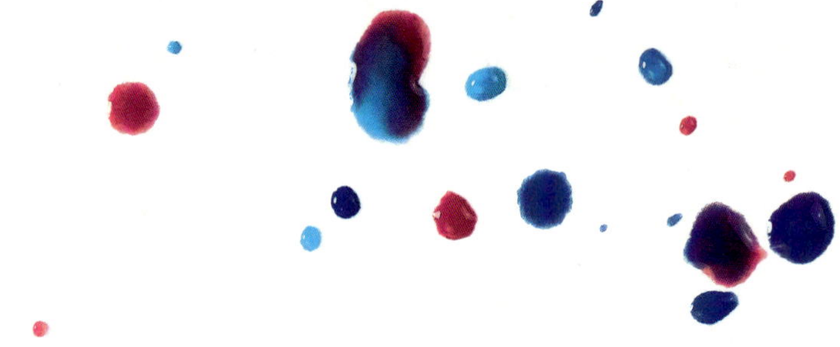

ACKNOWLEDGEMENTS

A huge thank you to the many distributors and galleries who, over the years, gave me a platform for my work and helped turn a pipe dream into reality. Particular gratitude goes to DeMontfort Fine Art, who allowed me to 'give up the day job' and become a full-time professional artist, and to Domestika who subsequently introduced me to a worldwide community of learners.

Thank you to the amazing team at Bloomsbury and Herbert Press for helping me to produce this book of which I'm immensely proud. Your patience, professionalism and expertise have been incredible.

I'm indebted to all the wonderful community of artists, students, collectors and creatives that I've met along the way, both online and face to face. Your support has meant that I can live out a rich and full life creating, learning and teaching.

I would also like to extend my appreciation to the many photographers who have very generously allowed me to use their photographs in this book and throughout my art career.

Finally, I cannot begin to express my thanks to my beautiful family and friends for all the love, patience and encouragement you have given me over the years, for all the artwork you critiqued, for every exhibition you attended, for the family pets and relatives you let me paint when I was finding my style, for the social media posts you shared, and for the mad ramblings you patiently listened to as I churned ideas over, often late into the night. I love you all so very much.

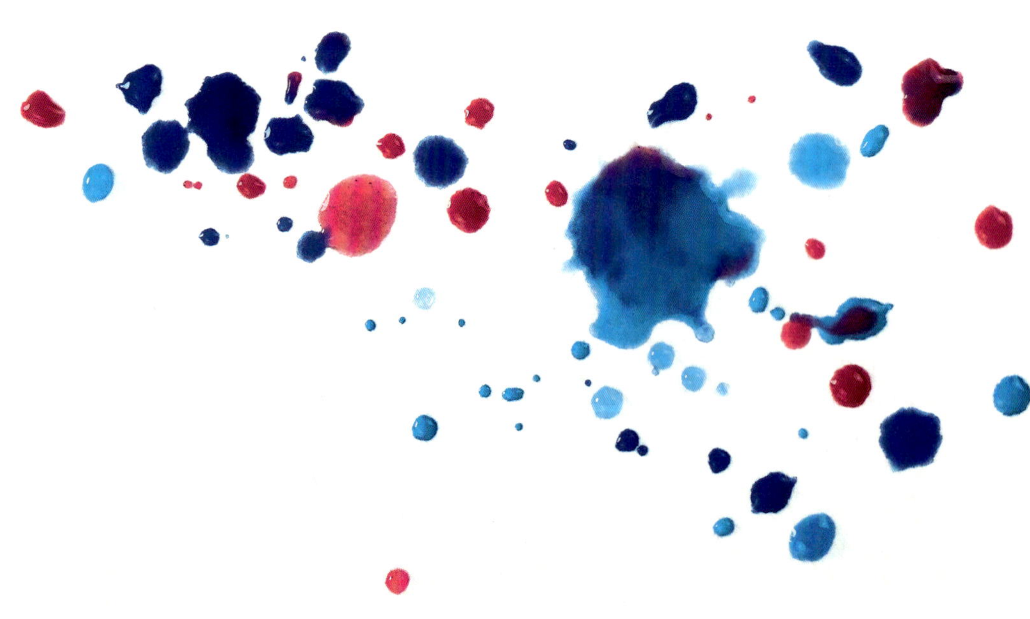